Welcome To Freedom

Let's All Get

HOPE

High

On [His]

Promises

Everyday

"I have placed **MY RAINBOW** in the clouds. It is the sign of **MY Covenant** with **You** and with all the earth."

◄ **Genesis 9:13** ► **[NLT]**

Natalie A. Lee-Walker

"I expect to pass through life but once. If, therefore, there be any kindness I can show, or any GOoD thing I can do to any fellow-being, let me do it now, and not defer or neglect it, as I shall not pass this way again."

- William Penn

This quote was the motto for my high school graduating class, and it became my personal mission statement when I made a promise to **GOD** that I would do my ultimate best to live up to it. I **HOPE** that **HE** is pleased with my continued efforts to serve **HIM** and my fellow man.

Another favorite quote that peaks my desire to create a new and better me is, ***"Life isn't about finding yourself. Life is about creating yourself."***

- George Bernard Shaw

Last but not least, in addition to daily reading the **WORD** of **GOD**, my dearly beloved spiritual mentor and advisor for over thirty-three years, Rev. Sylvia Radford, always prayed a version of this powerful prayer and I continue to recite it daily:

"*Infinite Spirit*, we are so happy and most grateful to be together with YOU, in THY sight and in THY Name. We ask that we may receive messages of guidance, helpfulness and wisdom. We ask that we may see, sense and hear, clearly and distinctly, that only the highest, the best and the truth may come through for us. We ask that our Angel warriors, guides, loved-ones and teachers draw closely to us, YOUR warrior Angels be here also. We ask for a special Blessing and a healing upon us, and upon those we love within our own home, knowing that with YOU all things are possible, and that it is so now, Amen!"

Welcome To Freedom: Let's All Get High

First Edition Printed in the United States 10 9 8 7 6 5 4 3 2 1

Cover design and Layout by: T. Jones Media

DISCLAIMER

Please note that this book is not intended to replace nor be a substitute for the Bible. The above referenced Bible Versions have been carefully selected in order to either introduce or reintroduce a variety of scriptures and published Bible translations. It is intended to provide options from which you may choose your favorite version for better clarification of the scriptures cited throughout this book.

Table of Contents

Acknowledgments

I want to extend a very special THANK YOU to **GOD** for dictating through Divine intervention this **GODuScript** (opposite of MANuscript); to my forever Boyfriend/Husband, Christopher Walker, humanitarian and accomplished singer/songwriter/musician extraordinaire, and our SuperStar son, Christopher "SkyWalker" II, who continues to give us reasons to be proud parents. I thank you for your love, encouragement, unyielding support and for believing in my abilities even when I detoured or procrastinated; for this **I AM** forever grateful.

I also thank **GOD** for my DearLEE beloved parents, Leona Virginia and Paul Harris Lee, for setting such a solid spiritual foundation for us to build on. To my siblings, Lisa Geralyn, Deirdra Letticia Marie, Kayla Christine, Enid Damita and Bradford Paul for your unwavering belief and faith in **GOD** and love of the Lee-family unit. To the Lee-men; Troy Landry (Enid), Theodore Kelly (Kayla), Marc Batte (Deirdra), and Steve Gardner (Lisa) who are instrumental and fundamental influences in the Lee-family's makeup.

To my only **GOD**daughter, Kelli Renee Elisabeth Charles (surrogate sister/niece), Trevor Paul Landry (nephew), Ian Leonard Lee (nephew), Tyler Noelle Kelly (niece), Jana Leigh Kelly (niece), Trent Matthew Landry (nephew), [Jana & Trent ~ Associate Editors/constructive critique], Zion Theodore Kelly (nephew) and Eden Virginia Landry (niece), for all of your individual past, present and future successes that continue to give our family opportunities to celebrate [both in-person & virtual] and have forced-family-fun, [#FFF].

To Carolyn and Ralph Jones for your unconditional love, contributions, unlimited guidance and emotional support throughout my adult life from the moment we first met; as well as my trustworthy friends Cheryl Russell, Gary Warfield, Elnora Conley, Esq., Denona Conley, and Lygia Blount Collins (my dearest L.A.D.), for your Light and amazing talents used to assist in the constructive-critique and proofreading phase; and to my **GOD**-sent Angel, Dr. Traneisha Jones, for your invaluable labor of Love and self-publishing subject matter expertise to manifest this book as **GOD** ordained.

About the Author

N.A.T.A.L.I.E.
Now Anointed To Activate Loving-light In Everyone

Natalie A. Lee-Walker, originally from St. Martinville, LA, now residing in a suburb of Houston, TX, is a Paralegal who holds two Bachelors and a Master's Degree, a wife, mother, sibling, aunt, loyal friend (*with an expiration date*), confidante, prayer warrior, **SOUL**-seeker, and Spiritual Ambassador for **GOD/JESUS/HOLY SPIRIT**, prophetically-gifted, published author, all with a huge heart for **GOD** that drives her immense desire to provide support, encouragement and service to others.

In 2012, she graduated Valedictorian from Full Sail University with a Master of Science Degree in Entertainment Business/Sports Management. As a prerequisite for graduation, she created a non-profit Business Plan entitled, "EagleWings DREAYM BYG Association", and won an award for best-submitted Business Plan. In 2014, the plan received 501c(3) credentials.

There is an anointing on her life and a mysterious and miraculous significance beginning with her **GOD**-ordained origin, past and present accomplishments, and the yet-to-be revealed future successes associated with this **Book**, which was prophesied over her life years ago, and contains the phenomenal pre**SCRIPT**ion that will encourage, empower and propel you to live your best
LIFE AFTER DELIVERANCE.

Introduction

GOD is Faithful and even in the face of tests, trials, troubles and tribulations, the Truth of HIS WORD assures us of HIS unconditional Love and that HE is always with us. Our Heavenly FATHER watches over us and waits for us to call on HIM using HIS WORD because HIS Promises provide the HOPE and help that we need to continue this journey and to fulfill our plans that align with HIS Purpose.

LET'S ALL GET

HIGH ON [HIS] PROMISES EVERYDAY

as we commit to praying for ourselves, for our families
and for each other daily.

"Be strong and let your heart take courage,
all You who HOPE in the LORD!"
◄ Psalm 31:24 ► [NASB]

Deliver Us From Evil

In my quest to seek more knowledge about **GOD**, desiring to ultimately have a closer relationship with **HIM**, and after many years of exploring different religions and spiritualties, I have finally discovered that the answers to my prayers are located throughout the **Scriptures**, which contain **HIS Promises** to us, and also found in the last phrase of **The LORD's Prayer**, which instructs us to ask for **Deliverance**.

"Our FATHER, WHO art in Heaven, hallowed by THY Name, THY Kingdom come, THY Will be done on earth as it is in Heaven, give us this day our daily bread and forgive us our debts/trespasses as we forgive our debtors/those who trespass against us and lead us not into temptation, but DELIVER US from evil!"

In 2016, I continued on my journey to find a local non-denominational church with a specific focus on a **Deliverance** ministry that was intent on saving **SOULS**. I had read several books, watched numerous curse-breaking videos on the internet, and had conversed with various Priests, Pastors, Apostles, Prophetess' and Prophets, as well as a variety of self-professed spiritualists. I had also watched supernatural, spiritual-based TV programs all in an effort to find the answers to unanswered questions. I had more questions: What happens in my Life After **Deliverance**? What is the meaning of the phrase, "***DELIVER US** from evil?*" I was truly amazed at how the answers were so clearly available to me the whole time.

While in my Prayer, Meditation, and Sacrifice room [a.k.a. my P.M.S. room], I was led to this answer: ***'To be Delivered from evil is to be freed, liberated, released from ALL curses, including generational curses, that binds a SOUL to darkness'.***

After years of searching, I located the ministry of a very well-known man of **GOD**, Apostle John Eckhardt, located in Chicago, IL. I began to watch his online videos, read many of his books and listened to all of his audio books. I had also prayed to either find a local, similar ministry, or thought I would have to travel to Chicago to visit his church in order to receive the **Deliverance** that I had been so desperately seeking.

In January 2017, **GOD** heard my prayers and it was truly life changing! Apostle Eckhardt was scheduled to appear as the headlining guest speaker at a Greater Grace Houston prayer retreat, formerly known as Greater Grace Outreach Church. My initial plan was to attend the program on Friday evening; however, it stormed so badly that I was not able to attend that day. Since I am sensitive to the presence of spirit and the possibility of spirit transference, I also debated whether I wanted to be present if/or when deliverance happened for other attendees. Instead, by the **Grace** of **GOD**, his visit was extended, and I attended the following Sunday's service.

Upon arriving, I asked **GOD** for a specific spiritual encounter to validate whether this was to become my new church home. **HIS** answer came to me so real-time that there was no room for doubt. This was the place where I was to receive **Deliverance**; and although I did not immediately join as a member, I began to attend weekly services.

On March 26, 2017, there was a visiting Pastor who sang one of my favorite songs, ***'A CHANGE IS GONNA COME'***. When it was nearing the end of the service, Bishop E. L. Usher, the Founding Pastor of Greater Grace, extended an *Altar-Call* invitation to anyone who either wanted intercessory prayers, to be baptized or re-baptized, or to join and become a member. I stood, picked up my backpack and decided that I would now exit the church. Instead, I somehow found myself mysteriously standing alone at the altar.

A lady approached me and asked whether I needed intercessory prayers or wanted to join. I was still confused as to how I was now standing at the altar and responded that I could not join at this time because I had a dilemma, but I would accept intercessory prayers.

As a side note, I must mention that as a Christian with strong ties to ultra-conservative Catholicism, I had foolishly convinced myself that I would never fall to the floor like that of others I had previously witnessed after the laying of hands in prayer. In my attempt to ensure that this would not happen to me, I intentionally wore a dress to church every Sunday.
Big Mistake!

Once the lady began praying over me, I was keenly aware that the First Lady and co-Pastor, Tawanda Usher, was standing next to me praying with another lady who was wailing so loudly I could not concentrate on the prayers being prayed for me. I also began to pray warfare prayers that I had learned from my spiritual advisor and rebuked any demon that would possibly exit that lady and try to transfer to me. No thank you, I had my own demons!

Next, I abruptly fell to the floor and the impact caused my eyeglasses to fall from my face. I slowly opened my eyes but could only see what looked like white clouds surrounding me. I remember repeating, *"I cannot see"* and someone gave the instruction, "*Get her glasses, she cannot see!"* My glasses were again placed over my eyes, but I could still only see white clouds surrounding me. I then heard a deeper female voice praying, ***"Let her go! You cannot have her SOUL! I command you in the Name of JESUS to release her now! Get thee behind me Satan in the Name of JESUS!"*** ...and on....and on...AND... then...... silence! I passed out!!

Then, the service had ended! When I came out of the trance (as it was later explained), the lights were now dimmed and almost everyone had exited the building, including some of the choir members, the guest speaker and his family, the Bishop and First Lady, ushers, greeters, media team, visitors and other church members. A female choir member and a male church member helped me to stand and I was escorted to a seat until I regained my composure. I began to cry uncontrollably because I had no knowledge or recollection of what happened after I passed out. I asked of those who remained whether they knew what transpired and no one could explain it.

Since I was not yet acquainted with any of the church members, I did not know whom I could contact to fill in the gap. I thought that either I had experienced a spiritual cleansing or was losing my mind. It was a scary feeling to be detached from my reality! The choir member handed a tissue to me with her phone number in the event I later wanted to speak with someone. She also informed me there was an ambulance outside, but she did not know for whom the ambulance had been dispatched.

When I was finally able to return to my vehicle, I began to drive away with the intention of heading home. I was driving for about an hour when Chris, my husband who was the Minister of Music at another local church at that time [hence my dilemma], called to determine our plans for lunch since we customarily met after Sunday service to either dine-in or get takeout. It was then I realized that I did not know where I was going.

After explaining that I believed I had experienced a transformation and that I only had partial recollection of the occurrence, he became very concerned because I was also not able to provide my current location. He was now aware that I was driving and asked if I needed him to meet me. I began to cry again because I wondered whether this is how it feels to have a mental breakdown because I felt so disconnected from my reality. He suggested that I find a familiar establishment and remain there until I was either comfortable enough to drive home or he would come to meet me, if necessary. Fast-forward, I was now an hour away from home on the northside of the city, and I located a familiar cafeteria-styled restaurant. I now realized I was closer to my place of employment, whereby I remained until after midnight.

Several weeks later when things returned to some semblance of normalcy, I decided to join as a member of Greater Grace Church. As a new member, I attended my first day of orientation class and we were asked to introduce ourselves and explain what led us to join the church. I introduced myself and explained that although it felt right, I had limited recollection of the day I accepted the *Altar-Call* invitation.

Another lady, who was attending the last day of her new-member's orientation class, introduced herself as Debra Solomon and stated that she would explain exactly what happened to me that day. To reward my obedience for accepting the call, **GOD** had placed us in this class at the same time in order that I would not only know that she was the lady who had interceded for my **SOUL's Deliverance** after I had fallen to the floor, but she was also the individual for whom the ambulance had been called that day.

She stated that after praying for me, her body began to convulse so aggressively that observers believed she was having an epileptic seizure and called 911 for help. After a thorough examination by the Emergency Medical Technicians, they determined it was not a seizure and she was released to drive home. Thank **YOU, JESUS,** I now know with certainty that **IT REALLY HAPPENED**!! I had truly received the **Deliverance** that I had been seeking and my **SOUL** was now **liberated** from years of bondage, both current and past generational curses!

So, what happens now? What is life after **Deliverance**? Who is here to instruct me on how to live my best life after **Deliverance**? Do I continue to attend services each Sunday to receive new **Deliverance**? How do I keep my **SOUL** connected to the **Light**, the **MOST POWERFUL PURE LOVING LIGHT**? All these questions and there was no one available to provide the answers that made sense to me. I went back to the **SOURCE** and prayed:

*"Dear **GOD**, please help me to complete this **Book** in order that I may help myself and others to live their best Life After **Deliverance**! Please also grant me **YOUR Amazing Power**, **Anointing**, **Authority** and **Wisdom** in **JESUS' Most Holy Name**. Amen."*

I was then led to read this **Scripture**:

> "Do not fear, for **I AM** with **You**; **I Will** bring your offspring from the east and gather **You** from the west. **I Will** say to the north, 'Give them up!' And to the south, 'Do not hold them back' Bring **MY** sons from afar and **MY** daughters from the ends of the earth, everyone who is called by **MY Name**, and whom **I** have created for **MY Glory**, whom **I** have formed, even whom **I** have made'." ◄ Isaiah 43:5-7 ► [NIV]

All Glory and Praise and Honor to

The BLESSED TRINITY ~

Our CREATOR, The Heavenly FATHER;
Our SAVIOR, The Messiah, JESUS; and
Our COMFORTER, The HOLY SPIRIT!

"**YOURS, O LORD**, is **The Greatness**, **The Power**, **The Glory**, **The Victory**, and **The Majesty**. Everything in the **Heavens** and on earth is **YOURS, O LORD**, and this is **YOUR Kingdom**. We adore **YOU** as **The ONE WHO** is over all things."
◄ 1 Chronicles 29:11 ► [NLT]

I. A.M.

IT'S ABOUT ME!

The Great I AM is GOD and HE is The PROMISE MAKER!

The one thing that remains certain is the belief that no matter where You are in your life, there is something better to be gained and You should be among the recipients. Because GOD wants us to know HIM more intimately, HE has revealed another hidden treasure through HIS Name, 'I AM'!

Although man has many different names for GOD, including:

Jehovah-Jireh,	**The LORD Will Provide,**
Jehovah-Rapha,	**The LORD Will Heal,**
Jehovah-Shalom,	**The LORD Our Peace,**
Jehovah-Nissi,	**The LORD Our Banner,**
Jehovah-Tsidkenu,	**The LORD Our Righteousness,**
Jehovah-Raah,	**The LORD Is Our Shepherd,**
Jehovah-Shammah,	**The LORD Is Always Present, et al,**

Scripture reflects that GOD and JESUS introduced themselves as

'I AM'

"GOD said unto Moses, 'I AM WHO I AM.' This is what You are to say to the Israelites: 'I AM has sent me to You'."

◄ Exodus 3:14 ► [CEV]

"JESUS answered, "I tell You for certain that even before Abraham was, I was, and I AM."

◄ John 8:58 ► [ESV]

The following Scriptures will provide more insight into the knowledge of WHO is GOD, The Promise Maker ~ The Great I AM!

Indeed, it is **ALL** about GOD and it is important to know that GOD wants You to have a personal relationship with HIM through JESUS, and it is then that HIS Purpose for You will be manifested.

Once You have a better understanding of the sole role of your SOUL on this journey [no pun intended], The Great I AM shall speak with a powerful breath from Heaven and give to You what HE has Promised in HIS Will. HE has given HIS WORD!

By the way, **Spoiler Aler**t! GOD knows You oh-so-well and HE knows that You want to make this journey all about YOU!
It is Not All About Y.O.U.!

HIS WORD instructs us to trust in the LORD and to not rely on your own ability to understand:

"Trust in the LORD with all your heart and do not depend on **Your Own Understanding** ~ Y.O.U.!"
◄ Proverbs 3:5 ► [NASB]

For GOD is saying, **IT'S ABOUT ME**

I. A.M. The Great I. A.M.

Therefore, each time that You refer to yourself using the WORDS 'I AM', You are calling on The SPIRIT of GOD that dwells in You and tapping into HIS POWER!

Call on GOD each day by decreeing and declaring:

I AM ANOINTED,
I AM AWESOME,
I AM FAITHFUL,
I AM GRATEFUL,
I AM HEALED,
I AM HOLY,
I AM MIGHTY,
I AM POWERFUL,
I AM PROMOTED,
I AM PROTECTED,
I AM REDEEMED,
I AM RIGHTEOUS,
I AM SAVED,
I AM VICTORIOUS,
I AM WONDERFUL….

I AM ALL THAT I AM…

IT'S ABOUT ME! ~ I AM THE ALMIGHTY GOD {EL-SHADDAI}!

"Now when Abram was ninety-nine years old, the LORD appeared to Abram and said to him, '**I AM GOD Almighty**';
Walk before ME and be blameless."
◄ Genesis 17:1 ► [NASB]

I. A.M.

IT'S ABOUT ME! ~ I AM THE BREAD OF LIFE
"JESUS said to them, 'I AM THE BREAD OF LIFE; he who comes to ME Will not hunger, and he who believes in ME Will never thirst'."
◀ John 6:35 ▶ [NASB]

IT'S ABOUT ME! ~ I AM THE BREAD OF LIFE
"I AM telling You the truth: he who believes has eternal life. I AM THE BREAD OF LIFE'!"
◀ John 6:47-48 ▶ [GNT]

IT'S ABOUT ME! ~ I AM THE LIGHT OF LIFE
"Then JESUS again spoke to them, saying, "I AM THE LIGHT of the world; he who follows ME Will not walk in the darkness, but will have the LIGHT OF LIFE."
◀ John 8:12 ▶ [NASB]

IT'S ABOUT ME! ~ I AM THE DOOR
"I AM THE DOOR; if anyone enters through ME, he will be saved, and will go in and out and find pasture."
◀ John 10:9 ▶ [NASB]

IT'S ABOUT ME! ~ I AM THE GOoD SHEPHERD
"I AM THE GOoD SHEPHERD; THE GOoD SHEPHERD, lays down HIS Life for the sheep."
◀ John 10:11 ▶ [NASB]

IT'S ABOUT ME! ~ I AM THE RESURRECTION and THE LIFE
"JESUS said to her, 'I AM THE RESURRECTION and THE LIFE; he who believes in ME Will live even if he dies."
◀ John 11:25 ▶ [NASB]

IT'S ABOUT ME! ~ I AM THE VINE
"I AM THE VINE, You are the branches; he who abides in ME and I in him, he bears much fruit, for apart from ME You can do nothing."
◀ John 15:5 ▶ [NIV]

IT'S ABOUT ME! ~ I AM THE WAY, THE TRUTH & THE LIFE
"JESUS said to him, "I AM THE WAY, THE TRUTH, and THE LIFE; no one comes to THE FATHER but through ME."
◀ John 14:6 ▶ [NASB]

I. A.M.

IT'S ABOUT ME! ~ I AM THE ALPHA AND THE OMEGA
"Then **HE** said to me, "It is done. **I AM THE ALPHA AND THE OMEGA**, the **Beginning** and the **End**. **I Will** give to the one who thirsts from the spring of the water of life without cost." ◄ Revelation 21:6 ► [NASB]

IT'S ABOUT ME! ~ I AM THE BEGINNING AND THE END
"**I AM THE ALPHA AND THE OMEGA**', says the **LORD GOD**, '**WHO** is and **WHO** was and **WHO** is to come, **THE ALMIGHTY**."
◄ Revelation 1:8 ► [NASB]

IT'S ABOUT ME! ~ I AM THE LIVING ONE
"**I AM THE LIVING ONE**! **I** was dead, but now **I AM ALIVE** forever and ever. **I** have authority over death and the world of the dead."
◄ Revelation 1:18 ► [GNT]

IT'S ABOUT ME! ~ I AM COMING SOON
"**I AM COMING SOON**. So, hold firmly to what **You** have, and no one will take away the crown **You** will be given as your reward."
◄ Revelation 3:11 ► [CEV]

IT'S ABOUT ME! ~ I AM COMING SOON
"The **ONE WHO** has spoken these things says, '**I AM COMING SOON**'!" So, **LORD JESUS**, please come **SOON**!" ◄ Revelation 22:20 ► [CEV]

IT'S ABOUT ME! ~ I AM MAKING EVERYTHING NEW
"And **HE WHO** was seated on the throne said, 'Behold, **I AM MAKING ALL THINGS NEW**'. Also, **HE** said, 'Write this down, for these **WORDS** are trustworthy and true." ◄ Revelation 21:5 ► [ESV]

B.O.A.T.S.

Have You ever personally experienced or watched a movie where someone was intentionally left out of the will for not doing something that was required of them? It is the same with GOD. In order to be an heir in the Will of GOD, You must meet / fulfill specific requirements.

As an heir in GOD's Will, You are here to acquire your inheritance. HE Loves You and wants You to possess those hidden treasures and riches stored in secret places. Just as a will is probated after death, JESUS has already died for us and The Will has been Probated for all who:

Believe HIM/ Obey HIM/ Ask HIM/ Trust HIM/ SEEK HIM.

"And HE got into one of the B.O.A.T.S., which was Simon's, and asked him to go out a little way from the land. JESUS sat down and began teaching the people from the B.O.A.T." ◄ Luke 5:3 ► [NASB]

BELIEVE HIM

"Therefore, I say to You, all things for which You pray and A.S.K, BELIEVE that You have received them, and they will be granted to You."

◄ Mark 11:24 ► [NASB]

OBEY HIM

"You have OBEYED ME, and so You and your descendants will be a Blessing to all nations on earth." ◄ Genesis 22:18 ► [CEV]

ASK HIM

"Whatever You ASK in MY Name, that will I do, so that the FATHER may be glorified in the SON." ◄ John 14:13 ► [NASB]

TRUST HIM

"When I am afraid, I will put my TRUST in YOU." ◄ Psalm 56:3 ► [NASB]

SEEK HIM

"But SEEK first HIS Kingdom and HIS Righteousness, and all these things will be added to You." ◄ Matthew 6:33 ► [NASB]

'I.F.F.Y.' CONDITIONS!

You, too, are a rightful heir in the Will of GOD and these same instructions to Believe, Obey, Ask, Trust, & Seek HIM were given to the Israelites in the past and continues to apply to You today. Since there are over 1,000 'IFs' in the Bible, the Bible is known for its 'IFFY' conditional Promises. One widely known conditional Promise is in John 3:16. Although GOD Loves us unconditionally and HE gave HIS Only SON as a sacrifice for the atonement of our sins; there is a conditional requirement that You must meet in order to receive the Blessing of Salvation.

"*Whoever believes* is synonymous with 'IF You believe
You shall not perish but have eternal life.'"

The number five [5] is a symbol of the Grace of GOD and Grace means undeserved 'Favor'. Of the Ten Commandments, the fifth commandment has an 'IF' provisional Promise:

"Honor your father and your mother, that your days may be prolonged in the land which the LORD your GOD gives You."
◄ Exodus 20:12 ► [NIV]

It is safe to say that GOD's Promises are 'quid pro quo', 'something for something' with specific 'I.F.F.Y.' conditional benefits. Ask yourself,
'AM I ready to Acquire My Inheritance?'

When the requirements have been fulfilled, You will see the manifestation of HIS Promises and You will then obtain your inheritance.
HE Will have an

IMPRESSIVE
FINISH
FOR
YOU!

GOD'S WILL ~ BE DONE

In Deuteronomy, the fifth book of the Bible, it reflects some of GOD's conditional Promises. Specifically, in Chapter 28, there are five 'IF' provisional requirements necessary to acquire the Promises in HIS Will:

The "LORD Will give You Abundance for GOoD"

IF You LISTEN diligently to the Voice …

IF You HEED the Voice of The LORD your GOD…

IF You KEEP the Commandments…

IF You DO GOoD…

IF You LISTEN to the Commandments of The LORD…

In ◀ Deuteronomy 28:1-3 ▶ [ONMB]

28:1 "And it Will be, IF You Will listen diligently to the voice of the LORD your GOD, to observe to do all HIS commandments, which I command You this day, that the LORD your GOD Will set You high above all nations of the earth."

Be obedient ~ listen to and observe HIS laws ~ You will be Promoted above all nations on the earth ~ Promotion comes from GOD!

28:2 "And all these BLESSINGS Will come upon You and overtake You, IF You heed the voice of the LORD your GOD."

Provisions Will be provided to You in abundance!

28:3 "BLESSED Will You be in the city and BLESSED Will You be in the field."

Productive in all your endeavors~ Success, Favor, Abundance and Bountiful Harvest.

In ◀ Deuteronomy 28:4-8 ▶ [ONMB]

28:4 "**BLESSED Will** be the fruit of your body, the fruit of your ground, the fruit of your cattle, the offspring of your oxen, and the increase of your flock."

HIS Provisions for all of your needs for every seed You have sown with your finances and your service to others will harvest!

28:5 "**BLESSED Will** be your basket and your kneading trough."

Overflow of resources to meet your desires and your needs!

28:6 "**BLESSED Will You** be when **You** come in and **BLESSED Will You** be when **You** go out."

The Mighty Hand of Favor is upon You wherever You go!

28:7 "The **LORD Will** cause your enemies who rise up against **You** to be stricken before your face. They **Will** come out against **You** one way and flee before **You** seven ways."

Your enemies will flee. The IMPENETRABLE SHIELD & HEDGE OF PROTECTION [I.S.H.O.P.] will be around You every day, VICTORY OVER ENEMIES!

28:8 "The **LORD Will** command the **BLESSING** upon **You** in your storehouses and in all that **You** undertake; and **HE Will BLESS You** in the land which the **LORD** your **GOD** gives **You**."

Provisions and Prosperity to overflowing capacities; everything You touch turns to Prophetic gold!

In ◀ Deuteronomy 28:9-12 ▶ [ONMB]

28:9 "The **LORD Will** establish **You** as a people **Holy** to **HIMSELF**, as **HE** has sworn to **You**, **IF You** keep the commandments of the **LORD** your **GOD** and walk in **HIS** ways."

You will be separated from the unholy for HIS Glory ~ always walking righteously~ boldly and confidently with HIM!

28:10 "And all the people of the earth will see that **You** are called by the **Name** of the **LORD** and they will stand in awe of **You**."

FAVOR IN THE PRESENCE OF ALL!

28:11 "And the **LORD Will** give **You Abundance for GOoD**, in the fruit of your body, in the fruit of your cattle, and in the fruit of your ground, in the land which the **LORD** swore to your fathers to give **You**."

Abundant Blessings for your faithfulness in doing GOoD!

28:12 "The **LORD Will** open to **You HIS GOoD** treasury, the **Heavens**, to give the rain of your land in its season and to **Bless** all the work of your hand. And **You** will lend to many nations, but **You** will not borrow."

The windows of heaven are open to You ~ Prosperity & success in all of your endeavors / a recipient and distributor of HIS Kingdom's wealth!

In ◀ Deuteronomy 28: 13-14 ▶ [ONMB]

28:13 "And the **LORD Will** make **You** the head and not the tail, and **You** will be above only and **You** will not be beneath, **IF You** will listen to the commandments of the **LORD** your **GOD**, which **I** command **You** this day, to observe and to do them."

HE is the KING of kings ~ as an heir You are to be Promoted with aristocratic rights & privileges!

28:14 "And **You** will not go aside from any of the **WORDS** which **I** command **You** this day, to the right hand or to the left, to go after other gods to serve them."

Do not serve or worship anyone or anything other than The CREATOR~ follow HIS laws and stay on the righteous path!

When **You** have a clearer understanding of **WHO GOD** is, **You** will have the **Freedom to Believe, Obey, Ask, Trust, & Seek HIS Purpose** for your life; be **Delivered** from oppression; and be abundantly **Blessed**. If **You** truly know that **GOD** is **The Kingdom**, **The Power** and **The Glory** forever and ever, **You** will also have confidence in **HIS SON, JESUS, WHO** died on the **Cross** for us in order to:

Justify
Every
Sinner
Under
Salvation

"They said, '**Believe** in the **LORD JESUS**, and **You** will be saved, **You** and your household'."
◀ Acts 16:31 [NASB]

A.M. I?
Acquiring My Inheritance

Then I heard the voice of the LORD, saying,
"Whom shall I send, and who will go for Us?"
Then I said, "Here AM I. Send me!"
◀ Isaiah 6:8 ▶ [NASB]

Now that **You** know more about **The Creator, The Great I AM**, and that **HIS Promises** are contained in **HIS Will**, **You** can further explore who **You** are and what is your sole role on this journey by answering the questions:

Who AM I? AM I a reflection of **The Great I AM**? Yes, **You** are! Tell yourself: "**I AM** confident in the knowledge that **GOD's Purpose** for me is that I **Acquire My Inheritance**.

If there has ever been a time when **You** were excluded or rejected; felt abandoned or neglected, just know that **You** are not alone. **You** are **Chosen** to be **ROSES** among **WEEDS** and the **THORNS** are there to protect the **ROSES**! For example, offensive and oppressive negative energy from the attacks of the enemy may cause mental trauma or severe emotional **PAIN.** This pain is your **SOUL's** warning signal that **You** are under attack from the Wicked, Evil, Envious Demonic Spirits trying to dwell in your temple / mind, which may block your spiritual growth.

Do not allow negative thoughts to occupy space in your mind or allow your **SOUL** to **D**well **I**n **N**egative **E**nergy [**D.I.N.E.**]. Feeding negative thoughts to your **SOUL** will prevent the elevation and the empowerment of your **SOUL** and hinder the manifestation of your best life.

Now ask yourself:

"AM I ready to **Acquire My Inheritance** as ROSES with THORNS among WEEDS?"

R.O.S.E.S. / T.H.O.R.N.S. / W.E.E.D.S.

ROSES are here to:

REBUKE/ RESIST/ REVERSE
OFFENSIVE/ OPPRESSIVE
SPIRITUAL
ENERGY with
SCRIPTURES

THORNS are here to protect You and make You stronger because:

TESTS/TRIALS/TRIBULATIONS/TROUBLES
HAPPEN
OFTEN
RESIST/REBUKE/REVERSE/RENOUNCE
NEGATIVE
SPIRITS

WEEDS are here to hinder your elevation and stifle your growth:

WICKED
EVIL
ENVIOUS
DEMONIC
SPIRITS

You must Peel Away Inner Negativity [P.A.I.N.] by daily renewing your mind with the WORD of GOD, which keeps the SOUL fed with positive energy. As believers, You now possess the KEYS to the Kingdom to Keep Empowering Your Soul every day.

"I Will give You the KEYS of the Kingdom of Heaven; and whatever You bind on earth shall have been bound in heaven, and whatever You loose on earth shall have been loosed in heaven." *◄ Matthew 16:19 ► [NASB]*

When **You A.S.K.**, Acquire **Scripture K**nowledge, and actually know **HIS WORD**, **You** now have the **Power**, the **Authority** and the **Wisdom** to destroy all **W**icked **E**vil **E**nvious **D**emonic **S**pirits! Since the **THORNS** are meant to protect the **ROSES** from harm and danger, the **T**ests, **T**rials, **T**ribulations, & **T**roubles **H**appen **O**ften, therefore, **R**esist / **R**ebuke / **R**everse **N**egative **S**pirits with **HIS WORD**.

In accordance with **GOD's Purpose**, be confident in the knowledge that **You** are strengthened with the **Power** and **Authority** to overcome all weapons formed against **You** because they will **NOT** prosper.

"Do not be conformed to this world, but be transformed by the Renewal of Your Mind, that by testing You may discern what is the Will of GOD, what is GOoD and acceptable and perfect." ◄ *Romans 12:2* ► *[ESV]*

WHAT'S ON YOUR MIND?

T.E.M.P.L.E.!

TO	**and**	**TEACH**
ELEVATE		**EVERY**
MEMORIZE{HIS}		**MIND{HIS}**
PROMISES		**PROMISES of**
LOYALLY		**LOVING-LIGHT**
EVERYDAY		**EVERYDAY**

Although **You** have been correctly informed that the **SPIRIT** of **GOD** lives in your **TEMPLE**, **You** have been incorrectly informed that your body is the **TEMPLE**. There is only one part of your body called the **TEMPLE**. It is the space located inside your head, behind the eyes, as it is commonly said that the eyes are the windows to the **SOUL**! When **GOD** first blew the **Breath of Life** in the nostrils of man, **HE** blew in **The SPIRIT Of** Unlimited Life. Therefore, the **TEMPLE** of **GOD** is the space where the **SOUL / Spirit** resides., which is the **Mind** and **NOT** in the body.

"Then the LORD GOD formed man of dust from the ground and breathed into his nostrils the Breath Of Life; and man became a living being."
◄ Genesis 2:7 ► [NASB]

The **SOUL** is here to guide **You** through your journey and is also the storage place for your thoughts. Remember, your **SOUL** is a valued and treasured possession and **You** are to protect it daily with the most powerful weapon, **HIS WORD**, because your thoughts feed your **SOUL**. As **Believers**, we are equipped with Divine Armor to defeat our enemies and all evil.

To guard the **TEMPLE** of **GOD** against negative thoughts, **You** must daily renew your mind and vibrate High On Positive Energy. This is the **H.O.P.E.** needed to Keep Empowering Yourself Spiritually, which are the **K.E.Y.S.** to the **Kingdom** contained in **HIS Promises** and necessary to unlock the truths of **HIS Purpose** for your life. This will **Free** your **SOUL** to soar like an eagle and tap into the **Power** for Manifestation.

WHAT IS A S.O.U.L.?

IT IS A

SPIRIT OF UNLIMITED LIFE

The SOUL is the only part of the human body that never dies, but it may live eternally in either Light or darkness. It is through the eyes, ears, and mouth that You can daily receive and distribute both positive and negative information and these messages are connected to energy.

If You are not walking righteously, which is boldly and confidently with **GOD, WHO is The SOURCE Of Unlimited Light,** You will find yourself wandering from one temporary fix to another trying to appease your physical desires and seeking to find that ultimate high. The most commonly sought temporary fixes are **Sex, Alcohol or Drugs** [S.A.D.]. These vices are known to cause addictions and may lead You to the dark side, which can indefinitely place your SOUL in an altered, oppressed, depressed or confined state of being.

"Why are You cast down, oh my SOUL and why are You in turmoil within me? H.O.P.E. in GOD; for I shall again praise HIM, my Salvation and my GOD."
◄ Psalm 43:5 ► [ESV]

Because these temporary S.A.D. vices are rooted in darkness, they will fill your mind, which is the TEMPLE, with negativity that deprives the SOUL of the Power of Light. Until You receive Deliverance from all dark vices and break Free from known and unknown generational curses, your SOUL will be in bondage to the devil.

"Why do you not understand what I say? It is because you cannot bear to hear MY WORD. For You are the children of your father the devil, and You love to do the evil things he does. He was a murderer from the beginning. He has always hated the Truth, because there is no truth in him. When he lies, it is consistent with his character; for he is a liar and the father of lies."
◄ John 8:43-44 ► [ESV]

Remember that GOD is Truth and the Devil Is A Liar ~with JESUS the **Devil Is Defeated ~ Inherit Truths**!

D.I.A.L. ~ JESUS D.I.D. I.T.

"GOD is not a man that HE might lie, or a son of man that HE might change HIS mind. Does HE speak and not act, or Promise and not fulfill?"

◄ Numbers 23:19 ► [CSB]

Your tangible possessions, including your physical health, are not as valuable as the wellbeing of your **Mind**, which is the space where your SOUL dwells. Yet, if You do not know how to protect the SOUL from the wiles, tricks, temptations and snares of the enemy, You will continue to diminish the Power inside of You. It is time that You learn how to tap into HIS Power that dwells and works within You!

"Now to HIM WHO is able to do exceedingly, abundantly, above all that we ASK or think, according to the POWER that works in us."

◄ Ephesians 3:20 ► [NKJV]

What Is the POWER?

The Power is GOD's LIGHT in your SOUL and a SOUL that contains LIGHT has the Power and Authority to accomplish the hard and seemingly impossible things. You may also be defeated if You focus on the physical things of the world like debt, poverty, epidemics, pandemics, racism, reparations, social injustices or conflicts with others, including friends, family, co-workers, acquaintances, society, etc.

Do not get distracted by the things of this world because this battle is not physical. This battle is a Spiritual warfare and You must remain aware that the daily battle that the enemy wages against You is to obtain control of and to possess the Power in your SOUL.

"This is what the LORD says: 'Do not be afraid or discouraged because of this vast number, for the battle is not yours, but GOD's."

◄ 2 Chronicles 20:15 ► [CSB]

You now have the knowledge that the battle is not yours, it belongs to GOD and You must daily entrust your SOUL to GOD so that the enemy will have no reason to continue to wage war against You. It is important to commit and recommit your SOUL to GOD daily. How do You do this? L.E.A.P. F.R.O.G. ~

LET EVERYONE ALWAYS PRAY~
FOR REAL! ONLY GOD!

In your immaturity [youth], You may have learned the prayer:

"Now I lay me down to sleep, I pray the LORD my SOUL to keep, if I should die before I wake, I pray the LORD my SOUL to take."
[Author Unknown]

Due to the continuous battle for the possession of your SOUL, this is a very POWERFUL prayer and we thank GOD that our ancestors / grandparents / parents / guardians knew enough to understand the importance of daily committing our SOULs to the CREATOR.

In your maturity, it is also imperative that You continue to commit your SOUL to GOD when You awake each day. JESUS spoke these last WORDS before HE took HIS last breath and died on the Cross:

"Then JESUS, calling out with a loud voice, said,
'FATHER, into YOUR Hands I commit MY SPIRIT'!"
And having said this HE breathed HIS last." ◄ Luke 23:46 ► [ESV]

JESUS understood the importance of committing HIS SPIRIT into GOD's Mighty and Powerful Hands because the devil wanted and continues to want the Power that dwells in HIS SOUL. Although JESUS spoke these words before HE died, HE was not the first to speak these WORDS as HE often quoted Scriptures. David first spoke these same WORDS in ancient times found in the Old Testament:

"Into YOUR Hand I commit my Spirit; YOU have Redeemed me,
O LORD GOD of Truth. ◄ Psalm 31:5 ► [NKJV]

Satan has always hated **Truth** and **GOD** is **Truth**! Once **You** daily commit your **SOUL / Spirit** to **GOD**, this battle is between **GOD** and Satan / the devil / the evil one; [it is right v. wrong; unity v. division; **GOoD** v. bad; virtuous v. evil, justice v. injustice, etc.].

To whom have **You** committed your **SOUL**? As long as **You** have the breath of life, **You** are able to daily commit and recommit your **SOUL** to **GOD**, our **CREATOR**. Each time **You** do so, **GOD Will Protect** and empower your **SOUL** with **HIS MOST POWERFUL PURE LOVING LIGHT**.

You have the **Freedom** to choose. Choose this day whom **You** will serve! Choose the **LIGHT**! Choose **GOD**!

"And if it seems evil to You to serve The LORD, choose for yourselves this day whom You will serve, whether the gods which your fathers served that were on the other side of the River, or the gods of the Amorites, in whose land You dwell.
But as for me and my house,
we will serve The LORD."
◄ Joshua 24:15 ► [NKJV]

GOD'S ANOINTING!

In ancient times, there were many individuals **Anointed** to fulfill **GOD's Purpose** and **HE Anoints** us with that same **Power** to fulfill **HIS Purpose** today. The following are some examples of the **Chosen** ones who received **GOD's Anointing**:

E.S.A.U. & J.A.C.O.B.

Esau was the elder of the twin sons of Isaac and Rebecca. Once when Esau was very hungry, he accepted an offer of a bowl of stew from his twin brother, Jacob, in exchange for his birthright. The birthright is a gift from **GOD**, which gives the right to be recognized as firstborn and has to do with both position and inheritance. By birthright, the firstborn inherits the leadership of the family and the authority of the father. Since Esau bartered his birthright in exchange for a bowl of stew, **E.S.A.U.** did not appreciate the value of **GOD's Anointing** on his life.

Elder Sibling's Anointing Undervalued

Unlike Esau, Jacob understood the value of the Anointing because **J.A.C.O.B.**

Joyfully Accepted Challenges, Opportunities & Blessings!!

"For YOU make him most Blessed forever;
YOU make him joyful with gladness in YOUR presence."
◄ Proverbs 18:22 ► [ESV]

It is important to know the value of **GOD's Anointing** on your life because when **You** do not know the value, **You** will not be able to fulfill **GOD's Purpose** for your life, which can cause long-term consequences like conflicts that ensued between Jacob and Esau's descendant nations.

R.U.T.H.

After Ruth was widowed, she remained with her mother-in-law, Naomi. Ruth is a symbol of abiding loyalty and devotion because she accepted the **GOD** of the Israelites as her **GOD** and the Israelite people as her own when she promised Naomi, *'Where You die, I will die—there will I be buried.'*

Ruth accompanied Naomi to Bethlehem, and because of her loyalty and devotion to Naomi, Naomi guided and prepared Ruth to receive her husband in order to continue the legacy. Ruth was later married to Boaz who was a distant relative of her deceased husband. **R.U.T.H** was

Righteously Ushered To [her] Husband!!

"He who finds a wife finds a GOoD thing and obtains favor from the LORD." ◀ Proverbs 18:22 ▶ [ESV]

D.A.V.I.D.

When **GOD** selected David to be **Anointed** as the king to replace Saul, he was a mere shepherd boy who was overlooked by everyone, including his own brothers and father. David was imperfectly human and only a lad, yet **GOD** favored him and chose him to conquer Goliath without using the typical warfare armor or weapons.

Although David was not trained by the military like his elder brothers, he spent most of his days in the field with only a slingshot and stones tending to and protecting the sheep from danger. When it was time for David to answer the call of **GOD** to free the oppressed people, Saul dressed David in his own military garments, a bronze helmet on his head and a coat of armor. David fastened the sword over the tunic but was not able to freely move around because he was not familiar with this heavy armor. He removed the armor and with only his own shepherd's staff and sling in hand, he chose five smooth stones from the stream, placed the stones in his shepherd's pouch and approached Goliath.

Accompanied by a soldier carrying a shield, Goliath approached David, but Goliath despised him because of his youth and **GOoD** looks. Goliath was also offended and insulted that David was not heavily armored for battle against him. David was confident in his walk with **GOD** and said, *"But I have come out to fight you in the Name of the **LORD ALL POWERFUL. HE** is the **GOD** of Israel's army and you have insulted **HIM** too!"*

After defeating Goliath, David was later **Promoted** from shepherd boy to the king and he became a warrior who killed tens of thousands. **GOD** chose him to **Free** those who were oppressed by the enemy and he showed great courage in the face of danger. **D.A.V.I.D.** was

DIVINELY

ARMORED

VALOR / VICTORIES

IMPRESSIVELY

DISPLAYED

"For Promotion cometh neither from the east, nor from the west, nor from the south. But GOD is the Judge: HE putteth down one, and setteth up another."

◄ Psalm 75:6-7 ► [KJV]

J.O.B.

It is important to know that Satan cannot bring financial and physical destruction upon **You** unless **GOD** permits it because **HE** has **Sovereign Power** over what Satan can and cannot do.

The Job **Anointing** is often associated with having the 'Patience of Job'. In order to have patience one must have an immense and unyielding degree of calm conviction, especially in the face of Tests, Trials, Troubles and Tribulations. Although Job had absolute trust and faith in **GOD**, he did not remain unshaken by the numerous afflictions set upon himself, his family, and his estate by Satan.

To the contrary, Job did not display patience as he accused **GOD** of acting unjustly and questioned why **GOD** would allow him to suffer. When Job decided to talk directly with **GOD** instead of talking with his friends, **GOD** reminded Job that the world is filled with both beauty and danger and although we will not always know why we suffer, we can always trust that **GOD** knows what **HE** is doing and we can bring our pain and grief to **HIM**.

Now, Job always prayed daily for himself and his family, and **GOD** accepted his prayers. The hidden treasure is in the knowledge that when **JOB PRAYED FOR HIS FRIENDS**, **GOD RESTORED** his fortunes giving him twice as much as he had before.

"And the LORD accepted Job's prayer. And the LORD RESTORED the fortunes of Job when he had prayed for his friends. And the LORD gave Job twice as much as he had before." ◄ Job 42:9-10 ► [ESV]

The Job **Anointing** is profound because it specifically reflects the preSCRIPTion for **GOD's RESTORATION**. The most fascinating aspect of the Job **Anointing** is the timing that **J.O.B.** again

JOYFULLY OBTAINED BLESSINGS!

JESUS S.T.O.O.D.!

In the Old Testament, GOD sent HIS messages through Prophets and sometimes directly to the individuals whom HE Divinely Anointed and Chose to do HIS Will and fulfill HIS Purpose.

JESUS was called 'The CHRIST', and although Christianity is one of the greatest professions of our faith in The FATHER, The SON and The Holy SPIRIT, HIS Purpose was not to create new religions or various denominations. HIS Purpose is to Free our SOULs from bondage by delivering us from evil / negativity; to teach us the WORD of GOD; and to unite us all under one covenant for eternal Salvation.

It is important to note that JESUS also Acquired Scripture Knowledge. As reflected in the New Testament, JESUS often referenced the Old Testament's teachings by prefacing HIS statements with, ***'FOR IT IS WRITTEN'.*** This is confirmation that JESUS did not come to earth to abolish the Old Covenant between GOD and man, but to include us in GOD's Will and empower us with the weapons of spiritual warfare, which are needed to defeat the enemy.

JESUS is The Greatest MAN to have ever walked this land and we thank GOD that we now have the Victory through HIS death and resurrection. The **S**ting is **T**aken **O**ut **O**f **D**eath because JESUS has already **S.T.O.O.D.** for us!

"But the LORD S.T.O.O.D. with me and strengthened me, so that through me the proclamation might be fully accomplished, and that all the Gentiles might hear; and I was rescued out of the lion's mouth."

◄ 2 Timothy 4:17 ► [NASB]

"O death, where is thy STING? O grave, where is thy Victory? The STING of death is sin; and the strength of sin is the law. But thanks be to GOD, which giveth us the victory through our LORD JESUS CHRIST."

◄ 1 Corinthians 15:55-57 ► [KJV]

Friends & Enemies!

R.O.D. & S.T.A.F.F.

If You do not know your GOD-given Purpose, just Acquire Scripture Knowledge and then ASK GOD for HIS Anointing on your life. HE Will Bless You and wants to be your Friend.

It is important to remember that on this journey You will have both friends and enemies. As a shepherd-boy in the field, David had a Staff when attending to the sheep, but he also had a ROD and STAFF that comforted him, and his name was Jonathan. Like David and Jonathan's brotherly-love friendship, we each need to have a R.O.D. [Ride-Or-Die] and S.T.A.F.F. [SOULs That Are Friends Forever] that comfort us.

"Even when I walk through the darkest valley, I will not be afraid, for YOU are close beside me. YOUR ROD and YOUR STAFF protect and comfort me."
◄ Psalm 23:4-5 ► [NLT]

David also reminds us that he has never witnessed GOD neglecting those who walked boldly and confidently with HIM, nor did he witness GOD neglecting their children.

"I have been young, and now am old, yet I have not seen the righteous forsaken or his children begging for bread."
◄ Psalm 37:25 ► [ESV]

"No longer do I call You servants, for the servant does not know what his master is doing; but I have called You Friends, for all that I have heard from MY FATHER I have made known to You."
◄ John 15:15 ► [ESV]

"You are My Friends if You do what I Command You."
◄ John 15:14 ► [NASB]

KNOW YOUR FRIENDS AND ALSO… KNOW YOUR ENEMIES!

Who are your enemies? It is also important to know your enemies. If You do not know your enemies, whom will You have as your witness at the preparation of your banquet table when You are being honored with Anointing oil and being filled to overflow with GOD's Blessings?

"YOU prepare a feast for me in the presence of my enemies. YOU honor me by Anointing my head with oil and my cup overflows with Blessings." ◄ Psalm 23:5 ► [NLT]

Saul was also Anointed and Chosen by GOD. Another of David's greatest strengths was his obedience and reverence to GOD when he spared the life of one of his biggest enemies, Saul. David had the utmost respect for the one Anointed by GOD.

You should also give the people in your life the respect they deserve, including your friends, acquaintances and family members, and give them the opportunity to choose whether they will be your ROD [**Ride-Or-Die**] and S.T.A.F.F. [**Souls That Are Friends Forever**], or your enemy W.E.E.D.S. [Wicked. Evil, Envious, Demonic Spirits].

Side note: Your enemies could be identified in your phone contact list as L.M.N.O.P. ~ i.e., LMNOP Jane Doe.

Lose My Number Opportunity Passed! [lol]

If GOD would give impressive victories to David in the presence of his enemies, be assured HE can and will also have an

Impressive Finish For You ~ If You

Believe HIM / Obey HIM / Ask HIM / Trust HIM / Seek HIM

B.O.A.T.S.

GOD'S TIMING IS S.O.O.N.

If You have prayed and asked and asked and prayed time and time again, but your prayers have not yet been answered, and You feel or have felt helpless or hopeless, be reminded of and take comfort in the knowledge that GOD's timing is not our timing.

"But You must not forget this one thing, dear Friends: A day is like a thousand years to the LORD, and a thousand years is like a day."
◄ 2 Peter 3:8 ► [NLT]

When You know **HIS WORD**, You know the **Truth**. Although the manifestation of **HIS Promises** may seem delayed, **IT** is **NOT** denied when your desires align with **HIS Will**. **GOD's 'NO'** is only the beginning of the words **NOT NOW**!

GOD is **NOT** a man; therefore, **HE** does **NOT** lie, nor does **HE** make **Promises** then fail to act or follow through because **HIS WORD** never returns void. Start to see yourself as **GOD** sees You! Be confident and **Trust** that You are now where You need to be in order to get where You are going, and it will happen S.O.O.N.! You can depend on **HIM** because **HE** is a **GOD WHO** is able to make

Something Out Of Nothing ~

"But You are the ones CHOSEN by GOD, CHOSEN for the high calling of priestly work, CHOSEN to be a Holy People, GOD's instruments to do HIS Work and speak out for HIM, to tell others of the night-and-day difference HE has made for You- from rejected to Accepted; From nothing to SOMETHING." ◄ 1 Peter 2:9-10 ► [TMB]

"This is what the Scriptures mean when GOD told him, "I have made You the father of many nations." This happened because Abraham believed in the GOD WHO brings the dead back to life and WHO creates NEW THINGS out of nothing." ◄ Romans 4:17 ► [NLT]

ANTIQUITY!

Relative to the importance and the influence of the number six [6] is the number of days **GOD** created the world with the spoken **WORD**. The number 6 is also symbolic of a **Loving** and caring nature. It is appropriately named the **Motherhood** number due to being associated with sacrificing, caring, healing, protecting and teaching others.

Although technology has the potential to become antiquated; to the contrary, the **WORD** of **GOD** never returns void nor is it outdated. Included in this power-filled **Book** is a compilation of over 2,196 **Promise Scriptures** divinely selected to help us daily obtain the knowledge of **ALL** of **GOD's Promises** and **HIS** instructions specific to the day we were born and every day of the year. The selected **Scriptures** are meant to enable us to pray for ourselves, our families, and each other [known and unknown] who were born on the current date. **HIS WORD** is **Truth** and it holds the **K.E.Y.S.** to our **Freedom**. The more **You Keep Empowering Yourself Scripturally**, **You** will gain what **HE** has **Promised**. However, the **Truth** will never set **You Free IF You DO NOT KNOW IT**!

"And You will Know the Truth, and the Truth will set You Free." ◄ John 8:32 ► [ESV]

Again, **HIS WORD** never returns void, and **HE Will** only give to **You** what **HE** has **Promised**. When **You** know what **HE** has **Promised**, **You** become empowered to manifest **HIS Promises.**

It is implied that if it was not **PROMISED You** should not expect to receive it. **You** must **KNOW** the **Truth**, which is the **Promised WORD** of **GOD** in order that your expectations may be valid and fulfilled. Otherwise, your expectations will only exceed your reality. **HE** is the **BREAD OF LIFE**; therefore, the **WORD** of **GOD** is food for the **SOUL**. We must feed our **SOULs** the **WORD** of **GOD** daily, which provides **IT** the **Power** of **LIGHT**. **GOD** is **LIGHT**!

"This is the message we have heard from HIM and announce to You, that GOD is LIGHT, and in HIM there is no darkness at all."
◄ 1 John 1:5 ► [NASB]

"Let this be recorded for future generations, so that a people not yet born will Praise the LORD." ◄ Psalm 102:18 ► [NLT]

'***For future generations'!*** Indeed, this is **ANTIQUITY**! The Ancient **Truths**! The **WORD** was written back then and still applies today ~ so **You** must know **IT**, own **IT** and teach **IT** to others in order that **IT** will continue **for future generations**. **HIS WORD** and **HIS Promises** are from generation to generation and we are the heirs in **HIS Will.** Let us **Inherit Truth ~ 'IT'**!

"Such things were written in the Scriptures long ago to teach us. And the Scriptures give us H.O.P.E. and encouragement as we wait patiently for GOD's Promises to be fulfilled." ◄ Romans 15:4 ► [NLT]

As **You** now know that **JESUS** often said, **'*For IT is written*'** before **HE** applied the **WORD** to the situation, the **Script** has already been written for **You** in the **Scriptures.** Therefore, all **You** need to do is learn the **Script** ~ **Know HIS WORD, Own HIS WORD**, **ASK** for the **Promises** in **HIS WORD**, and be **Blessed** by **HIS WORD.**

Accept with certainty that no matter your race, color, creed, date or year **You** were born, **You** each have a specific birthdate between January 1 through December 31, including February 29th, in LEAP year (every four years). The following birthday **ANTIQUITY Scriptures** were divinely ordained and selected to empower **You** each day of the year and to enable **You** to **Pray** for yourself, your family and for others. Own the **WORD** of **GOD**. That's right, **You Own IT**!!

GOD hears when You Pray for yourself and your family, but when You Pray for your friends, acquaintances and even your enemies, your RESTORATION will be released twofold.

There is nothing new under the sun!! Therefore, since it happened in the ancient past, understanding the past will help You to better understand the present, the future and your SOUL's role in this life.

In addition to the following divinely selected birthday Scriptures, which contains HIS Truths and HIS Promises, I have also added a Powerful Manifestation Prayer that is KEY for protection as You pray for yourself, your family and for others. When You say this prayer, You will daily receive the covering of HIS

Impenetrable Shield & Hedge Of Protection.

#ISHOP

Learn HIS WORD because You will be put to the test~

"Do your best to present yourself to GOD as one approved, a worker who has no need to be ashamed, rightly handling the WORD of Truth."
◄ 2 Timothy 2:15 ► [ESV]

"But You, be strong and do not lose courage, for there is reward for your work."
◄ 2 Chronicles 15:7 ► [NASB]

"Therefore, since GOD in HIS Mercy has given us this new way, WE NEVER GIVE UP."
◄ 2 Corinthians 4:1 ► [NLT]

ANTIQUITY

WHY DO YOU HAVE NOT?

"You do not have because You do not A.S.K.."
◀ James 4:2 ▶ [NASB]

Do You know how to **A.S.K.?**

~

A.CQUIRE
S.CRIPTURE
K.NOWLEDGE

"And this is the testimony: GOD has given us eternal life, and this life is in HIS SON. Whoever has the SON has life; whoever does not have the SON OF GOD does not have life. I write these things to You who BELIEVE in the Name of the SON OF GOD so that You may know that You have eternal life. This is the confidence we have in approaching GOD that IF we A.S.K. anything according to HIS Will, HE hears us. And IF we know that HE hears us—whatever we A.S.K. —we know that we have what we A.S.K. of HIM."
◀ John 5:11-15 ▶ [NIV]

A.S.K.
And You Shall Receive…

Are You Ready To

A.**CQUIRE**
S.**CRIPTURE**
K.**NOWLEDGE?**

K.E.Y.S.

Keep Empowering Your Soul
&

Unlock the door to the Kingdom with
HIS AMAZING POWER,
ANOINTING, AUTHORITY & WISDOM

January
1

~ I **Pray** for **You** and **You Pray** for Me!

"After Job had prayed for his friends, the **LORD** restored his fortunes and gave him twice as much as he had before." ◄ Job 42:10 ► [NIV]

"**You** haven't done this before. **A.S.K.** using **MY NAME**, and **You** will receive, and **You** will have abundant joy." ◄ John 16:24 ► [NLT]

Powerful Manifestation Prayer:

I BLESS myself, my family and everyone born in this month with GOD's MOST POWERFUL PURE LOVING LIGHT, HIS MOST POWERFUL PURE SOURCE HEALING ENERGY, and an ABUNDANCE OF HIS AMAZING GREATER GRACE in the POWER, the ANOINTING, the AUTHORITY and the WISDOM of the HOLY SPIRIT, in JESUS' MOST HOLY NAME.
AMEN INDEED!

A.S.K.- Additional Scripture Knowledge

Write Additional Scriptures here.

Day 1
1:1

"In the beginning, GOD created the Heavens and the earth." ◀ Genesis 1:1 ▶ [NASB]

"In the beginning was the WORD, and the WORD was with GOD, and the WORD was GOD." ◀ John 1:1 ▶ [ESV]

"Blessed is the man who walks not in the counsel of the wicked, nor stands in the way of sinners, nor sits in the seat of scoffers." ◀ Psalm 1:1 ▶ [ESV]

"I was not appointed by any group of people or any human authority, but by JESUS CHRIST HIMSELF and by GOD The FATHER, WHO raised JESUS from the dead." ◀ Galatians 1:1 ▶ [NLT]

"In the past GOD spoke to our ancestors through the prophets at many times and in various ways." ◀ Hebrews 1:1 ▶ [NIV]

"This man was blameless and upright; he feared GOD and shunned evil." ◀ Job 1:1 ▶ [NIV]

Powerful Manifestation Prayer:

I BLESS myself, my family and everyone born on this date with GOD's MOST POWERFUL PURE LOVING LIGHT, HIS MOST POWERFUL PURE SOURCE HEALING ENERGY, and an ABUNDANCE OF HIS AMAZING GREATER GRACE in the POWER, the ANOINTING, the AUTHORITY and the WISDOM of the HOLY SPIRIT, in JESUS' MOST HOLY NAME. AMEN INDEED!

Day 2
1:2

"The earth was without form and void, and darkness was over the face of the deep. And the SPIRIT OF GOD was hovering over the face of the waters." ◄ Genesis 1:2 ► [ESV]

"Count it all joy, my brothers, when You meet trials of various kinds." ◄ James 1:2 ► [ESV]

"Beloved, I pray that all may go well with You and that You may be in GOoD health, as it goes well with your Soul." ◄ 3 John 1:2 ► [ESV]

"The LORD is a jealous GOD, filled with vengeance and rage. HE takes revenge on all who oppose HIM and continues to rage against HIS enemies!" ◄ Nahum 1:2 ► [NIV]

"But they delight in the Law of the LORD, meditating on it day and night." ◄ Psalm 1:2 ► [NLT]

"Grace and peace to You from GOD our FATHER and the LORD JESUS CHRIST." ◄ Ephesians 1:2 ► [NIV]

Powerful Manifestation Prayer:

I BLESS myself, my family and everyone born on this date with GOD's MOST POWERFUL PURE LOVING LIGHT, HIS MOST POWERFUL PURE SOURCE HEALING ENERGY, and an ABUNDANCE OF HIS AMAZING GREATER GRACE in the POWER, the ANOINTING, the AUTHORITY and the WISDOM of the HOLY SPIRIT, in JESUS' MOST HOLY NAME. AMEN INDEED!

Day 3
1:3

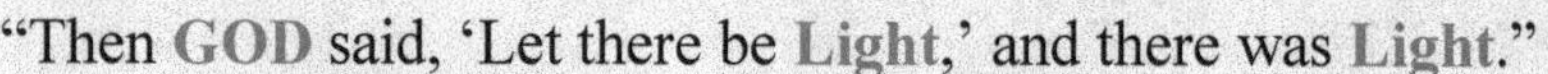

"Then GOD said, 'Let there be Light,' and there was Light." ◀ Genesis 1:3 ▶ [NASB]

"Blessed be the GOD and FATHER of our LORD JESUS CHRIST, WHO has Blessed us in CHRIST with every Spiritual Blessing in the Heavenly places." ◀ Ephesians 1:3 ▶ [ESV]

"Praise be to the GOD and FATHER of our LORD JESUS CHRIST, the FATHER of compassion and the GOD of all comfort." ◀ 2 Corinthians 1:3 ▶ [NIV]

"HIS Divine Power has granted to us all things that pertain to life and GODliness, through the Knowledge of HIM WHO called us to HIS OWN Glory and Excellence." ◀ 2 Peter 1:3 ▶ [ESV]

"That person is like a tree planted by streams of water, which yields its fruit in season and whose leaf does not wither-- whatever they do prospers." ◀ Psalm 1:3 ▶ [NIV]

"Their purpose is to teach people to live disciplined and successful lives, to help them do what is right, just, and fair." ◀ Proverbs 1:3 ▶ [NLT]

Powerful Manifestation Prayer:

I BLESS myself, my family and everyone born on this date with GOD's MOST POWERFUL PURE LOVING LIGHT, HIS MOST POWERFUL PURE SOURCE HEALING ENERGY, and an ABUNDANCE OF HIS AMAZING GREATER GRACE in the POWER, the ANOINTING, the AUTHORITY and the WISDOM of the HOLY SPIRIT, in JESUS' MOST HOLY NAME. AMEN INDEED!

Day 4
1:4

"In HIM was life, and that life was the LIGHT of men." ◀ John 1:4 ▶ [ESV]

"Even as HE Chose us in HIM before the foundation of the world, that we should be Holy and blameless before HIM. In Love." ◀ Ephesians 1:4 ▶ [ESV]

"And WHO through the SPIRIT of Holiness was appointed the SON of GOD in Power by HIS resurrection from the dead: JESUS CHRIST our LORD." ◀ Romans 1:4 ▶ [NIV]

"WHO comforts us in all our affliction so that we will be able to comfort those who are in any affliction with the comfort with which we ourselves are comforted by GOD." ◀ 2 Corinthians 1:4 ▶ [NASB]

"Through these HE has given us HIS very great and precious Promises so that through them You may participate in the divine nature, having escaped the corruption in the world caused by evil desires." ◀ 2 Peter 1:4 ▶ [NIV]

"And let endurance have its perfect result, so that You may be perfect and complete, lacking in nothing." ◀ James 1:4 ▶ [NASB]

Powerful Manifestation Prayer:

I BLESS myself, my family and everyone born on this date with GOD's MOST POWERFUL PURE LOVING LIGHT, HIS MOST POWERFUL PURE SOURCE HEALING ENERGY, and an ABUNDANCE OF HIS AMAZING GREATER GRACE in the POWER, the ANOINTING, the AUTHORITY and the WISDOM of the HOLY SPIRIT, in JESUS' MOST HOLY NAME. AMEN INDEED!

Day 5
1:5

"No one will be able to stand against You all the days of your life. As I was with Moses, so I Will be with You; I Will never leave You nor forsake You." ◀ Joshua 1:5 ▶ [NIV]

"If any of You lacks Wisdom, You should ASK GOD, WHO gives generously to all without finding fault, and it will be given to You." ◀ James 1:5 ▶ [NIV]

"This is the message we have heard from HIM and announce to You, that GOD is LIGHT, and in HIM there is no darkness at all." ◀ 1 John 1:5 ▶ [NASB]

"A wise man will hear and increase in learning, and a man of understanding will acquire wise counsel." ◀ Proverbs 1:5 ▶ [NASB]

"HE predestined us for adoption to HIMSELF as sons through JESUS CHRIST, according to the Purpose of HIS Will." ◀ Ephesians 1:5 ▶ [ESV]

"Look among the nations! Observe! Be astonished! Wonder! Because I AM doing something in your days—You would not believe if You were told." ◀ Habakkuk 1:5 ▶ [NASB]

Powerful Manifestation Prayer:

I BLESS myself, my family and everyone born on this date with GOD's MOST POWERFUL PURE LOVING LIGHT, HIS MOST POWERFUL PURE SOURCE HEALING ENERGY, and an ABUNDANCE OF HIS AMAZING GREATER GRACE in the POWER, the ANOINTING, the AUTHORITY and the WISDOM of the HOLY SPIRIT, in JESUS' MOST HOLY NAME. AMEN INDEED!

Day 6
1:6

"Being confident of this, that HE WHO began a GOoD work in You will carry it on to completion until the day of CHRIST JESUS." ◀ Philippians 1:6 ▶ [NIV]

"But he must ASK in Faith without any doubting, for the one who doubts is like the surf of the sea, driven and tossed by the wind." ◀ James 1:6 ▶ [NASB]

"For the LORD watches over the way of the righteous, but the way of the wicked leads to destruction." ◀ Psalm 1:6 ▶ [NIV]

"If we say we have fellowship with HIM while we walk in darkness, we lie and do not practice the Truth." ◀ 1 John 1:6 ▶ [ESV]

"And I Will destroy those who used to worship ME but now no longer do. They no longer ASK for the LORD's guidance or seek MY Blessings." ◀ Zephaniah1:6 ▶ [NIV]

"But everything I said through MY servants the prophets happened to your ancestors, just as I said. As a result, they repented and said, 'We have received what we deserved from the LORD of Heaven's Armies. HE has done what HE said HE would do." ◀ Zechariah 1:6 ▶ [NLT]

Powerful Manifestation Prayer:

I BLESS myself, my family and everyone born on this date with GOD's MOST POWERFUL PURE LOVING LIGHT, HIS MOST POWERFUL PURE SOURCE HEALING ENERGY, and an ABUNDANCE OF HIS AMAZING GREATER GRACE in the POWER, the ANOINTING, the AUTHORITY and the WISDOM of the HOLY SPIRIT, in JESUS' MOST HOLY NAME. AMEN INDEED!

Day 7
1:7

"The LORD is GOoD, a refuge in times of trouble. HE cares for those who trust in HIM."
◀ Nahum 1:7 ▶ [NIV]

"The fear of the LORD is the beginning of Knowledge, but fools despise Wisdom and instruction."
◀ Proverbs 1:7 ▶ [NIV]

"Be strong and very courageous. Be careful to obey all the Laws MY servant Moses gave You; do not turn from it to the right or to the left, that You may be successful wherever You go."
◀ Joshua 1:7 ▶ [NIV]

"Be silent before the LORD GOD! For the day of the LORD is near, For the LORD has prepared a sacrifice, HE has consecrated HIS guests."
◀ Zephaniah 1:7 ▶ [NASB]

"But if we walk in the LIGHT, as HE is in the LIGHT, we have fellowship with one another, and the BLOOD OF JESUS, HIS SON, cleanses us from all sin."
◀ 1 John 1:7 ▶ [ESV]

"And our HOPE for You is firm, because we know that just as You share in our sufferings, so also You share in our comfort."
◀ 2 Corinthians 1:7 ▶ [NIV]

Powerful Manifestation Prayer:

I BLESS myself, my family and everyone born on this date with GOD's MOST POWERFUL PURE LOVING LIGHT, HIS MOST POWERFUL PURE SOURCE HEALING ENERGY, and an ABUNDANCE OF HIS AMAZING GREATER GRACE in the POWER, the ANOINTING, the AUTHORITY and the WISDOM of the HOLY SPIRIT, in JESUS' MOST HOLY NAME. AMEN INDEED!

Day 8

1:8

"I AM the Alpha and the Omega," says the LORD GOD, "WHO is, and WHO was, and WHO is to come, the ALMIGHTY." ◀ Revelation 1:8 ▶ [NASB]

"This book of the Law shall not depart from your mouth, but You shall meditate on it day and night, so that You may be careful to do according to all that is written in it; for then You will make your way prosperous, and then You will have success." ◀ Joshua 1:8 ▶ [NASB]

"Now we know that the Law is GOoD if one uses it lawfully." ◀ 1 Timothy 1:8 ▶ [ESV]

"YOUR throne, O GOD, is forever and ever, the scepter of uprightness is the scepter of YOUR Kingdom." ◀ Hebrews 1:8 ▶ [ESV]

"My child, listen when your father corrects You. Don't neglect your mother's instruction." ◀ Proverbs 1:8 ▶ [NLT]

"HE Will keep You strong to the end so that You will be Free from all blame on the day when our LORD JESUS CHRIST returns." ◀ 1 Corinthians 1:8 ▶ [NLT]

Powerful Manifestation Prayer:

I BLESS myself, my family and everyone born on this date with GOD's MOST POWERFUL PURE LOVING LIGHT, HIS MOST POWERFUL PURE SOURCE HEALING ENERGY, and an ABUNDANCE OF HIS AMAZING GREATER GRACE in the POWER, the ANOINTING, the AUTHORITY and the WISDOM of the HOLY SPIRIT, in JESUS' MOST HOLY NAME. AMEN INDEED!

Day 9
1:9

"For this reason, also, since the day we heard of it, we have not ceased to **Pray** for **You** and to **ASK** that **You** may be filled with the **Knowledge** of **HIS Will** in all **Spiritual Wisdom** and understanding."
◀ Colossians 1:9 ▶ [NASB]

"If we confess our sins, **HE** is **Faithful** and just to forgive us our sins and to cleanse us from all unrighteousness."
◀ 1 John 1:9 ▶ [ESV]

"Have **I** not commanded **You**? Be strong and courageous! Do not tremble or be dismayed, for the **LORD** your **GOD** is with **You** wherever **You** go."
◀ Joshua 1:9 ▶ [NASB]

"He must hold firmly to the trustworthy message as it has been taught, so that **You** can encourage others by sound doctrine and refute those who oppose it."
◀ Titus 1:9 ▶ [NIV]

"What has been will be again, what has been done will be done again; there is nothing new under the sun."
◀ Ecclesiastes 1:9 ▶ [NIV]

"Then the **LORD** stretched out **HIS Hand** and touched my mouth, and the **LORD** said to me, "Behold, **I** have put **MY WORDS** in your mouth."
◀ Jeremiah 1:9 ▶ [NASB]

Powerful Manifestation Prayer:

I BLESS myself, my family and everyone born on this date with GOD's MOST POWERFUL PURE LOVING LIGHT, HIS MOST POWERFUL PURE SOURCE HEALING ENERGY, and an ABUNDANCE OF HIS AMAZING GREATER GRACE in the POWER, the ANOINTING, the AUTHORITY and the WISDOM of the HOLY SPIRIT, in JESUS' MOST HOLY NAME. AMEN INDEED!

Day 10
1:10

"Is there anything of which one might say, "See this, it is new"? Already it has existed for ages which were before us." ◄ Ecclesiastes 1:10 ► [NASB]

"Give me **Wisdom** and **Knowledge**, that I may lead this people, for who is able to govern this great people of **YOURS**?" ◄ 2 Chronicles 1:10 ► [NIV]

"Have **YOU** not put a hedge around him and his house and all that he has, on every side? **YOU** have **Blessed** the work of his hands, and his possessions have increased in the land." ◄ Job 1:10 ► [ESV]

"**HE** was in the world, and the world was made through **HIM**, yet the world did not know **HIM**." ◄ John 1:10 ► [ESV]

"**HE** delivered us from such a deadly peril, and **HE Will** deliver us. On **HIM** we have set our **HOPE** that **HE Will** deliver us again." ◄ 2 Corinthians 1:10 ► [ESV]

"The **LORD** your **GOD** has increased your numbers so that today **You** are as numerous as the stars in the sky." ◄ Deuteronomy 1:10 ► [NIV]

Powerful Manifestation Prayer:

I BLESS myself, my family and everyone born on this date with GOD's MOST POWERFUL PURE LOVING LIGHT, HIS MOST POWERFUL PURE SOURCE HEALING ENERGY, and an ABUNDANCE OF HIS AMAZING GREATER GRACE in the POWER, the ANOINTING, the AUTHORITY and the WISDOM of the HOLY SPIRIT, in JESUS' MOST HOLY NAME. AMEN INDEED!

Day 11
1:11

"I want You to know, brothers and sisters, that the Gospel I preached is not of human origin."
◀ Galatians 1:11 ▶ [NIV]

"For I long to see You, that I may impart to You some Spiritual gift to strengthen You."
◀ Romans 1:11 ▶ [ESV]

"O LORD, let YOUR ear be attentive to the prayer of YOUR servant, and to the prayer of YOUR servants who delight to fear YOUR Name, and give success to YOUR servant today, and grant him mercy in the sight of this man." Now I was cupbearer to the king." ◀ Nehemiah 1:11 ▶ [ESV]

"As You help us by your prayers. Then many will give thanks on our behalf for the Gracious Favor granted us in answer to the prayers of many." ◀ 2 Corinthians 1:11 ▶ [NIV]

"And an Angel of the LORD appeared to him, standing to the right of the altar of incense."
◀ Luke 1:11 ▶ [NASB]

"And a voice came from Heaven: "YOU are My Beloved SON; with YOU I AM well pleased."
◀ Mark 1:11 ▶ [ESV]

Powerful Manifestation Prayer:

I BLESS myself, my family and everyone born on this date with GOD's MOST POWERFUL PURE LOVING LIGHT, HIS MOST POWERFUL PURE SOURCE HEALING ENERGY, and an ABUNDANCE OF HIS AMAZING GREATER GRACE in the POWER, the ANOINTING, the AUTHORITY and the WISDOM of the HOLY SPIRIT, in JESUS' MOST HOLY NAME. AMEN INDEED!

Day 12
1:12

"Now I want **You** to know, brothers and sisters, that what has happened to me has actually served to advance the **Gospel**."
◀ Philippians 1:12 ▶ [NIV]

"**Blessed** is the one who perseveres under trial because, having **STOOD** the test, that person will receive the crown of life that the **LORD** has **Promised** to those who love **HIM**."
◀ James 1:12 ▶ [NIV]

"But do not gloat over the day of your brother in the day of his misfortune; do not rejoice over the people of Judah in the day of their ruin; do not boast in the day of distress."
◀ Obadiah 1:12 ▶ [ESV]

"I thank **HIM WHO** has given me strength, **CHRIST JESUS** our **LORD**, because **HE** judged me **Faithful**, appointing me to **HIS** service."
◀ 1 Timothy 1:12 ▶ [ESV]

"But to all who have received **HIM**—those who believe in **HIS Name**—**HE** has given the right to become **GOD's** children."
◀ John 1:12 ▶ [NET]

"**Wisdom** and **Knowledge** have been granted to **You**. And **I Will** give **You** riches and wealth and honor, such as none of the kings who were before **You** has possessed nor those who will come after **You**."
◀ 2 Chronicles 1:12 ▶ [NASB]

Powerful Manifestation Prayer:

I BLESS myself, my family and everyone born on this date with GOD's MOST POWERFUL PURE LOVING LIGHT, HIS MOST POWERFUL PURE SOURCE HEALING ENERGY, and an ABUNDANCE OF HIS AMAZING GREATER GRACE in the POWER, the ANOINTING, the AUTHORITY and the WISDOM of the HOLY SPIRIT, in JESUS' MOST HOLY NAME. AMEN INDEED!

Day 13
1:13

"Children born not of natural descent, nor of human decision or a husband's will, but born of GOD."
◀ John 1:13 ▶ [NIV]

"Where HE was tempted by Satan for forty days. HE was out among the wild animals, and Angels took care of HIM."
◀ Mark 1:13 ▶ [NLT]

"YOUR eyes are too pure to look on evil; YOU cannot tolerate wrongdoing. Why then do YOU tolerate the treacherous? Why are YOU silent while the wicked swallow up those more righteous than themselves?"
◀ Habakkuk 1:13 ▶ [NIV]

"And You also were included in CHRIST when You heard the message of Truth, the Gospel of your Salvation. When You believed, You were marked in HIM with a seal, the Promised HOLY SPIRIT."
◀ Ephesians 1:13 ▶ [NIV]

"I applied my mind to study and to explore by Wisdom all that is done under the Heavens. What a heavy burden GOD has laid on mankind!"
◀ Ecclesiastes 1:13 ▶ [NIV]

"So, prepare your minds for action and exercise self-control. Put all your HOPE in the Gracious Salvation that will come to You when JESUS CHRIST is revealed to the world."
◀ 1 Peter 1:13 ▶ [NLT]

"Hold on to the pattern of wholesome teaching You learned from me—a pattern shaped by the Faith and Love that You have in CHRIST JESUS."
◀ 2 Timothy 1:13 ▶ [NLT]

Powerful Manifestation Prayer:

I BLESS myself, my family and everyone born on this date with GOD's MOST POWERFUL PURE LOVING LIGHT, HIS MOST POWERFUL PURE SOURCE HEALING ENERGY, and an ABUNDANCE OF HIS AMAZING GREATER GRACE in the POWER, the ANOINTING, the AUTHORITY and the WISDOM of the HOLY SPIRIT, in JESUS' MOST HOLY NAME. AMEN INDEED!

Day 14
1:14

"So, You must live as GOD's obedient children. Don't slip back into your old ways of living to satisfy your own desires. You didn't know any better then." ◀ 1 Peter 1:14 ▶ [NLT]

"And the WORD became Flesh and dwelt among us, and we have seen HIS Glory, Glory as of the ONLY SON from the FATHER, full of Grace and Truth." ◀ John 1:14 ▶ [ESV]

"The SPIRIT is GOD's guarantee that HE Will give us the inheritance HE Promised and that HE has purchased us to be HIS OWN people. HE did this so we would praise and glorify HIM." ◀ Ephesians 1:14 ▶ [NLT]

"And You will have joy and gladness, and many will rejoice at his birth." ◀ Luke 1:14 ▶ [ESV]

"And because of my chains, most of the brothers and sisters have become confident in the LORD and dare all the more to proclaim the Gospel without fear." ◀ Philippians 1:14 ▶ [NIV]

"And the Grace of our LORD was more than abundant, with the Faith and Love which are found in CHRIST JESUS." ◀ 1 Timothy 1:14 ▶ [NASB]

"After John was put in prison, JESUS went into Galilee, proclaiming the GOoD News of GOD." ◀ Mark 1:14 ▶ [NIV]

Powerful Manifestation Prayer:

I BLESS myself, my family and everyone born on this date with GOD's MOST POWERFUL PURE LOVING LIGHT, HIS MOST POWERFUL PURE SOURCE HEALING ENERGY, and an ABUNDANCE OF HIS AMAZING GREATER GRACE in the POWER, the ANOINTING, the AUTHORITY and the WISDOM of the HOLY SPIRIT, in JESUS' MOST HOLY NAME. AMEN INDEED!

Day 15
1:15

"HE is the image of the invisible GOD, the Firstborn of all creation." ◄ Colossians 1:15 ► [NASB]

"Some indeed preach CHRIST from envy and rivalry, but others from GOoD will."
◄ Philippians 1:15 ► [ESV]

"My child, don't go along with them! Stay far away from their paths." ◄ Proverbs 1:15 ► [NLT]

"For the day of the LORD is near upon all the nations. As You have done, it shall be done to You; your deeds shall return on your own head." ◄ Obadiah 1:15 ► [ESV]

"And I will also be diligent that at any time after my departure You will be able to call these things to mind." ◄ 2 Peter 1:15 ► [NASB]

"The time has come, HE said. 'The Kingdom of GOD has come near. Repent and believe the GOoD News!'" ◄ Mark 1:15 ► [NIV]

Powerful Manifestation Prayer:

I BLESS myself, my family and everyone born on this date with GOD's MOST POWERFUL PURE LOVING LIGHT, HIS MOST POWERFUL PURE SOURCE HEALING ENERGY, and an ABUNDANCE OF HIS AMAZING GREATER GRACE in the POWER, the ANOINTING, the AUTHORITY and the WISDOM of the HOLY SPIRIT, in JESUS' MOST HOLY NAME. AMEN INDEED!

Day 16
1:16

"Because it is written, 'You shall be Holy, for I AM HOLY." ◀ 1 Peter 1:16 ▶ [NASB]

"For I am not ashamed of the Gospel, for it is the Power of GOD for Salvation to everyone who believes, to the Jew first and also to the Greek." ◀ Romans 1:16 ▶ [NASB]

"Do not take YOUR servant for a wicked woman; I have been praying here out of my great anguish and grief." ◀ 1 Samuel 1:16 ▶ [NIV]

"I said in my heart, "I have acquired great Wisdom, surpassing all who were over Jerusalem before me, and my heart has had great experience of Wisdom and Knowledge." ◀ Ecclesiastes 1:16 ▶ [ESV]

"And he will turn many of the children of Israel to the LORD their GOD." ◀ Luke 1:16 ▶ [ESV]

"For we were not making up clever stories when we told You about the Powerful coming of our LORD JESUS CHRIST. We saw HIS majestic splendor with our own eyes." ◀ 2 Peter 1:16 ▶ [NLT]

Powerful Manifestation Prayer:

I BLESS myself, my family and everyone born on this date with GOD's MOST POWERFUL PURE LOVING LIGHT, HIS MOST POWERFUL PURE SOURCE HEALING ENERGY, and an ABUNDANCE OF HIS AMAZING GREATER GRACE in the POWER, the ANOINTING, the AUTHORITY and the WISDOM of the HOLY SPIRIT, in JESUS' MOST HOLY NAME. AMEN INDEED!

Day 17
1:17

"Get yourself ready! Stand up and say to them whatever I command You. Do not be terrified by them, or I Will terrify You before them." ◄ Jeremiah 1:17 ► [NIV]

"Every GOoD thing given and every perfect gift is from above, coming down from the FATHER of Lights, with WHOM there is no variation or shifting shadow." ◄ James 1:17 ► [NASB]

"And he will go on before the LORD, in the Spirit and power of Elijah, to turn the hearts of the parents to their children and the disobedient to the Wisdom of the righteous—to make ready a people prepared for the LORD." ◄ Luke 1:17 ► [NIV]

"Now to the King eternal, immortal, invisible, the only GOD, be Honor and Glory forever and ever. Amen." ◄ 1 Timothy 1:17 ► [NASB]

"For the Gospel reveals the Righteousness of GOD that comes by Faith from start to finish, just as it is written: "The righteous will live by Faith." ◄ Romans 1:17 ► [BSB]

"Then JESUS said to them, "Follow ME, and I Will make You become fishers of men." ◄ Mark 1:17 ► [NKJV]

Powerful Manifestation Prayer:

I BLESS myself, my family and everyone born on this date with GOD's MOST POWERFUL PURE LOVING LIGHT, HIS MOST POWERFUL PURE SOURCE HEALING ENERGY, and an ABUNDANCE OF HIS AMAZING GREATER GRACE in the POWER, the ANOINTING, the AUTHORITY and the WISDOM of the HOLY SPIRIT, in JESUS' MOST HOLY NAME. AMEN INDEED!

Acquire Scripture Knowledge

Day 18
1:18

"**HE** is also **Head** of the **Body**, the **Church**; and **HE** is the **Beginning**, the **Firstborn** from the dead, so that **HE HIMSELF Will** come to have first place in everything." ◄ Colossians 1:18 ► [NASB]

"**HE** wanted us to be **HIS OWN** special people, and so **HE** sent the **True** message to give us new birth." ◄ James 1:18 ► [CEV]

"For **You** know that it was not with perishable things such as silver or gold that **You** were redeemed from the empty way of life handed down to **You** from your ancestors." ◄ 1 Peter 1:18 ► [NIV]

"The message about the **Cross** doesn't make any sense to lost people. But for those of us who are being saved, it is **GOD's Power** at work." ◄ 1 Corinthians 1:18 ► [CEV]

"What does it matter? Only that in every way, whether from false motives or **True**, **CHRIST** is proclaimed, and in this I rejoice. Yes, and I will continue to rejoice." ◄ Philippians 1:18 ► [CSB]

"Let **YOUR** servant find **Favor** in **YOUR** eyes." ◄ 1 Samuel 1:18 ► [ESV]

Powerful Manifestation Prayer:

I BLESS myself, my family and everyone born on this date with GOD's MOST POWERFUL PURE LOVING LIGHT, HIS MOST POWERFUL PURE SOURCE HEALING ENERGY, and an ABUNDANCE OF HIS AMAZING GREATER GRACE in the POWER, the ANOINTING, the AUTHORITY and the WISDOM of the HOLY SPIRIT, in JESUS' MOST HOLY NAME. AMEN INDEED!

Day 19
1:19

"They will fight against You, but they shall not prevail against You. For I AM with You," says the LORD, "to deliver You."
◀ Jeremiah 1:19 ▶ [NKJV]

"For I know that through your prayers and the help of the SPIRIT of JESUS CHRIST this will turn out for my deliverance."
◀ Philippians 1:19 ▶ [ESV]

"My dear brothers and sisters, understand this: Everyone should be quick to listen, slow to speak, and slow to anger."
◀ James 1:19 ▶ [CSB]

"If You are willing and obedient, You will eat the GOoD things of the land."
◀ Isaiah 1:19 ▶ [CSB]

"The Angel answered and said to him, "I am Gabriel, who stands in the presence of GOD, and I have been sent to speak to You and to bring You this GOoD News."
◀ Luke 1:19 ▶ [NASB]

"And so we have the prophetic WORD confirmed, which You do well to heed as a Light that shines in a dark place, until the day dawns and the morning star rises in your hearts."
◀ 2 Peter 1:19 ▶ [NKJV]

Powerful Manifestation Prayer:

I BLESS myself, my family and everyone born on this date with GOD's MOST POWERFUL PURE LOVING LIGHT, HIS MOST POWERFUL PURE SOURCE HEALING ENERGY, and an ABUNDANCE OF HIS AMAZING GREATER GRACE in the POWER, the ANOINTING, the AUTHORITY and the WISDOM of the HOLY SPIRIT, in JESUS' MOST HOLY NAME. AMEN INDEED!

Day 20
1:20

"Immediately **HE** called them; and they left their father Zebedee in the **BOAT** with the hired servants, and went away to follow **HIM**."
◄ Mark 1:20 ► [NASB]

"My eager expectation and **HOPE** is that I will not be ashamed about anything, but that now as always, with all courage, **CHRIST Will** be highly honored in my body, whether by life or by death."
◄ Philippians 1:20 ► [CSB]

"For all the **Promises** of **GOD** find their **Yes** in **HIM**. That is why it is through **HIM** that we utter our **Amen** to **GOD** for **HIS Glory**."
◄ 2 Corinthians 1:20 ► [ESV]

"And behold, **You** shall be silent and unable to speak until the day when these things take place, because **You** did not believe **MY WORDS**, which will be fulfilled in their proper time."
◄ Luke 1:20 ► [NASB]

"But know this first of all, that no prophecy of **Scripture** is a matter of one's own interpretation."
◄ 2 Peter 1:20 ► [NASB]

"**HE** was known before the foundation of the world, but was revealed in the last times for your sake."
◄ 1 Peter 1:20 ► [BSB]

Powerful Manifestation Prayer:

I BLESS myself, my family and everyone born on this date with GOD's MOST POWERFUL PURE LOVING LIGHT, HIS MOST POWERFUL PURE SOURCE HEALING ENERGY, and an ABUNDANCE OF HIS AMAZING GREATER GRACE in the POWER, the ANOINTING, the AUTHORITY and the WISDOM of the HOLY SPIRIT, in JESUS' MOST HOLY NAME. AMEN INDEED!

Day 21
1:21

"For to me, to live is CHRIST and to die is gain." ◀ Philippians 1:21 ▶ [NASB]

"And he said, "Naked I came from my mother's womb, and naked shall I return. The LORD gave, and the LORD has taken away; Blessed be the Name of the LORD." ◀ Job 1:21 ▶ [ESV]

"And so GOD makes it possible for You and us to stand firmly together with CHRST. GOD is also the ONE WHO Chose us." ◀ 2 Corinthians 1:21 ▶ [CEV]

"Keep yourselves in the Love of GOD, waiting anxiously for the mercy of our LORD JESUS CHRIST to eternal life." ◀ Jude 1:21 ▶ [NASB]

"Therefore, get rid of all moral filth and every expression of evil, and humbly accept the WORD planted in You, which can save your Souls." ◀ James 1:21 ▶ [BSB]

"Look, the LORD your GOD has set the land before You; go up and possess it, as the LORD GOD of your fathers has spoken to You; do not fear or be discouraged." ◀ Deuteronomy 1:21 ▶ [NKJV]

Powerful Manifestation Prayer:

I BLESS myself, my family and everyone born on this date with GOD's MOST POWERFUL PURE LOVING LIGHT, HIS MOST POWERFUL PURE SOURCE HEALING ENERGY, and an ABUNDANCE OF HIS AMAZING GREATER GRACE in the POWER, the ANOINTING, the AUTHORITY and the WISDOM of the HOLY SPIRIT, in JESUS' MOST HOLY NAME. AMEN INDEED!

Day 22
1:22

"Foolish people! How long do **You** want to be foolish? How long will **You** enjoy making fun of **Knowledge?** Will **You** never learn?"
◄ Proverbs 1:22 ► [GNT]

"But if I am to live on in the flesh, this will mean fruitful labor for me; and I do not know which to choose."
◄ Philippians 1:22 ► [NASB]

"And **GOD** placed all things under **HIS** feet and appointed **HIM** to be **Head** over everything for the **Church**."
◄ Ephesians 1:22 ► [NIV]

"Do not deceive yourselves by just listening to **HIS WORD**; instead, put it into practice."
◄ James 1:22 ► [GNT]

"**HE** has also put **HIS Seal** on us and given us the **SPIRIT** in our hearts as a down payment."
◄ 2 Corinthians 1:22 ► [CSB]

"Having purified your **Souls** by your obedience to the **Truth** for a sincere brotherly love, love one another earnestly from a pure heart."
◄ 1 Peter 1:22 ► [ESV]

Powerful Manifestation Prayer:

I BLESS myself, my family and everyone born on this date with GOD's MOST POWERFUL PURE LOVING LIGHT, HIS MOST POWERFUL PURE SOURCE HEALING ENERGY, and an ABUNDANCE OF HIS AMAZING GREATER GRACE in the POWER, the ANOINTING, the AUTHORITY and the WISDOM of the HOLY SPIRIT, in JESUS' MOST HOLY NAME. AMEN INDEED!

Day 23
1:23

"But I am hard-pressed from both directions, having the desire to depart and be with CHRIST, for that is very much better." ◀ Philippians 1:23 ▶ [NASB]

"For You have been born again not of seed which is perishable but imperishable, that is, through the living and enduring WORD of GOD." ◀ 1 Peter 1:23 ▶ [NASB]

"The virgin will conceive and give birth to a SON, and they will call HIM IMMANUEL (which means GOD with us)." ◀ Matthew 1:23 ▶ [NIV]

"But You must continue to believe this Truth and stand firmly in it. Don't drift away from the assurance You received when You heard the GOoD News. The GOoD News has been preached all over the world, and I, Paul, have been appointed as GOD's servant to proclaim it."
◀ Colossians 1:23 ▶ [NLT]

"Saul and Jonathan, beloved and pleasant in their life, And in their death they were not parted; They were swifter than eagles, They were stronger than lions." ◀ 2 Samuel 1:23 ▶ [NASB]

"If You respond to MY warning, then I Will pour out MY SPIRIT on You and teach You MY WORDS." ◀ Proverbs 1:23 ▶ [CSB]

Powerful Manifestation Prayer:

I BLESS myself, my family and everyone born on this date with GOD's MOST POWERFUL PURE LOVING LIGHT, HIS MOST POWERFUL PURE SOURCE HEALING ENERGY, and an ABUNDANCE OF HIS AMAZING GREATER GRACE in the POWER, the ANOINTING, the AUTHORITY and the WISDOM of the HOLY SPIRIT, in JESUS' MOST HOLY NAME. AMEN INDEED!

Day 24
1:24

"Therefore, the LORD declares, the LORD of hosts, the MIGHTY ONE of Israel: "Ah, I Will get relief from MY enemies and avenge MYSELF on MY foes." ◀ Isaiah 1:24 ▶ [ESV]

"What have YOU to do with us, JESUS of Nazareth? Have YOU come to destroy us? I know WHO YOU are— the HOLY ONE of GOD!" ◀ Mark 1:24 ▶ [ESV]

"And they prayed and said, "YOU, LORD, WHO know the hearts of all men, show which one of these two YOU have Chosen." ◀ Acts 1:24 ▶ [NASB]

"To HIM WHO is able to keep You from stumbling and to present You before HIS Glorious presence without fault and with great joy." ◀ Jude 1:24 ▶ [NIV]

"Now I rejoice in my sufferings for your sake, and in my flesh, I do my share on behalf of HIS Body, which is the Church, in filling up what is lacking in CHRIST's afflictions."
◀ Colossians 1:24 ▶ [NASB]

"Not that we lord it over your Faith, but we work with You for your joy, for You stand firm in your Faith." ◀ 2 Corinthians 1:24 ▶ [ESV]

Powerful Manifestation Prayer:

I BLESS myself, my family and everyone born on this date with GOD's MOST POWERFUL PURE LOVING LIGHT, HIS MOST POWERFUL PURE SOURCE HEALING ENERGY, and an ABUNDANCE OF HIS AMAZING GREATER GRACE in the POWER, the ANOINTING, the AUTHORITY and the WISDOM of the HOLY SPIRIT, in JESUS' MOST HOLY NAME. AMEN INDEED!

Day 25
1:25

"To GOD our Savior, WHO Alone is wise, be Glory and Majesty, Dominion and Power, both now and forever. Amen."
◄ Jude 1:25 ► [NKJV]

"The Grace of the LORD JESUS CHRIST be with your Spirit." ◄ Philemon 1:25 ► [ESV]

"The LORD has done this for me," she said. "In these days HE has shown HIS Favor and taken away my disgrace among the people."
◄ Luke 1:25 ► [NIV]

"But the WORD of the LORD remains forever." And that WORD is the GOoD News that was preached to You."
◄ 1 Peter 1:25 ► [ESV]

"GOD's plan was to make me a servant of HIS Church and to send me to preach HIS complete message to You."
◄ Colossians 1:25 ► [CEV]

"But the one who looks into the perfect Law, the Law of liberty, and perseveres, being no hearer who forgets but a doer who acts, he will be Blessed in his doing." ◄ James 1:25 ► [ESV]

Powerful Manifestation Prayer:

I BLESS myself, my family and everyone born on this date with GOD's MOST POWERFUL PURE LOVING LIGHT, HIS MOST POWERFUL PURE SOURCE HEALING ENERGY, and an ABUNDANCE OF HIS AMAZING GREATER GRACE in the POWER, the ANOINTING, the AUTHORITY and the WISDOM of the HOLY SPIRIT, in JESUS' MOST HOLY NAME. AMEN INDEED!

Day 26
1:26

"Jonathan, I miss You most! I loved You like a brother. You were truly loyal to me, more Faithful than a wife to her husband."
◄ 2 Samuel 1:26 ► [CEV]

"I Will restore your leaders as in days of old, your rulers as at the beginning. Afterward You will be called the City of Righteousness, the Faithful City."
◄ Isaiah 1:26 ► [NIV]

"For ages and ages this message was kept secret from everyone, but now it has been explained to GOD's people."
◄ Colossians 1:26 ► [CEV]

"If anyone thinks himself to be religious, and yet does not bridle his tongue but deceives his own heart, this man's religion is worthless."
◄ James 1:26 ► [NASB]

"John answered them, 'I baptize with water, but among You stands ONE You do not know'."
◄ John 1:26 ► [ESV]

"Then, when I visit You again, You will have GOoD reason to take great pride in CHRIST JESUS because of me."
◄ Philippians 1:26 ► [CEV]

Powerful Manifestation Prayer:

I BLESS myself, my family and everyone born on this date with GOD's MOST POWERFUL PURE LOVING LIGHT, HIS MOST POWERFUL PURE SOURCE HEALING ENERGY, and an ABUNDANCE OF HIS AMAZING GREATER GRACE in the POWER, the ANOINTING, the AUTHORITY and the WISDOM of the HOLY SPIRIT, in JESUS' MOST HOLY NAME. AMEN INDEED!

Day 27
1:27

"GOD created man in HIS OWN Image, in the Image of GOD HE created him; male and female HE created them."
◄ Genesis 1:27 ► [NASB]

"But GOD Chose what is foolish in the world to shame the wise; GOD Chose what is weak in the world to shame the strong."
◄ 1 Corinthians 1:27 ► [ESV]

"For this child I prayed, and the LORD has granted me my petition which I asked of HIM."
◄ 1 Samuel 1:27 ► [NKJV]

"HE is the ONE coming after me, WHOSE sandal strap I'm not worthy to untie."
◄ John 1:27 ► [CSB]

"To them GOD Chose to make known how great among the Gentiles are the riches of the Glory of this mystery, which is CHRIST in You, the HOPE of Glory."
◄ Colossians 1:27 ► [ESV]

"Religion that GOD our FATHER accepts as pure and faultless is this: to look after orphans and widows in their distress and to keep oneself from being polluted by the world."
◄ James 1:27 ► [NIV]

Powerful Manifestation Prayer:

I BLESS myself, my family and everyone born on this date with GOD's MOST POWERFUL PURE LOVING LIGHT, HIS MOST POWERFUL PURE SOURCE HEALING ENERGY, and an ABUNDANCE OF HIS AMAZING GREATER GRACE in the POWER, the ANOINTING, the AUTHORITY and the WISDOM of the HOLY SPIRIT, in JESUS' MOST HOLY NAME. AMEN INDEED!

Day 28
1:28

"Greetings, You who are highly Favored! The LORD is with You." ◀ Luke 1:28 ▶ [NIV]

"GOD Blessed them; and GOD said to them, "Be fruitful and multiply, and fill the earth, and subdue it; and rule over the fish of the sea and over the birds of the sky and over every living thing that moves on the earth."" ◀ Genesis 1:28 ▶ [NASB]

"GOD Chose the lowly things of this world and the despised things—and the things that are not—to nullify the things that are." ◀ 1 Corinthians 1:28 ▶ [NIV]

"But rebels and sinners will both be broken, and those who forsake the LORD Will perish." ◀ Isaiah 1:28 ▶ [NIV]

"So, we tell others about CHRIST, warning everyone and teaching everyone with all the Wisdom GOD has given us. We want to present them to GOD, perfect in their relationship to CHRIST." ◀ Colossians 1:28 ▶ [NLT]

"The appearance of the Brilliant Light all around was like that of a rainbow in a cloud on a rainy day. This was the appearance of the likeness of the LORD's Glory. When I saw IT, I fell facedown and heard A Voice speaking." ◀ Ezekiel 1:28 ▶ [CSB]

"News about JESUS quickly spread all over Galilee." ◀ Mark 1:28 ▶ [CEV]

Powerful Manifestation Prayer:

I BLESS myself, my family and everyone born on this date with GOD's MOST POWERFUL PURE LOVING LIGHT, HIS MOST POWERFUL PURE SOURCE HEALING ENERGY, and an ABUNDANCE OF HIS AMAZING GREATER GRACE in the POWER, the ANOINTING, the AUTHORITY and the WISDOM of the HOLY SPIRIT, in JESUS' MOST HOLY NAME. AMEN INDEED!

Day 29
1:29

"For they hated Knowledge and chose not to fear the LORD." ◀ Proverbs 1.29 ▶ [NLT]

"Then I said to You, 'Do not be terrified or afraid of them." ◀ Deuteronomy 1:29 ▶ [NKJV]

"As surely as the LORD lives, WHO has delivered me out of every trouble." ◀ 1 Kings 1:29 ▶ [NIV]

"To this end I strenuously contend with all the energy, CHRIST so powerfully works in me."
◀ Colossians 1:29 ▶ [NIV]

"For to You it has been granted for CHRIST's sake, not only to believe in HIM, but also to suffer for HIS sake."
◀ Philippians 1:29 ▶ [NASB]

"The next day John saw JESUS coming toward him and said, "Look, The LAMB of GOD, WHO takes away the sins of the world!"
◀ John 1:29 ▶ [NIV]

Powerful Manifestation Prayer:

I BLESS myself, my family and everyone born on this date with GOD's MOST POWERFUL PURE LOVING LIGHT, HIS MOST POWERFUL PURE SOURCE HEALING ENERGY, and an ABUNDANCE OF HIS AMAZING GREATER GRACE in the POWER, the ANOINTING, the AUTHORITY and the WISDOM of the HOLY SPIRIT, in JESUS' MOST HOLY NAME. AMEN INDEED!

Day 30
1:30

"I will surely carry out this very day what I swore to You by the LORD, the GOD of Israel: Solomon your son shall be king after me, and he will sit on my throne in my place."
◄ 1 Kings 1:30 ► [NIV]

"They are backstabbers, haters of GOD, insolent, proud, and boastful. They invent new ways of sinning, and they disobey their parents." ◄ Romans 1:30 ► [NLT]

"But the Angel said to her, "Do not be afraid, Mary; You have found Favor with GOD."
◄ Luke 1:30 ► [NIV]

"'The LORD your GOD WHO goes before You will HIMSELF fight on your behalf, just as HE did for You in Egypt before your eyes." ◄ Deuteronomy 1:30 ► [NASB]

"It is because of HIM that You are in CHRIST JESUS, WHO has become for us Wisdom from GOD, that is, our Righteousness, holiness and redemption." ◄ 1 Corinthians 1:30 ► [NIV]

"This is the ONE I meant when I said, 'A MAN WHO comes after me has surpassed me because HE was before me'." ◄ John 1:30 ► [NIV]

Powerful Manifestation Prayer:

I BLESS myself, my family and everyone born on this date with GOD's MOST POWERFUL PURE LOVING LIGHT, HIS MOST POWERFUL PURE SOURCE HEALING ENERGY, and an ABUNDANCE OF HIS AMAZING GREATER GRACE in the POWER, the ANOINTING, the AUTHORITY and the WISDOM of the HOLY SPIRIT, in JESUS' MOST HOLY NAME. AMEN INDEED!

Day 31
1:31

"**GOD** saw all that **HE** had made, and behold, it was very **GOoD**. And there was evening and there was morning, the **Sixth** day."
◄ Genesis 1:31 ► [NASB]

"And **You** saw how the **LORD** your **GOD** cared for **You** all along the way as **You** traveled through the wilderness, just as a father cares for his child. Now **HE** has brought **You** to this place."
◄ Deuteronomy 1:31 ► [NLT]

"Therefore, they shall eat the fruit of their way, and have their fill of their own devices."
◄ Proverbs 1:31 ► [ESV]

"Your strongest leaders will be like dry wood set on fire by their idols. No one will be able to help, as they all go up in flames."
◄ Isaiah 1:31 ► [CEV]

"And **HE** came to her and raised her up, taking her by the hand, and the fever left her, and she waited on **Them**."
◄ Mark 1:31 ► [NASB]

"So, if **You** want to brag, do what the **Scriptures** say and brag about the **LORD**."
◄ 1 Corinthians 1:31 ► [CEV]

Powerful Manifestation Prayer:

I BLESS myself, my family and everyone born on this date with GOD's MOST POWERFUL PURE LOVING LIGHT, HIS MOST POWERFUL PURE SOURCE HEALING ENERGY, and an ABUNDANCE OF HIS AMAZING GREATER GRACE in the POWER, the ANOINTING, the AUTHORITY and the WISDOM of the HOLY SPIRIT, in JESUS' MOST HOLY NAME. AMEN INDEED!

February
2

~ I Pray for You and You Pray for Me!

"After Job had prayed for his friends, the LORD restored his fortunes and gave him twice as much as he had before." ◄ Job 42:10 ► [NIV]

"You haven't done this before. A.S.K. using MY NAME, and You will receive, and You will have abundant joy." ◄ John 16:24 ► [NLT]

Powerful Manifestation Prayer:

I BLESS myself, my family and everyone born in this month with GOD's MOST POWERFUL PURE LOVING LIGHT, HIS MOST POWERFUL PURE SOURCE HEALING ENERGY, and an ABUNDANCE OF HIS AMAZING GREATER GRACE in the POWER, the ANOINTING, the AUTHORITY and the WISDOM of the HOLY SPIRIT, in JESUS' MOST HOLY NAME.
AMEN INDEED!

A.S.K.- Additional Scripture Knowledge

Write Additional Scriptures here.

Day 32
2:1

"First of all, then, I urge that supplications, prayers, intercessions, and thanksgivings be made for all people."
◀ 1 Timothy 2:1 ▶ [ESV]

"You, therefore, have no excuse, You who pass judgment on someone else, for at whatever point You judge another, You are condemning yourself, because You who pass judgment do the same things."
◀ Romans 2:1 ▶ [NIV]

"My heart rejoices in the LORD; in the LORD my horn is lifted high. My mouth boasts over my enemies, for I delight in YOUR deliverance."
◀ 1 Samuel 2:1 ▶ [NIV]

"Woe to those who devise wickedness and work evil on their beds! When the morning dawns, they perform it, because it is in the power of their hand."
◀ Micah 2:1 ▶ [ESV]

"The one who scatters has come up against You. Man the fortress, watch the road;
Strengthen your back, summon all your strength."
◀ Nahum 2:1 ▶ [NASB]

"You then, my child, be strengthened by the Grace that is in CHRIST JESUS."
◀ 2 Timothy 2:1 ▶ [ESV]

Powerful Manifestation Prayer:

I BLESS myself, my family and everyone born on this date with GOD's MOST POWERFUL PURE LOVING LIGHT, HIS MOST POWERFUL PURE SOURCE HEALING ENERGY, and an ABUNDANCE OF HIS AMAZING GREATER GRACE in the POWER, the ANOINTING, the AUTHORITY and the WISDOM of the HOLY SPIRIT, in JESUS' MOST HOLY NAME. AMEN INDEED!

Day 33
2:2

"By the seventh day **GOD** had finished the work **HE** had been doing; so on the seventh day **HE** rested from all **HIS** work." ◀ Genesis 2:2 ▶ [NIV]

"In my distress, O **LORD**, I called to **YOU**, and **YOU** answered me. From deep in the world of the dead I cried for help, and **YOU** heard me." ◀ Jonah 2:2 ▶ [GNT]

"Where is **HE WHO** has been born **King** of the Jews? For we saw **HIS Star** in the east and have come to worship **HIM**." ◀ Matthew 2:2 ▶ [NASB]

"And many were gathered together, so that there was no longer room, not even near the door; and **HE** was speaking the **WORD** to them." ◀ Mark 2:2 ▶ [NASB]

"And suddenly there came from **Heaven** a sound like a mighty rushing wind, and it filled the entire house where they were sitting." ◀ Acts 2:2 ▶ [NIV]

"There is no one **Holy** like the **LORD**; there is no one besides **YOU**; there is no **Rock** like our **GOD**." ◀ 1 Samuel 2:2 ▶ [ESV]

Powerful Manifestation Prayer:

I BLESS myself, my family and everyone born on this date with GOD's MOST POWERFUL PURE LOVING LIGHT, HIS MOST POWERFUL PURE SOURCE HEALING ENERGY, and an ABUNDANCE OF HIS AMAZING GREATER GRACE in the POWER, the ANOINTING, the AUTHORITY and the WISDOM of the HOLY SPIRIT, in JESUS' MOST HOLY NAME. AMEN INDEED!

Day 34
2:3

"So GOD Blessed the seventh day and made it Holy, because on it GOD rested from all HIS work that HE had done in creation."
◄ Genesis 2:3 ► [ESV]

"Seek the LORD, all You humble of the land, who do HIS just commands; seek Righteousness; seek humility; perhaps You may be hidden on the day of the anger of the LORD."
◄ Zephaniah 2:3 ► [ESV]

"Do nothing from selfishness or empty conceit, but with humility of mind regard one another as more important than yourselves."
◄ Philippians 2:3 ► [NASB]

"Many people shall come and say, "Come, and let us go up to the mountain of the LORD, To the house of the GOD of Jacob; HE Will teach us HIS ways, and we shall walk in HIS paths."
◄ Isaiah 2:3 ► [NKJV]

"Boast no more so very proudly, do not let arrogance come out of your mouth; For the LORD is a GOD of Knowledge, and with HIM actions are weighed."
◄ 1 Samuel 2:3 ► [NASB]

"Keep the charge of the LORD your GOD, to walk in HIS Ways, to keep HIS Statutes, HIS Commandments, HIS Ordinances, and HIS Testimonies, according to what is written in the Law of Moses, that You may succeed in all that You do and wherever You turn."
◄ 1 Kings 2:3 ► [NASB]

Powerful Manifestation Prayer:

I BLESS myself, my family and everyone born on this date with GOD's MOST POWERFUL PURE LOVING LIGHT, HIS MOST POWERFUL PURE SOURCE HEALING ENERGY, and an ABUNDANCE OF HIS AMAZING GREATER GRACE in the POWER, the ANOINTING, the AUTHORITY and the WISDOM of the HOLY SPIRIT, in JESUS' MOST HOLY NAME. AMEN INDEED!

Day 35
2:4

"But now be strong, … declares the LORD. 'Be strong, …. Be strong, all You people of the land,' declares the LORD, 'and work. For I AM with You,' declares the LORD ALMIGHTY."

◀ Haggai 2:4 ▶ [NIV]

"Our LORD, YOU break the bows of warriors, but YOU give strength to everyone who stumbles."

◀ 1 Samuel 2:4 ▶ [CEV]

"And that the LORD may keep HIS Promise to me: 'If your descendants watch how they live, and if they walk Faithfully before ME with all their heart and Soul, You will never fail to have a successor on the throne of Israel.'"

◀ 1 Kings 2:4 ▶ [NIV]

"Hear the WORD of the LORD, O house of Jacob, and all the families of the house of Israel."

◀ Jeremiah 2:4 ▶ [NASB]

"Then I said, 'I am driven away from YOUR sight; yet I shall again look upon YOUR Holy Temple.'"

◀ Jonah 2:4 ▶ [ESV]

"And they were all filled with the HOLY SPIRIT and began to speak with other tongues, as the SPIRIT was giving them utterance."

◀ Acts 2:4 ▶ [NASB]

Powerful Manifestation Prayer:

I BLESS myself, my family and everyone born on this date with GOD's MOST POWERFUL PURE LOVING LIGHT, HIS MOST POWERFUL PURE SOURCE HEALING ENERGY, and an ABUNDANCE OF HIS AMAZING GREATER GRACE in the POWER, the ANOINTING, the AUTHORITY and the WISDOM of the HOLY SPIRIT, in JESUS' MOST HOLY NAME. AMEN INDEED!

Day 36
2:5

"For there is One **GOD**, and there is One **Mediator** between **GOD** and men, the **MAN CHRIST JESUS**." ◀ 1 Timothy 2:5 ▶ [ESV]

"Come, house of Jacob, and let us walk in the **Light** of the **LORD**." ◀ Isaiah 2:5 ▶ [NASB]

"The house which I am about to build will be great, for greater is our **GOD** than all the gods." ◀ 2 Chronicles 2:5 ▶ [NASB]

"Then **You** will understand the fear of the **LORD** and find the **Knowledge** of **GOD**." ◀ Proverbs 2:5 ▶ [ESV]

"As for them, whether they hear or whether they refuse—for they are a rebellious house—yet they will know that a **Prophet** has been among them." ◀ Ezekiel 2:5 ▶ [NKJV]

"Just as **I Promised** your ancestors when **I** brought them out of Egypt. Don't worry. **MY SPIRIT** is right here with **You**!" ◀ Haggai 2:5 ▶ [CEV]

Powerful Manifestation Prayer:

I BLESS myself, my family and everyone born on this date with GOD's MOST POWERFUL PURE LOVING LIGHT, HIS MOST POWERFUL PURE SOURCE HEALING ENERGY, and an ABUNDANCE OF HIS AMAZING GREATER GRACE in the POWER, the ANOINTING, the AUTHORITY and the WISDOM of the HOLY SPIRIT, in JESUS' MOST HOLY NAME. AMEN INDEED!

Day 37
2:6

"**You** have accepted **CHRIST JESUS** as your **LORD**. Now keep on following **HIM**."
◀ Colossians 2:6 ▶ [CEV]

"**WHO** gave **HIMSELF** to redeem the whole human race. That was the proof at the right time that **GOD** wants everyone to be saved." ◀ 1 Timothy 2:6 ▶ [GNT]

"Then Elijah said to him, 'Please stay here, for the **LORD** has sent me to the Jordan.' And he said, 'As the **LORD** lives, and as **You** yourself live, I will not leave **You**'. So, the two of them went on."
◀ 2 Kings 2:6 ▶ [NASB]

"For it stands in **Scripture**: "Behold, **I AM** laying in Zion a **Stone,** a **Cornerstone Chosen** and **Precious**, and whoever believes in **HIM Will** not be put to shame."" ◀ 1 Peter 2:6 ▶ [ESV]

"I descended to the roots of the mountains. The earth with its bars was around me forever, but **YOU** have brought up my life from the pit, O **LORD** my **GOD**." ◀ Jonah 2:6 ▶ [NASB]

"For the **LORD** gives **Wisdom**; from **HIS Mouth** come **Knowledge** and **Understanding**."
◀ Proverbs 2:6 ▶ [NASB]

Powerful Manifestation Prayer:

I BLESS myself, my family and everyone born on this date with GOD's MOST POWERFUL PURE LOVING LIGHT, HIS MOST POWERFUL PURE SOURCE HEALING ENERGY, and an ABUNDANCE OF HIS AMAZING GREATER GRACE in the POWER, the ANOINTING, the AUTHORITY and the WISDOM of the HOLY SPIRIT, in JESUS' MOST HOLY NAME. AMEN INDEED!

Day 38
2:7

"For this I was appointed a preacher and an apostle (I am telling the **Truth**, I am not lying) as a teacher of the Gentiles in **Faith** and **Truth**." ◀ 1 Timothy 2:7 ▶ [NASB]

"So the honor is for **You** who believe, but for those who do not believe, "The **Stone** that the builders rejected has become the **Cornerstone**." ◀ 1 Peter 2:7 ▶ [ESV]

"For the **LORD** your **GOD** has **Blessed You** in all that **You** have done; **HE** has known your wanderings through this great wilderness. These forty years the **LORD** your **GOD** has been with **You**; **You** have not lacked a thing." ◀ Deuteronomy 2:7 ▶ [NASB]

"And the people served the **LORD** all the days of Joshua, and all the days of the elders who outlived Joshua, who had seen all the great work that the **LORD** had done for Israel." ◀ Judges 2:7 ▶ [ESV]

"The **LORD** makes poor and rich; **HE** brings low, **HE** also exalts." ◀ 1 Samuel 2:7 ▶ [NASB]

"I will tell the **Promise** that the **LORD** made to me: '**You** are **MY** son, because today **I** have become your **FATHER**.'" ◀ Psalm 2:7 ▶ [CEV]

Powerful Manifestation Prayer:

I BLESS myself, my family and everyone born on this date with GOD's MOST POWERFUL PURE LOVING LIGHT, HIS MOST POWERFUL PURE SOURCE HEALING ENERGY, and an ABUNDANCE OF HIS AMAZING GREATER GRACE in the POWER, the ANOINTING, the AUTHORITY and the WISDOM of the HOLY SPIRIT, in JESUS' MOST HOLY NAME. AMEN INDEED!

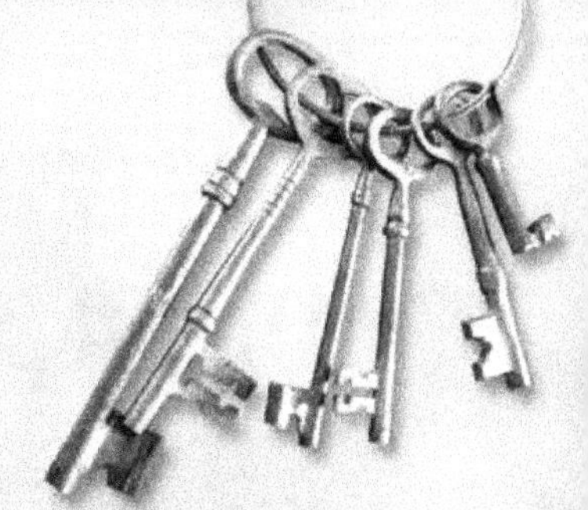

Day 39
2:8

"Being found in appearance as a MAN, HE humbled HIMSELF by becoming obedient to the point of death, even death on a Cross."
◄ Philippians 2:8 ► [NASB]

"ASK of ME, and I Will surely give the nations as your inheritance, and the very ends of the earth as your possession."
◄ Psalm 2:8 ► [NASB]

"HE raises up the poor from the dust; HE lifts the needy from the ash heap to make them sit with princes and inherit a seat of honor. For the pillars of the earth are the LORD's, and on them HE has set the world."
◄ 1 Samuel 2:8 ► [ESV]

"Now You, son of man, listen to what I AM speaking to You; do not be rebellious like that rebellious house. Open your mouth and eat what I AM giving You."
◄ Ezekiel 2:8 ► [NASB]

"For thus says the LORD of Hosts, "After Glory HE has sent ME against the nations which plunder You, for he who touches You, touches the apple of HIS eye.""
◄ Zechariah 2:8 ► [NASB]

"For by Grace You have been saved through Faith. And this is not your own doing; it is the gift of GOD."
◄ Ephesians 2:8 ► [ESV]

Powerful Manifestation Prayer:

I BLESS myself, my family and everyone born on this date with GOD's MOST POWERFUL PURE LOVING LIGHT, HIS MOST POWERFUL PURE SOURCE HEALING ENERGY, and an ABUNDANCE OF HIS AMAZING GREATER GRACE in the POWER, the ANOINTING, the AUTHORITY and the WISDOM of the HOLY SPIRIT, in JESUS' MOST HOLY NAME. AMEN INDEED!

Day 40
2:9

"But You are a chosen race, a royal priesthood, a holy nation, a people for HIS OWN possession, that You may proclaim the excellencies of HIM WHO called You out of darkness into HIS marvelous Light."
◄ 1 Peter 2:9 ► [ESV]

"But I will sacrifice to YOU with the voice of thanksgiving. That which I have vowed I will pay. Salvation is from the LORD."
◄ Jonah 2:9 ► [NASB]

"The latter Glory of this house will be greater than the former,' says the LORD of Hosts, 'and in this place I Will give peace,' declares the LORD of Hosts."
◄ Haggai 2:9 ► [NASB]

"Then You will understand Righteousness and justice and equity, every GOoD path."
◄ Proverbs 2:9 ► [ESV]

"So, I became great and surpassed all who were before me in Jerusalem. Also, my Wisdom remained with me."
◄ Ecclesiastes 2:9 ► [ESV]

"However, as **IT IS WRITTEN**: 'What no eye has seen, what no ear has heard, and what no human mind has conceived'— the things GOD has prepared for those who Love HIM."
◄ 1 Corinthians 2:9 ► [NIV]

Powerful Manifestation Prayer:

I BLESS myself, my family and everyone born on this date with GOD's MOST POWERFUL PURE LOVING LIGHT, HIS MOST POWERFUL PURE SOURCE HEALING ENERGY, and an ABUNDANCE OF HIS AMAZING GREATER GRACE in the POWER, the ANOINTING, the AUTHORITY and the WISDOM of the HOLY SPIRIT, in JESUS' MOST HOLY NAME. AMEN INDEED!

Day 41
2:10

"For we are HIS workmanship, created in CHRIST JESUS for GOoD works, which GOD prepared beforehand so that we would walk in them." ◄ Ephesians 2:10 ► [NASB]

"And You have been given full life in union with HIM. HE is Supreme over every Spiritual ruler and authority." ◄ Colossians 2:10 ► [GNT]

"If we Love others, we live in the Light, and so there is nothing in us that will cause someone else to sin." ◄ 1 John 2:10 ► [GNT]

"At one time You were not GOD's people, but now You are HIS people; at one time You did not know GOD's mercy, but now You have received HIS mercy." ◄ 1 Peter 2:10 ► [GNT]

"So, at the Name of JESUS everyone will bow down, those in Heaven, on earth, and under the earth." ◄ Philippians 2:10 ► [CEV]

"Do not be afraid of what You are about to suffer. I tell You; the devil will put some of You in prison to test You, and You will suffer persecution for ten days. Be Faithful, even to the point of death, and I Will give You life as your victor's crown." ◄ Revelations 2:10 ► [NIV]

Powerful Manifestation Prayer:

I BLESS myself, my family and everyone born on this date with GOD's MOST POWERFUL PURE LOVING LIGHT, HIS MOST POWERFUL PURE SOURCE HEALING ENERGY, and an ABUNDANCE OF HIS AMAZING GREATER GRACE in the POWER, the ANOINTING, the AUTHORITY and the WISDOM of the HOLY SPIRIT, in JESUS' MOST HOLY NAME. AMEN INDEED!

Day 42
2:11

"Hiram sent his answer back to Solomon: I know that the **LORD** must **Love HIS** people, because **HE** has **Chosen You** to be their king." ◄ 2 Chronicles 2:11 ► [CEV]

"Worship the **LORD** with reverence and rejoice with trembling." ◄ Psalm 2:11 ► [NASB]

"Beloved, I urge **You** as aliens and strangers to abstain from fleshly lusts which wage war against the **Soul**." ◄ 1 Peter 2:11 ► [NASB]

"And as soon as we heard it, our hearts melted, and there was no **Spirit** left in any man because of **You**, for the **LORD** your **GOD**, **HE** is **GOD** in the **Heavens** above and on the earth beneath." ◄ Joshua 2:11 ► [ESV]

"And that every tongue will confess that **JESUS CHRIST** is **LORD**, to the **Glory** of **GOD** the **FATHER**." ◄ Philippians 2:11 ► [NASB]

"Your insight and understanding will protect **You**." ◄ Proverbs 2:11 ► [GNT]

Powerful Manifestation Prayer:

I BLESS myself, my family and everyone born on this date with GOD's MOST POWERFUL PURE LOVING LIGHT, HIS MOST POWERFUL PURE SOURCE HEALING ENERGY, and an ABUNDANCE OF HIS AMAZING GREATER GRACE in the POWER, the ANOINTING, the AUTHORITY and the WISDOM of the HOLY SPIRIT, in JESUS' MOST HOLY NAME. AMEN INDEED!

Day 43
2:12

"Yet even now," declares the LORD, "Return to ME with all your heart, and with fasting, weeping and mourning."" ◀ Joel 2:12 ▶ [NASB]

"For the LORD of Hosts has a day against all that is proud and lofty, against all that is lifted up—and it shall be brought low." ◀ Isaiah 2:12 ▶ [ESV]

"May the LORD reward your work, and your wages be full from the LORD, the GOD of Israel, under WHOSE Wings You have come to seek refuge." ◀ Ruth 2:12 ▶ [NASB]

"We exhorted each one of You and encouraged You and charged You to walk in a manner worthy of GOD, WHO calls You into HIS OWN Kingdom and Glory."
◀ 1 Thessalonians 2:12 ▶ [ESV]

"Wisdom will protect You from evil schemes and from those liars." ◀ Proverbs 2:12 ▶ [CEV]

"Now we have received, not the spirit of the world, but the SPIRIT WHO is from GOD, so that we may know the things Freely given to us by GOD." ◀ 1 Corinthians 2:12 ▶ [NASB]

Powerful Manifestation Prayer:

I BLESS myself, my family and everyone born on this date with GOD's MOST POWERFUL PURE LOVING LIGHT, HIS MOST POWERFUL PURE SOURCE HEALING ENERGY, and an ABUNDANCE OF HIS AMAZING GREATER GRACE in the POWER, the ANOINTING, the AUTHORITY and the WISDOM of the HOLY SPIRIT, in JESUS' MOST HOLY NAME. AMEN INDEED!

Day 44
2:13

"For it is GOD WHO is at work in You, both to will and to work for HIS GOoD pleasure."
◄ Philippians 2:13 ► [NASB]

"Don't rip your clothes to show your sorrow. Instead, turn back to ME with broken hearts. I AM merciful, kind, and caring. I don't easily lose MY temper, and I don't like to punish."
◄ Joel 2:13 ► [CEV]

"For this reason we also constantly thank GOD that when You received the WORD of GOD which You heard from us, You accepted it not as the word of men, but for what it really is, the WORD of GOD, which also performs its work in You who believe."
◄ 1 Thessalonians 2:13 ► [NASB]

"For it is not the hearers of the Law who are righteous before GOD, but the doers of the Law who will be justified."
◄ Romans 2:13 ► [ESV]

"But now in CHRIST JESUS You who formerly were far off have been brought near by the BLOOD OF CHRIST."
◄ Ephesians 2:13 ► [NASB]

"When You were dead in your transgressions and the uncircumcision of your flesh, HE made You alive together with HIM, having forgiven us all our transgressions."
◄ Colossians 2:13 ► [NASB]

Powerful Manifestation Prayer:

I BLESS myself, my family and everyone born on this date with GOD's MOST POWERFUL PURE LOVING LIGHT, HIS MOST POWERFUL PURE SOURCE HEALING ENERGY, and an ABUNDANCE OF HIS AMAZING GREATER GRACE in the POWER, the ANOINTING, the AUTHORITY and the WISDOM of the HOLY SPIRIT, in JESUS' MOST HOLY NAME. AMEN INDEED!

Day 45
2:14

"Do everything without complaining or arguing." ◀ Philippians 2:14 ▶ [GNT]

"Glory to GOD in the highest, and on earth peace among those with whom HE is pleased!" ◀ Luke 2:14 ▶ [ESV]

"For the earth will be filled with the Knowledge of the Glory of the LORD as the waters cover the sea." ◀ Habakkuk 2:14 ▶ [ESV]

"HE gave HIMSELF to rescue us from everything evil and to make our hearts pure. HE wanted us to be HIS OWN people and to be eager to do right." ◀ Titus 2:14 ▶ [CEV]

"Remind them of these things, and solemnly charge them in the presence of GOD not to wrangle about words, which is useless and leads to the ruin of the hearers." ◀ 2 Timothy 2:14 ▶ [NASB]

"By canceling the record of debt that **STOOD** against us with its legal demands. This HE set aside, nailing it to the Cross." ◀ Colossians 2:14 ▶ [ESV]

Powerful Manifestation Prayer:

I BLESS myself, my family and everyone born on this date with GOD's MOST POWERFUL PURE LOVING LIGHT, HIS MOST POWERFUL PURE SOURCE HEALING ENERGY, and an ABUNDANCE OF HIS AMAZING GREATER GRACE in the POWER, the ANOINTING, the AUTHORITY and the WISDOM of the HOLY SPIRIT, in JESUS' MOST HOLY NAME. AMEN INDEED!

Day 46
2:15

"Do not love the world nor the things in the world. If anyone loves the world, the Love of the FATHER is not in him." ◄ 1 John 2:15 ► [NASB]

"For GOD wants You to silence the ignorant talk of foolish people by the GOoD things You do." ◄ 1 Peter 2:15 ► [GNT]

"For we are a fragrance of CHRIST to GOD among those who are being saved and among those who are perishing." ◄ 2 Corinthians 2:15 ► [NASB]

"Be diligent to present yourself approved to GOD as a workman who does not need to be ashamed, accurately handling the WORD of Truth." ◄ 2 Timothy 2:15 ► [NASB]

"That You may be blameless and innocent, children of GOD without blemish in the midst of a crooked and twisted generation, among whom You shine as Lights in the world." ◄ Philippians 2:15 ► [ESV]

"Teach these things, as You use your full authority to encourage and correct people. Make sure You earn everyone's respect." ◄ Titus 2:15 ► [CEV]

"She did not request anything except what Hegai, the king's eunuch who was in charge of the women, advised. And Esther found Favor in the eyes of all who saw her." ◄ Esther 2:15 ► [NASB]

Powerful Manifestation Prayer:

I BLESS myself, my family and everyone born on this date with GOD's MOST POWERFUL PURE LOVING LIGHT, HIS MOST POWERFUL PURE SOURCE HEALING ENERGY, and an ABUNDANCE OF HIS AMAZING GREATER GRACE in the POWER, the ANOINTING, the AUTHORITY and the WISDOM of the HOLY SPIRIT, in JESUS' MOST HOLY NAME. AMEN INDEED!

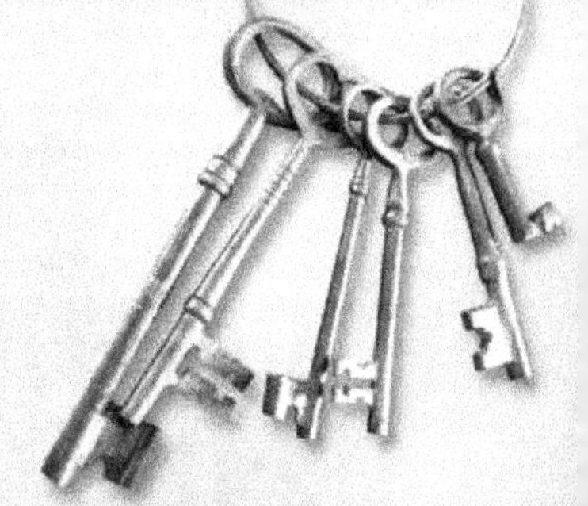

Day 47
2:16

"Now may our **LORD JESUS CHRIST HIMSELF** and **GOD** our **FATHER, WHO** has **Loved** us and given us eternal comfort and **GOoD HOPE** by **Grace**. [comfort and strengthen your hearts in every good work and word." ◀ 2 Thessalonians 2:16 ▶ [NASB]

"Live as people who are **Free**, not using your **Freedom** as a cover-up for evil, but living as servants of **GOD**." ◀ 1 Peter 2:16 ▶ [ESV]

"For all that is in the world, the lust of the flesh and the lust of the eyes and the boastful pride of life, is not from the **FATHER**, but is from the world." ◀ 1 John 2:16 ▶ [NASB]

"For **I** hate divorce!" says the **LORD**, the **GOD** of Israel. "To divorce your wife is to overwhelm her with cruelty," says the **LORD** of **Heaven's Armies**. "So guard your heart; do not be unfaithful to your wife." ◀ Malachi 2:16 ▶ [NLT]

"On that day when, according to my **Gospel**, **GOD** judges the secrets of men by **CHRIST JESUS**." ◀ Romans 2:16 ▶ [ESV]

"Know that a person is not justified by the works of the **Law**, but by **Faith** in **JESUS CHRIST**. So we, too, have put our **Faith** in **CHRIST JESUS** that we may be justified by **Faith**." ◀ Galatians 2:16 ▶ [NIV]

Powerful Manifestation Prayer:

I BLESS myself, my family and everyone born on this date with GOD's MOST POWERFUL PURE LOVING LIGHT, HIS MOST POWERFUL PURE SOURCE HEALING ENERGY, and an ABUNDANCE OF HIS AMAZING GREATER GRACE in the POWER, the ANOINTING, the AUTHORITY and the WISDOM of the HOLY SPIRIT, in JESUS' MOST HOLY NAME. AMEN INDEED!

Day 48
2:17

"The world and the desires it causes are disappearing. But if we obey GOD, we will live forever."
◄ 1 John 2:17 ► [CEV]

"And the haughtiness of man shall be humbled, and the lofty pride of men shall be brought low, and the LORD Alone Will be exalted in that day." ◄ Isaiah 2:17 ► [ESV]

"Have You not brought this upon yourself by forsaking the LORD your GOD, when HE led You in the way?" ◄ Jeremiah 2:17 ► [ESV]

"And hearing this, JESUS said to them, "It is not those who are healthy who need a physician, but those who are sick; I did not come to call the righteous, but sinners."" ◄ Mark 2:17 ► [NASB]

"'In the last days, GOD says, I Will pour out MY SPIRIT on all people. Your sons and daughters will prophesy, your young men will see visions, your old men will dream dreams.'"
◄ Acts 2:17 ► [NIV]

"For we are not, like so many, peddlers of GOD's WORD, but as men of sincerity, as commissioned by GOD, in the sight of GOD we speak in CHRIST." ◄ 2 Corinthians 2:17 ► [ESV]

Powerful Manifestation Prayer:

I BLESS myself, my family and everyone born on this date with GOD's MOST POWERFUL PURE LOVING LIGHT, HIS MOST POWERFUL PURE SOURCE HEALING ENERGY, and an ABUNDANCE OF HIS AMAZING GREATER GRACE in the POWER, the ANOINTING, the AUTHORITY and the WISDOM of the HOLY SPIRIT, in JESUS' MOST HOLY NAME. AMEN INDEED!

Day 49
2:18

"But Samuel, though he was only a boy, served the **LORD**. He wore a linen garment like that of a priest." ◀ 1 Samuel 2:18 ▶ [NLT]

"And I told them of the **Hand** of my **GOD** that had been upon me for **GOoD**, and also of the words that the king had spoken to me. And they said, "Let us rise up and build." So they strengthened their hands for the **GOoD** work." ◀ Nehemiah 2:18 ▶ [ESV]

"Don't be cheated by people who make a show of acting humble and who worship angels. They brag about seeing visions. But it is all nonsense, because their minds are filled with selfish desires." ◀ Colossians 2:18 ▶ [CEV]

"For in that **HE HIMSELF** has suffered, being tempted, **HE** is able to aid those who are tempted." ◀ Hebrews 2:18 ▶ [NKJV]

"And **I Will** agree to let **You** live in peace—**You** will no longer be attacked by wild animals and birds or by weapons of war." ◀ Hosea 2:18 ▶ [CEV]

"And because of **CHRIST**, all of us can come to the **FATHER** by the same **SPIRIT**." ◀ Ephesians 2:18 ▶ [CEV]

Powerful Manifestation Prayer:

I BLESS myself, my family and everyone born on this date with GOD's MOST POWERFUL PURE LOVING LIGHT, HIS MOST POWERFUL PURE SOURCE HEALING ENERGY, and an ABUNDANCE OF HIS AMAZING GREATER GRACE in the POWER, the ANOINTING, the AUTHORITY and the WISDOM of the HOLY SPIRIT, in JESUS' MOST HOLY NAME. AMEN INDEED!

Day 50
2:19

"What can **You** learn from idols covered with silver or gold? They can't even breathe. Pity anyone who says to an idol of wood or stone, "Get up and do something." ◀ Habakkuk 2:19 ▶ [CEV]

"Your own sins will punish **You**, because it was a bitter mistake for **You** to reject **ME** without fear of punishment. **I**, the **LORD All-Powerful**, have spoken." ◀ Jeremiah 2:19 ▶ [CEV]

"Get up and pray for help all through the night. Pour out your feelings to the **LORD**, as **You** would pour water out of a jug. Beg **HIM** to save your people, who are starving to death at every street crossing." ◀ Lamentations 2:19 ▶ [CEV]

"In answer to their prayers **HE** said, "**I Will** give **You** enough grain, wine, and olive oil to satisfy your needs. No longer will **I** let **You** be insulted by the nations."" ◀ Joel 2:19 ▶ [CEV]

"**I Will** make **You MY** wife forever, showing **You Righteousness** and justice, unfailing **Love** and compassion." ◀ Hosea 2:19 ▶ [NLT]

"So then **You** are no longer strangers and aliens, but **You** are fellow citizens with the saints, and are of **GOD's** household." ◀ Ephesians 2:19 ▶ [NASB]

Powerful Manifestation Prayer:

I BLESS myself, my family and everyone born on this date with GOD's MOST POWERFUL PURE LOVING LIGHT, HIS MOST POWERFUL PURE SOURCE HEALING ENERGY, and an ABUNDANCE OF HIS AMAZING GREATER GRACE in the POWER, the ANOINTING, the AUTHORITY and the WISDOM of the HOLY SPIRIT, in JESUS' MOST HOLY NAME. AMEN INDEED!

Day 51
2:20

"But the LORD is in HIS Holy Temple. Let all the earth be silent before HIM."
◄ Habakkuk 2:20 ► [NASB]

"I Will be Faithful to You and make You MINE, and You will finally know ME as the LORD."
◄ Hosea 2:20 ► [NLT]

"I answered, "The GOD of Heaven Will give us success. We are HIS servants, and we are going to start building. But You have no right to any property in Jerusalem, and You have no share in its traditions.""
◄ Nehemiah 2:20 ► [GNT]

"Daniel said, "Let the Name of GOD be Blessed forever and ever, For Wisdom and Power belong to HIM."
◄ Daniel 2:20 ► [NASB]

"Naomi replied. "He has shown that he is still loyal to the living and to the dead. Boaz is a close relative, one of those who is supposed to look after us."
◄ Ruth 2:20 ► [CEV]

"So, You will walk in the way of the GOoD and keep to the paths of the righteous."
◄ Proverbs 2:20 ► [ESV]

Powerful Manifestation Prayer:

I BLESS myself, my family and everyone born on this date with GOD's MOST POWERFUL PURE LOVING LIGHT, HIS MOST POWERFUL PURE SOURCE HEALING ENERGY, and an ABUNDANCE OF HIS AMAZING GREATER GRACE in the POWER, the ANOINTING, the AUTHORITY and the WISDOM of the HOLY SPIRIT, in JESUS' MOST HOLY NAME. AMEN INDEED!

Day 52
2:21

"And it shall come to pass that everyone who calls upon the **Name** of the **LORD** shall be saved."
◄ Acts 2:21 ► [ESV]

"For You have been called for this purpose, since **CHRIST** also suffered for **You**, leaving **You** an example for **You** to follow in **HIS** steps."
◄ 1 Peter 2:21 ► [NASB]

"Fear not, O land; be glad and rejoice, for the **LORD** has done great things!" ◄ Joel 2:21 ► [ESV]

"**HE** changes times and seasons; **HE** removes kings and sets up kings; **HE** gives **Wisdom** to the wise and **Knowledge** to those who have understanding."
◄ Daniel 2:21 ► [ESV]

"It would have been much better for them never to have known the way of **Righteousness** than to know it and then turn away from the sacred command that was given them."
◄ 2 Peter 2:21 ► [GNT]

"For the upright will live in the land, and the blameless will remain in it." ◄ Proverbs 2:21 ► [NKJV]

Powerful Manifestation Prayer:

I BLESS myself, my family and everyone born on this date with GOD's MOST POWERFUL PURE LOVING LIGHT, HIS MOST POWERFUL PURE SOURCE HEALING ENERGY, and an ABUNDANCE OF HIS AMAZING GREATER GRACE in the POWER, the ANOINTING, the AUTHORITY and the WISDOM of the HOLY SPIRIT, in JESUS' MOST HOLY NAME. AMEN INDEED!

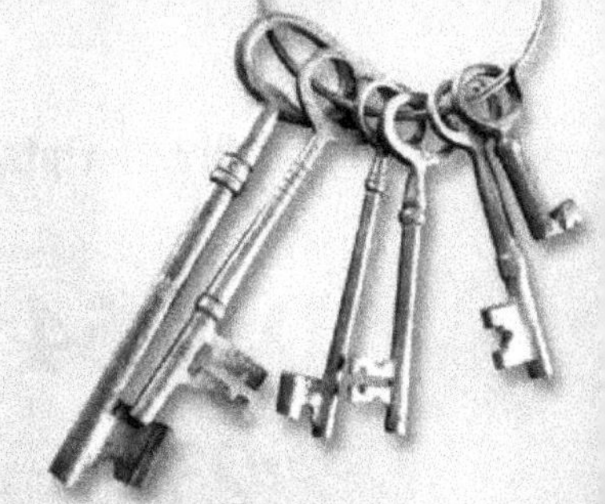

Day 53
2:22

"Stop trusting the power of humans. They are all going to die, so how can they help?"
◀ Isaiah 2:22 ▶ [CEV]

"Now, listen to what I have to say about JESUS from Nazareth. GOD proved HE sent JESUS to You by having HIM work miracles, wonders, and signs. All of You know this." ◀ Acts 2:22 ▶ [CEV]

"I Will overthrow the thrones of kingdoms and destroy the power of the kingdoms of the nations; and I Will overthrow the chariots and their riders, and the horses and their riders will go down, everyone by the sword of another." ◀ Haggai 2:22 ▶ [NASB]

"Joshua left those nations to test Israel. I wanted to see whether or not the people would carefully walk in the path marked out by the LORD, as their ancestors were careful to do." ◀ Judges 2:22 ▶ [NET]

"HE committed no sin, neither was deceit found in HIS mouth." ◀ 1 Peter 2:22 ▶ [ESV]

"HE reveals deep and hidden things; HE knows what is in the darkness, and the LIGHT dwells with HIM." ◀ Daniel 2:22 ▶ [ESV]

Powerful Manifestation Prayer:

I BLESS myself, my family and everyone born on this date with GOD's MOST POWERFUL PURE LOVING LIGHT, HIS MOST POWERFUL PURE SOURCE HEALING ENERGY, and an ABUNDANCE OF HIS AMAZING GREATER GRACE in the POWER, the ANOINTING, the AUTHORITY and the WISDOM of the HOLY SPIRIT, in JESUS' MOST HOLY NAME. AMEN INDEED!

Day 54
2:23

"GOD had already planned and decided that JESUS would be handed over to You. So, You took HIM and had evil men put HIM to death on a Cross. ◀ Acts 2:23 ▶ [CEV]

"Although HE was abused, HE never tried to get even. And when HE suffered, HE made no threats. Instead, HE had Faith in GOD, WHO judges fairly." ◀1 Peter 2:23 ▶ [CEV]

"I Will establish MY people in the land and make them prosper. I Will show Love to those who were called "Unloved," and to those who were called "Not-MY-People" I Will say, 'You are MY people,' and they will answer, 'YOU are our GOD'!" ◀ Hosea 2:23 ▶ [GNT]

"To YOU, O GOD, of my fathers, I give thanks and praise, For YOU have given me Wisdom and Power; Even now YOU have made known to me what we requested of YOU, For YOU have made known to us the king's matter." ◀ Daniel 2:23 ▶ [NASB]

"People of Zion, celebrate in honor of the LORD your GOD! HE is generous and has sent the autumn and spring rains in the proper seasons." ◀ Joel 2:23 ▶ [CEV]

"Abraham believed GOD, and GOD counted him as righteous because of his Faith." He was called even the Friend of GOD." ◀ James 2:23 ▶ [NLT]

Powerful Manifestation Prayer:

I BLESS myself, my family and everyone born on this date with GOD's MOST POWERFUL PURE LOVING LIGHT, HIS MOST POWERFUL PURE SOURCE HEALING ENERGY, and an ABUNDANCE OF HIS AMAZING GREATER GRACE in the POWER, the ANOINTING, the AUTHORITY and the WISDOM of the HOLY SPIRIT, in JESUS' MOST HOLY NAME. AMEN INDEED!

Day 55
2:24

"So GOD heard their groaning, and GOD remembered HIS covenant with Abraham, with Isaac, and with Jacob." ◀ Exodus 2:24 ▶ [NKJV]

"And they said to Joshua, "Truly the LORD has given all the land into our hands. And also, all the inhabitants of the land melt away because of us." ◀ Joshua 2:24 ▶ [ESV]

"And HE HIMSELF bore our sins in HIS Body on the Cross, so that we might die to sin and live to Righteousness; for by HIS wounds You were healed." ◀ 1 Peter 2:24 ▶ [NASB]

"But GOD raised HIM up again, putting an end to the agony of death, since it was impossible for HIM to be held in its power." ◀ Acts 2:24 ▶ [NASB]

"And the LORD's servant must not be quarrelsome but kind to everyone, able to teach, patiently enduring evil." ◀ 2 Timothy 2:24 ▶ [ESV]

"Let what You heard from the beginning abide in You. If what You heard from the beginning abides in You, then You, too, will abide in the SON and in the FATHER." ◀ 1 John 2:24 ▶ [ESV]

Powerful Manifestation Prayer:

I BLESS myself, my family and everyone born on this date with GOD's MOST POWERFUL PURE LOVING LIGHT, HIS MOST POWERFUL PURE SOURCE HEALING ENERGY, and an ABUNDANCE OF HIS AMAZING GREATER GRACE in the POWER, the ANOINTING, the AUTHORITY and the WISDOM of the HOLY SPIRIT, in JESUS' MOST HOLY NAME. AMEN INDEED!

Day 56
2:25

"For You were straying like sheep but have now returned to the Shepherd and Overseer of your Souls."
◄ 1 Peter 2:25 ► [ESV]

"From today on I Will make people everywhere afraid of You. Everyone will tremble with fear at the mention of your name."
◄ Deuteronomy 2:25 ► [GNT]

"So I Will restore to You the years that the swarming locust has eaten, The crawling locust, the consuming locust, and the chewing locust, MY great army which I sent among You."
◄ Joel 2:25 ► [NKJV]

"What David said are really the WORDS of JESUS, "I always see the LORD near me, and I will not be afraid with HIM at my right side."
◄ Acts 2:25 ► [CEV]

"This is the Promise which HE HIMSELF made to us: ETERNAL LIFE."
◄ 1 John 2:25 ► [NASB]

"'Nevertheless, what You have, hold fast until I come.'"
◄ Revelations 2:25 ► [NASB]

Powerful Manifestation Prayer:

I BLESS myself, my family and everyone born on this date with GOD's MOST POWERFUL PURE LOVING LIGHT, HIS MOST POWERFUL PURE SOURCE HEALING ENERGY, and an ABUNDANCE OF HIS AMAZING GREATER GRACE in the POWER, the ANOINTING, the AUTHORITY and the WISDOM of the HOLY SPIRIT, in JESUS' MOST HOLY NAME. AMEN INDEED!

Day 57
2:26

"You shall eat in plenty and be satisfied, and Praise the name of the LORD your GOD, WHO has dealt wondrously with You. And MY people shall never again be put to shame."
◀ Joel 2:26 ▶ [ESV]

"And they may come to their senses and escape from the snare of the devil, having been held captive by him to do his will."
◀ 2 Timothy 2:26 ▶ [NASB]

"For to the one who pleases HIM GOD has given Wisdom and Knowledge and Joy, but to the sinner HE has given the business of gathering and collecting, only to give to one who pleases GOD. This also is vanity and a striving after wind."
◀ Ecclesiastes 2:26 ▶ [ESV]

"Therefore, my heart was glad, and my tongue rejoiced; my flesh also will dwell in HOPE."
◀ Acts 2:26 ▶ [ESV]

"Now the boy Samuel continued to grow both in stature and in Favor with the LORD and also with man."
◀ 1 Samuel 2:26 ▶ [ESV]

"For just as the body without the Spirit is dead, so also Faith without works is dead."
◀ James 2:26 ▶ [NASB]

Powerful Manifestation Prayer:

I BLESS myself, my family and everyone born on this date with GOD's MOST POWERFUL PURE LOVING LIGHT, HIS MOST POWERFUL PURE SOURCE HEALING ENERGY, and an ABUNDANCE OF HIS AMAZING GREATER GRACE in the POWER, the ANOINTING, the AUTHORITY and the WISDOM of the HOLY SPIRIT, in JESUS' MOST HOLY NAME. AMEN INDEED!

Day 58
2:27

"For indeed he was sick to the point of death, but GOD had mercy on him, and not on him only but also on me, so that I would not have sorrow upon sorrow." ◀ Philippians 2:27 ▶ [NASB]

"For YOU Will not leave my Soul among the dead or allow YOUR Holy One to rot in the grave." ◀ Acts 2:27 ▶ [NLT]

"You will all be disgraced—You that say that a tree is your father and that a rock is your mother. This will happen because You turned away from ME instead of turning to ME. But when You are in trouble, You ASK ME to come and save You." ◀ Jeremiah 2:27 ▶ [GNT]

"Thus, You will know that I AM in the midst of Israel, And that I AM the LORD your GOD, And there is no other; And MY people will never be put to shame." ◀ Joel 2:27 ▶ [NASB]

"Then JESUS said to them, "The Sabbath was made to meet the needs of people, and not people to meet the requirements of the Sabbath." ◀ Mark 2:27 ▶ [NLT]

"But as for You, CHRIST has poured out HIS SPIRIT on You. As long as HIS SPIRIT remains in You, You do not need anyone to teach You. For HIS SPIRIT teaches You about everything, and what HE teaches is True, not false. Obey the SPIRIT's teaching, then, and remain in union with CHRIST." ◀ 1 John 2:27 ▶ [GNT]

Powerful Manifestation Prayer:

I BLESS myself, my family and everyone born on this date with GOD's MOST POWERFUL PURE LOVING LIGHT, HIS MOST POWERFUL PURE SOURCE HEALING ENERGY, and an ABUNDANCE OF HIS AMAZING GREATER GRACE in the POWER, the ANOINTING, the AUTHORITY and the WISDOM of the HOLY SPIRIT, in JESUS' MOST HOLY NAME. AMEN INDEED!

Day 59
2:28

"But where are your gods that You made for yourself? Let them arise, if they can save You, in your time of trouble; for as many as your cities are your gods, O Judah." ◄ Jeremiah 2:28 ► [ESV]

"So, the SON of Man is LORD even of the Sabbath." ◄ Mark 2:28 ► [NASB]

"It will come about after this that I Will pour out MY SPIRIT on all mankind; And your sons and daughters will prophesy, Your old men will dream dreams, Your young men will see visions." ◄ Joel 2:28 ► [NASB]

"They will have the same authority I received from MY FATHER, and I Will also give them the Morning Star!" ◄ Revelations 2:28 ► [NLT]

"Yes, my children, remain in union with HIM, so that when HE appears, we may be full of courage and need not hide in shame from HIM on the Day HE comes." ◄ 1 John 2:28 ► [GNT]

"YOU have made known to me the ways of life; YOU Will make me full of joy in YOUR presence." ◄ Acts 2:28 ► [NKJV]

Powerful Manifestation Prayer:

I BLESS myself, my family and everyone born on this date with GOD's MOST POWERFUL PURE LOVING LIGHT, HIS MOST POWERFUL PURE SOURCE HEALING ENERGY, and an ABUNDANCE OF HIS AMAZING GREATER GRACE in the POWER, the ANOINTING, the AUTHORITY and the WISDOM of the HOLY SPIRIT, in JESUS' MOST HOLY NAME. AMEN INDEED!

Day 60
2:29

L.E.A.P. YEAR
LET EVERYONE ALWAYS PRAY

"Even on the male and female servants **I Will** pour out **MY SPIRIT** in those days."
◄ Joel 2:29 ► [NASB]

"As for **You**… while on your bed your thoughts turned to what would take place in the future; and **HE WHO** reveals mysteries has made known to **You** what will take place."
◄ Daniel 2:29 ► [NASB]

"Rather, the real Jew is the person who is a Jew on the inside, that is, whose heart has been circumcised, and this is the work of **GOD's SPIRIT**, not of the written **Law**. Such a person receives **Praise** from **GOD**, not from human beings."
◄ Romans 2:29 ► [GNT]

"Be sure to give him a cheerful welcome, just as people who serve the **LORD** deserve."
◄ Philippians 2:29 ► [CEV]

"If **You** know that **HE** is righteous, **You** know that everyone also who practices **Righteousness** is born of **HIM**."
◄ 1 John 2:29 ► [NASB]

"**LORD**, I am **YOUR** servant, and now I can die in peace, because **YOU** have kept **YOUR Promise** to me."
◄ Luke 2:29 ► [CEV]

Powerful Manifestation Prayer:

I BLESS myself, my family and everyone born on this date with GOD's MOST POWERFUL PURE LOVING LIGHT, HIS MOST POWERFUL PURE SOURCE HEALING ENERGY, and an ABUNDANCE OF HIS AMAZING GREATER GRACE in the POWER, the ANOINTING, the AUTHORITY and the WISDOM of the HOLY SPIRIT, in JESUS' MOST HOLY NAME. AMEN INDEED!

March
3

~ I **Pray** for **You** and **You Pray** for Me!

"After Job had prayed for his friends, the **LORD** restored his fortunes and gave him twice as much as he had before." ◀ Job 42:10 ▶ [NIV]

"**You** haven't done this before. **A.S.K.** using **MY NAME**, and **You** will receive, and **You** will have abundant joy." ◀ John 16:24 ▶ [NLT]

Powerful Manifestation Prayer:

I BLESS myself, my family and everyone born in this month with GOD's MOST POWERFUL PURE LOVING LIGHT, HIS MOST POWERFUL PURE SOURCE HEALING ENERGY, and an ABUNDANCE OF HIS AMAZING GREATER GRACE in the POWER, the ANOINTING, the AUTHORITY and the WISDOM of the HOLY SPIRIT, in JESUS' MOST HOLY NAME.
AMEN INDEED!

A.S.K.- Additional Scripture Knowledge

Write Additional Scriptures here.

Day 60
3:1

"I have so many enemies, LORD, so many who turn against me!" ◄ Psalm 3:1 ► [GNT]

"Therefore, if You have been raised up with CHRIST, keep seeking the things above where CHRIST is, seated at the Right Hand of GOD." ◄ Colossians 3:1 ► [NASB]

"Remind them to be subject to rulers, to authorities, to be obedient, to be ready for every GOoD deed." ◄ Titus 3:1 ► [NASB]

"There is an appointed time for everything. And there is a time for every event under heaven--." ◄ Ecclesiastes 3:1 ► [NASB]

"MY child, remember MY teachings and instructions and obey them completely." ◄ Proverbs 3:1 ► [CEV]

"See how great a Love the FATHER has bestowed on us, that we would be called children of GOD; and such we are. For this reason, the world does not know us, because it did not know HIM." ◄ 1 John 3:1 ► [NASB]

Powerful Manifestation Prayer:

I BLESS myself, my family and everyone born on this date with GOD's MOST POWERFUL PURE LOVING LIGHT, HIS MOST POWERFUL PURE SOURCE HEALING ENERGY, and an ABUNDANCE OF HIS AMAZING GREATER GRACE in the POWER, the ANOINTING, the AUTHORITY and the WISDOM of the HOLY SPIRIT, in JESUS' MOST HOLY NAME. AMEN INDEED!

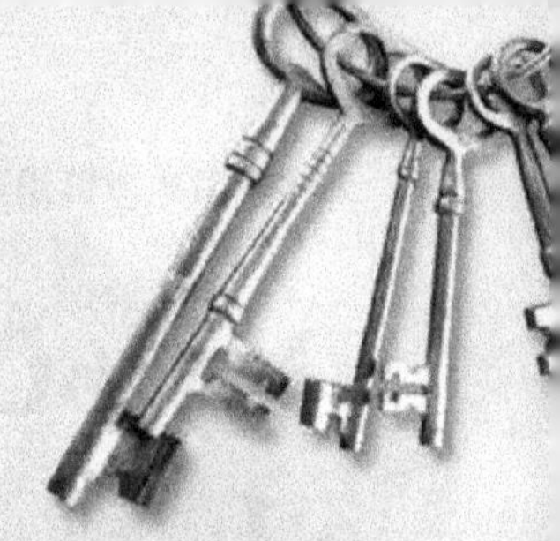

Day 61
3:2

"This man came to JESUS by night and said to HIM, "RABBI, we know that YOU are a TEACHER come from GOD, for no one can do these signs that YOU do unless GOD is with HIM."
◀ John 3:2 ▶ [ESV]

"I want You to remember the WORDS that were spoken long ago by the Holy Prophets, and the command from the LORD and SAVIOR which was given You by YOUR apostles."
◀ 2 Peter 3:2 ▶ [GNT]

"An overseer, then, must be above reproach, the husband of one wife, temperate, prudent, respectable, hospitable, able to teach." ◀ 1 Timothy 3:2 ▶ [NASB]

"Set your minds on things that are above, not on the things that are on earth."
◀ Colossians 3:2 ▶ [ESV]

"MY teaching will give You a long and prosperous life." ◀ Proverbs 3:2 ▶ [GNT]

"My dear friends, we are now GOD's children, but it is not yet clear what we shall become. But we know that when CHRIST appears, we shall be like HIM, because we shall see HIM as HE really is."
◀ 1 John 3:2 ▶ [GNT]

Powerful Manifestation Prayer:

I BLESS myself, my family and everyone born on this date with GOD's MOST POWERFUL PURE LOVING LIGHT, HIS MOST POWERFUL PURE SOURCE HEALING ENERGY, and an ABUNDANCE OF HIS AMAZING GREATER GRACE in the POWER, the ANOINTING, the AUTHORITY and the WISDOM of the HOLY SPIRIT, in JESUS' MOST HOLY NAME. AMEN INDEED!

Day 62
3:3

"For You have died, and your life is hidden with CHRIST in GOD." ◄ Colossians 3:3 ► [ESV]

"But the LORD is Faithful, and HE Will strengthen and protect You from the evil one."
◄ 2 Thessalonians 3:3 ► [NASB]

"But YOU, O LORD, are always my shield from danger; YOU give me victory and restore my courage."
◄ Psalm 3:3 ► [GNT]

"JESUS answered HIM, "Truly, truly, I say to You, unless one is born again he cannot see the Kingdom of GOD."
◄ John 3:3 ► [ESV]

"Remember, then, what You were taught and what You heard; obey it and turn from your sins. If You do not wake up, I Will come upon You like a thief, and You will not even know the time when I Will come."
◄ Revelation 3:3 ► [GNT]

"Do not let kindness and Truth leave You; Bind them around your neck, Write them on the tablet of your heart."
◄ Proverbs 3:3 ► [NASB]

Powerful Manifestation Prayer:

I BLESS myself, my family and everyone born on this date with GOD's MOST POWERFUL PURE LOVING LIGHT, HIS MOST POWERFUL PURE SOURCE HEALING ENERGY, and an ABUNDANCE OF HIS AMAZING GREATER GRACE in the POWER, the ANOINTING, the AUTHORITY and the WISDOM of the HOLY SPIRIT, in JESUS' MOST HOLY NAME. AMEN INDEED!

Day 63
3:4

"When CHRIST, WHO is our life, is revealed, then You also will be revealed with HIM in Glory."
◄ Colossians 3:4 ► [NASB]

"He must be one who manages his own household well, keeping his children under control with all dignity."
◄ 1 Timothy 3:4 ► [NASB]

"Of course not! GOD is TRUE, even if everyone else is a liar. As it is written, 'You are right when You speak, and win your case when You go into court'."
◄ Romans 3:4 ► [ISV]

"I call to the LORD for help, and from HIS Sacred Hill HE answers me." ◄ Psalm 3:4 ► [GNT]

"Be beautiful in your heart by being gentle and quiet. This kind of beauty will last, and GOD considers it very special."
◄ 1 Peter 3:4 ► [CEV]

"So, You will find Favor and GOoD repute in the sight of GOD and man."
◄ Proverbs 3:4 ► [NASB]

Powerful Manifestation Prayer:

I BLESS myself, my family and everyone born on this date with GOD's MOST POWERFUL PURE LOVING LIGHT, HIS MOST POWERFUL PURE SOURCE HEALING ENERGY, and an ABUNDANCE OF HIS AMAZING GREATER GRACE in the POWER, the ANOINTING, the AUTHORITY and the WISDOM of the HOLY SPIRIT, in JESUS' MOST HOLY NAME. AMEN INDEED!

Day 64

3:5

"Even though they will make a show of being religious, their religion won't be real. Don't have anything to do with such people."
◄ 2 Timothy 3:5 ► [CEV]

"Afterward the sons of Israel will return and seek the **LORD** their **GOD** and David their king; and they will come trembling to the **LORD** and to **HIS GOoDness** in the last days."
◄ Hosea 3:5 ► [NASB]

"**HE** saved us, not on the basis of deeds which we have done in **Righteousness**, but according to **HIS Mercy**, by the washing of regeneration and renewing by the **HOLY SPIRIT**."
◄ Titus 3:5 ► [NASB]

"Trust in the **LORD** with all your heart, and do not lean on **Your Own Understanding** ~ [Y.O.U.]."
◄ Proverbs 3:5 ► [ESV]

"May the **LORD** direct your hearts into the **Love** of **GOD** and into the steadfastness of **CHRIST**."
◄ 2 Thessalonians 3:5 ► [NASB]

"I lay down and slept; I woke again, for the **LORD** sustained me." ◄ Psalm 3:5 ► [ESV]

Powerful Manifestation Prayer:

I BLESS myself, my family and everyone born on this date with GOD's MOST POWERFUL PURE LOVING LIGHT, HIS MOST POWERFUL PURE SOURCE HEALING ENERGY, and an ABUNDANCE OF HIS AMAZING GREATER GRACE in the POWER, the ANOINTING, the AUTHORITY and the WISDOM of the HOLY SPIRIT, in JESUS' MOST HOLY NAME. AMEN INDEED!

Day 65
3:6

"GOD poured out the HOLY SPIRIT abundantly on us through JESUS CHRIST our SAVIOR."
◀ Titus 3:6 ▶ [GNT]

"I will not be afraid of many thousands of people who have set themselves against me all around."
◀ Psalm 3:6 ▶ [ESV]

"Always let HIM lead You, and HE Will clear the road for You to follow." ◀ Proverbs 3:6 ▶ [CEV]

"Our friends, we command You in the Name of our LORD JESUS CHRIST to keep away from all Believers who are living a lazy life and who do not follow the instructions that we gave them."
◀ 2 Thessalonians 3:6 ▶ [GNT]

"Humans give life to their children. Yet only GOD's SPIRIT can change You into a child of GOD."
◀ John 3:6 ▶ [CEV]

"I AM The LORD, and I do not change. And so, You, the descendants of Jacob, are not yet completely lost."
◀ Malachi 3:6 ▶ [GNT]

Powerful Manifestation Prayer:

I BLESS myself, my family and everyone born on this date with GOD's MOST POWERFUL PURE LOVING LIGHT, HIS MOST POWERFUL PURE SOURCE HEALING ENERGY, and an ABUNDANCE OF HIS AMAZING GREATER GRACE in the POWER, the ANOINTING, the AUTHORITY and the WISDOM of the HOLY SPIRIT, in JESUS' MOST HOLY NAME. AMEN INDEED!

Day 66

3:7

"You should realize, then, that the real descendants of Abraham are the people who have Faith."
◄ Galatians 3:7 ► [GNT]

"Do not be wise in your own eyes; fear the LORD and turn away from evil."
◄ Proverbs 3:7 ► [NASB]

"So that being justified by HIS Grace we would be made heirs according to the HOPE of ETERNAL LIFE."
◄ Titus 3:7 ► [NASB]

"Arise, O LORD save me, O my GOD! For YOU have smitten all my enemies on the cheek; YOU have shattered the teeth of the wicked."
◄ Psalm 3:7 ► [NASB]

"Return to ME, and I Will return to You,' says the LORD of Hosts."
◄ Malachi 3:7 ► [ESV]

"HE WHO is Holy, WHO is TRUE, WHO has the KEY of David, WHO opens and no one will shut, and WHO shuts and no one opens."
◄ Revelation 3:7 ► [NASB]

Powerful Manifestation Prayer:

I BLESS myself, my family and everyone born on this date with GOD's MOST POWERFUL PURE LOVING LIGHT, HIS MOST POWERFUL PURE SOURCE HEALING ENERGY, and an ABUNDANCE OF HIS AMAZING GREATER GRACE in the POWER, the ANOINTING, the AUTHORITY and the WISDOM of the HOLY SPIRIT, in JESUS' MOST HOLY NAME. AMEN INDEED!

Day 67
3:8

"The LORD said: Just wait for the day when I accuse You nations. I have decided on a day, when I Will bring together every nation and kingdom and punish them all in MY fiery anger. I Will become furious and destroy the earth."
◄ Zephaniah 3:8 ► [CEV]

"Nothing is as wonderful as knowing CHRIST JESUS my LORD. I have given up everything else and count it all as garbage. All I want is CHRIST."
◄ Philippians 3:8 ► [CEV]

"This is a trustworthy statement; and concerning these things I want to speak confidently, so that those who have believed GOD Will be careful to engage in GOoD deeds. These things are GOoD and profitable for men."
◄ Titus 3:8 ► [NASB]

"'I know your deeds. Behold, I have put before You an open door which no one can shut, because You have a little power, and have kept MY WORD, and have not denied MY Name."
◄ Revelations 3:8 ► [NASB]

"If You do, it will be like GOoD medicine, healing your wounds and easing your pains."
◄ Proverbs 3:8 ► [GNT]

"Salvation belongs to the LORD; YOUR Blessing be upon YOUR people! Selah."
◄ Psalm 3:8 ► [NASB]

Powerful Manifestation Prayer:

I BLESS myself, my family and everyone born on this date with GOD's MOST POWERFUL PURE LOVING LIGHT, HIS MOST POWERFUL PURE SOURCE HEALING ENERGY, and an ABUNDANCE OF HIS AMAZING GREATER GRACE in the POWER, the ANOINTING, the AUTHORITY and the WISDOM of the HOLY SPIRIT, in JESUS' MOST HOLY NAME. AMEN INDEED!

Day 68
3:9

"I was **Chosen** to explain to everyone this mysterious plan that **GOD**, **The CREATOR** of all things, had kept secret from the beginning." ◀ Ephesians 3:9 ▶ [NLT]

"Don't be hateful and insult people just because they are hateful and insult **You**. Instead, treat everyone with kindness. **You** are **GOD's Chosen Ones**, and **HE Will Bless You**." ◀ 1 Peter 3:9 ▶ [CEV]

"The **LORD** is not slow about **HIS Promise**, as some count slowness, but is patient toward **You**, not wishing for any to perish but for all to come to repentance." ◀ 2 Peter 3:9 ▶ [NASB]

"Honor the **LORD** with your wealth and with the first fruits of all your produce." ◀ Proverbs 3:9 ▶ [ESV]

"Do not lie to one another, since **You** laid aside the old self with its evil practices." ◀ Colossians 3:9 ▶ [NASB]

"No one who is born of **GOD** practices sin, because **HIS Seed** abides in him; and he cannot sin, because he is born of **GOD**." ◀ 1 John 3:9 ▶ [NASB]

Powerful Manifestation Prayer:

I BLESS myself, my family and everyone born on this date with GOD's MOST POWERFUL PURE LOVING LIGHT, HIS MOST POWERFUL PURE SOURCE HEALING ENERGY, and an ABUNDANCE OF HIS AMAZING GREATER GRACE in the POWER, the ANOINTING, the AUTHORITY and the WISDOM of the HOLY SPIRIT, in JESUS' MOST HOLY NAME. AMEN INDEED!

Day 69
3:10

"I AM the LORD All-Powerful, and I challenge You to put ME to the test. Bring the entire ten percent into the storehouse, so there will be food in MY house. Then I Will open the windows of Heaven and flood You with Blessing after Blessing." ◄ Malachi 3:10 ► [CEV]

"Even now the ax of GOD's judgment is poised, ready to sever the roots of the trees. Yes, every tree that does not produce GOoD fruit will be chopped down and thrown into the fire."
◄ Matthew 3:10 ► [NLT]

"As for a person who stirs up division, after warning him once and then twice, have nothing more to do with him." ◄ Titus 3:10 ► [ESV]

"By this it is evident who are the children of GOD, and who are the children of the devil: whoever does not practice Righteousness is not of GOD, nor is the one who does not Love his brother."
◄ 1 John 3:10 ► [ESV]

"All I want is to know CHRIST and to experience the POWER of HIS resurrection, to share in HIS sufferings and become like HIM in HIS death." ◄ Philippians 3:10 ► [GNT]

"Each of You is now a new person. You are becoming more and more like your CREATOR, and You will understand HIM better." ◄ Colossians 3:10 ► [CEV]

Powerful Manifestation Prayer:

I BLESS myself, my family and everyone born on this date with GOD's MOST POWERFUL PURE LOVING LIGHT, HIS MOST POWERFUL PURE SOURCE HEALING ENERGY, and an ABUNDANCE OF HIS AMAZING GREATER GRACE in the POWER, the ANOINTING, the AUTHORITY and the WISDOM of the HOLY SPIRIT, in JESUS' MOST HOLY NAME. AMEN INDEED!

Day 70
3:11

"I Will rebuke the devourer for You, so that it will not destroy the fruits of your soil, and your vine in the field shall not fail to bear, says the LORD of Hosts. ◄ Malachi 3:11 ► [ESV]

"I baptize You with water for repentance, but HE WHO is coming after me is mightier than I, WHOSE sandals I am not worthy to carry. HE Will baptize You with the HOLY SPIRIT and fire." ◄ Matthew 3:11 ► [ESV]

"It doesn't matter if You are a Greek or a Jew, or if You are circumcised or not. You may even be a barbarian or a Scythian, and You may be a slave or a Free person. Yet CHRIST is all that matters, and HE Lives in all of us." ◄ Colossians 3:11 ► [CEV]

"For this is the message that You have heard from the beginning, that we should Love one another." ◄ 1 John 3:11 ► [ESV]

"In the HOPE that I myself will be raised from death to life!" ◄ Philippians 3:11 ► [GNT]

"I AM coming **S.O.O.N.**! So hold firmly to what You have, and no one will take away the crown You will be given as your reward." ◄ Revelations 3:11 ► [CEV]

Powerful Manifestation Prayer:

I BLESS myself, my family and everyone born on this date with GOD's MOST POWERFUL PURE LOVING LIGHT, HIS MOST POWERFUL PURE SOURCE HEALING ENERGY, and an ABUNDANCE OF HIS AMAZING GREATER GRACE in the POWER, the ANOINTING, the AUTHORITY and the WISDOM of the HOLY SPIRIT, in JESUS' MOST HOLY NAME. AMEN INDEED!

Day 71
3:12

"GOD replied, 'I Will be with You. And You will know that I AM The ONE WHO sent You, when You worship ME on this mountain after You have led MY people out of Egypt."
◄ Exodus 3:12 ► [CEV]

"Then GOD's SPIRIT lifted me up, and I heard behind me the loud roar of a voice that said, "Praise the Glory of the LORD in Heaven above!"
◄ Ezekiel 3:12 ► [GNT]

"GOD Loves You and has Chosen You as HIS OWN special people. So be gentle, kind, humble, meek, and patient."
◄ Colossians 3:12 ► [CEV]

"But I, the LORD, won't destroy any of your people who are truly humble and turn to ME for safety."
◄ Zephaniah 3:12 ► [CEV]

"Not that I have already obtained this or am already perfect, but I press on to make IT my own, because CHRIST JESUS has made me HIS OWN."
◄ Philippians 3:12 ► [ESV]

"All the nations will call You Blessed, for You shall be a delightful land," says the LORD of Hosts."
◄ Malachi 3:12 ► [NASB]

Powerful Manifestation Prayer:

I BLESS myself, my family and everyone born on this date with GOD's MOST POWERFUL PURE LOVING LIGHT, HIS MOST POWERFUL PURE SOURCE HEALING ENERGY, and an ABUNDANCE OF HIS AMAZING GREATER GRACE in the POWER, the ANOINTING, the AUTHORITY and the WISDOM of the HOLY SPIRIT, in JESUS' MOST HOLY NAME. AMEN INDEED!

Day 72
3:13

"No, dear brothers and sisters, I have not achieved it, but I focus on this one thing: Forgetting the past and looking forward to what lies ahead."
◄ Philippians 3:13 ► [NLT]

"Be tolerant with one another and forgive one another whenever any of **You** has a complaint against someone else. **You** must forgive one another just as the **LORD** has forgiven **You**."
◄ Colossians 3:13 ► [GNT]

"In this way **HE Will** strengthen **You**, and **You** will be perfect and **Holy** in the presence of our **GOD** and **FATHER** when our **LORD JESUS** comes with all who belong to **HIM**."
◄ 1 Thessalonians 3:13 ► [GNT]

"**Blessed** is the one who finds **Wisdom**, and the one who gets understanding."
◄ Proverbs 3:13 ► [ESV]

"Who among **You** is wise and understanding? Let him show by his **GOoD** behavior his deeds in the gentleness of **Wisdom**."
◄ James 3:13 ► [NASB]

"And the quality of each person's work will be seen when the Day of **CHRIST** exposes it. For on that Day fire will reveal everyone's work; the fire will test it and show its real quality."
◄ 1 Corinthians 3:13 ► [GNT]

"**JESUS** decided to **ASK** some of **HIS** disciples to go up on a mountain with **HIM**, and they went."
◄ Mark 3:13 ► [CEV]

Powerful Manifestation Prayer:

I BLESS myself, my family and everyone born on this date with GOD's MOST POWERFUL PURE LOVING LIGHT, HIS MOST POWERFUL PURE SOURCE HEALING ENERGY, and an ABUNDANCE OF HIS AMAZING GREATER GRACE in the POWER, the ANOINTING, the AUTHORITY and the WISDOM of the HOLY SPIRIT, in JESUS' MOST HOLY NAME. AMEN INDEED!

Day 73
3:14

"But even if **You** should suffer for **Righteousness'** sake, **You** will be **Blessed**. Have no fear of them, nor be troubled." ◀ 1 Peter 3:14 ▶ [ESV]

"Our people must also learn to engage in **GOoD** deeds to meet pressing needs, so that they will not be unfruitful." ◀ Titus 3:14 ▶ [NASB]

"I run toward the goal, so I can win the prize of being called to **Heaven**. This is the prize **GOD** offers because of what **CHRIST JESUS** has done." ◀ Philippians 3:14 ▶ [CEV]

"Everything **GOD** has done will last forever; nothing **HE** does can ever be changed. **GOD** has done all this, so that we will worship **HIM**." ◀ Ecclesiastes 3:14 ▶ [CEV]

"And if **You** follow **ME** and obey **MY** decrees and **MY** commands as your father, David, did, **I Will** give **You** a long life." ◀ 1 Kings 3:14 ▶ [NLT]

"For this reason I fall on my knees before the **FATHER**." ◀ Ephesians 3:14 ▶ [GNT]

Powerful Manifestation Prayer:

I BLESS myself, my family and everyone born on this date with GOD's MOST POWERFUL PURE LOVING LIGHT, HIS MOST POWERFUL PURE SOURCE HEALING ENERGY, and an ABUNDANCE OF HIS AMAZING GREATER GRACE in the POWER, the ANOINTING, the AUTHORITY and the WISDOM of the HOLY SPIRIT, in JESUS' MOST HOLY NAME. AMEN INDEED!

Day 74
3:15

"Everything that happens has happened before, and all that will be has already been-- **GOD** does everything over and over again."
◀ Ecclesiastes 3:15 ▶ [CEV]

"And **I Will** give **You** shepherds after **MY OWN Heart**, who will feed **You** with **Knowledge** and understanding."
◀ Jeremiah 3:15 ▶ [ESV]

"And to have authority to cast out demons."
◀ Mark 3:15 ▶ [NASB]

"And that from childhood **You** have known the sacred writings which are able to give **You** the **Wisdom** that leads to **Salvation** through **Faith** which is in **CHRIST JESUS**."
◀ 2 Timothy 3:15 ▶ [NASB]

"Let the peace of **CHRIST** rule in your hearts, to which indeed **You** were called in **One Body**; and be thankful."
◀ Colossians 3:15 ▶ [NASB]

"The **LORD** has taken away **HIS** judgments against **You**, **HE** has cleared away your enemies. The **King** of Israel, the **LORD**, is in your midst; **You** will fear disaster no more."
◀ Zephaniah 3:15 ▶ [NASB]

Powerful Manifestation Prayer:

I BLESS myself, my family and everyone born on this date with GOD's MOST POWERFUL PURE LOVING LIGHT, HIS MOST POWERFUL PURE SOURCE HEALING ENERGY, and an ABUNDANCE OF HIS AMAZING GREATER GRACE in the POWER, the ANOINTING, the AUTHORITY and the WISDOM of the HOLY SPIRIT, in JESUS' MOST HOLY NAME. AMEN INDEED!

Day 75
3:16

"All Scripture is inspired by GOD and profitable for teaching, for reproof, for correction, for training in Righteousness."
◄ 2 Timothy 3:16 ► [NASB]

"For GOD so Loved the world, that HE gave HIS ONLY begotten SON, that whoever believes in HIM shall not perish, but have ETERNAL LIFE."
◄ John 3:16 ► [NASB]

"Let the WORD of CHRIST richly dwell within You, with all Wisdom teaching and admonishing one another with psalms and hymns and Spiritual songs, singing with thankfulness in your hearts to GOD."
◄ Colossians 3:16 ► [NASB]

"For where jealousy and selfish ambition exist, there is disorder and every evil thing."
◄ James 3:16 ► [NASB]

"Do You not know that You are GOD's Temple and that GOD's SPIRIT dwells in You?"
◄ 1 Corinthians 3:16 ► [ESV]

"Give a kind and respectful answer and keep your conscience clear. This way You will make people ashamed for saying bad things about your GOoD conduct as a follower of CHRIST."
◄ 1 Peter 3:16 ► [CEV]

Powerful Manifestation Prayer:

I BLESS myself and everyone born on this date with GOD's MOST POWERFUL PURE LOVING LIGHT, HIS MOST POWERFUL PURE SOURCE HEALING ENERGY, and an ABUNDANCE OF HIS AMAZING GREATER GRACE in the POWER, the ANOINTING, the AUTHORITY and the WISDOM of the HOLY SPIRIT, in JESUS' MOST HOLY NAME. AMEN INDEED!

Day 76
3:17

"Together You are GOD's Holy Temple, and GOD Will destroy anyone who destroys HIS Temple."
◄ 1 Corinthians 3:17 ► [CEV]

"And I Pray that CHRIST Will make HIS Home in your hearts through Faith. I Pray that You may have your roots and foundation in Love."
◄ Ephesians 3:17 ► [GNT]

"Whatever You do in WORD or deed, do all in the Name of the LORD JESUS, giving thanks through HIM to GOD the FATHER."
◄ Colossians 3:17 ► [NASB]

"Now the LORD is the SPIRIT, and where the SPIRIT of the LORD is, there is Freedom."
◄ 2 Corinthians 3:17 ► [ESV]

"They will be MY people," says the LORD Almighty. "On the day when I act, they will be MY very OWN. I Will be merciful to them as parents are merciful to the children who serve them."
◄ Malachi 3:17 ► [NASB]

"The LORD your GOD is with You, the Mighty Warrior WHO saves. HE Will take great delight in You; in HIS Love HE Will no longer rebuke You but will rejoice over You with singing."
◄ Zephaniah 3:17 ► [NIV]

"And a Voice from Heaven said, "This is MY SON, WHOM I Love; with HIM I AM well pleased."
◄ Matthew 3:17 ► [NIV]

Powerful Manifestation Prayer:

I BLESS myself, my family and everyone born on this date with GOD's MOST POWERFUL PURE LOVING LIGHT, HIS MOST POWERFUL PURE SOURCE HEALING ENERGY, and an ABUNDANCE OF HIS AMAZING GREATER GRACE in the POWER, the ANOINTING, the AUTHORITY and the WISDOM of the HOLY SPIRIT, in JESUS' MOST HOLY NAME. AMEN INDEED!

Day 77
3:18

"Dear children, let's not merely say that we Love each other; let us show the Truth by our actions."
◀ 1 John 3:18 ▶ [NLT]

"Whoever believes in HIM is not condemned, but whoever does not believe is condemned already, because he has not believed in the Name of the ONLY SON of GOD." ◀ John 3:18 ▶ [ESV]

"Yet I will rejoice in the LORD; I will take joy in the GOD of my Salvation."
◀ Habakkuk 3:18 ▶ [GNT]

"When peacemakers plant seeds of peace, they will harvest justice." ◀ James 3:18 ▶ [CEV]

"A wife must put her husband first. This is her duty as a follower of the LORD."
◀ Colossians 3:18 ▶ [CEV]

"The LORD has Promised: Your sorrow has ended, and You can celebrate."
◀ Zephaniah 3:18 ▶ [CEV]

Powerful Manifestation Prayer:

I BLESS myself, my family and everyone born on this date with GOD's MOST POWERFUL PURE LOVING LIGHT, HIS MOST POWERFUL PURE SOURCE HEALING ENERGY, and an ABUNDANCE OF HIS AMAZING GREATER GRACE in the POWER, the ANOINTING, the AUTHORITY and the WISDOM of the HOLY SPIRIT, in JESUS' MOST HOLY NAME. AMEN INDEED!

Day 78
3:19

"By the sweat of your face **You** will eat bread, till **You** return to the ground, because from it **You** were taken; For **You** are dust, and to dust **You** shall return." ◄ Genesis 3:19 ► [NASB]

"Husbands, **Love** your wives, and do not be harsh with them." ◄ Colossians 3:19 ► [ESV]

"**GOD**, the **LORD**, is my strength; **HE** makes my feet like the deer's; **HE** makes me tread on my high places." ◄ Habakkuk 3:19 ► [ESV]

"When we **Love** others, we know we belong to the **Truth**, and we feel at ease in the presence of **GOD**." ◄ 1 John 3:19 ► [CEV]

"Therefore, repent and return, so that your sins may be wiped away, in order that times of refreshing may come from the presence of the **LORD**." ◄ Acts 3:19 ► [NASB]

"**I** correct and punish everyone **I Love**. So, make up your minds to turn away from your sins." ◄ Revelations 3:19 ► [CEV]

Powerful Manifestation Prayer:

I BLESS myself, my family and everyone born on this date with GOD's MOST POWERFUL PURE LOVING LIGHT, HIS MOST POWERFUL PURE SOURCE HEALING ENERGY, and an ABUNDANCE OF HIS AMAZING GREATER GRACE in the POWER, the ANOINTING, the AUTHORITY and the WISDOM of the HOLY SPIRIT, in JESUS' MOST HOLY NAME. AMEN INDEED!

Day 79
3:20

"Children, obey your parents in everything, for this pleases the **LORD**."
◄ Colossians 3:20 ► [ESV]

"All go to the same place. All came from the dust and all return to the dust."
◄ Ecclesiastes 3:20 ► [NASB]

"If our conscience condemns us, we know that **GOD** is greater than our conscience and that **HE** knows everything."
◄ 1 John 3:20 ► [GNT]

"**I Will** lead **You** home, and with your own eyes **You** will see **ME Bless You** with all **You** once owned. Then **You** will be famous everywhere on this earth. **I**, the **LORD**, have spoken!"
◄ Zephaniah 3:20 ► [CEV]

"Behold, **I** stand at the door and knock. If anyone hears **MY Voice** and opens the door, **I Will** come to him and dine with him, and **HE** with **ME**."
◄ Revelation 3:20 ► [NKJV]

"Now to **HIM WHO** is able to do exceedingly abundantly above all that we **ASK** or think, according to the **Power** that works in us."
◄ Ephesians 3:20 ► [NKJV]

Powerful Manifestation Prayer:

I BLESS myself, my family and everyone born on this date with GOD's MOST POWERFUL PURE LOVING LIGHT, HIS MOST POWERFUL PURE SOURCE HEALING ENERGY, and an ABUNDANCE OF HIS AMAZING GREATER GRACE in the POWER, the ANOINTING, the AUTHORITY and the WISDOM of the HOLY SPIRIT, in JESUS' MOST HOLY NAME. AMEN INDEED!

Day 80
3:21

"Baptism, which corresponds to this, now saves You, not as a removal of dirt from the body but as an appeal to GOD for a GOoD conscience, through the resurrection of JESUS CHRIST."
◀ 1 Peter 3:21 ▶ [ESV]

"Now when all the people were baptized, JESUS was also baptized, and while HE was praying, Heaven was opened."
◀ Luke 3:21 ▶ [NASB]

"HE must remain in Heaven until the time comes for all things to be made new, as GOD announced through HIS Holy Prophets of long ago."
◀ Acts 3:21 ▶ [GNT]

"Fathers, do not provoke your children, lest they become discouraged." ◀ Colossians 3:21 ▶ [ESV]

"But those who do what is True come to the Light in order that the Light may show that what they did was in obedience to GOD."
◀ John 3:21 ▶ [GNT]

"To GOD be the Glory in the church and in CHRIST JESUS for all time, forever and ever! Amen."
◀ Ephesians 3:21 ▶ [GNT]

Powerful Manifestation Prayer:

I BLESS myself, my family and everyone born on this date with GOD's MOST POWERFUL PURE LOVING LIGHT, HIS MOST POWERFUL PURE SOURCE HEALING ENERGY, and an ABUNDANCE OF HIS AMAZING GREATER GRACE in the POWER, the ANOINTING, the AUTHORITY and the WISDOM of the HOLY SPIRIT, in JESUS' MOST HOLY NAME. AMEN INDEED!

Day 81
3:22

"The **LORD** your **GOD Will** choose one of your own people to be a prophet, just as **HE Chose** me. Listen to everything he tells **You**."
◀ Acts 3:22 ▶ [CEV]

"The **Righteousness** of **GOD** is through **Faith** in **JESUS CHRIST** to all **WHO** believe, since there is no distinction."
◀ Romans 3:22 ▶ [CSB]

"**You** shall not fear them, for it is the **LORD** your **GOD** who fights for **You**."
◀ Deuteronomy 3:22 ▶ [ESV]

"And whatever we **ASK** we receive from **HIM**, because we keep **HIS** commandments and do the things that are pleasing in **HIS Sight**."
◀ 1 John 3:22 ▶ [NASB]

"But the **Scripture** imprisoned everything under sin, so that the **Promise** by **Faith** in **JESUS CHRIST** might be given to those who believe."
◀ Galatians 3:22 ▶ [ESV]

"The **LORD's Loving Kindness** indeed never cease, for **HIS** compassions never fail."
◀ Lamentations 3:22 ▶ [NASB]

Powerful Manifestation Prayer:

I BLESS myself, my family and everyone born on this date with GOD's MOST POWERFUL PURE LOVING LIGHT, HIS MOST POWERFUL PURE SOURCE HEALING ENERGY, and an ABUNDANCE OF HIS AMAZING GREATER GRACE in the POWER, the ANOINTING, the AUTHORITY and the WISDOM of the HOLY SPIRIT, in JESUS' MOST HOLY NAME. AMEN INDEED!

Day 82
3:23

"Before the way of Faith in CHRIST was available to us, we were placed under guard by the Law. We were kept in protective custody, so to speak, until the way of Faith was revealed."
◄ Galatians 3:23 ► [NLT]

"Why is Life given to those with no future, those whom GOD has surrounded with difficulties?"
◄ Job 3:23 ► [NLT]

"All of us have sinned and fallen short of GOD's Glory." ◄ Romans 3:23 ► [CEV]

"The LORD can always be trusted to show mercy each morning." ◄ Lamentations 3:23 ► [CEV]

"Whatever You do, work at it with all your heart, as though You were working for the LORD and not for people."
◄ Colossians 3:23 ► [GNT]

"And You belong to CHRIST, and CHRIST belongs to GOD." ◄ 1 Corinthians 3:23 ► [CEV]

Powerful Manifestation Prayer:

I BLESS myself, my family and everyone born on this date with GOD's MOST POWERFUL PURE LOVING LIGHT, HIS MOST POWERFUL PURE SOURCE HEALING ENERGY, and an ABUNDANCE OF HIS AMAZING GREATER GRACE in the POWER, the ANOINTING, the AUTHORITY and the WISDOM of the HOLY SPIRIT, in JESUS' MOST HOLY NAME. AMEN INDEED!

Day 83
3:24

"Those who obey GOD's commands live in union with GOD and GOD Lives in union with them. And because of the SPIRIT that GOD has given us we know that GOD Lives in union with us."
◄ 1 John 3:24 ► [GNT]

"If You lie down, You will not be afraid; when You lie down, your sleep will be sweet."
◄ Proverbs 3:24 ► [ESV]

"Samuel and all the other prophets who came later also spoke about what is now happening."
◄ Acts 3:24 ► [CEV]

"But GOD treats us much better than we deserve, and because of CHRIST JESUS, HE Freely accepts us and sets us Free from our sins." ◄ Romans 3:24 ► [CEV]

"Our LORD, it seems that YOU have just begun to show me YOUR Great Power. No other GOD in the sky or on earth is able to do the Mighty things that YOU do."
◄ Deuteronomy 3:24 ► [CEV]

"The LORD is my portion," says my Soul, "therefore I will HOPE in HIM."
◄ Lamentations 3:24 ► [ESV]

Powerful Manifestation Prayer:

I BLESS myself, my family and everyone born on this date with GOD's MOST POWERFUL PURE LOVING LIGHT, HIS MOST POWERFUL PURE SOURCE HEALING ENERGY, and an ABUNDANCE OF HIS AMAZING GREATER GRACE in the POWER, the ANOINTING, the AUTHORITY and the WISDOM of the HOLY SPIRIT, in JESUS' MOST HOLY NAME. AMEN INDEED!

Day 84
3:25

"The **Promises** of **GOD** through **HIS Prophets** are for **You**, and **You** share in the covenant which **GOD** made with your ancestors. As **HE** said to Abraham, 'Through your descendants **I Will Bless** all the people on earth.'"

◀ Acts 3:25 ▶ [GNT]

"Whom **GOD** put forward as a propitiation by **HIS Blood**, to be received by **Faith**. This was to show **GOD's Righteousness**, because in **HIS Divine** forbearance **HE** had passed over former sins."

◀ Romans 3:25 ▶ [ESV]

"For the thing I greatly feared has come upon me, and what I dreaded has happened to me."

◀ Job 3:25 ▶ [NKJV]

"But **CHRIST** has no favorites! **HE Will** punish evil people, just as they deserve."

◀ Colossians 3:25 ▶ [CEV]

"And if a house is divided against itself, that house will not be able to stand."

◀ Mark 3:25 ▶ [ESV]

"The **LORD** is **GOoD** to those who wait for **HIM**, to the person who seeks **HIM**."

◀ Lamentations 3:25 ▶ [NASB]

Powerful Manifestation Prayer:

I BLESS myself, my family and everyone born on this date with GOD's MOST POWERFUL PURE LOVING LIGHT, HIS MOST POWERFUL PURE SOURCE HEALING ENERGY, and an ABUNDANCE OF HIS AMAZING GREATER GRACE in the POWER, the ANOINTING, the AUTHORITY and the WISDOM of the HOLY SPIRIT, in JESUS' MOST HOLY NAME. AMEN INDEED!

Day 85
3:26

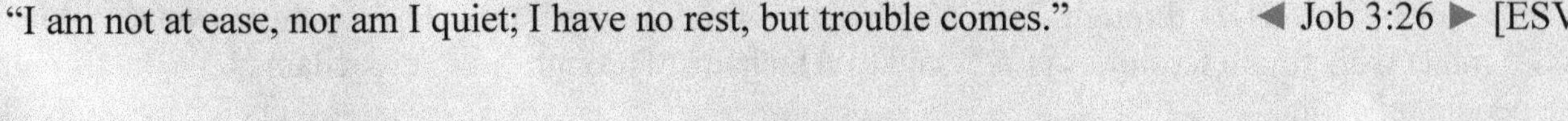

"I am not at ease, nor am I quiet; I have no rest, but trouble comes." ◀ Job 3:26 ▶ [ESV]

"So, if Satan fights against himself, that will be the end of him." ◀ Mark 3:26 ▶ [CEV]

"It is **GOoD** that one should wait quietly for the **Salvation** of the **LORD**."
◀ Lamentations 3:26 ▶ [ESV]

"**GOD**, having raised up **HIS** servant, sent **HIM** to **You** first, to **Bless You** by turning every one of **You** from your wickedness."
◀ Acts 3:26 ▶ [ESV]

"For **You** are all sons of **GOD** through **Faith** in **CHRIST JESUS**." ◀ Galatians 3:26 ▶ [NASB]

"**You** can be sure that the **LORD Will** protect **You** from harm." ◀ Proverbs 3:26 ▶ [CEV]

Powerful Manifestation Prayer:

I BLESS myself, my family and everyone born on this date with GOD's MOST POWERFUL PURE LOVING LIGHT, HIS MOST POWERFUL PURE SOURCE HEALING ENERGY, and an ABUNDANCE OF HIS AMAZING GREATER GRACE in the POWER, the ANOINTING, the AUTHORITY and the WISDOM of the HOLY SPIRIT, in JESUS' MOST HOLY NAME. AMEN INDEED!

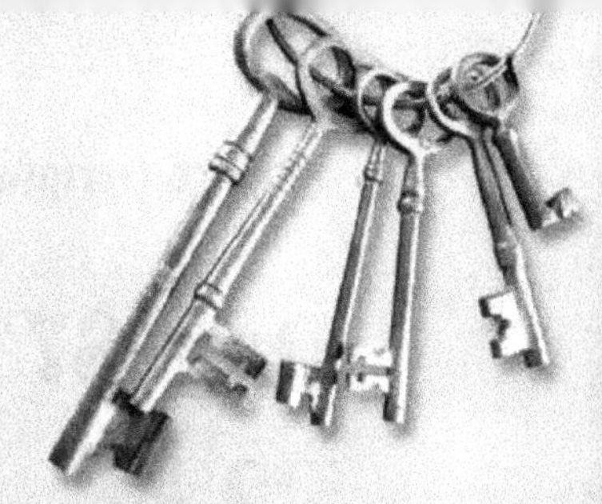

Day 86
3:27

"But the time will come, when I Will tell You what to say, and You will again be able to speak MY message. Some of them will listen; others will be stubborn and refuse to listen."

◀ Ezekiel 3:27 ▶ [CEV]

"Do not withhold GOoD from those to whom it is due, when it is in your power to do it."

◀ Proverbs 3:27 ▶ [ESV]

"What, then, can we boast about? Nothing! And what is the reason for this? Is it that we obey the Law? No, but that we believe."

◀ Romans 3:27 ▶ [GNT]

"John answered, "A person cannot receive even one thing unless it is given him from Heaven."

◀ John 3:27 ▶ [ESV]

"And it is best to learn this patience in our youth."

◀ Lamentations 3:27 ▶ [GNT]

"For all of You who were baptized into CHRIST have clothed yourselves with CHRIST."

◀ Galatians 3:27 ▶ [NASB]

Powerful Manifestation Prayer:

I BLESS myself, my family and everyone born on this date with GOD's MOST POWERFUL PURE LOVING LIGHT, HIS MOST POWERFUL PURE SOURCE HEALING ENERGY, and an ABUNDANCE OF HIS AMAZING GREATER GRACE in the POWER, the ANOINTING, the AUTHORITY and the WISDOM of the HOLY SPIRIT, in JESUS' MOST HOLY NAME. AMEN INDEED!

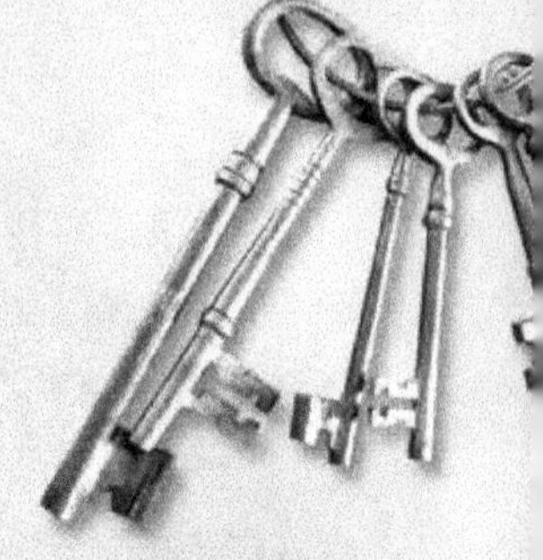

Day 87
3:28

"And all Israel heard of the judgment which the king had rendered; and they feared the king, for they saw that the **Wisdom** of **GOD** was in him to administer justice." ◀ 1 Kings 3:28 ▶ [NKJV]

"When we suffer, we should sit alone in silent patience." ◀ Lamentations 3:28 ▶ [GNT]

"Do not say to your neighbor, "Go, and come again, tomorrow I will give it"—when **You** have it with **You**." ◀ Proverbs 3:28 ▶ [ESV]

"**I Promise You** that any of the sinful things **You** say or do can be forgiven, no matter how terrible those things are." ◀ Mark 3:28 ▶ [CEV]

"**Faith** in **CHRIST JESUS** is what makes each of **You** equal with each other, whether **You** are a Jew or a Greek, a slave or a **Free** person, a man or a woman." ◀ Galatians 3:28 ▶ [CEV]

"We see that people are acceptable to **GOD** because they have **Faith**, and not because they obey the **Law**." ◀ Romans 3:28 ▶ [CEV]

Powerful Manifestation Prayer:

I BLESS myself, my family and everyone born on this date with GOD's MOST POWERFUL PURE LOVING LIGHT, HIS MOST POWERFUL PURE SOURCE HEALING ENERGY, and an ABUNDANCE OF HIS AMAZING GREATER GRACE in the POWER, the ANOINTING, the AUTHORITY and the WISDOM of the HOLY SPIRIT, in JESUS' MOST HOLY NAME. AMEN INDEED!

Day 88
3:29

"Or is **GOD** the **GOD** of the Jews only? Is **HE** not the **GOD** of the Gentiles also? Of course, **HE** is."
◀ Romans 3:29 ▶ [GNT]

"Let him put his mouth in the dust— There may yet be **HOPE**." ◀ Lamentations 3:29 ▶ [NKJV]

"Don't plan anything that will hurt your neighbors; they live beside **You**, trusting **You**."
◀ Proverbs 3:29 ▶ [GNT]

"If **You** belong to **CHRIST**, then **You** are the descendants of Abraham and will receive what **GOD** has **Promised**."
◀ Galatians 3:29 ▶ [GNT]

"Therefore. I make a decree that any people, nation or tongue that speaks anything offensive against the **GOD** of Shadrach, Meshach and Abednego shall be torn limb from limb and their houses reduced to a rubbish heap, inasmuch as there is no other god who is able to deliver in this way."
◀ Daniel 3:29 ▶ [NASB]

"But whoever says evil things against the **HOLY SPIRIT** will never be forgiven, because he has committed an eternal sin."
◀ Mark 3:29 ▶ [GNT]

Powerful Manifestation Prayer:

I BLESS myself, my family and everyone born on this date with GOD's MOST POWERFUL PURE LOVING LIGHT, HIS MOST POWERFUL PURE SOURCE HEALING ENERGY, and an ABUNDANCE OF HIS AMAZING GREATER GRACE in the POWER, the ANOINTING, the AUTHORITY and the WISDOM of the HOLY SPIRIT, in JESUS' MOST HOLY NAME. AMEN INDEED!

Day 89
3:30

"Don't argue with others for no reason when they have never done You any harm."
◀ Proverbs 3:30 ▶ [GNT]

"JESUS said this because the people were saying that HE had an evil spirit in HIM."
◀ Mark 3:30 ▶ [CEV]

"Though beaten and insulted, we should accept it all." ◀ Lamentations 3:30 ▶ [GNT]

"HE must increase, but I must decrease." ◀ John 3:30 ▶ [ESV]

"After this happened, the king appointed Shadrach, Meshach, and Abednego to even higher positions in Babylon Province."
◀ Daniel 3:30 ▶ [CEV]

"There is ONLY ONE GOD, and HE accepts Gentiles as well as Jews, simply because of their Faith."
◀ Romans 3:30 ▶ [CEV]

Powerful Manifestation Prayer:

I BLESS myself, my family and everyone born on this date with GOD's MOST POWERFUL PURE LOVING LIGHT, HIS MOST POWERFUL PURE SOURCE HEALING ENERGY, and an ABUNDANCE OF HIS AMAZING GREATER GRACE in the POWER, the ANOINTING, the AUTHORITY and the WISDOM of the HOLY SPIRIT, in JESUS' MOST HOLY NAME. AMEN INDEED!

Day 90
3:31

"Do we destroy the **Law** by our **Faith**? Not at all! We make it even more powerful."
◄ Romans 3:31 ► [CEV]

"Do not envy a man of violence and do not choose any of his ways." ◄ Proverbs 3:31 ► [ESV]

"Show your sorrow by tearing your clothes and wearing sackcloth!" ◄ 2 Samuel 3:31 ► [CEV]

"Then **JESUS' Mother** and **Brothers** arrived. **They** stood outside the house and sent in a message, asking for **HIM**." ◄ Mark 3:31 ► [GNT]

"**GOD's SON** comes from **Heaven** and is above all others. Everyone who comes from the earth belongs to the earth and speaks about earthly things. The **ONE WHO** comes from **Heaven** is above all others." ◄ John 3:31 ► [CEV]

"The **LORD** is merciful and will not reject us forever." ◄ Lamentations 3:31 ► [GNT]

Powerful Manifestation Prayer:

I BLESS myself, my family and everyone born on this date with GOD's MOST POWERFUL PURE LOVING LIGHT, HIS MOST POWERFUL PURE SOURCE HEALING ENERGY, and an ABUNDANCE OF HIS AMAZING GREATER GRACE in the POWER, the ANOINTING, the AUTHORITY and the WISDOM of the HOLY SPIRIT, in JESUS' MOST HOLY NAME. AMEN INDEED!

April
4

~ I **Pray** for **You** and **You Pray** for Me!

"After Job had prayed for his friends, the **LORD** restored his fortunes and gave him twice as much as he had before." ◄ Job 42:10 ► [NIV]

"**You** haven't done this before. **A.S.K.** using **MY NAME**, and **You** will receive, and **You** will have abundant joy." ◄ John 16:24 ► [NLT]

Powerful Manifestation Prayer:

I BLESS myself, my family and everyone born in this month with GOD's MOST POWERFUL PURE LOVING LIGHT, HIS MOST POWERFUL PURE SOURCE HEALING ENERGY, and an ABUNDANCE OF HIS AMAZING GREATER GRACE in the POWER, the ANOINTING, the AUTHORITY and the WISDOM of the HOLY SPIRIT, in JESUS' MOST HOLY NAME.
AMEN INDEED!

A.S.K.- Additional Scripture Knowledge

Write Additional Scriptures here.

Day 91
4:1

"**GOD's Promise** of entering **HIS** rest still stands, so we ought to tremble with fear that some of **You** might fail to experience it."
◄ Hebrews 4:1 ► [NLT]

"Answer me when I pray, O **GOD**, my **Defender**! When I was in trouble, **YOU** helped me. Be kind to me now and hear my prayer."
◄ Psalm 4:1 ► [GNT]

"Dear **Friends**, don't believe everyone who claims to have the **SPIRIT** of **GOD**. Test them all to find out if they really do come from **GOD**. Many false prophets have already gone out into the world.
◄ 1 John 4:1 ► [CEV]

"The **LORD** said: 'Israel, if **You** really want to come back to **ME**, get rid of those disgusting idols."
◄ Jeremiah 4:1 ► [CEV]

"My children listen to what your father teaches **You**. Pay attention, and **You** will have understanding."
◄ Proverbs 4:1 ► [GNT]

"Therefore, since **GOD** in **HIS** mercy has given us this new way, **WE NEVER GIVE UP."**
◄ 2 Corinthians 4:1 ► [NLT]

Powerful Manifestation Prayer:

I BLESS myself, my family and everyone born on this date with GOD's MOST POWERFUL PURE LOVING LIGHT, HIS MOST POWERFUL PURE SOURCE HEALING ENERGY, and an ABUNDANCE OF HIS AMAZING GREATER GRACE in the POWER, the ANOINTING, the AUTHORITY and the WISDOM of the HOLY SPIRIT, in JESUS' MOST HOLY NAME. AMEN INDEED!

Day 92
4:2

"Be completely humble and gentle; be patient, bearing with one another in **Love**."
◀ Ephesians 4:2 ▶ [NIV]

"Preach the **WORD**; be prepared in season and out of season; correct, rebuke and encourage—with great patience and careful instruction."
◀ 2 Timothy 4:2 ▶ [NIV]

"Devote yourselves to **Prayer**, being watchful and thankful."
◀ Colossians 4:2 ▶ [NIV]

"But we have renounced the hidden things of shame, not walking in craftiness nor handling the **WORD** of **GOD** deceitfully, but by manifestation of the **Truth** commending ourselves to every man's conscience in the sight of **GOD**."
◀ 2 Corinthians 4:2 ▶ [NKJV]

"Make **Promises** only in **MY Name**, and do what **You Promise**! Then all nations will **Praise ME**, and **I Will Bless** them."
◀ Jeremiah 4:2 ▶ [CEV]

"By this **You** will know the **SPIRIT** of **GOD**: Every **Spirit** that confesses that **JESUS CHRIST** has come in the flesh is from **GOD**."
◀ 1 John 4:2 ▶ [ESV]

"For **I** give **You** sound teaching; Do not abandon **MY** instruction."
◀ Proverbs 4:2 ▶ [NASB]

Powerful Manifestation Prayer:

I BLESS myself, my family and everyone born on this date with GOD's MOST POWERFUL PURE LOVING LIGHT, HIS MOST POWERFUL PURE SOURCE HEALING ENERGY, and an ABUNDANCE OF HIS AMAZING GREATER GRACE in the POWER, the ANOINTING, the AUTHORITY and the WISDOM of the HOLY SPIRIT, in JESUS' MOST HOLY NAME. AMEN INDEED!

Day 93
4:3

"The **LORD** says to the people of Judah and Jerusalem, 'Plow up your unplowed fields; do not plant your seeds among **THORNS**'."
◀ Jeremiah 4:3 ▶ [GNT]

"But every spirit that does not acknowledge **JESUS** is not from **GOD**. This is the spirit of the antichrist, which **You** have heard is coming and even now is already in the world."
◀ 1 John 4:3 ▶ [NIV]

"Such people teach that it is wrong to marry and to eat certain foods. But **GOD** created those foods to be eaten, after a **Prayer** of thanks, by those who are **Believers** and have come to know the **Truth**."
◀ 1 Timothy 4:3 ▶ [GNT]

"For a time is coming when people will no longer listen to sound and wholesome teaching. They will follow their own desires and will look for teachers who will tell them whatever their itching ears want to hear."
◀ 2 Timothy 4:3 ▶ [NLT]

"Try your best to let **GOD's SPIRIT** keep your hearts united. Do this by living at peace."
◀ Ephesians 4:3 ▶ [CEV]

"**GOD** wants **You** to be **Holy** and completely **Free** from sexual immorality."
◀ 1 Thessalonians 4:3 ▶ [GNT]

Powerful Manifestation Prayer:

I BLESS myself, my family and everyone born on this date with GOD's MOST POWERFUL PURE LOVING LIGHT, HIS MOST POWERFUL PURE SOURCE HEALING ENERGY, and an ABUNDANCE OF HIS AMAZING GREATER GRACE in the POWER, the ANOINTING, the AUTHORITY and the WISDOM of the HOLY SPIRIT, in JESUS' MOST HOLY NAME. AMEN INDEED!

Day 94
4:4

"Then he taught me and said to me, "Let your heart hold fast **MY WORDS**; Keep **MY Commandments** and live."
◀ Proverbs 4:4 ▶ [NASB]

"But **JESUS** answered, "The **Scripture** says, 'Human beings cannot live on bread alone, but need every **WORD** that **GOD** speaks."
◀ Matthew 4:4 ▶ [GNT]

"For everything created by **GOD** is **GOoD**, and nothing is to be rejected if it is received with gratitude."
◀ 1 Timothy 4:4 ▶ [NASB]

"Everyone will find rest beneath their own fig trees or grape vines, and they will live in peace. This is a **Solemn Promise** of the **LORD All-Powerful**."
◀ Micah 4:4 ▶ [CEV]

"But **You** who held fast to the **LORD** your **GOD** are alive today, every one of **You**."
◀ Deuteronomy 4:4 ▶ [NASB]

"**You** are from **GOD**, little children, and have overcome them; because greater is **HE WHO** is in **You** than he who is in the world."
◀ 1 John 4:4 ▶ [NASB]

Powerful Manifestation Prayer:

I BLESS myself, my family and everyone born on this date with GOD's MOST POWERFUL PURE LOVING LIGHT, HIS MOST POWERFUL PURE SOURCE HEALING ENERGY, and an ABUNDANCE OF HIS AMAZING GREATER GRACE in the POWER, the ANOINTING, the AUTHORITY and the WISDOM of the HOLY SPIRIT, in JESUS' MOST HOLY NAME. AMEN INDEED!

Day 95
4:5

"But You must keep control of yourself in all circumstances; endure suffering, do the work of a preacher of the GOoD News, and perform your whole duty as a servant of GOD. ◀ 2 Timothy 4:5 ▶ [NLT]

"Each nation worships and obeys its own god, but we will worship and obey the LORD our GOD forever and ever." ◀ Micah 4:5 ▶ [GNT]

"Acquire Wisdom! Acquire Understanding! Do not forget nor turn away from the WORDS of MY Mouth." ◀ Proverbs 4:5 ▶ [NASB]

"Therefore, do not go on passing judgment before the time, but wait until the LORD comes WHO Will both bring to Light the things hidden in the darkness and disclose the motives of men's hearts and then each man's Praise will come to him from GOD." ◀ 1 Corinthians 4:5 ▶ [NASB]

"You see, we don't go around preaching about ourselves. We preach that JESUS CHRIST is LORD, and we ourselves are your servants for JESUS' sake." ◀ 2 Corinthians 4:5 ▶ [NLT]

"Offer the sacrifices of Righteousness, and trust in the LORD." ◀ Psalm 4:5 ▶ [NASB]

Powerful Manifestation Prayer:

I BLESS myself, my family and everyone born on this date with GOD's MOST POWERFUL PURE LOVING LIGHT, HIS MOST POWERFUL PURE SOURCE HEALING ENERGY, and an ABUNDANCE OF HIS AMAZING GREATER GRACE in the POWER, the ANOINTING, the AUTHORITY and the WISDOM of the HOLY SPIRIT, in JESUS' MOST HOLY NAME. AMEN INDEED!

Day 96

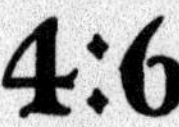

4:6

"Is not your fear of GOD your confidence, and the integrity of your ways your HOPE?"
◀ Job 4:6 ▶ [NASB]

"But HE gives us more Grace. That is why Scripture says: 'GOD opposes the proud but shows Favor to the humble'."
◀ James 4:6 ▶ [NIV]

"Be anxious for nothing, but in everything by Prayer and supplication with thanksgiving let your requests be made known to GOD."
◀ Philippians 4:6 ▶ [NASB]

"We are from GOD; he who knows GOD listens to us; he who is not from GOD does not listen to us. By this we know the SPIRIT of Truth and the spirit of error."
◀ 1 John 4:6 ▶ [NASB]

"For GOD, WHO said, "Let there be Light in the darkness," has made this Light shine in our hearts so we could know the Glory of GOD that is seen in the Face of JESUS CHRIST."
◀ 2 Corinthians 4:6 ▶ [NLT]

"Do not abandon Wisdom, and she will protect You; Love her, and she will keep You safe."
◀ Proverbs 4:6 ▶ [GNT]

Powerful Manifestation Prayer:

I BLESS myself, my family and everyone born on this date with GOD's MOST POWERFUL PURE LOVING LIGHT, HIS MOST POWERFUL PURE SOURCE HEALING ENERGY, and an ABUNDANCE OF HIS AMAZING GREATER GRACE in the POWER, the ANOINTING, the AUTHORITY and the WISDOM of the HOLY SPIRIT, in JESUS' MOST HOLY NAME. AMEN INDEED!

Day 97
4:7

"Yet we who have this **Spiritual Treasure** are like common clay pots, in order to show that the **Supreme Power** belongs to **GOD**, not to us." ◄ 2 Corinthians 4:7 ► [GNT]

"Happy are those whose wrongs are forgiven; whose sins are pardoned."
◄ Romans 4:7 ► [GNT]

"And the **Peace** of **GOD** which surpasses all understanding, will guard your hearts and your minds in **CHRIST JESUS**." ◄ Philippians 4:7 ► [ESV]

"Submit therefore to **GOD**. Resist the devil and he will flee from **You**." ◄ James 4:7 ► [NASB]

"**GOD** again set a certain day, calling it 'Today'. This **HE** did when a long time later **HE** spoke through David, as in the passage already quoted: 'Today, if **You** hear **HIS Voice**, do not harden your hearts'." ◄ Hebrews 4:7 ► [NIV]

"I have fought the **GOoD** fight, I have finished the race, I have kept the **Faith**."
◄ 2 Timothy 4:7 ► [ESV]

Powerful Manifestation Prayer:

I BLESS myself, my family and everyone born on this date with GOD's MOST POWERFUL PURE LOVING LIGHT, HIS MOST POWERFUL PURE SOURCE HEALING ENERGY, and an ABUNDANCE OF HIS AMAZING GREATER GRACE in the POWER, the ANOINTING, the AUTHORITY and the WISDOM of the HOLY SPIRIT, in JESUS' MOST HOLY NAME. AMEN INDEED!

Day 98
4:8

"We often suffer, but we are never crushed. Even when we don't know what to do, **WE NEVER GIVE UP**."
◄ 2 Corinthians 4:8 ► [CEV]

"Draw near to GOD and HE Will draw near to You. Cleanse your hands, You sinners; and purify your hearts, You double-minded."
◄ James 4:8 ► [NASB]

"And now there is waiting for me the victory prize of being put right with GOD, which the LORD, the Righteous Judge, Will give me on that day--and not only to me, but to all those who wait with Love for HIM to appear."
◄ 2 Timothy 4:8 ► [GNT]

"This is why it says: "When HE ascended on high, HE took many captives and gave gifts to HIS people.""
◄ Ephesians 4:8 ► [NIV]

"The one who does not Love does not know GOD, for GOD is Love." ◄ 1 John 4:8 ► [NASB]

"In peace I will both lie down and sleep, for YOU Alone, O LORD, make me to dwell in safety."
◄ Psalm 4:8 ► [NASB]

Powerful Manifestation Prayer:

I BLESS myself, my family and everyone born on this date with GOD's MOST POWERFUL PURE LOVING LIGHT, HIS MOST POWERFUL PURE SOURCE HEALING ENERGY, and an ABUNDANCE OF HIS AMAZING GREATER GRACE in the POWER, the ANOINTING, the AUTHORITY and the WISDOM of the HOLY SPIRIT, in JESUS' MOST HOLY NAME. AMEN INDEED!

Day 99
4:9

"There are many enemies, but we are never without a **FRIEND**; and though badly hurt at times, we are not destroyed."
◄ 2 Corinthians 4:9 ► [GNT]

"David answered them, "I take a vow by the **Living LORD**, **WHO** has saved me from all dangers!"
◄ 2 Samuel 4:9 ► [GNT]

"By the breath of **GOD**, they perish, and by the blast of **HIS** anger they come to an end."
◄ Job 4:9 ► [NASB]

"In this the **Love** of **GOD** was made manifest among us, that **GOD** sent **HIS Only Son** into the world, so that we might live through **HIM**."
◄ 1 John 4:9 ► [ESV]

"**You** must be very careful not to forget the things **You** have seen **GOD** do for **You**. Keep reminding yourselves and tell your children and grandchildren as well."
◄ Deuteronomy 4:9 ► [CEV]

"The things **You** have learned and received and heard and seen in me, practice these things, and the **GOD** of **Peace** will be with **You**."
◄ Philippians 4:9 ► [NIV]

Powerful Manifestation Prayer:

I BLESS myself, my family and everyone born on this date with GOD's MOST POWERFUL PURE LOVING LIGHT, HIS MOST POWERFUL PURE SOURCE HEALING ENERGY, and an ABUNDANCE OF HIS AMAZING GREATER GRACE in the POWER, the ANOINTING, the AUTHORITY and the WISDOM of the HOLY SPIRIT, in JESUS' MOST HOLY NAME. AMEN INDEED!

Day 100
4:10

"This is real **Love**—not that we **Loved GOD**, but that **HE Loved** us and sent **HIS SON** as a **Sacrifice** to take away our sins." ◀ 1 John 4:10 ▶ [NLT]

"Humble yourselves in the presence of the **LORD**, and **HE Will** exalt **You**."
◀ James 4:10 ▶ [NASB]

"For all who have entered into **GOD's** rest have rested from their labors, just as **GOD** did after creating the world." ◀ Hebrews 4:10 ▶ [NLT]

"Assemble the people before **ME** to hear **MY WORDS** so that they may learn to revere **ME** as long as they live in the land and may teach them to their children." ◀ Deuteronomy 4:10 ▶ [NIV]

"If **You** fall, your friend can help **You** up. But if **You** fall without having a friend nearby, **You** are really in trouble." ◀ Ecclesiastes 4:10 ▶ [CEV]

"**MY** child, if **You** listen and obey **MY Teachings**, **You** will live a long time." ◀ Proverbs 4:10 ▶ [CEV]

Powerful Manifestation Prayer:

I BLESS myself, my family and everyone born on this date with GOD's MOST POWERFUL PURE LOVING LIGHT, HIS MOST POWERFUL PURE SOURCE HEALING ENERGY, and an ABUNDANCE OF HIS AMAZING GREATER GRACE in the POWER, the ANOINTING, the AUTHORITY and the WISDOM of the HOLY SPIRIT, in JESUS' MOST HOLY NAME. AMEN INDEED!

Day 101
4:11

"YOU are worthy, our LORD and GOD, to receive Glory and Honor and Power, for YOU created all things, and by YOUR Will they were created and have their being." ◄ Revelation 4:11 ► [NIV]

"Dear friends, if this is how GOD Loved us, then we should Love one another."
◄ 1 John 4:11 ► [GNT]

"I have directed You in the way of Wisdom; I have led You in upright paths."
◄ Proverbs 4:11 ► [NASB]

"I am not complaining about having too little. I have learned to be satisfied with whatever I have."
◄ Philippians 4:11 ► [CEV]

"Make it your goal to live a quiet life, minding your own business and working with your hands, just as we instructed You before." ◄ 1 Thessalonians 4:11 ► [CEV]

"If anyone speaks, let it be as one who speaks GOD's WORDS; if anyone serves, let it be from the strength GOD provides, so that GOD may be Glorified through JESUS CHRIST in everything. To HIM be the Glory and the Power forever and ever. Amen." ◄ 1 Peter 4:11 ► [CSB]

Powerful Manifestation Prayer:

I BLESS myself, my family and everyone born on this date with GOD's MOST POWERFUL PURE LOVING LIGHT, HIS MOST POWERFUL PURE SOURCE HEALING ENERGY, and an ABUNDANCE OF HIS AMAZING GREATER GRACE in the POWER, the ANOINTING, the AUTHORITY and the WISDOM of the HOLY SPIRIT, in JESUS' MOST HOLY NAME. AMEN INDEED!

Day 102
4:12

"No one has ever seen GOD. If we Love one another, GOD remains in us and HIS Love is made complete in us." ◄ 1 John 4:12 ► [CSB]

"For the WORD of GOD is living and active and sharper than any two-edged sword and piercing as far as the division of Soul and Spirit, of both joints and marrow, and able to judge the thoughts and intentions of the heart." ◄ Hebrews 4:12 ► [NASB]

"My dear friends, do not be surprised at the painful test You are suffering, as though something unusual were happening to You." ◄ 1 Peter 4:12 ► [GNT]

"I know what it is to be poor or to have plenty, and I have lived under all kinds of conditions. I know what it means to be full or to be hungry, to have too much or too little." ◄ Philippians 4:12 ► [CEV]

"Nothing will stand in your way if You walk wisely, and You will not stumble when You run." ◄ Proverbs 4:12 ► [GNT]

"Now go! When You speak, I Will be with You and give You the Words to say." ◄ Exodus 4:12 ► [CEV]

Powerful Manifestation Prayer:

I BLESS myself, my family and everyone born on this date with GOD's MOST POWERFUL PURE LOVING LIGHT, HIS MOST POWERFUL PURE SOURCE HEALING ENERGY, and an ABUNDANCE OF HIS AMAZING GREATER GRACE in the POWER, the ANOINTING, the AUTHORITY and the WISDOM of the HOLY SPIRIT, in JESUS' MOST HOLY NAME. AMEN INDEED!

Day 103
4:13

"HE told You what You must do to keep the covenant HE made with You -- You must obey the Ten Commandments, which HE wrote on two stone tablets." ◀ Deuteronomy 4:13 ▶ [GNT]

"Always remember what You have learned. Your education is your life--guard it well."
◀ Proverbs 4:13 ▶ [GNT]

"After the devil had finished testing JESUS in every way possible, he left HIM for a while."
◀ Luke 4:13 ▶ [CEV]

"There is nothing that can be hid from GOD; everything in all creation is exposed and lies open before HIS eyes. And it is to HIM that we must all give an account of ourselves." ◀ Hebrews 4:13 ▶ [GNT]

"Be glad for the chance to suffer as CHRIST suffered. It will prepare You for even greater happiness when HE makes HIS Glorious return." ◀ 1 Peter 4:13 ▶ [CEV]

"By this we know that we abide in HIM and HE in us, because HE has given us of HIS SPIRIT."
◀ 1 John 4:13 ▶ [NASB]

"I can do all things through CHRIST WHO strengthens me." ◀ Philippians 4:13 ▶ [NKJV]

Powerful Manifestation Prayer:

I BLESS myself, my family and everyone born on this date with GOD's MOST POWERFUL PURE LOVING LIGHT, HIS MOST POWERFUL PURE SOURCE HEALING ENERGY, and an ABUNDANCE OF HIS AMAZING GREATER GRACE in the POWER, the ANOINTING, the AUTHORITY and the WISDOM of the HOLY SPIRIT, in JESUS' MOST HOLY NAME. AMEN INDEED!

Day 104
4:14

"For if what **GOD Promise** is to be given to those who obey the **Law**, then **Faith** means nothing, and **GOD's Promise** is worthless." ◄ Romans 4:14 ► [GNT]

"And we have seen and tell others that the **FATHER** sent **HIS SON** to be the **Savior** of the world." ◄ 1 John 4:14 ► [GNT]

"Let us, then, hold firmly to the **Faith** we profess. For we have a **Great High Priest WHO** has gone into the very presence of **GOD** -- **JESUS** the **SON** of **GOD**." ◄ Hebrews 4:14 ► [GNT]

"Do not enter the path of the wicked, and do not walk in the way of the evil." ◄ Proverbs 4:14 ► [ESV]

"And the **LORD** commanded me at that time to teach **You** statutes and rules, that **You** might do them in the land that **You** are going over to possess." ◄ Deuteronomy 4:14 ► [ESV]

"If **You** are insulted for the **Name** of **CHRIST**, **You** are **Blessed**, because the **SPIRIT** of **Glory** and of **GOD** rests upon **You**." ◄ 1 Peter 4:14 ► [ESV]

Powerful Manifestation Prayer:

I BLESS myself, my family and everyone born on this date with GOD's MOST POWERFUL PURE LOVING LIGHT, HIS MOST POWERFUL PURE SOURCE HEALING ENERGY, and an ABUNDANCE OF HIS AMAZING GREATER GRACE in the POWER, the ANOINTING, the AUTHORITY and the WISDOM of the HOLY SPIRIT, in JESUS' MOST HOLY NAME. AMEN INDEED!

Day 105
4:15

"For we do not have a high priest who is unable to empathize with our weaknesses, but we have **ONE WHO** has been tempted in every way, just as we are—yet **HE** did not sin."
◀ Hebrews 4:15 ▶ [NIV]

"Instead **You** ought to say, "If the **LORD Wills**, we will live and do this or that."
◀ James 4:15 ▶ [ESV]

"Whoever confesses that **JESUS** is the **SON** of **GOD, GOD** abides in him, and he in **GOD**."
◀ 1 John 4:15 ▶ [NASB]

"When our enemies heard that it was known to us, and that **GOD** had frustrated their plan, then all of us returned to the wall, each one to his work." ◀ Nehemiah 4:15 ▶ [NASB]

"Don't do it! Keep away from evil! Refuse it and go on your way." ◀ Proverbs 4:15 ▶ [GNT]

"Indeed, everything is for your benefit so that, as **Grace** extends through more and more people, it may cause thanksgiving to increase to the **Glory** of **GOD**." ◀ 2 Corinthians 4:15 ▶ [CSB]

Powerful Manifestation Prayer:

I BLESS myself, my family and everyone born on this date with GOD's MOST POWERFUL PURE LOVING LIGHT, HIS MOST POWERFUL PURE SOURCE HEALING ENERGY, and an ABUNDANCE OF HIS AMAZING GREATER GRACE in the POWER, the ANOINTING, the AUTHORITY and the WISDOM of the HOLY SPIRIT, in JESUS' MOST HOLY NAME. AMEN INDEED!

Day 106
4:16

"Therefore, **WE DO NOT GIVE UP**. Even though our outer person is being destroyed, our inner person is being renewed day by day." ◄ 2 Corinthians 4:16 ► [CSB]

"Let us then with confidence draw near to the throne of **Grace**, that we may receive mercy and find **Grace** to help in time of need." ◄ Hebrews 4:16 ► [ESV]

"We know how much **GOD Loves** us, and we have put our trust in **HIS Love**. **GOD** is **LOVE**, and all who live in **Love**, live in **GOD**, and **GOD Lives** in them." ◄ 1 John 4:16 ► [NLT]

"For they cannot sleep unless they do evil; and they are robbed of sleep unless they make someone stumble." ◄ Proverbs 4:16 ► [NASB]

"So do not corrupt yourselves by making an idol in any form—whether of a man or a woman." ◄ Deuteronomy 4:16 ► [NLT]

"Yet if anyone suffers as a **Christian**, let him not be ashamed, but let him **Glorify GOD** in that **Name**." ◄ 1 Peter 4:16 ► [ESV]

Powerful Manifestation Prayer:

I BLESS myself, my family and everyone born on this date with GOD's MOST POWERFUL PURE LOVING LIGHT, HIS MOST POWERFUL PURE SOURCE HEALING ENERGY, and an ABUNDANCE OF HIS AMAZING GREATER GRACE in the POWER, the ANOINTING, the AUTHORITY and the WISDOM of the HOLY SPIRIT, in JESUS' MOST HOLY NAME. AMEN INDEED!

Day 107
4:17

"Can a mortal be more righteous than GOD? Can even a strong man be more pure than HIS Maker?"
◀ Job 4:17 ▶ [NIV]

"But since they don't have deep roots, they don't last long. They fall away as **SOON** as they have problems or are persecuted for believing GOD's WORD." ◀ Mark 4:17 ▶ [NLT]

"And as we live in GOD, our Love grows more perfect. So we will not be afraid on the Day of Judgment, but we can face HIM with confidence because we live like JESUS here in this world."
◀ 1 John 4:17 ▶ [NLT]

"Then JESUS started preaching, 'Turn back to GOD! The Kingdom of Heaven will **SOON** be here.'"
◀ Matthew 4:17 ▶ [CEV]

"Then we who are alive and remain will be caught up together with them in the clouds to meet the LORD in the air, and so we shall always be with the LORD." ◀ 1 Thessalonians 4:17 ▶ [GNT]

"Therefore, to one who knows the right thing to do and does not do it, to him it is sin."
◀ James 4:17 ▶ [NASB]

Powerful Manifestation Prayer:

I BLESS myself, my family and everyone born on this date with GOD's MOST POWERFUL PURE LOVING LIGHT, HIS MOST POWERFUL PURE SOURCE HEALING ENERGY, and an ABUNDANCE OF HIS AMAZING GREATER GRACE in the POWER, the ANOINTING, the AUTHORITY and the WISDOM of the HOLY SPIRIT, in JESUS' MOST HOLY NAME. AMEN INDEED!

Day 108
4:18

"Abraham believed and hoped, even when there was no reason for hoping, and so became "the father of many nations." Just as the **Scripture** says, "Your descendants will be as many as the stars."
◀ Romans 4:18 ▶ [GNT]

"There is no fear in **Love**; instead, perfect **Love** drives out fear, because fear involves punishment. So, the one who fears is not complete in **Love**."
◀ 1 John 4:18 ▶ [CSB]

"The road the righteous travel is like the sunrise, getting brighter and brighter until daylight has come."
◀ Proverbs 4:18 ▶ [GNT]

"The **LORD's SPIRIT** has come to me, because **HE** has **Chosen** me to tell the **GOoD News** to the poor. The **LORD** has sent me to announce **Freedom** for prisoners, to give sight to the blind, to **Free** everyone who suffers."
◀ Luke 4:18 ▶ [CEV]

"I have been paid back everything, and with interest. I am completely satisfied with the gifts **You** sent … They are like a sweet-smelling offering or like the right kind of sacrifice that pleases **GOD**."
◀ Philippians 4:18 ▶ [CEV]

"Therefore encourage one another with these **WORDS**."
◀ 1 Thessalonians 4:18 ▶ [ESV]

Powerful Manifestation Prayer:

I BLESS myself, my family and everyone born on this date with GOD's MOST POWERFUL PURE LOVING LIGHT, HIS MOST POWERFUL PURE SOURCE HEALING ENERGY, and an ABUNDANCE OF HIS AMAZING GREATER GRACE in the POWER, the ANOINTING, the AUTHORITY and the WISDOM of the HOLY SPIRIT, in JESUS' MOST HOLY NAME. AMEN INDEED!

Day 109
4:19

"When You look to the Heavens and see the sun, moon, and stars--all the stars in the sky--do not be led astray to bow in worship to them and serve them. The LORD your GOD has provided them for all people everywhere under Heaven." ◀ Deuteronomy 4:19 ▶ [CSB]

"Do You think GOD wants us to obey You or to obey HIM?" ◀ Acts 4:19 ▶ [CEV]

"But the worries of the world, and the deceitfulness of riches, and the desires for other things enter in and choke the WORD, and it becomes unfruitful." ◀ Mark 4:19 ▶ [NASB]

"Therefore, let those who suffer according to GOD's Will entrust their Souls to a Faithful CREATOR while doing GOoD." ◀ 1 Peter 4:19 ▶ [ESV]

"And my GOD Will supply all your needs according to HIS Riches in Glory in CHRIST JESUS." ◀ Philippians 4:19 ▶ [NASB]

"We Love, because HE first Loved us." ◀ 1 John 4:19 ▶ [NASB]

Powerful Manifestation Prayer:

I BLESS myself, my family and everyone born on this date with GOD's MOST POWERFUL PURE LOVING LIGHT, HIS MOST POWERFUL PURE SOURCE HEALING ENERGY, and an ABUNDANCE OF HIS AMAZING GREATER GRACE in the POWER, the ANOINTING, the AUTHORITY and the WISDOM of the HOLY SPIRIT, in JESUS' MOST HOLY NAME. AMEN INDEED!

Day 110
4:20

"If someone says, "I Love GOD," and hates his brother, he is a liar; for the one who does not Love his brother whom he has seen, cannot Love GOD WHOM he has not seen."

◀ 1 John 4:20 ▶ [NASB]

"Yet, with respect to the Promise of GOD, he did not waver in unbelief but grew strong in Faith, giving Glory to GOD." ◀ Romans 4:20 ▶ [NASB]

"But the LORD has taken You and brought You out of the iron furnace, out of Egypt, to be a people of HIS OWN inheritance, as You are this day." ◀ Deuteronomy 4:20 ▶ [ESV]

"MY Child, pay attention to what I say. Listen to MY WORDS." ◀ Proverbs 4:20 ▶ [GNT]

"For we cannot stop speaking about what we have seen and heard." ◀ Acts 4:20 ▶ [NASB]

"Now to our GOD and FATHER be Glory forever and ever. Amen." ◀ Philippians 4:20 ▶ [NASB]

Powerful Manifestation Prayer:

I BLESS myself, my family and everyone born on this date with GOD's MOST POWERFUL PURE LOVING LIGHT, HIS MOST POWERFUL PURE SOURCE HEALING ENERGY, and an ABUNDANCE OF HIS AMAZING GREATER GRACE in the POWER, the ANOINTING, the AUTHORITY and the WISDOM of the HOLY SPIRIT, in JESUS' MOST HOLY NAME. AMEN INDEED!

Day 111
4:21

"And we have this command from **HIM**: The one who **Loves GOD** must also **Love** his brother and sister."
◄ 1 John 4:21 ► [CSB]

"What do **You** want me to do when I arrive? Do **You** want me to be hard on **You** or to be kind and gentle?"
◄ 1 Corinthians 4:21 ► [CEV]

"After threatening them further, they released them. They found no way to punish them because the people were all giving **Glory** to **GOD** over what had been done."
◄ Acts 4:21 ► [CSB]

"Then **JESUS** asked them, "Would anyone light a lamp and then put it under a basket or under a bed? Of course not! A lamp is placed on a stand, where its light will shine."
◄ Mark 4:21 ► [NLT]

"**HE** began by saying to them, "Today as **You** listen, this **Scripture** has been fulfilled."
◄ Luke 4:21 ► [CSB]

"Let **Them** [**HIS WORDS**] not escape from your sight; keep **Them** within your heart."
◄ Proverbs 4:21 ► [ESV]

Powerful Manifestation Prayer:

I BLESS myself, my family and everyone born on this date with GOD's MOST POWERFUL PURE LOVING LIGHT, HIS MOST POWERFUL PURE SOURCE HEALING ENERGY, and an ABUNDANCE OF HIS AMAZING GREATER GRACE in the POWER, the ANOINTING, the AUTHORITY and the WISDOM of the HOLY SPIRIT, in JESUS' MOST HOLY NAME. AMEN INDEED!

Day 112
4:22

"So get rid of your old self, which made You live as You used to--the old self that was being destroyed by its deceitful desires." ◄ Ephesians 4:22 ► [GNT]

"When a ruler inadvertently sins, disobeying any one of the commands of the LORD his GOD that should not be violated, he will be guilty." ◄ Leviticus 4:22 ► [ISV]

"It is You, O king; for You have become great and grown strong, and your majesty has become great and reached to the sky and your dominion to the end of the earth." ◄ Daniel 4:22 ► [NASB]

"And all spoke well of HIM and marveled at the Gracious WORDS that were coming from HIS mouth. And they said, "Is not this Joseph's SON?" ◄ Luke 4:22 ► [ESV]

"Knowing these teachings will mean True life and GOoD health for You."
◄ Proverbs 4:22 ► [CEV]

"The LORD be with your Spirit. Grace be with You." ◄ 2 Timothy 4:22 ► [NASB]

"I heard the LORD say, "My people ignore me. They are foolish children who do not understand that they will be punished. All they know is how to sin." ◄ Jeremiah 4:22 ► [CEV]

Powerful Manifestation Prayer:

I BLESS myself, my family and everyone born on this date with GOD's MOST POWERFUL PURE LOVING LIGHT, HIS MOST POWERFUL PURE SOURCE HEALING ENERGY, and an ABUNDANCE OF HIS AMAZING GREATER GRACE in the POWER, the ANOINTING, the AUTHORITY and the WISDOM of the HOLY SPIRIT, in JESUS' MOST HOLY NAME. AMEN INDEED!

Day 113
4:23

"**JESUS** was going throughout all Galilee, teaching in their synagogues and proclaiming the **Gospel** of the **Kingdom**, and healing every kind of disease and every kind of sickness among the people."
◄ Matthew 4:23 ► [NASB]

"Be certain that **You** do not forget the **Covenant** that the **LORD** your **GOD** made with **You**. Obey **HIS Command** not to make yourselves any kind of idol." ◄ Deuteronomy 4:23 ► [GNT]

"Be careful how **You** think; your life is shaped by your thoughts." ◄ Proverbs 4:23 ► [GNT]

"But an hour is coming, and now is, when the **True** worshipers will worship the **FATHER** in the **Spirit** and in **Truth**; for such people the **FATHER** seeks to be **HIS** worshipers."
◄ John 4:23 ► [NASB]

"And that **You** be renewed in the **Spirit** of your mind." ◄ Ephesians 4:23 ► [NASB]

"The **Grace** of the **LORD JESUS CHRIST** be with your **Spirit**." ◄ Philippians 4:23 ► [NASB]

Powerful Manifestation Prayer:

I BLESS myself, my family and everyone born on this date with GOD's MOST POWERFUL PURE LOVING LIGHT, HIS MOST POWERFUL PURE SOURCE HEALING ENERGY, and an ABUNDANCE OF HIS AMAZING GREATER GRACE in the POWER, the ANOINTING, the AUTHORITY and the WISDOM of the HOLY SPIRIT, in JESUS' MOST HOLY NAME. AMEN INDEED!

Day 114
4:24

"For the LORD your GOD is a Consuming Fire, a Jealous GOD."
◀ Deuteronomy 4:24 ▶ [NASB]

"Never tell lies or be deceitful in what You say." ◀ Proverbs 4:24 ▶ [CEV]

"Put on your new nature, created to be like GOD—truly Righteous and Holy."
◀ Ephesians 4:24 ▶ [NLT]

"And HE said to them, "Pay attention to what You hear: with the measure You use, it will be measured to You, and still more will be added to You." ◀ Mark 4:24 ▶ [ESV]

"That all the peoples of the earth may know that the Hand of the LORD is Mighty, so that You may fear the LORD your GOD forever." ◀ Joshua 4:24 ▶ [NASB]

"GOD is SPIRIT, and those who worship HIM must worship in SPIRIT and Truth."
◀ John 4:24 ▶ [NASB]

Powerful Manifestation Prayer:

I BLESS myself, my family and everyone born on this date with GOD's MOST POWERFUL PURE LOVING LIGHT, HIS MOST POWERFUL PURE SOURCE HEALING ENERGY, and an ABUNDANCE OF HIS AMAZING GREATER GRACE in the POWER, the ANOINTING, the AUTHORITY and the WISDOM of the HOLY SPIRIT, in JESUS' MOST HOLY NAME. AMEN INDEED!

Day 115
4:25

"Let your eyes look directly forward, and your gaze be straight before You."
◀ Proverbs 4:25 ▶ [ESV]

"No more lying, then! Each of You must tell the Truth to the other Believer, because we are all members together in the Body of CHRIST."
◀ Ephesians 4:25 ▶ [GNT]

"For whoever has, to him more shall be given; and whoever does not have, even what he has shall be taken away from him."
◀ Mark 4:25 ▶ [NASB]

"The woman said to him, "I know that the MESSIAH is coming" (WHO is called CHRIST). "When HE comes, HE Will explain everything to us."
◀ John 4:25 ▶ [CSB]

"GOD gave JESUS to die for our sins, and HE raised HIM to life, so that we would be made acceptable to GOD."
◀ Romans 4:25 ▶ [CEV]

"Even when You have been in the land a long time and have children and grandchildren, do not sin by making for yourselves an idol in any form at all. This is evil in the LORD's sight, and it will make HIM angry."
◀ Deuteronomy 4:25 ▶ [GNT]

Powerful Manifestation Prayer:

I BLESS myself, my family and everyone born on this date with GOD's MOST POWERFUL PURE LOVING LIGHT, HIS MOST POWERFUL PURE SOURCE HEALING ENERGY, and an ABUNDANCE OF HIS AMAZING GREATER GRACE in the POWER, the ANOINTING, the AUTHORITY and the WISDOM of the HOLY SPIRIT, in JESUS' MOST HOLY NAME. AMEN INDEED!

Day 116
4:26

"I looked, and the fertile field was a wilderness. All its cities were torn down because of the LORD and HIS burning anger." ◀ Jeremiah 4:26 ▶ [CSB]

"Again, JESUS said: GOD's Kingdom is like what happens when a farmer scatters seed in a field." ◀ Mark 4:26 ▶ [CEV]

"Carefully consider the path for your feet, and all your ways will be established." ◀ Proverbs 4:26 ▶ [CSB]

"If You become angry, do not let your anger lead You into sin, and do not stay angry all day." ◀ Ephesians 4:26 ▶ [GNT]

"Then JESUS declared, 'I, the ONE speaking to You--I AM HE'." ◀ John 4:26 ▶ [NIV]

"At that time people began to call on the Name of the LORD." ◀ Genesis 4:26 ▶ [CSB]

Powerful Manifestation Prayer:

I BLESS myself, my family and everyone born on this date with GOD's MOST POWERFUL PURE LOVING LIGHT, HIS MOST POWERFUL PURE SOURCE HEALING ENERGY, and an ABUNDANCE OF HIS AMAZING GREATER GRACE in the POWER, the ANOINTING, the AUTHORITY and the WISDOM of the HOLY SPIRIT, in JESUS' MOST HOLY NAME. AMEN INDEED!

Day 117
4:27

"When any of You ordinary people disobey ME without meaning to, You are still guilty."
◄ Leviticus 4:27 ► [CEV]

"The LORD Will scatter You among other nations, where only a few of You will survive."
◄ Deuteronomy 4:27 ► [GNT]

"The LORD has said that the whole earth will become a wasteland, but that HE Will not completely destroy it."
◄ Jeremiah 4:27 ► [GNT]

"Do not swerve to the right or to the left; turn your foot away from evil."
◄ Proverbs 4:27 ► [ESV]

"And do not give the devil an opportunity." ◄ Ephesians 4:27 ► [NASB]

"For the Scripture says, "Be happy, You childless woman! Shout and cry with joy, You who never felt the pains of childbirth! For the woman who was deserted will have more children than the woman whose husband never left her."
◄ Galatians 4:27 ► [GNT]

Powerful Manifestation Prayer:

I BLESS myself, my family and everyone born on this date with GOD's MOST POWERFUL PURE LOVING LIGHT, HIS MOST POWERFUL PURE SOURCE HEALING ENERGY, and an ABUNDANCE OF HIS AMAZING GREATER GRACE in the POWER, the ANOINTING, the AUTHORITY and the WISDOM of the HOLY SPIRIT, in JESUS' MOST HOLY NAME. AMEN INDEED!

Day 118
4:28

"For this the earth shall mourn and the **Heavens** above be dark, because **I** have spoken, **I** have purposed, and **I Will** not change **MY** mind, nor will **I** turn from it." ◀ Jeremiah 4:28 ▶ [NASB]

"Moses told Aaron what **GOD** had sent him to say; he also told him about the miracles **GOD** had given him the **Power** to perform." ◀ Exodus 4:28 ▶ [CEV]

"They did what **YOU** in **YOUR Power** and **Wisdom** had already decided would happen." ◀ Acts 4:28 ▶ [CEV]

"And **You**, dear brothers and sisters, are children of the **Promise**, just like Isaac." ◀ Galatians 4:28 ▶ [NLT]

"Let the thief no longer steal, but rather let him labor, doing honest work with his own hands, so that he may have something to share with anyone in need." ◀ Ephesians 4:28 ▶ [ESV]

"Stand up for what is right, even if it costs **You** your life; the **LORD GOD Will** be fighting on your side." ◀ Sirach 4:28 ▶ [GNT]

Powerful Manifestation Prayer:

I BLESS myself, my family and everyone born on this date with GOD's MOST POWERFUL PURE LOVING LIGHT, HIS MOST POWERFUL PURE SOURCE HEALING ENERGY, and an ABUNDANCE OF HIS AMAZING GREATER GRACE in the POWER, the ANOINTING, the AUTHORITY and the WISDOM of the HOLY SPIRIT, in JESUS' MOST HOLY NAME. AMEN INDEED!

Day 119
4:29

"But when the grain is ripe, at once he puts in the sickle, because the harvest has come."
◀ Mark 4:29 ▶ [ESV]

"Let no unwholesome word proceed from your mouth, but only such a Word as is GOoD for edification according to the need of the moment, so that it will give Grace to those who hear."
◀ Ephesians 4:29 ▶ [NASB]

"But from there You will seek the LORD your GOD, and You will find HIM if You search for HIM with all your heart and all your Soul."
◀ Deuteronomy 4:29 ▶ [NASB]

"At that time the son who was born in the usual way persecuted the ONE WHO was born because of GOD's SPIRIT; and it is the same now."
◀ Galatians 4:29 ▶ [GNT]

"Come and see the MAN WHO told me everything I have ever done. Could HE be The MESSIAH?"
◀ John 4:29 ▶ [GNT]

"And now, LORD, take notice of the threats they have made, and allow us, YOUR Servants, to speak YOUR Message with all boldness."
◀ Acts 4:29 ▶ [GNT]

Powerful Manifestation Prayer:

I BLESS myself, my family and everyone born on this date with GOD's MOST POWERFUL PURE LOVING LIGHT, HIS MOST POWERFUL PURE SOURCE HEALING ENERGY, and an ABUNDANCE OF HIS AMAZING GREATER GRACE in the POWER, the ANOINTING, the AUTHORITY and the WISDOM of the HOLY SPIRIT, in JESUS' MOST HOLY NAME. AMEN INDEED!

Day 120
4:30

"Solomon's Wisdom was greater than the Wisdom of all the people of the East, greater than all the Wisdom of Egypt." ◀ 1 Kings 4:30 ▶ [CSB]

"When You are in distress and all these things have come upon You, in the latter days You will return to the LORD your GOD and listen to HIS Voice." ◀ Deuteronomy 4:30 ▶ [NASB]

"And do not grieve the HOLY SPIRIT of GOD, by WHOM You were sealed for the day of redemption." ◀ Ephesians 4:30 ▶ [ESV]

"Show your Mighty Power, as we heal people and work Miracles and Wonders in the Name of YOUR HOLY SERVANT JESUS." ◀ Acts 4:30 ▶ [CEV]

"Everyone in town went out to see JESUS." ◀ John 4:30 ▶ [CEV]

"But HE walked through the middle of the crowd and went HIS way." ◀ Luke 4:30 ▶ [GNT]

Powerful Manifestation Prayer:

I BLESS myself, my family and everyone born on this date with GOD's MOST POWERFUL PURE LOVING LIGHT, HIS MOST POWERFUL PURE SOURCE HEALING ENERGY, and an ABUNDANCE OF HIS AMAZING GREATER GRACE in the POWER, the ANOINTING, the AUTHORITY and the WISDOM of the HOLY SPIRIT, in JESUS' MOST HOLY NAME. AMEN INDEED!

May
5

~ I **Pray** for **You** and **You** **Pray** for Me!

"After Job had prayed for his friends, the **LORD** restored his fortunes and gave him twice as much as he had before." ◀ Job 42:10 ▶ [NIV]

"**You** haven't done this before. **A.S.K.** using **MY NAME**, and **You** will receive, and **You** will have abundant joy." ◀ John 16:24 ▶ [NLT]

Powerful Manifestation Prayer:

I BLESS myself, my family and everyone born in this month with GOD's MOST POWERFUL PURE LOVING LIGHT, HIS MOST POWERFUL PURE SOURCE HEALING ENERGY, and an ABUNDANCE OF HIS AMAZING GREATER GRACE in the POWER, the ANOINTING, the AUTHORITY and the WISDOM of the HOLY SPIRIT, in JESUS' MOST HOLY NAME.
AMEN INDEED!

A.S.K.- Additional Scripture Knowledge

Write Additional Scriptures here.

Day 121
5:1

"Guard your steps when You go to the house of GOD. To draw near to listen is better than to offer the sacrifice of fools, for they do not know that they are doing evil." ◄ Ecclesiastes 5:1 ► [ESV]

"Therefore, be imitators of GOD, as dearly Loved children." ◄ Ephesians 5:1 ► [CSB]

"LORD, remember what has happened to us. Look, and see our disgrace!" ◄ Lamentations 5:1 ► [CSB]

"Come now, You rich people, weep and wail over the miseries that are coming on You." ◄ James 5:1 ► [CSB]

"Search Jerusalem for honest people who try to be Faithful. If You can find even one, I'll forgive the whole city." ◄ Jeremiah 5:1 ► [CEV]

"Everyone who believes that JESUS is the CHRIST has been born of GOD, and everyone who Loves the FATHER also Loves the ONE born of HIM." ◄ 1 John 5:1 ► [CSB]

Powerful Manifestation Prayer:

I BLESS myself, my family and everyone born on this date with GOD's MOST POWERFUL PURE LOVING LIGHT, HIS MOST POWERFUL PURE SOURCE HEALING ENERGY, and an ABUNDANCE OF HIS AMAZING GREATER GRACE in the POWER, the ANOINTING, the AUTHORITY and the WISDOM of the HOLY SPIRIT, in JESUS' MOST HOLY NAME. AMEN INDEED!

Day 122
5:2

"And treat older women as You would your own mother. Show the same respect to younger women that You would to your sister." ◀ 1 Timothy 5:2 ▶ [CEV]

"For indeed in this house we groan, longing to be clothed with our dwelling from Heaven." ◀ 2 Corinthians 5:2 ▶ [NASB]

"We have also obtained access through HIM by Faith into this Grace in which we stand, and we rejoice in the HOPE of the Glory of GOD." ◀ Romans 5:2 ▶ [CSB]

"He is able to deal gently with those who are ignorant and are going astray, since he is also clothed with weakness." ◀ Hebrews 5:2 ▶ [CSB]

"You are guilty and unfit to worship ME if You accidentally touch the dead body of any kind of unclean animal." ◀ Leviticus 5:2 ▶ [CEV]

"And walk in Love, as CHRIST Loved us and gave HIMSELF up for us, a fragrant offering and sacrifice to GOD." ◀ Ephesians 5:2 ▶ [ESV]

Powerful Manifestation Prayer:

I BLESS myself, my family and everyone born on this date with GOD's MOST POWERFUL PURE LOVING LIGHT, HIS MOST POWERFUL PURE SOURCE HEALING ENERGY, and an ABUNDANCE OF HIS AMAZING GREATER GRACE in the POWER, the ANOINTING, the AUTHORITY and the WISDOM of the HOLY SPIRIT, in JESUS' MOST HOLY NAME. AMEN INDEED!

Day 123
5:3

"In the morning, LORD, YOU hear my voice; in the morning I plead my case to YOU and watch expectantly."
◄ Psalm 5:3 ► [CSB]

"And not only that, but we also rejoice in our afflictions, because we know that affliction produces endurance."
◄ Romans 5:3 ► [CSB]

"Support widows who are genuinely in need." ◄ 1 Timothy 5:3 ► [CSB]

"Since You are GOD's people, it is not right that any matters of sexual immorality or indecency or greed should even be mentioned among You." ◄ Ephesians 5:3 ► [GNT]

"O LORD, do not YOUR eyes look for Truth? YOU have struck them down, but they felt no anguish; YOU have consumed them, but they refused to take correction. They have made their faces harder than rock; they have refused to repent." ◄ Jeremiah 5:3 ► [ESV]

"Happy are those who know they are Spiritually poor; the Kingdom of Heaven belongs to them!"
◄ Matthew 5:3 ► [GNT]

Powerful Manifestation Prayer:

I BLESS myself, my family and everyone born on this date with GOD's MOST POWERFUL PURE LOVING LIGHT, HIS MOST POWERFUL PURE SOURCE HEALING ENERGY, and an ABUNDANCE OF HIS AMAZING GREATER GRACE in the POWER, the ANOINTING, the AUTHORITY and the WISDOM of the HOLY SPIRIT, in JESUS' MOST HOLY NAME. AMEN INDEED!

Day 124
5:4

"**GOD Blesses** those people who grieve. They will find comfort!" ◀ Matthew 5:4 ▶ [CEV]

"When **You** make a vow to **GOD**, do not be late in paying it; for **HE** takes no delight in fools. Pay what **You** vow!" ◀ Ecclesiastes 5:4 ▶ [NASB]

"And endurance develops strength of character, and character strengthens our confident **HOPE** of **Salvation**." ◀ Romans 5:4 ▶ [NLT]

"He will stand and shepherd them in the strength of the **LORD**, in the **Majestic Name** of the **LORD** his **GOD**. They will live securely, for then **HIS Greatness Will** extend to the ends of the earth." ◀ Micah 5:4 ▶ [CSB]

"But if any widow has children or grandchildren, let them learn to practice godliness toward their own family first and to repay their parents, for this pleases **GOD**." ◀ 1 Timothy 5:4 ▶ [CSB]

"Nor is it fitting for **You** to use language, which is obscene, profane, or vulgar. Rather **You** should give thanks to **GOD**." ◀ Ephesians 5:4 ▶ [GNT]

"And no one takes the honor to himself but receives it when he is called by **GOD**." ◀ Ephesians 5:4 ▶ [NASB]

Powerful Manifestation Prayer:

I BLESS myself, my family and everyone born on this date with GOD's MOST POWERFUL PURE LOVING LIGHT, HIS MOST POWERFUL PURE SOURCE HEALING ENERGY, and an ABUNDANCE OF HIS AMAZING GREATER GRACE in the POWER, the ANOINTING, the AUTHORITY and the WISDOM of the HOLY SPIRIT, in JESUS' MOST HOLY NAME. AMEN INDEED!

Day 125
5:5

"For You are all children of Light, children of the Day. We are not of the night or of the darkness."
◀ 1 Thessalonians 5:5 ▶ [ESV]

"It is better that You should not vow than that You should vow and not pay."
◀ Ecclesiastes 5:5 ▶ [NASB]

"For through the SPIRIT, by Faith, we ourselves eagerly wait for the HOPE of Righteousness."
◀ Galatians 5:5 ▶ [ESV]

"HE WHO has prepared us for this very thing is GOD, WHO has given us the SPIRIT as a guarantee."
◀ 2 Corinthians 5:5 ▶ [ESV]

"For know and recognize this: Every sexually immoral or impure or greedy person, who is an idolater, does not have an inheritance in the Kingdom of CHRIST and of GOD." ◀ Ephesians 5:5 ▶ [CSB]

"The widow who is truly in need and left all alone has put her HOPE in GOD and continues night and day in her petitions and Prayers." ◀ 1 Timothy 5:5 ▶ [CSB]

Powerful Manifestation Prayer:

I BLESS myself, my family and everyone born on this date with GOD's MOST POWERFUL PURE LOVING LIGHT, HIS MOST POWERFUL PURE SOURCE HEALING ENERGY, and an ABUNDANCE OF HIS AMAZING GREATER GRACE in the POWER, the ANOINTING, the AUTHORITY and the WISDOM of the HOLY SPIRIT, in JESUS' MOST HOLY NAME. AMEN INDEED!

Day 126
5:6

"Therefore, humble yourselves under the **Mighty Hand** of **GOD**, that **HE** may exalt **You** at the proper time."
◀ 1 Peter 5:6 ▶ [NASB]

"Let no one deceive **You** with empty words, for because of these things the wrath of **GOD** comes upon the sons of disobedience."
◀ Ephesians 5:6 ▶ [NASB]

"**Blessed** are those who hunger and thirst for **Righteousness**, for they shall be satisfied."
◀ Matthew 5:6 ▶ [NASB]

"When we were utterly helpless, **CHRIST** came at just the right time and died for us sinners."
◀ Romans 5:6 ▶ [NLT]

"**I AM** the **LORD** your **GOD**, **WHO** brought **You** out of the land of Egypt, out of the house of slavery."
◀ Deuteronomy 5:6 ▶ [NASB]

"Whatever **You ASK** will be given to **You**. Whatever **You** want, even to half the kingdom, will be done!"
◀ Esther 5:6 ▶ [CSB]

Powerful Manifestation Prayer:

I BLESS myself, my family and everyone born on this date with GOD's MOST POWERFUL PURE LOVING LIGHT, HIS MOST POWERFUL PURE SOURCE HEALING ENERGY, and an ABUNDANCE OF HIS AMAZING GREATER GRACE in the POWER, the ANOINTING, the AUTHORITY and the WISDOM of the HOLY SPIRIT, in JESUS' MOST HOLY NAME. AMEN INDEED!

Day 127
5:7

"A few of Jacob's descendants survived and are scattered among the nations. But the **LORD Will** let them cover the earth like dew and rain that refreshes the soil." ◀ Micah 5:7 ▶ [CEV]

"**You** were running well; who hindered **You** from obeying the **Truth**?" ◀ Galatians 5:7 ▶ [NASB]

"For when dreams increase and words grow many, there is vanity; but **GOD** is the **ONE You** must fear." ◀ Ecclesiastes 5:7 ▶ [ESV]

"**Blessed** are the merciful, for they shall receive mercy." ◀ Matthew 5:7 ▶ [NASB]

"Because of **YOUR Great Mercy**, I come to **YOUR House**, **LORD**, and I am filled with wonder as I bow down to worship at **YOUR Holy Temple**." ◀ Psalm 5:7 ▶ [CEV]

"For we walk by **Faith**, not by sight." ◀ 2 Corinthians 5:7 ▶ [NASB]

Powerful Manifestation Prayer:

I BLESS myself, my family and everyone born on this date with GOD's MOST POWERFUL PURE LOVING LIGHT, HIS MOST POWERFUL PURE SOURCE HEALING ENERGY, and an ABUNDANCE OF HIS AMAZING GREATER GRACE in the POWER, the ANOINTING, the AUTHORITY and the WISDOM of the HOLY SPIRIT, in JESUS' MOST HOLY NAME. AMEN INDEED!

Day 128
5:8

"Be on your guard and stay awake. Your enemy, the devil, is like a roaring lion, sneaking around to find someone to attack."
◄ 1 Peter 5:8 ► [CEV]

"However, if I were **You**, I would appeal to **GOD** and would present my case to **HIM**."
◄ Job 5:8 ► [CSB]

"Lead me, O **LORD**, in **YOUR Righteousness** because of my enemies; make **YOUR** way straight before me."
◄ Psalm 5:8 ► [ESV]

"But **GOD** shows **HIS Love** for us in that while we were still sinners, **CHRIST** died for us."
◄ Romans 5:8 ► [ESV]

"In fact, we are confident, and we would prefer to be away from the body and at home with the **LORD**."
◄ 2 Corinthians 5:8 ► [CSB]

"**Blessed** are the pure in heart, for they shall see **GOD**." ◄ Matthew 5:8 ► [NASB]

Powerful Manifestation Prayer:

I BLESS myself, my family and everyone born on this date with GOD's MOST POWERFUL PURE LOVING LIGHT, HIS MOST POWERFUL PURE SOURCE HEALING ENERGY, and an ABUNDANCE OF HIS AMAZING GREATER GRACE in the POWER, the ANOINTING, the AUTHORITY and the WISDOM of the HOLY SPIRIT, in JESUS' MOST HOLY NAME. AMEN INDEED!

Day 129
5:9

"But the **LORD All-Powerful** has made this **Promise** to me: Those large and beautiful homes will be left empty, with no one to take care of them." ◀ Isaiah 5:9 ▶ [CEV]

"But **You** must resist the devil and stay strong in your **Faith**. **You** know that all over the world the **LORD's** followers are suffering just as **You** are." ◀ 1 Peter 5:9 ▶ [CEV]

"He brings destruction on the mighty and their strongholds." ◀ Amos 5:9 ▶ [GNT]

"Much more then, having now been justified by **HIS Blood,** we shall be saved from the wrath of **GOD** through **HIM**." ◀ Romans 5:9 ▶ [NASB]

"But whether we are at **Home** with the **LORD** or away from **HIM**, we still try our best to please **HIM**." ◀ 2 Corinthians 5:9 ▶ [CEV]

"**Blessed** are the peacemakers, for they shall be called **Sons** of **GOD**." ◀ Matthew 5:9 ▶ [NASB]

Powerful Manifestation Prayer:

I BLESS myself, my family and everyone born on this date with GOD's MOST POWERFUL PURE LOVING LIGHT, HIS MOST POWERFUL PURE SOURCE HEALING ENERGY, and an ABUNDANCE OF HIS AMAZING GREATER GRACE in the POWER, the ANOINTING, the AUTHORITY and the WISDOM of the HOLY SPIRIT, in JESUS' MOST HOLY NAME. AMEN INDEED!

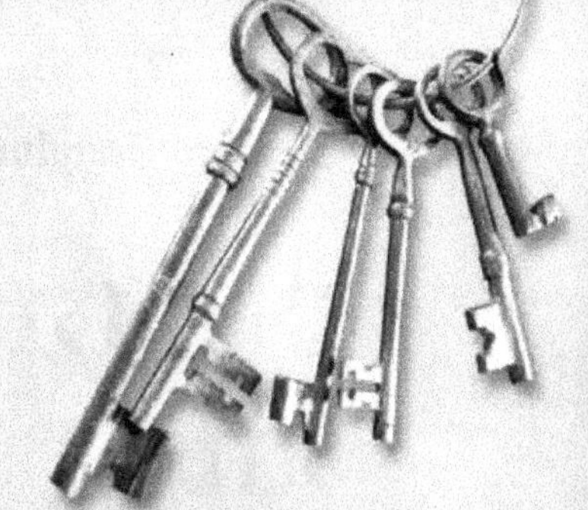

Day 130
5:10

"The GOD of all Grace, WHO called You to HIS Eternal Glory in CHRIST, Will HIMSELF restore, establish, strengthen, and support You after You have suffered a little while."
◀ 1 Peter 5:10 ▶ [CSB]

"For we must all appear before the judgment seat of CHRIST, so that each one may receive what is due for what he has done in the body, whether GOoD or evil." ◀ 2 Corinthians 5:10 ▶ [ESV]

"But I still feel confident about You. Our life in union with the LORD makes me confident that You will not take a different view and that whoever is upsetting You will be punished by GOD."
◀ Galatians 5:10 ▶ [GNT]

"Blessed are those who have been persecuted for the sake of Righteousness, for theirs is the Kingdom of Heaven." ◀ Matthew 5:10 ▶ [NASB]

"His partners James and John, the sons of Zebedee, were surprised too. JESUS told Simon, "Don't be afraid! From now on You will bring in people instead of fish!" ◀ Luke 5:10 ▶ [CEV]

"We were GOD's enemies, but HE made us HIS Friends through the death of HIS SON. Now that we are GOD's Friends, how much more will we be saved by CHRIST's Life!"
◀ Romans 5:10 ▶ [NLT]

Powerful Manifestation Prayer:

I BLESS myself, my family and everyone born on this date with GOD's MOST POWERFUL PURE LOVING LIGHT, HIS MOST POWERFUL PURE SOURCE HEALING ENERGY, and an ABUNDANCE OF HIS AMAZING GREATER GRACE in the POWER, the ANOINTING, the AUTHORITY and the WISDOM of the HOLY SPIRIT, in JESUS' MOST HOLY NAME. AMEN INDEED!

Day 131
5:11

"**Blessed** are **You** when people insult **You** and persecute **You**, and falsely say all kinds of evil against **You** because of **ME**."
◄ Matthew 5:11 ► [NASB]

"Therefore encourage one another and build up one another, just as **You** also are doing."
◄ 1 Thessalonians 5:11 ► [NASB]

"So that **HE** sets on high those who are lowly, and those who mourn are lifted to safety."
◄ Job 5:11 ► [NASB]

"But let all who take refuge in **YOU** rejoice; let them ever sing for joy, and spread **YOUR** protection over them, that those who **Love YOUR Name** may exult in **YOU**."
◄ Psalm 5:11 ► [ESV]

"**You** shall not take the **Name** of the **LORD** your **GOD** in vain, for the **LORD Will** not leave him unpunished who takes **HIS Name** in vain."
◄ Deuteronomy 5:11 ► [NASB]

"To **HIM** be the **Glory** and the **Dominion** forever and ever. Amen."
◄ 1 Peter 5:11 ► [NKJV]

Powerful Manifestation Prayer:

I BLESS myself, my family and everyone born on this date with GOD's MOST POWERFUL PURE LOVING LIGHT, HIS MOST POWERFUL PURE SOURCE HEALING ENERGY, and an ABUNDANCE OF HIS AMAZING GREATER GRACE in the POWER, the ANOINTING, the AUTHORITY and the WISDOM of the HOLY SPIRIT, in JESUS' MOST HOLY NAME. AMEN INDEED!

Day 132
5:12

"Observe the **Sabbath Day** to keep it **Holy**, as the **LORD** your **GOD** has commanded **You**."
◄ Deuteronomy 5:12 ► [NASB]

"He who has the **SON** has the life; he who does not have the **SON** of **GOD** does not have the life."
◄ 1 John 5:12 ► [NASB]

"For it is **YOU WHO Blesses** the **Righteous** man, O **LORD**, **YOU** surround him with **Favor** as with a shield."
◄ Psalm 5:12 ► [NASB]

"**I Will** destroy the magic charms **You** use and leave **You** without any fortunetellers."
◄ Micah 5:12 ► [GNT]

"For it is shameful even to speak of the things that they do in secret."
◄ Ephesians 5:12 ► [ESV]

"Saying with a loud voice, "Worthy is the **LAMB** that was slain to receive **Power** and **Riches** and **Wisdom** and **Might** and **Honor** and **Glory** and **Blessing**."
◄ Revelations 5:12 ► [NASB]

Powerful Manifestation Prayer:

I BLESS myself, my family and everyone born on this date with GOD's MOST POWERFUL PURE LOVING LIGHT, HIS MOST POWERFUL PURE SOURCE HEALING ENERGY, and an ABUNDANCE OF HIS AMAZING GREATER GRACE in the POWER, the ANOINTING, the AUTHORITY and the WISDOM of the HOLY SPIRIT, in JESUS' MOST HOLY NAME. AMEN INDEED!

Day 133
5:13

"GOD judges outsiders. Remove the evil person from among You."
◀ 1 Corinthians 5:13 ▶ [CSB]

"I Will cut off your carved images and your sacred pillars from among You so that You will no longer bow down to the work of your hands."
◀ Micah 5:13 ▶ [NASB]

"But all things become visible when they are exposed by the Light, for everything that becomes visible is Light."
◀ Ephesians 5:13 ▶ [NASB]

"Therefore, those who have insight will keep silent at such a time, for the days are evil."
◀ Amos 5:13 ▶ [CSB]

"For You were called to be Free, brothers and sisters; only don't use this Freedom as an opportunity for the flesh but serve one another through Love."
◀ Galatians 5:13 ▶ [CSB]

"These things I have written to You who believe in the Name of the SON of GOD, so that You may know that You have Eternal Life."
◀ 1 John 5:13 ▶ [NASB]

Powerful Manifestation Prayer:

I BLESS myself, my family and everyone born on this date with GOD's MOST POWERFUL PURE LOVING LIGHT, HIS MOST POWERFUL PURE SOURCE HEALING ENERGY, and an ABUNDANCE OF HIS AMAZING GREATER GRACE in the POWER, the ANOINTING, the AUTHORITY and the WISDOM of the HOLY SPIRIT, in JESUS' MOST HOLY NAME. AMEN INDEED!

Day 134
5:14

"If You really want to live, You must stop doing wrong and start doing right. I, the LORD GOD All-Powerful, Will then be on your side, just as You claim I AM." ◀ Amos 5:14 ▶ [CEV]

"For the whole Law is fulfilled in one statement: Love **your neighbor as yourself**."
◀ Galatians 5:14 ▶ [CSB]

"You are the Light of the world. A city set on a hill cannot be hidden."
◀ Matthew 5:14 ▶ [NASB]

"For this reason it says, "Awake, sleeper, and arise from the dead, and CHRIST Will shine on You."
◀ Ephesians 5:14 ▶ [NASB]

"Is anyone among You sick? Then he must call for the elders of the church and they are to Pray over him, Anointing him with oil in the Name of the LORD." ◀ James 5:14 ▶ [NASB]

"Greet one another with a kiss of Love. Peace be to You all who are in CHRIST."
◀ 1 Peter 5:14 ▶ [NASB]

Powerful Manifestation Prayer:

I BLESS myself, my family and everyone born on this date with GOD's MOST POWERFUL PURE LOVING LIGHT, HIS MOST POWERFUL PURE SOURCE HEALING ENERGY, and an ABUNDANCE OF HIS AMAZING GREATER GRACE in the POWER, the ANOINTING, the AUTHORITY and the WISDOM of the HOLY SPIRIT, in JESUS' MOST HOLY NAME. AMEN INDEED!

Day 135
5:15

"See that no one repays another with evil for evil, but always seek after that which is GOoD for one another and for all people."
◀ 1 Thessalonians 5:15 ▶ [NASB]

"And the Prayer of Faith will save the one who is sick, and the LORD Will raise him up. And if he has committed sins, he will be forgiven."
◀ James 5:15 ▶ [ESV]

"But if You bite and devour one another, take care that You are not consumed by one another."
◀ Galatians 5:15 ▶ [NASB]

"And in anger and wrath I Will execute vengeance on the nations that did not obey."
◀ Micah 5:15 ▶ [ESV]

"For some have already turned aside to follow Satan."
◀ 1 Timothy 5:15 ▶ [NASB]

"Hate evil and Love what is GOoD; turn your courts into true halls of justice. Perhaps even yet the LORD GOD of Heaven's Armies Will have mercy on the remnant of HIS people."
◀ Amos 5:15 ▶ [NLT]

Powerful Manifestation Prayer:

I BLESS myself, my family and everyone born on this date with GOD's MOST POWERFUL PURE LOVING LIGHT, HIS MOST POWERFUL PURE SOURCE HEALING ENERGY, and an ABUNDANCE OF HIS AMAZING GREATER GRACE in the POWER, the ANOINTING, the AUTHORITY and the WISDOM of the HOLY SPIRIT, in JESUS' MOST HOLY NAME. AMEN INDEED!

Day 136
5:16

"Respect your father and your mother, as I, the LORD your GOD, command You, so that all may go well with You and so that You may live a long time in the land that I AM giving You."
◀ Deuteronomy 5:16 ▶ [GNT]

"If any believing woman has widows in her family, let her help them. Let the church not be burdened, so that it can help widows in genuine need."
◀ 1 Timothy 5:16 ▶ [CSB]

"In the same way, let your Light shine before others, so that they may see your GOoD works and give Glory to your FATHER in Heaven."
◀ Matthew 5:16 ▶ [CSB]

"Therefore, confess your sins to one another, and Pray for one another so that You may be healed. The effective Prayer of a righteous man can accomplish much."
◀ James 5:16 ▶ [NASB]

"But I say, walk by the SPIRIT, and You will not carry out the desire of the flesh."
◀ Galatians 5:16 ▶ [NASB]

"Rejoice always!"
◀ 1 Thessalonians 5:16 ▶ [NASB]

"Make GOoD use of every opportunity You have, because these are evil days."
◀ Ephesians 5:16 ▶ [GNT]

Powerful Manifestation Prayer:

I BLESS myself, my family and everyone born on this date with GOD's MOST POWERFUL PURE LOVING LIGHT, HIS MOST POWERFUL PURE SOURCE HEALING ENERGY, and an ABUNDANCE OF HIS AMAZING GREATER GRACE in the POWER, the ANOINTING, the AUTHORITY and the WISDOM of the HOLY SPIRIT, in JESUS' MOST HOLY NAME. AMEN INDEED!

Day 137
5:17

"You shall not murder." ◀ Deuteronomy 5:17 ▶ [NASB]

"For the desires of the flesh are against the SPIRIT, and the SPIRIT are against the flesh, for these are opposed to each other, to keep You from doing the things You want to do."
◀ Galatians 5:17 ▶ [ESV]

"The elders who are GOoD leaders are to be considered worthy of double honor, especially those who work hard at preaching and teaching." ◀ 1 Timothy 5:17 ▶ [CSB]

"Blessed is the one whom GOD corrects; so do not despise the discipline of the ALMIGHTY."
◀ Job 5:17 ▶ [NIV]

"Do not think that I came to abolish the Law or the Prophets; I did not come to abolish but to fulfill."
◀ Matthew 5:17 ▶ [NASB]

"And never stop Praying." ◀ 1 Thessalonians 5:17 ▶ [CEV]

Powerful Manifestation Prayer:

I BLESS myself, my family and everyone born on this date with GOD's MOST POWERFUL PURE LOVING LIGHT, HIS MOST POWERFUL PURE SOURCE HEALING ENERGY, and an ABUNDANCE OF HIS AMAZING GREATER GRACE in the POWER, the ANOINTING, the AUTHORITY and the WISDOM of the HOLY SPIRIT, in JESUS' MOST HOLY NAME. AMEN INDEED!

Day 138
5:18

"For the **Scripture** says, "Do not muzzle an ox when **You** are using it to thresh grain" and "Workers should be given their pay."
◄ 1 Timothy 5:18 ► [GNT]

"For truly **I** tell **You**, until **Heaven** and earth pass away, not the smallest letter or one stroke of a letter will pass away from the **Law** until all things are accomplished."
◄ Matthew 5:18 ► [CSB]

"Do not get drunk with wine, which will only ruin **You**; instead, be filled with the **SPIRIT**."
◄ Ephesians 5:18 ► [GNT]

"**You** shall not commit adultery."
◄ Deuteronomy 5:18 ► [NASB]

"Then the priest will make atonement on his behalf for the error he has committed unintentionally, and he will be forgiven."
◄ Leviticus 5:18 ► [CSB]

"In everything give thanks; for this is **GOD's Will** for **You** in **CHRIST JESUS**."
◄ 1 Thessalonians 5:18 ► [NASB]

Powerful Manifestation Prayer:

I BLESS myself, my family and everyone born on this date with GOD's MOST POWERFUL PURE LOVING LIGHT, HIS MOST POWERFUL PURE SOURCE HEALING ENERGY, and an ABUNDANCE OF HIS AMAZING GREATER GRACE in the POWER, the ANOINTING, the AUTHORITY and the WISDOM of the HOLY SPIRIT, in JESUS' MOST HOLY NAME. AMEN INDEED!

Day 139
5:19

"People's desires make them give in to immoral ways, filthy thoughts, and shameful deeds."
◀ Galatians 5:19 ▶ [CEV]

"Do not receive an accusation against an elder except on the basis of two or three witnesses."
◀ 1 Timothy 5:19 ▶ [NASB]

"**You** shall not steal." ◀ Deuteronomy 5:19 ▶ [NASB]

"So, if **You** ignore the least commandment and teach others to do the same, **You** will be called the least in the **Kingdom** of **Heaven**. But anyone who obeys **GOD's Laws** and teaches them will be called great in the **Kingdom** of **Heaven**." ◀ Matthew 5:19 ▶ [NLT]

"Remember, O my **GOD**, all that I have done for these people, and **Bless** me for it."
◀ Nehemiah 5:19 ▶ [NLT]

"Go in peace…" ◀ 2 Kings 5:19 ▶ [NASB]

Powerful Manifestation Prayer:

I BLESS myself, my family and everyone born on this date with GOD's MOST POWERFUL PURE LOVING LIGHT, HIS MOST POWERFUL PURE SOURCE HEALING ENERGY, and an ABUNDANCE OF HIS AMAZING GREATER GRACE in the POWER, the ANOINTING, the AUTHORITY and the WISDOM of the HOLY SPIRIT, in JESUS' MOST HOLY NAME. AMEN INDEED!

Day 140
5:20

"We know that JESUS CHRIST the SON of GOD has come and has shown us the True GOD. And because of JESUS, we now belong to the True GOD WHO gives eternal life."
◄ 1 John 5:20 ► [CEV]

"For I tell You, unless your Righteousness exceeds that of the scribes and Pharisees, You will never enter the Kingdom of Heaven."
◄ Matthew 5:20 ► [ESV]

"Therefore, we are ambassadors for CHRIST as though GOD were making an appeal through us; we beg You on behalf of CHRIST, be reconciled to GOD."
◄ 2 Corinthians 5:20 ► [NASB]

"If You turn sinners from the wrong way, You will save them from death, and many of their sins will be forgiven."
◄ James 5:20 ► [CEV]

"When JESUS saw their Faith, HE said, "Friends, your sins are forgiven."
◄ Luke 5:20 ► [NIV]

"Giving thanks always and for everything to GOD the FATHER in the Name of our LORD JESUS CHRIST."
◄ Ephesians 5:20 ► [ESV]

Powerful Manifestation Prayer:

I BLESS myself, my family and everyone born on this date with GOD's MOST POWERFUL PURE LOVING LIGHT, HIS MOST POWERFUL PURE SOURCE HEALING ENERGY, and an ABUNDANCE OF HIS AMAZING GREATER GRACE in the POWER, the ANOINTING, the AUTHORITY and the WISDOM of the HOLY SPIRIT, in JESUS' MOST HOLY NAME. AMEN INDEED!

Day 141
5:21

"**You** shall not covet your neighbor's wife, and **You** shall not desire your neighbor's house, his field or his male servant or his female servant, his ox or his donkey or anything that belongs to your neighbor." ◄ Deuteronomy 5:21 ► [NASB]

"Envy, drunkenness, carousing, and anything similar. I am warning **You** about these things--as I warned **You** before--that those who practice such things will not inherit the **Kingdom** of **GOD**." ◄ Galatians 5:21 ► [CSB]

"Dear children, keep away from anything that might take **GOD's** place in your hearts." ◄ 1 John 5:21 ► [NLT]

"For the ways of a man are before the eyes of the **LORD**, and **HE** watches all his paths." ◄ Proverbs 5:21 ► [NASB]

"Sin ruled by means of death. But **GOD's Gift** of **Grace** now rules, and **GOD** has accepted us because of **JESUS CHRIST** our **LORD**. This means that we will have **Eternal Life**." ◄ Romans 5:21 ► [CEV]

"**CHRIST** was without sin, but for our sake **GOD** made him share our sin in order that in union with **HIM** we might share the **Righteousness** of **GOD**." ◄ 2 Corinthians 5:21 ► [GNT]

Powerful Manifestation Prayer:

I BLESS myself, my family and everyone born on this date with GOD's MOST POWERFUL PURE LOVING LIGHT, HIS MOST POWERFUL PURE SOURCE HEALING ENERGY, and an ABUNDANCE OF HIS AMAZING GREATER GRACE in the POWER, the ANOINTING, the AUTHORITY and the WISDOM of the HOLY SPIRIT, in JESUS' MOST HOLY NAME. AMEN INDEED!

Day 142
5:22

"I AM the LORD; why don't You fear me? Why don't You tremble before ME? I placed the sand as the boundary of the sea, a permanent boundary that it cannot cross. The sea may toss, but it cannot go beyond it; the waves may roar, but they cannot break through." ◀ Jeremiah 5:22 ▶ [CEV]

"Stay away from every kind of evil." ◀ 1 Thessalonians 5:22 ▶ [CSB]

"But the Fruit of the SPIRIT is Love, Joy, Peace, Patience, Kindness, GOoDness, Faithfulness." ◀ Galatians 5:22 ▶ [NASB]

"Wives, submit to your own husbands, as to the LORD." ◀ Ephesians 5:22 ▶ [ESV]

"Nor does the FATHER HIMSELF judge anyone. HE has given HIS SON the full right to judge." ◀ John 5:22 ▶ [GNT]

"These WORDS the LORD spoke to all your assembly at the mountain from the midst of the fire, of the cloud and of the thick gloom, with a Great Voice, and HE added no more. HE wrote them on two tablets of stone and gave them to me." ◀ Deuteronomy 5:22 ▶ [NASB]

"Do not lay hands upon anyone too hastily and thereby share responsibility for the sins of others; keep yourself Free from sin." ◀ 1 Timothy 5:22 ▶ [NASB]

Powerful Manifestation Prayer:

I BLESS myself, my family and everyone born on this date with GOD's MOST POWERFUL PURE LOVING LIGHT, HIS MOST POWERFUL PURE SOURCE HEALING ENERGY, and an ABUNDANCE OF HIS AMAZING GREATER GRACE in the POWER, the ANOINTING, the AUTHORITY and the WISDOM of the HOLY SPIRIT, in JESUS' MOST HOLY NAME. AMEN INDEED!

Day 143
5:23

"But You have not honored the GOD WHO gives You the Breath of Life and controls your destiny!"
◄ Daniel 5:23 ► [NLT]

"Now may the GOD of peace HIMSELF sanctify You completely and may your whole Spirit and Soul and body be kept blameless at the coming of our LORD JESUS CHRIST."
◄ 1 Thessalonians 5:23 ► [ESV]

"A husband is the head of his wife, as CHRIST is the Head and the Savior of the Church, which is HIS OWN Body."
◄ Ephesians 5:23 ► [CEV]

"He pleaded earnestly with HIM, 'My little daughter is dying. Please come and put YOUR Hands on her so that she will be healed and live."
◄ Mark 5:23 ► [NIV]

"He dies for lack of discipline, and because of his great folly he is led astray."
◄ Proverbs 5:23 ► [ESV]

"So that all will Honor the SON even as they Honor the FATHER. He who does not Honor the SON does not Honor the FATHER WHO sent HIM."
◄ John 5:23 ► [NASB]

Powerful Manifestation Prayer:

I BLESS myself, my family and everyone born on this date with GOD's MOST POWERFUL PURE LOVING LIGHT, HIS MOST POWERFUL PURE SOURCE HEALING ENERGY, and an ABUNDANCE OF HIS AMAZING GREATER GRACE in the POWER, the ANOINTING, the AUTHORITY and the WISDOM of the HOLY SPIRIT, in JESUS' MOST HOLY NAME. AMEN INDEED!

Day 144
5:24

"Behold, the LORD our GOD has shown us HIS Glory and HIS Greatness, and we have heard HIS Voice from the midst of the fire; we have seen today that GOD Speaks with man, yet he lives."
◄ Deuteronomy 5:24 ► [NASB]

"You will know that your home is safe. When You survey your possessions, nothing will be missing."
◄ Job 5:24 ► [NLT]

"Truly I tell You, anyone who hears MY WORD and believes HIM WHO sent ME has Eternal Life and will not come under judgment but has passed from death to life." ◄ John 5:24 ► [CSB]

"The sins of some men are quite evident, going before them to judgment; for others, their sins follow after."
◄ 1 Timothy 5:24 ► [NASB]

"But let justice flow like water, and Righteousness, like an unfailing stream." ◄ Amos 5:24 ► [CSB]

"GOD Will make this happen, for HE WHO calls You is Faithful."
◄ 1 Thessalonians 5:24 ► [NLT]

Powerful Manifestation Prayer:

I BLESS myself, my family and everyone born on this date with GOD's MOST POWERFUL PURE LOVING LIGHT, HIS MOST POWERFUL PURE SOURCE HEALING ENERGY, and an ABUNDANCE OF HIS AMAZING GREATER GRACE in the POWER, the ANOINTING, the AUTHORITY and the WISDOM of the HOLY SPIRIT, in JESUS' MOST HOLY NAME. AMEN INDEED!

Day 145
5:25

"Dear brothers and sisters, **Pray** for us." ◀ 1 Thessalonians 5:25 ▶ [NLT]

"Truly I tell **You**, an hour is coming, and is now here, when the dead will hear the **Voice** of the **SON** of **GOD**, and those who hear will live." ◀ John 5:25 ▶ [CSB]

"**You** will also know that your offspring will be many and your descendants like the grass of the earth." ◀ Job 5:25 ▶ [CSB]

"If we live by the **SPIRIT**, let us also walk by the **SPIRIT**." ◀ Galatians 5:25 ▶ [NASB]

"In the same way, the **GOoD** deeds of some people are obvious. And the **GOoD** deeds done in secret will someday come to **Light**." ◀ 1 Timothy 5:25 ▶ [NLT]

"Husbands, **Love** your wives, just as **CHRIST** also **Loved** the **Church** and gave **HIMSELF** up for her." ◀ Ephesians 5:25 ▶ [NASB]

Powerful Manifestation Prayer:

I BLESS myself, my family and everyone born on this date with GOD's MOST POWERFUL PURE LOVING LIGHT, HIS MOST POWERFUL PURE SOURCE HEALING ENERGY, and an ABUNDANCE OF HIS AMAZING GREATER GRACE in the POWER, the ANOINTING, the AUTHORITY and the WISDOM of the HOLY SPIRIT, in JESUS' MOST HOLY NAME. AMEN INDEED!

Day 146
5:26

"Greet all the **Believers** with the kiss of **Peace**." ◀ 1 Thessalonians 5:26 ▶ [GNT]

"Let us not become boastful, challenging one another, envying one another."
◀ Galatians 5:26 ▶ [NASB]

"**HE** made the **Church Holy** by the **Power** of **HIS WORD**, and **HE** made it pure by washing it with water." ◀ Ephesians 5:26 ▶ [CEV]

"And amazement seized them all, and they **Glorified GOD** and were filled with awe, saying, "We have seen extraordinary things today." ◀ Luke 5:26 ▶ [ESV]

"Just as the **FATHER** is **HIMSELF** the **Source** of **Life**, in the same way **HE** has made **HIS SON** to be the **Source** of **Life**." ◀ John 5:26 ▶ [GNT]

"**You** will live a very long life, and your body will be strong until the day **You** die."
◀ Job 5:26 ▶ [CEV]

Powerful Manifestation Prayer:

I BLESS myself, my family and everyone born on this date with GOD's MOST POWERFUL PURE LOVING LIGHT, HIS MOST POWERFUL PURE SOURCE HEALING ENERGY, and an ABUNDANCE OF HIS AMAZING GREATER GRACE in the POWER, the ANOINTING, the AUTHORITY and the WISDOM of the HOLY SPIRIT, in JESUS' MOST HOLY NAME. AMEN INDEED!

Day 147
5:27

"I urge **You** by the authority of the **LORD** to read this letter to all the **Believers**."
◀ 1 Thessalonians 5:27 ▶ [GNT]

"None of them grows weary or stumbles; no one slumbers or sleeps. No belt is loose and no sandal strap broken."
◀ Isaiah 5:27 ▶ [CSB]

"Go near and hear all that the **LORD** our **GOD** says; then speak to us all that the **LORD** our **GOD** speaks to **You**, and we will hear and do it."
◀ Deuteronomy 5:27 ▶ [NASB]

"**You** have heard that it was said, '**You** shall not commit adultery'."
◀ Matthew 5:27 ▶ [ESV]

"**CHRIST** did this, so **HE** would have a **Glorious** and **Holy Church**, without faults or spots or wrinkles or any other flaws."
◀ Ephesians 5:27 ▶ [CEV]

"Behold, this we have searched out; it is **True**. Hear, and know it for your **GOoD**."
◀ Job 5:27 ▶ [ESV]

Powerful Manifestation Prayer:

I BLESS myself, my family and everyone born on this date with GOD's MOST POWERFUL PURE LOVING LIGHT, HIS MOST POWERFUL PURE SOURCE HEALING ENERGY, and an ABUNDANCE OF HIS AMAZING GREATER GRACE in the POWER, the ANOINTING, the AUTHORITY and the WISDOM of the HOLY SPIRIT, in JESUS' MOST HOLY NAME. AMEN INDEED!

Day 148
5:28

"For she thought to herself, "If I can just touch **HIS** robe, I will be healed."

◄ Mark 5:28 ► [NLT]

"The **LORD** heard your words when **You** spoke to me. **HE** said to me, '**I** have heard the words that these people have spoken to **You**. Everything they have said is right."

◄ Deuteronomy 5:28 ► [CSB]

"Their arrows are sharpened, and all their bows strung. Their horses' hooves are like flint; their chariot wheels are like a whirlwind."

◄ Isaiah 5:28 ► [CSB]

"But **I** say to **You** that everyone who looks at a woman with lust for her has already committed adultery with her in his heart."

◄ Matthew 5:28 ► [NASB]

"In the same way, husbands are to **Love** their wives as their own bodies. He who **Loves** his wife **Loves** himself."

◄ Ephesians 5:28 ► [CSB]

"The **Grace** of our **LORD JESUS CHRIST** be with **You**."

◄ 1 Thessalonians 5:28 ► [NASB]

Powerful Manifestation Prayer:

I BLESS myself, my family and everyone born on this date with GOD's MOST POWERFUL PURE LOVING LIGHT, HIS MOST POWERFUL PURE SOURCE HEALING ENERGY, and an ABUNDANCE OF HIS AMAZING GREATER GRACE in the POWER, the ANOINTING, the AUTHORITY and the WISDOM of the HOLY SPIRIT, in JESUS' MOST HOLY NAME. AMEN INDEED!

Day 149
5:29

"Her wise attendants find an answer for her; in fact, she tells the same words to herself."
◀ Judges 5:29 ▶ [ISV]

"We must obey **GOD** rather than people!" ◀ Acts 5:29 ▶ [CSB]

"If your right eye causes **You** to sin, tear it out and throw it away. For it is better that **You** lose one of your members than that your whole body be thrown into hell." ◀ Matthew 5:29 ▶ [ESV]

"And come out--those who have done **GOoD** things, to the resurrection of life, but those who have done wicked things, to the resurrection of condemnation." ◀ John 5:29 ▶ [CSB]

"For no one ever hated his own flesh, but nourishes and cherishes it, just as **CHRIST** does the **Church**." ◀Ephesians 5:29 ▶ [ESV]

"If only they had such a heart to fear **ME** and keep all **MY Commands** always, so that they and their children would prosper forever." ◀ Deuteronomy 5:29 ▶ [CSB]

Powerful Manifestation Prayer:

I BLESS myself, my family and everyone born on this date with GOD's MOST POWERFUL PURE LOVING LIGHT, HIS MOST POWERFUL PURE SOURCE HEALING ENERGY, and an ABUNDANCE OF HIS AMAZING GREATER GRACE in the POWER, the ANOINTING, the AUTHORITY and the WISDOM of the HOLY SPIRIT, in JESUS' MOST HOLY NAME. AMEN INDEED!

Day 150
5:30

"Why do You eat and drink with such scum?" ◄ Luke 5:30 ► [NLT]

"And if your right hand causes You to sin, cut it off and throw it away. For it is better that You lose one of the parts of your body than for your whole body to go into hell." ◄ Matthew 5:30 ► [CSB]

"I can do nothing on MY Own initiative. As I hear, I judge; and MY judgment is just, because I do not seek MY Own Will, but the Will of HIM WHO sent ME." ◄ John 5:30 ► [NASB]

"At that moment JESUS felt Power go out from HIM. HE turned to the crowd and asked, 'Who touched MY clothes'?" ◄ Mark 5:30 ► [CEV]

"The GOD of our ancestors raised JESUS from the dead after You killed HIM by nailing HIM to a Cross." ◄ Acts 5:30 ► [GNT]

"For we are members of HIS Body, of HIS flesh and of HIS bones." ◄ Ephesians 5:30 ► [NASB]

Powerful Manifestation Prayer:

I BLESS myself, my family and everyone born on this date with GOD's MOST POWERFUL PURE LOVING LIGHT, HIS MOST POWERFUL PURE SOURCE HEALING ENERGY, and an ABUNDANCE OF HIS AMAZING GREATER GRACE in the POWER, the ANOINTING, the AUTHORITY and the WISDOM of the HOLY SPIRIT, in JESUS' MOST HOLY NAME. AMEN INDEED!

Day 151
5:31

"It was also said, 'Whoever divorces his wife must give her a written notice of divorce'."
◀ Matthew 5:31 ▶ [CSB]

"Moreover, the man will be Free from guilt, but that woman shall bear her guilt."
◀ Numbers 5:31 ▶ [NASB]

"But as for You, stand here by ME that I may speak to You all the commandments and the statutes and the judgments which You shall teach them, that they may observe them in the land which I give them to possess."
◀ Deuteronomy 5:31 ▶ [NASB]

"If I testify about MYSELF, MY testimony is not true."
◀ John 5:31 ▶ [CSB]

"JESUS replied to them, 'It is not those who are healthy who need a doctor, but those who are sick'."
◀ Luke 5:31 ▶ [CSB]

"GOD exalted HIM at HIS Right Hand as Leader and Savior, to give repentance to Israel and forgiveness of sins."
◀ Acts 5:31 ▶ [ESV]

Powerful Manifestation Prayer:

I BLESS myself, my family and everyone born on this date with GOD's MOST POWERFUL PURE LOVING LIGHT, HIS MOST POWERFUL PURE SOURCE HEALING ENERGY, and an ABUNDANCE OF HIS AMAZING GREATER GRACE in the POWER, the ANOINTING, the AUTHORITY and the WISDOM of the HOLY SPIRIT, in JESUS' MOST HOLY NAME. AMEN INDEED!

June
6

~ I Pray for You and You Pray for Me!

"After Job had prayed for his friends, the LORD restored his fortunes and gave him twice as much as he had before." ◀ Job 42:10 ▶ [NIV]

"You haven't done this before. A.S.K. using MY NAME, and You will receive, and You will have abundant joy." ◀ John 16:24 ▶ [NLT]

Powerful Manifestation Prayer:

I BLESS myself, my family and everyone born in this month with GOD's MOST POWERFUL PURE LOVING LIGHT, HIS MOST POWERFUL PURE SOURCE HEALING ENERGY, and an ABUNDANCE OF HIS AMAZING GREATER GRACE in the POWER, the ANOINTING, the AUTHORITY and the WISDOM of the HOLY SPIRIT, in JESUS' MOST HOLY NAME.
AMEN INDEED!

A.S.K.- Additional Scripture Knowledge

Write Additional Scriptures here.

Day 152
6:1

"My friends, You are Spiritual. So, if someone is trapped in sin, You should gently lead that person back to the right path. But watch out, and don't be tempted yourself." ◀ Galatians 6:1 ▶ [CEV]

"Hear now what the LORD is saying, 'Arise, plead your case before the mountains, and let the hills hear your voice." ◀ Micah 6:1 ▶ [NASB]

"Beware of practicing your Righteousness before men to be noticed by them; otherwise You have no reward with your FATHER WHO is in Heaven." ◀ Matthew 6:1 ▶ [NASB]

"How terrible it will be for You that have such an easy life in Zion and for You that feel safe in Samaria-- You great leaders of this great nation Israel, You to whom the people go for help!" ◀ Amos 6:1 ▶ [GNT]

"LORD, do not rebuke me in YOUR anger or discipline me in YOUR wrath." ◀ Psalm 6:1 ▶ [ESV]

"So let us stop going over the basic teachings about CHRIST again and again. Let us go on instead and become mature in our understanding." ◀ Hebrews 6:1 ▶ [NLT]

Powerful Manifestation Prayer:

I BLESS myself, my family and everyone born on this date with GOD's MOST POWERFUL PURE LOVING LIGHT, HIS MOST POWERFUL PURE SOURCE HEALING ENERGY, and an ABUNDANCE OF HIS AMAZING GREATER GRACE in the POWER, the ANOINTING, the AUTHORITY and the WISDOM of the HOLY SPIRIT, in JESUS' MOST HOLY NAME. AMEN INDEED!

Day 153
6:2

"Honor your father and mother"—which is the first commandment with a **Promise**."
◀ Ephesians 6:2 ▶ [ESV]

"That **You** may fear the **LORD** your **GOD**, **You** and your son and your son's son, by keeping all **HIS Statutes** and **HIS Commandments**, which **I** command **You**, all the days of your life, and that your days may be long."
◀ Deuteronomy 6:2 ▶ [ESV]

"So, when **You** give to the poor, do not sound a trumpet before **You**, as the hypocrites do in the synagogues and in the streets, so that they may be honored by men. Truly **I** say to **You**, they have their reward in full."
◀ Matthew 6:2 ▶ [NASB]

"Bear one another's burdens, and thereby fulfill the **Law** of **CHRIST**." ◀ Galatians 6:2 ▶ [NASB]

"Be gracious to me, **LORD**, for I am weak; heal me, **LORD**, for my bones are shaking."
◀ Psalm 6:2 ▶ [CSB]

"**HE Will** revive us after two days, and on the third day **HE Will** raise us up so we can live in **HIS** presence."
◀ Hosea 6:2 ▶ [CSB]

Powerful Manifestation Prayer:

I BLESS myself, my family and everyone born on this date with GOD's MOST POWERFUL PURE LOVING LIGHT, HIS MOST POWERFUL PURE SOURCE HEALING ENERGY, and an ABUNDANCE OF HIS AMAZING GREATER GRACE in the POWER, the ANOINTING, the AUTHORITY and the WISDOM of the HOLY SPIRIT, in JESUS' MOST HOLY NAME. AMEN INDEED!

Day 154
6:3

"And my whole being is deeply troubled. How long, O LORD, Will YOU wait to help me?"
◀ Psalm 6:3 ▶ [GNT]

"Let's do our best to know the LORD. HIS coming is as certain as the morning sun; HE Will refresh us like rain renewing the earth in the springtime."
◀ Hosea 6:3 ▶ [CEV]

"Listen, Israel, and be careful to follow them, so that You may prosper and multiply greatly, because the LORD, the GOD of your fathers, has Promised You a land flowing with milk and honey."
◀ Deuteronomy 6:3 ▶ [CSB]

"But when You give to the poor, do not let your left hand know what your right hand is doing."
◀ Matthew 6:3 ▶ [NASB]

"For if anyone considers himself to be something when he is nothing, he deceives himself."
◀ Galatians 6:3 ▶ [CSB]

"We put no obstacle in anyone's way, so that no fault may be found with our ministry."
◀ 2 Corinthians 6:3 ▶ [ESV]

Powerful Manifestation Prayer:

I BLESS myself, my family and everyone born on this date with GOD's MOST POWERFUL PURE LOVING LIGHT, HIS MOST POWERFUL PURE SOURCE HEALING ENERGY, and an ABUNDANCE OF HIS AMAZING GREATER GRACE in the POWER, the ANOINTING, the AUTHORITY and the WISDOM of the HOLY SPIRIT, in JESUS' MOST HOLY NAME. AMEN INDEED!

Day 155
6:4

"Hear, O Israel! The **LORD** is our **GOD**, the **LORD** is **ONE**!" ◄ Deuteronomy 6:4 ► [NASB]

"Turn, **LORD**! Rescue me; save me because of your **Faithful Love**." ◄ Psalm 6:4 ► [CSB]

"Fathers, do not provoke your children to anger, but bring them up in the discipline and instruction of the **LORD**." ◄ Ephesians 6:4 ► [NASB]

"But in everything and in every way we show we truly are **GOD's** servants. We have always been patient, though we have had a lot of trouble, suffering, and hard times." ◄ 2 Corinthians 6:4 ► [CEV]

"But each one must examine his own work, and then he will have reason for boasting in regard to himself alone, and not in regard to another." ◄ Galatians 6:4 ► [NASB]

"But we will devote ourselves to **Prayer** and to the ministry of the **WORD**." ◄ Acts 6:4 ► [ESV]

Powerful Manifestation Prayer:

I BLESS myself, my family and everyone born on this date with GOD's MOST POWERFUL PURE LOVING LIGHT, HIS MOST POWERFUL PURE SOURCE HEALING ENERGY, and an ABUNDANCE OF HIS AMAZING GREATER GRACE in the POWER, the ANOINTING, the AUTHORITY and the WISDOM of the HOLY SPIRIT, in JESUS' MOST HOLY NAME. AMEN INDEED!

Day 156
6:5

"Furthermore, I have heard the groaning of the sons of Israel, because the Egyptians are holding them in bondage, and I have remembered **MY Covenant**." ◀ Exodus 6:5 ▶ [NASB]

"Bondservants, obey your earthly masters with fear and trembling, with a sincere heart, as **You** would **CHRIST**." ◀ Ephesians 6:5 ▶ [ESV]

"We have been beaten, jailed, and mobbed; we have been overworked and have gone without sleep or food." ◀ 2 Corinthians 6:5 ▶ [GNT]

"For each person will have to carry his own load." ◀ Galatians 6:5 ▶ [CSB]

"**You** shall **Love** the **LORD** your **GOD** with all your heart and with all your **Soul** and with all your might." ◀ Deuteronomy 6:5 ▶ [NASB]

"For if we have been united with **HIM** in the likeness of **HIS** death, we will certainly also be in the likeness of **HIS** resurrection." ◀ Romans 6:5 ▶ [CSB]

Powerful Manifestation Prayer:

I BLESS myself, my family and everyone born on this date with GOD's MOST POWERFUL PURE LOVING LIGHT, HIS MOST POWERFUL PURE SOURCE HEALING ENERGY, and an ABUNDANCE OF HIS AMAZING GREATER GRACE in the POWER, the ANOINTING, the AUTHORITY and the WISDOM of the HOLY SPIRIT, in JESUS' MOST HOLY NAME. AMEN INDEED!

Day 157
6:6

"I AM the LORD and I Will bring You out from under the burdens of the Egyptians, and I Will deliver You from slavery to them, and I Will redeem You with an outstretched arm and with great acts of judgment."
◄ Exodus 6:6 ► [NLT]

"But when You Pray, go to your room, close the door, and Pray to your FATHER, WHO is unseen. And your FATHER, WHO sees what You do in private, will reward You."
◄ Matthew 6:6 ► [GNT]

"And who then turn away from GOD? It is impossible to bring such people back to repentance; by rejecting the SON of GOD, they themselves are nailing HIM to the Cross once again and holding HIM up to public shame."
◄ Hebrews 6:6 ► [NLT]

"But GODliness with contentment is great gain." ◄ 1 Timothy 6:6 ► [CSB]

"Those who are taught the WORD of GOD should provide for their teachers, sharing all GOoD things with them."
◄ Galatians 6:6 ► [NLT]

"These WORDS, which I AM commanding You today, shall be on your heart."
◄ Deuteronomy 6:6 ► [NASB]

Powerful Manifestation Prayer:

I BLESS myself, my family and everyone born on this date with GOD's MOST POWERFUL PURE LOVING LIGHT, HIS MOST POWERFUL PURE SOURCE HEALING ENERGY, and an ABUNDANCE OF HIS AMAZING GREATER GRACE in the POWER, the ANOINTING, the AUTHORITY and the WISDOM of the HOLY SPIRIT, in JESUS' MOST HOLY NAME. AMEN INDEED!

Day 158
6:7

"You shall teach Them [GOD's WORDS] diligently to your sons and shall talk of them when You sit in your house and when You walk by the way and when You lie down and when You rise up."
◄ Deuteronomy 6:7 ► [NASB]

"Then I Will take You for MY People, and I Will be your GOD; and You shall know that I AM the LORD your GOD, WHO brought You out from under the burdens of the Egyptians."
◄ Exodus 6:7 ► [NASB]

"HE touched my lips with the burning coal and said, 'This has touched your lips, and now your guilt is gone, and your sins are forgiven." ◄ Isaiah 6:7 ► [GNT]

"For we brought nothing into the world, and we can take nothing out." ◄ 1 Timothy 6:7 ► [CSB]

"For when we died with CHRIST, we were set Free from the power of sin." ◄ Romans 6:7 ► [NLT]

"Do not be deceived, GOD is not mocked; for whatever a man sows, this he will also reap."
◄ Galatians 6:7 ► [NASB]

Powerful Manifestation Prayer:

I BLESS myself, my family and everyone born on this date with GOD's MOST POWERFUL PURE LOVING LIGHT, HIS MOST POWERFUL PURE SOURCE HEALING ENERGY, and an ABUNDANCE OF HIS AMAZING GREATER GRACE in the POWER, the ANOINTING, the AUTHORITY and the WISDOM of the HOLY SPIRIT, in JESUS' MOST HOLY NAME. AMEN INDEED!

Day 159
6:8

“Then I heard the voice of the LORD, saying, "Whom shall I send, and who will go for Us?" Then I said, "Here AM I. Send me!" ◀ Isaiah 6:8 ▶ [NASB]

“The LORD GOD All-Powerful has sworn by HIS OWN Name: ‘You descendants of Jacob make ME angry by your pride, and I hate your fortresses. And so, I Will surrender your city and possessions to your enemies.” ◀ Amos 6:8 ▶ [CEV]

“I Will bring You to the land which I swore to give to Abraham, Isaac, and Jacob, and I Will give it to You for a possession; I AM the LORD.” ◀ Exodus 6:8 ▶ [NASB]

“But Noah found Favor in the eyes of the LORD.” ◀ Genesis 6:8 ▶ [NASB]

“Stephen, a man richly Blessed by GOD and full of Power, performed great miracles and wonders among the people.” ◀ Acts 6:8 ▶ [GNT]

“For the one who sows to his own flesh will from the flesh reap corruption, but the one who sows to the SPIRIT will from the SPIRIT reap Eternal Life.” ◀ Galatians 6:8 ▶ [NASB]

Powerful Manifestation Prayer:

I BLESS myself, my family and everyone born on this date with GOD’s MOST POWERFUL PURE LOVING LIGHT, HIS MOST POWERFUL PURE SOURCE HEALING ENERGY, and an ABUNDANCE OF HIS AMAZING GREATER GRACE in the POWER, the ANOINTING, the AUTHORITY and the WISDOM of the HOLY SPIRIT, in JESUS’ MOST HOLY NAME. AMEN INDEED!

Day 160
6:9

"The Voice of the LORD cries to the city— and it is sound Wisdom to fear YOUR Name: "Hear of the ROD and of HIM WHO appointed it!" ◄ Micah 6:9 ► [ESV]

"Pray, then, in this way: 'Our FATHER WHO is in Heaven, Hallowed be YOUR Name." ◄ Matthew 6:9 ► [NASB]

"We know that death no longer has any power over CHRIST. HE died and was raised to life, never again to die." ◄ Romans 6:9 ► [CEV]

"The LORD has heard my plea for help; the LORD accepts my Prayer." ◄ Psalm 6:9 ► [CSB]

"But those who want to be rich fall into temptation, a trap, and many foolish and harmful desires, which plunge people into ruin and destruction." ◄ 1 Timothy 6:9 ► [CSB]

"And let us not grow weary of doing GOoD, for in due season we will reap, if **WE DO NOT GIVE UP**." ◄ Galatians 6:9 ► [ESV]

Powerful Manifestation Prayer:

I BLESS myself, my family and everyone born on this date with GOD's MOST POWERFUL PURE LOVING LIGHT, HIS MOST POWERFUL PURE SOURCE HEALING ENERGY, and an ABUNDANCE OF HIS AMAZING GREATER GRACE in the POWER, the ANOINTING, the AUTHORITY and the WISDOM of the HOLY SPIRIT, in JESUS' MOST HOLY NAME. AMEN INDEED!

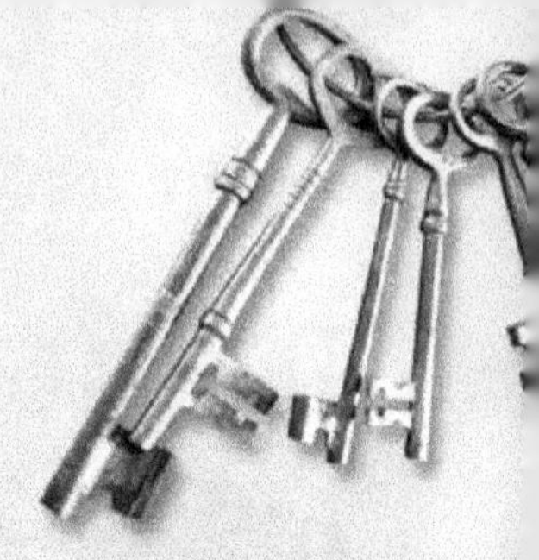

Day 161
6:10

"For the love of money is a root of all sorts of evil, and some by longing for it have wandered away from the **Faith** and pierced themselves with many griefs." ◀ 1 Timothy 6:10 ▶ [NASB]

"All my enemies will be ashamed and greatly dismayed; They shall turn back; they will suddenly be ashamed." ◀ Psalm 6:10 ▶ [NASB]

"But they were no match for Stephen, who spoke with the great **Wisdom** that the **SPIRIT** gave him." ◀ Acts 6:10 ▶ [CEV]

"For **GOD** is not unjust so as to forget your work and the **Love** which **You** have shown toward **HIS Name**, in having ministered and in still ministering to the saints." ◀ Hebrews 6:10 ▶ [NASB]

"Finally, be strong in the **LORD** and in the strength of **HIS Might**." ◀ Ephesians 6:10 ▶ [NASB]

"For the death that **HE** died, **HE** died to sin once for all; but the life that **HE** lives, **HE** lives to **GOD**." ◀ Romans 6:10 ▶ [NASB]

Powerful Manifestation Prayer:

I BLESS myself, my family and everyone born on this date with GOD's MOST POWERFUL PURE LOVING LIGHT, HIS MOST POWERFUL PURE SOURCE HEALING ENERGY, and an ABUNDANCE OF HIS AMAZING GREATER GRACE in the POWER, the ANOINTING, the AUTHORITY and the WISDOM of the HOLY SPIRIT, in JESUS' MOST HOLY NAME. AMEN INDEED!

Day 162
6:11

"Give us this day our daily bread." ◀ Matthew 6:11 ▶ [NASB]

"The houses will be richly stocked with **GOoDs You** did not produce. **You** will draw water from cisterns **You** did not dig, and **You** will eat from vineyards and olive trees **You** did not plant."
◀ Deuteronomy 6:11 ▶ [NLT]

"Even so consider yourselves to be dead to sin, but alive to **GOD** in **CHRIST JESUS**."
◀ Romans 6:11 ▶ [NASB]

"Such were some of **You**; but **You** were washed, but **You** were sanctified, but **You** were justified in the **Name** of the **LORD JESUS CHRIST** and in the **SPIRIT** of our **GOD**."
◀ 1 Corinthians 6:11 ▶ [NASB]

"But flee from these things, **You** man of **GOD**, and pursue **Righteousness**, **GODliness**, **Faith**, **Love**, perseverance and gentleness." ◀ 1 Timothy 6:11 ▶ [NASB]

"Put on the full armor of **GOD**, so that **You** will be able to stand firm against the schemes of the devil." ◀ Ephesians 6:11 ▶ [NASB]

Powerful Manifestation Prayer:

I BLESS myself, my family and everyone born on this date with GOD's MOST POWERFUL PURE LOVING LIGHT, HIS MOST POWERFUL PURE SOURCE HEALING ENERGY, and an ABUNDANCE OF HIS AMAZING GREATER GRACE in the POWER, the ANOINTING, the AUTHORITY and the WISDOM of the HOLY SPIRIT, in JESUS' MOST HOLY NAME. AMEN INDEED!

Day 163
6:12

"The people ate all they wanted, and **JESUS** told **HIS Disciples** to gather up the leftovers, so that nothing would be wasted."
◄ John 6:12 ► [CEV]

"Some of **You** say, "We can do anything we want to." But I tell **You** not everything is **GOoD** for us. So, I refuse to let anything have power over me."
◄ 1 Corinthians 6:12 ► [CEV]

"How can anyone know what is best for us in this short, useless life of ours--a life that passes like a shadow? How can we know what will happen in the world after we die?"
◄ Ecclesiastes 6:12 ► [GNT]

"Therefore, do not let sin reign in your mortal body, so that **You** obey its desires."
◄ Romans 6:12 ► [CSB]

"For our struggle is not against flesh and blood, but against the rulers, against the powers, against the world forces of this darkness, against the spiritual forces of wickedness in the heavenly places."
◄ Ephesians 6:12 ► [NASB]

"Then say to him, 'Thus says the **LORD** of **Hosts**, "Behold, a **Man Whose Name** is **Branch**, for **HE Will** branch out from where **HE** is; and **HE Will** build the **Temple of the LORD**."
◄ Zechariah 6:12 ► [NASB]

Powerful Manifestation Prayer:

I BLESS myself, my family and everyone born on this date with GOD's MOST POWERFUL PURE LOVING LIGHT, HIS MOST POWERFUL PURE SOURCE HEALING ENERGY, and an ABUNDANCE OF HIS AMAZING GREATER GRACE in the POWER, the ANOINTING, the AUTHORITY and the WISDOM of the HOLY SPIRIT, in JESUS' MOST HOLY NAME. AMEN INDEED!

Day 164
6:13

"Since I cannot help myself, the HOPE, for success has been banished from me."
◀ Job 6:13 ▶ [CSB]

"And they were casting out many demons and were Anointing with oil many sick people and healing them."
◀ Mark 6:13 ▶ [NASB]

"And do not go on presenting the members of your body to sin as instruments of unrighteousness; but present yourselves to GOD as those alive from the dead, and your members as instruments of Righteousness to GOD."
◀ Romans 6:13 ▶ [NASB]

"Yes, it is HE WHO Will build the Temple of the LORD, and HE WHO Will bear the Honor and sit and rule on HIS Throne. Thus, HE Will be a Priest on HIS Throne, and the counsel of Peace will be between the two offices."
◀ Zechariah 6:13 ▶ [NASB]

"Fear the LORD your GOD, worship HIM, and take your oaths in HIS Name."
◀ Deuteronomy 6:13 ▶ [CSB]

"And do not lead us into temptation but **Deliver Us From Evil**. For YOURS is the Kingdom, and the Power, and the Glory forever. Amen."
◀ Matthew 6:13 ▶ [NASB]

Powerful Manifestation Prayer:

I BLESS myself, my family and everyone born on this date with GOD's MOST POWERFUL PURE LOVING LIGHT, HIS MOST POWERFUL PURE SOURCE HEALING ENERGY, and an ABUNDANCE OF HIS AMAZING GREATER GRACE in the POWER, the ANOINTING, the AUTHORITY and the WISDOM of the HOLY SPIRIT, in JESUS' MOST HOLY NAME. AMEN INDEED!

Day 165
6:14

"Do not follow other gods, the gods of the peoples around **You**."

◄ Deuteronomy 6:14 ► [CSB]

"Do not try to work together as equals with unbelievers, for it cannot be done. How can right and wrong be partners? How can **Light** and darkness live together?" ◄ 2 Corinthians 6:14 ► [GNT]

"For if **You** forgive others for their transgressions, your **Heavenly FATHER Will** also forgive **You**."

◄ Matthew 6:14 ► [NASB]

"Sin must not be your master; for **You** do not live under **Law** but under **GOD's Grace**."

◄ Romans 6:14 ► [GNT]

"But as for me, I will never boast about anything except the **Cross** of our **LORD JESUS CHRIST**. The world has been crucified to me through the **Cross**, and I to the world."

◄ Galatians 6:14 ► [CSB]

"He said, "**I Promise You** that **I Will Bless You** and give **You** many descendants."

◄ Hebrews 6:14 ► [GNT]

Powerful Manifestation Prayer:

I BLESS myself, my family and everyone born on this date with GOD's MOST POWERFUL PURE LOVING LIGHT, HIS MOST POWERFUL PURE SOURCE HEALING ENERGY, and an ABUNDANCE OF HIS AMAZING GREATER GRACE in the POWER, the ANOINTING, the AUTHORITY and the WISDOM of the HOLY SPIRIT, in JESUS' MOST HOLY NAME. AMEN INDEED!

Day 166
6:15

"What, then? Shall we sin, because we are not under **Law** but under **GOD's Grace**? By no means!"
◀ Romans 6:15 ▶ [GNT]

"How can **CHRIST** and the devil agree? What does a **Believer** have in common with an unbeliever?"
◀ 2 Corinthians 6:15 ▶ [GNT]

"For the **LORD** your **GOD**, **WHO** is among **You**, is a jealous **GOD**. Otherwise, the **LORD** your **GOD Will** become angry with **You** and obliterate **You** from the face of the earth."
◀ Deuteronomy 6:15 ▶ [CSB]

"It doesn't matter if **You** are circumcised or not. All that matters is that **You** are a new person."
◀ Galatians 6:15 ▶ [CEV]

"For shoes, put on the **Peace** that comes from the **GOoD News** so that **You** will be fully prepared."
◀ Ephesians 6:15 ▶ [NLT]

"And so, having patiently waited, he obtained the **Promise**." ◀ Hebrews 6:15 ▶ [NASB]

Powerful Manifestation Prayer:

I BLESS myself, my family and everyone born on this date with GOD's MOST POWERFUL PURE LOVING LIGHT, HIS MOST POWERFUL PURE SOURCE HEALING ENERGY, and an ABUNDANCE OF HIS AMAZING GREATER GRACE in the POWER, the ANOINTING, the AUTHORITY and the WISDOM of the HOLY SPIRIT, in JESUS' MOST HOLY NAME. AMEN INDEED!

Day 167
6:16

"You shall not put the LORD your GOD to the test, as You tested HIM at Massah."
◀ Deuteronomy 6:16 ▶ [NASB]

"Or do You not know that he who is joined to a prostitute becomes one body with her? For, as it is written, "The two will become one flesh."
◀ 1 Corinthians 6:16 ▶ [ESV]

"Don't You realize that You become the slave of whatever You choose to obey? You can be a slave to sin, which leads to death, or You can choose to obey GOD, which leads to righteous living."
◀ Romans 6:16 ▶ [NLT]

"In addition to all, taking up the shield of Faith with which You will be able to extinguish all the flaming arrows of the evil one."
◀ Ephesians 6:16 ▶ [NASB]

"For people swear by something greater than themselves, and for them a confirming oath ends every dispute."
◀ Hebrews 6:16 ▶ [CSB]

"As for those who follow this rule in their lives, may Peace and Mercy be with them--with them and with all of GOD's People."
◀ Galatians 6:16 ▶ [GNT]

Powerful Manifestation Prayer:

I BLESS myself, my family and everyone born on this date with GOD's MOST POWERFUL PURE LOVING LIGHT, HIS MOST POWERFUL PURE SOURCE HEALING ENERGY, and an ABUNDANCE OF HIS AMAZING GREATER GRACE in the POWER, the ANOINTING, the AUTHORITY and the WISDOM of the HOLY SPIRIT, in JESUS' MOST HOLY NAME. AMEN INDEED!

Day 168
6:17

"You should diligently keep the Commandments of the LORD your GOD, and HIS Testimonies and HIS Statutes which HE has commanded You." ◀ Deuteronomy 6:17 ▶ [NASB]

"But when You fast, Anoint your head and wash your face." ◀ Matthew 6:17 ▶ [ESV]

"But thanks be to GOD that though You were slaves of sin, You became obedient from the heart to that form of teaching to which You were committed." ◀ Romans 6:17 ▶ [NASB]

"Take the helmet of Salvation and the Sword of the SPIRIT --which is the WORD of GOD." ◀ Ephesians 6:17 ▶ [CSB]

"From now on let no one cause me trouble, for I bear on my body the marks of JESUS." ◀ Galatians 6:17 ▶ [ESV]

"But the one who joins himself to the LORD is ONE SPIRIT with HIM." ◀ 1 Corinthians 6:17 ▶ [NASB]

Powerful Manifestation Prayer:

I BLESS myself, my family and everyone born on this date with GOD's MOST POWERFUL PURE LOVING LIGHT, HIS MOST POWERFUL PURE SOURCE HEALING ENERGY, and an ABUNDANCE OF HIS AMAZING GREATER GRACE in the POWER, the ANOINTING, the AUTHORITY and the WISDOM of the HOLY SPIRIT, in JESUS' MOST HOLY NAME. AMEN INDEED!

Day 169
6:18

"Flee from sexual immorality. Every other sin a person commits is outside the body, but the sexually immoral person sins against his own body." ◄ 1 Corinthians 6:18 ► [ESV]

"You shall do what is right and GOoD in the sight of the LORD, that it may be well with You and that You may go in and possess the GOoD land which the LORD swore to give your fathers." ◄ Deuteronomy 6:18 ► [NASB]

"Never stop Praying, especially for others. Always Pray by the Power of the SPIRIT. Stay alert and keep Praying for GOD's People." ◄ Ephesians 6:18 ► [CEV]

"Instruct them to do GOoD, to be rich in GOoD works, to be generous and ready to share." ◄ 1 Timothy 6:18 ► [NASB]

"That your fasting may not be seen by others but by your FATHER WHO is in secret. And your FATHER WHO sees in secret will reward You." ◄ Matthew 6:18 ► [ESV]

"Brothers and sisters, the Grace of our LORD JESUS CHRIST be with your Spirit. Amen." ◄ Galatians 6:18 ► [CSB]

Powerful Manifestation Prayer:

I BLESS myself, my family and everyone born on this date with GOD's MOST POWERFUL PURE LOVING LIGHT, HIS MOST POWERFUL PURE SOURCE HEALING ENERGY, and an ABUNDANCE OF HIS AMAZING GREATER GRACE in the POWER, the ANOINTING, the AUTHORITY and the WISDOM of the HOLY SPIRIT, in JESUS' MOST HOLY NAME. AMEN INDEED!

Day 170
6:19

"**Pray** also for me, that the message may be given to me when I open my mouth to make known with boldness the mystery of the **Gospel**." ◀ Ephesians 6:19 ▶ [CSB]

"And **You** will drive out your enemies, as **HE Promised**." ◀ Deuteronomy 6:19 ▶ [GNT]

"Do not store up for yourselves treasures on earth, where moth and rust destroy, and where thieves break in and steal." ◀ Matthew 6:19 ▶ [NASB]

"Thus, storing up treasure for themselves as a **GOoD** foundation for the future, so that they may take hold of that which is truly life." ◀ 1 Timothy 6:19 ▶ [ESV]

"Then, when they had rowed about three or four miles, they saw **JESUS** walking on the sea and drawing near to the **BOAT**; and they were frightened." ◀ John 6:19 ▶ [NASB]

"And all the people were trying to touch **HIM**, for **Power** was coming from **HIM** and healing them all." ◀ Luke 6:19 ▶ [NASB]

Powerful Manifestation Prayer:

I BLESS myself, my family and everyone born on this date with GOD's MOST POWERFUL PURE LOVING LIGHT, HIS MOST POWERFUL PURE SOURCE HEALING ENERGY, and an ABUNDANCE OF HIS AMAZING GREATER GRACE in the POWER, the ANOINTING, the AUTHORITY and the WISDOM of the HOLY SPIRIT, in JESUS' MOST HOLY NAME. AMEN INDEED!

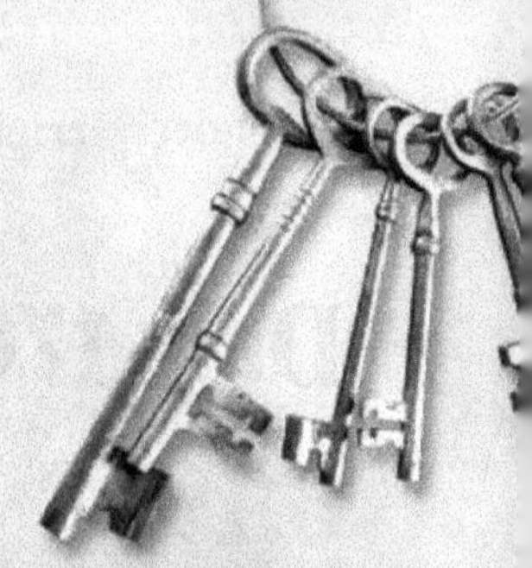

Day 171
6:20

"My son, observe the commandment of your father and do not forsake the teaching of your mother."
◀ Proverbs 6:20 ▶ [NASB]

"That **YOUR** eye may be open toward this house day and night, toward the place of which **YOU** have said that **YOU** would put **YOUR Name** there, to listen to the **Prayer** which **YOUR** servant shall **Pray** toward this place."
◀ 2 Chronicles 6:20 ▶ [NASB]

"Guard what has been entrusted to **You**, avoiding worldly and empty chatter and the opposing arguments of what is falsely called **Knowledge**."
◀ 1 Timothy 6:20 ▶ [NASB]

"But **HE** said, '**I AM JESUS**! Don't be afraid'!"
◀ John 6:20 ▶ [CEV]

"**GOD** paid a **Great Price** for **You**. So, use your body to **Honor GOD**."
◀ 1 Corinthians 6:20 ▶ [CEV]

"**JESUS** has entered there on our behalf as a **Forerunner**, because **HE** has become a **High Priest** forever according to the order of **Melchizedek**."
◀ Hebrews 6:20 ▶ [CSB]

Powerful Manifestation Prayer:

I BLESS myself, my family and everyone born on this date with GOD's MOST POWERFUL PURE LOVING LIGHT, HIS MOST POWERFUL PURE SOURCE HEALING ENERGY, and an ABUNDANCE OF HIS AMAZING GREATER GRACE in the POWER, the ANOINTING, the AUTHORITY and the WISDOM of the HOLY SPIRIT, in JESUS' MOST HOLY NAME. AMEN INDEED!

Day 172
6:21

"If You Promise an offering beyond what your vow requires You to give, You must fulfill exactly the Promise You made." ◀ Numbers 6:21 ▶ [GNT]

"For where your treasure is, there your heart will be also." ◀ Matthew 6:21 ▶ [CSB]

"Some people have even lost their Faith by believing this talk. I Pray that the LORD Will be kind to all of You!" ◀ 1 Timothy 6:21 ▶ [CEV]

"Hear the petitions of YOUR servant and YOUR people Israel, which they Pray toward this place. May YOU hear in YOUR dwelling place in Heaven. May YOU hear and forgive." ◀ 2 Chronicles 6:21 ▶ [CSB]

"Then You shall say to your son, "We were slaves to Pharaoh in Egypt, and the LORD brought us from Egypt with a Mighty Hand."" ◀ Deuteronomy 6:21 ▶ [NASB]

"Blessed are You who hunger now, for You shall be satisfied. Blessed are You who weep now, for You shall laugh." ◀ Luke 6:21 ▶ [NASB]

Powerful Manifestation Prayer:

I BLESS myself, my family and everyone born on this date with GOD's MOST POWERFUL PURE LOVING LIGHT, HIS MOST POWERFUL PURE SOURCE HEALING ENERGY, and an ABUNDANCE OF HIS AMAZING GREATER GRACE in the POWER, the ANOINTING, the AUTHORITY and the WISDOM of the HOLY SPIRIT, in JESUS' MOST HOLY NAME. AMEN INDEED!

Day 173
6:22

"The eye is the lamp of the body; so then if your eye is clear, your whole body will be full of LIGHT."
◀ Matthew 6:22 ▶ [NASB]

"GOD sent HIS Angel to shut the mouths of the lions so that they would not hurt me. HE did this because HE knew that I was innocent and because I have not wronged You, Your Majesty."
◀ Daniel 6:22 ▶ [GNT]

"I have sent him to You for this very purpose, so that You may know about us, and that he may comfort your hearts." ◀ Ephesians 6:22 ▶ [NASB]

"But now, since You have been set Free from sin and have become enslaved to GOD, You have your fruit, which results in sanctification--and the outcome is Eternal Life!" ◀ Romans 6:22 ▶ [CSB]

"Blessed are You when people hate You, when they exclude You, insult You, and slander your name as evil because of the SON of Man." ◀ Luke 6:22 ▶ [CSB]

"ASK me for whatever You want and I will give it to You." ◀ Mark 6:22 ▶ [NASB]

Powerful Manifestation Prayer:

I BLESS myself, my family and everyone born on this date with GOD's MOST POWERFUL PURE LOVING LIGHT, HIS MOST POWERFUL PURE SOURCE HEALING ENERGY, and an ABUNDANCE OF HIS AMAZING GREATER GRACE in the POWER, the ANOINTING, the AUTHORITY and the WISDOM of the HOLY SPIRIT, in JESUS' MOST HOLY NAME. AMEN INDEED!

Day 174
6:23

"For a command is a **Lamp**, teaching is a **Light**, and corrective discipline is the way to life."
◄ Proverbs 6:23 ► [CSB]

"But if your eye is bad, your whole body will be full of darkness. If then the **Light** that is in **You** is darkness, how great is the darkness."
◄ Matthew 6:23 ► [NASB]

"For the wages of sin is death, but the **Free Gift** of **GOD** is **Eternal Life** in **CHRIST JESUS** our **LORD**."
◄ Romans 6:23 ► [NASB]

"**HE** brought us out from there in order to bring us in, to give us the land which **HE** had sworn to our fathers."
◄ Deuteronomy 6:23 ► [NASB]

"But the **LORD** said to him, '**Peace** to **You**. Don't be afraid, for **You** will not die."
◄ Judges 6:23 ► [CSB]

"**Peace** to the brothers and sisters, and **Love** with **Faith**, from **GOD** the **FATHER** and the **LORD JESUS CHRIST**."
◄ Ephesians 6:23 ► [CSB]

Powerful Manifestation Prayer:

I BLESS myself, my family and everyone born on this date with GOD's MOST POWERFUL PURE LOVING LIGHT, HIS MOST POWERFUL PURE SOURCE HEALING ENERGY, and an ABUNDANCE OF HIS AMAZING GREATER GRACE in the POWER, the ANOINTING, the AUTHORITY and the WISDOM of the HOLY SPIRIT, in JESUS' MOST HOLY NAME. AMEN INDEED!

Day 175
6:24

"But woe to **You** who are rich, for **You** are receiving your comfort in full." ◀ Luke 6:24 ▶ [NASB]

"No one can serve two masters, for either he will hate the one and **Love** the other, or he will be devoted to the one and despise the other. **You** cannot serve **GOD** and money." ◀ Matthew 6:24 ▶ [ESV]

"Then the **LORD** our **GOD** commanded us to obey all these **Laws** and to **Honor HIM**. If we do, **HE Will** always watch over our nation and keep it prosperous." ◀ Deuteronomy 6:24 ▶ [GNT]

"Then Gideon built an altar there to **The LORD** and named it **The LORD** is **Peace**."
◀ Judges 6:24 ▶ [NASB]

"May **GOD's Grace** be with all those who **Love** our **LORD JESUS CHRIST** with undying **Love**."
◀ Ephesians 6:24 ▶ [GNT]

"May the **LORD Bless You** and protect **You**." ◀ Numbers 6:24 ▶ [CSB]

Powerful Manifestation Prayer:

I BLESS myself, my family and everyone born on this date with GOD's MOST POWERFUL PURE LOVING LIGHT, HIS MOST POWERFUL PURE SOURCE HEALING ENERGY, and an ABUNDANCE OF HIS AMAZING GREATER GRACE in the POWER, the ANOINTING, the AUTHORITY and the WISDOM of the HOLY SPIRIT, in JESUS' MOST HOLY NAME. AMEN INDEED!

Day 176
6:25

"How painful are honest words! But what does your argument prove?" ◀ Job 6:25 ▶ [NASB]

"Do not focus on her beauty in your mind, nor allow her to take You prisoner with her flirting eyes." ◀ Proverbs 6:25 ▶ [ISV]

"Listen from your Home in Heaven. Forgive them and bring them back to the land YOU gave their ancestors." ◀ 2 Chronicles 6:25 ▶ [CEV]

"For this reason, I say to You, do not be worried about your life, as to what You will eat or what You will drink; nor for your body, as to what You will put on. Is not life more than food, and the body more than clothing?" ◀ Matthew 6:25 ▶ [NASB]

"It will be Righteousness for us if we are careful to observe all this commandment before the LORD our GOD, just as HE commanded us." ◀ Deuteronomy 6:25 ▶ [NASB]

"The LORD make HIS Face shine on You, and be gracious to You." ◀ Numbers 6:25 ▶ [NASB]

Powerful Manifestation Prayer:

I BLESS myself, my family and everyone born on this date with GOD's MOST POWERFUL PURE LOVING LIGHT, HIS MOST POWERFUL PURE SOURCE HEALING ENERGY, and an ABUNDANCE OF HIS AMAZING GREATER GRACE in the POWER, the ANOINTING, the AUTHORITY and the WISDOM of the HOLY SPIRIT, in JESUS' MOST HOLY NAME. AMEN INDEED!

Day 177
6:26

"JESUS answered, "Truly I tell You, You are looking for ME, not because You saw the signs, but because You ate the loaves and were filled." ◀ John 6:26 ▶ [CSB]

"How terrible when all people speak well of You; their ancestors said the very same things about the false prophets." ◀ Luke 6:26 ▶ [GNT]

"Do You think that You can disprove my words or that a despairing man's words are mere wind?" ◀ Job 6:26 ▶ [CSB]

"Look at the birds of the air, that they do not sow, nor reap nor gather into barns, and yet your Heavenly FATHER feeds them. Are You not worth much more than they?" ◀ Matthew 6:26 ▶ [NASB]

"I make a decree that in all the dominion of my kingdom men are to fear and tremble before the GOD of Daniel; For HE is the Living GOD and enduring forever, and HIS Kingdom is one which will not be destroyed, and HIS Dominion Will be forever." ◀ Daniel 6:26 ▶ [NASB]

"May the LORD look with Favor on You and give You Peace." ◀ Numbers 6:26 ▶ [CSB]

Powerful Manifestation Prayer:

I BLESS myself, my family and everyone born on this date with GOD's MOST POWERFUL PURE LOVING LIGHT, HIS MOST POWERFUL PURE SOURCE HEALING ENERGY, and an ABUNDANCE OF HIS AMAZING GREATER GRACE in the POWER, the ANOINTING, the AUTHORITY and the WISDOM of the HOLY SPIRIT, in JESUS' MOST HOLY NAME. AMEN INDEED!

Day 178
6:27

"Do not work for the food which perishes, but for the food which endures to **Eternal Life**, which the **SON** of **Man Will** give to **You**, for on **HIM** the **FATHER**, **GOD**, has set **HIS** seal."

◀ John 6:27 ▶ [NASB]

"So, shall they put **MY Name** upon the people of Israel, and **I Will Bless** them."

◀ Numbers 6:27 ▶ [ESV]

"Then hear in **Heaven** and forgive the sin of **YOUR Servants** and **YOUR People** Israel, indeed, teach them the **GOoD** way in which they should walk. And send rain on **YOUR** land which **YOU** have given to **YOUR People** for an inheritance." ◀ 2 Chronicles 6:27 ▶ [NASB]

"Can any one of **You** by worrying add a single hour to your life?" ◀ Matthew 6:27 ▶ [NIV]

"But I say to **You** who hear, **Love** your enemies, do **GOoD** to those who hate **You**."

◀ Luke 6:27 ▶ [NASB]

"So, the **LORD** was with Joshua, and his fame was in all the land." ◀ Joshua 6:27 ▶ [NASB]

Powerful Manifestation Prayer:

I BLESS myself, my family and everyone born on this date with GOD's MOST POWERFUL PURE LOVING LIGHT, HIS MOST POWERFUL PURE SOURCE HEALING ENERGY, and an ABUNDANCE OF HIS AMAZING GREATER GRACE in the POWER, the ANOINTING, the AUTHORITY and the WISDOM of the HOLY SPIRIT, in JESUS' MOST HOLY NAME. AMEN INDEED!

Day 179
6:28

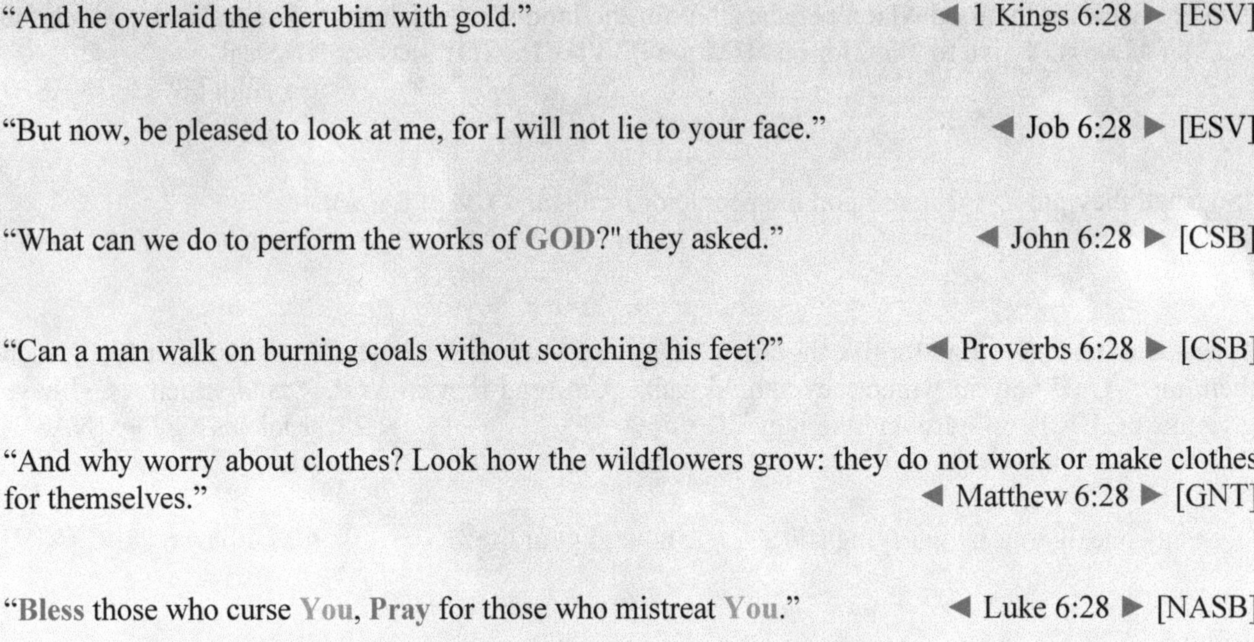

"And he overlaid the cherubim with gold." ◄ 1 Kings 6:28 ► [ESV]

"But now, be pleased to look at me, for I will not lie to your face." ◄ Job 6:28 ► [ESV]

"What can we do to perform the works of **GOD**?" they asked." ◄ John 6:28 ► [CSB]

"Can a man walk on burning coals without scorching his feet?" ◄ Proverbs 6:28 ► [CSB]

"And why worry about clothes? Look how the wildflowers grow: they do not work or make clothes for themselves." ◄ Matthew 6:28 ► [GNT]

"**Bless** those who curse **You**, **Pray** for those who mistreat **You**." ◄ Luke 6:28 ► [NASB]

Powerful Manifestation Prayer:

I BLESS myself, my family and everyone born on this date with GOD's MOST POWERFUL PURE LOVING LIGHT, HIS MOST POWERFUL PURE SOURCE HEALING ENERGY, and an ABUNDANCE OF HIS AMAZING GREATER GRACE in the POWER, the ANOINTING, the AUTHORITY and the WISDOM of the HOLY SPIRIT, in JESUS' MOST HOLY NAME. AMEN INDEED!

Day 180
6:29

"Please listen when anyone in Israel truly feels sorry and sincerely **Prays** with arms lifted toward **YOUR Temple.**"
◄ 2 Chronicles 6:29 ► [CEV]

"That the **LORD** spoke to Moses, saying, '**I AM** the **LORD**; speak to Pharaoh king of Egypt all that **I** speak to **You.**"
◄ Exodus 6:29 ► [NASB]

"Whoever hits **You** on the cheek, offer him the other also; and whoever takes away your coat, do not withhold your shirt from him either."
◄ Luke 6:29 ► [NASB]

"So, it is with the one who sleeps with another man's wife; no one who touches her will go unpunished."
◄ Proverbs 6:29 ► [CSB]

"Repent! Let there be no injustice; Change your ways! My vindication is at stake."
◄ Job 6:29 ► [ISV]

"**JESUS** answered and said to them, 'This is the work of **GOD**, that **You Believe** in **HIM WHOM HE** has sent'."
◄ John 6:29 ► [NASB]

Powerful Manifestation Prayer:

I BLESS myself, my family and everyone born on this date with GOD's MOST POWERFUL PURE LOVING LIGHT, HIS MOST POWERFUL PURE SOURCE HEALING ENERGY, and an ABUNDANCE OF HIS AMAZING GREATER GRACE in the POWER, the ANOINTING, the AUTHORITY and the WISDOM of the HOLY SPIRIT, in JESUS' MOST HOLY NAME. AMEN INDEED!

Day 181
6:30

"People do not despise a thief if he steals to satisfy his appetite when he is hungry."
◀ Proverbs 6:30 ▶ [ESV]

"Do You think I am lying? Don't I know the difference between right and wrong?"
◀ Job 6:30 ▶ [NLT]

"So, they said to HIM, 'Then what sign do YOU do, that we may see and believe YOU? What work do YOU perform'?"
◀ John 6:30 ▶ [ESV]

"Give to everyone who asks of You, and whoever takes away what is yours, do not demand it back."
◀ Luke 6:30 ▶ [NASB]

"YOU know what is in everyone's heart. So, from YOUR Home in Heaven answer their Prayers, according to what they do and what is in their hearts."
◀ 2 Chronicles 6:30 ▶ [CEV]

"If that is how GOD clothes the grass of the field, which is here today and tomorrow is thrown into the fire, will HE not much more clothe You—O You of little Faith?"
◀ Matthew 6:30 ▶ [ESV]

Powerful Manifestation Prayer:

I BLESS myself, my family and everyone born on this date with GOD's MOST POWERFUL PURE LOVING LIGHT, HIS MOST POWERFUL PURE SOURCE HEALING ENERGY, and an ABUNDANCE OF HIS AMAZING GREATER GRACE in the POWER, the ANOINTING, the AUTHORITY and the WISDOM of the HOLY SPIRIT, in JESUS' MOST HOLY NAME. AMEN INDEED!

July
7

~ I **Pray** for **You** and **You Pray** for Me!

"After Job had prayed for his friends, the **LORD** restored his fortunes and gave him twice as much as he had before." ◀ Job 42:10 ▶ [NIV]

"**You** haven't done this before. **A.S.K.** using **MY NAME**, and **You** will receive, and **You** will have abundant joy." ◀ John 16:24 ▶ [NLT]

Powerful Manifestation Prayer:

I BLESS myself, my family and everyone born in this month with GOD's MOST POWERFUL PURE LOVING LIGHT, HIS MOST POWERFUL PURE SOURCE HEALING ENERGY, and an ABUNDANCE OF HIS AMAZING GREATER GRACE in the POWER, the ANOINTING, the AUTHORITY and the WISDOM of the HOLY SPIRIT, in JESUS' MOST HOLY NAME.
AMEN INDEED!

A.S.K.- Additional Scripture Knowledge

Write Additional Scriptures here.

Day 182
7:1

"**O LORD** my **GOD**, in **YOU** I have taken refuge; Save me from all those who pursue me and deliver me!"
◀ Psalm 7:1 ▶ [NASB]

"When King Solomon finished his **Prayer**, fire came down from **Heaven** and burned up the sacrifices that had been offered, and the dazzling **Light** of the **LORD's** presence filled the Temple."
◀ 2 Chronicles 7:1 ▶ [GNT]

"**MY** child, remember what **I** say and never forget what **I** tell **You** to do."
◀ Proverbs 7:1 ▶ [GNT]

"Do not judge others, so that **GOD Will** not judge **You**." ◀ Matthew 7:1 ▶ [GNT]

"My friends, **GOD** has made us these **Promises**. So, we should stay away from everything that keeps our bodies and **Spirits** from being clean. We should honor **GOD** and try to be completely like **HIM**."
◀ 2 Corinthians 7:1 ▶ [CEV]

"This **Melchizedek** was king of Salem and a **Priest** of the **Most High GOD**. As Abraham was coming back from the battle in which he defeated the four kings, **Melchizedek** met him and **Blessed** him."
◀ Hebrews 7:1 ▶[GNT]

Powerful Manifestation Prayer:

I BLESS myself, my family and everyone born on this date with GOD's MOST POWERFUL PURE LOVING LIGHT, HIS MOST POWERFUL PURE SOURCE HEALING ENERGY, and an ABUNDANCE OF HIS AMAZING GREATER GRACE in the POWER, the ANOINTING, the AUTHORITY and the WISDOM of the HOLY SPIRIT, in JESUS' MOST HOLY NAME. AMEN INDEED!

Day 183
7:2

"The priests could not enter into the house of the **LORD** because the **Glory** of the **LORD** filled the **LORD's** house."
◄ 2 Chronicles 7:2 ► [NASB]

"Then Abraham gave him a tenth of everything he had. The meaning of the name **Melchizedek** is "King of Justice." But since Salem means "**Peace**," he is also "King of **Peace**."
◄ Hebrews 7:2 ► [CEV]

"Stand in the gate of the **LORD's** house and proclaim there this **WORD** and say, 'Hear the **WORD** of the **LORD**, all **You** of Judah, who enter by these gates to worship the **LORD**!"
◄ Jeremiah 7:2 ► [NASB]

"It never enters their heads that **I Will** remember all this evil; but their sins surround them, and **I** cannot avoid seeing them."
◄ Hosea 7:2 ► [GNT]

"For **GOD Will** judge **You** in the same way **You** judge others, and **HE Will** apply to **You** the same rules **You** apply to others."
◄ Matthew 7:2 ► [GNT]

"Obey **ME**, and **You** will live! Let **MY** instructions be your greatest treasure."
◄ Proverbs 7:2 ► [CEV]

Powerful Manifestation Prayer:

I BLESS myself, my family and everyone born on this date with GOD's MOST POWERFUL PURE LOVING LIGHT, HIS MOST POWERFUL PURE SOURCE HEALING ENERGY, and an ABUNDANCE OF HIS AMAZING GREATER GRACE in the POWER, the ANOINTING, the AUTHORITY and the WISDOM of the HOLY SPIRIT, in JESUS' MOST HOLY NAME. AMEN INDEED!

Day 184
7:3

"Sorrow is better than laughter, for by sadness of face the heart is made glad."
◀ Ecclesiastes 7:3 ▶ [ESV]

"There is no record of Melchizedek's father or mother or of any of his ancestors; no record of his birth or of his death. He is like the SON of GOD; he remains a Priest forever." ◀ Hebrews 7:3 ▶ [GNT]

"The Angel said, "Do not harm the earth, the sea, or the trees, until we mark the servants of our GOD with a seal on their foreheads." ◀ Revelation 7:3 ▶ [NLT]

"Why, then, do You look at the speck in your brother's eye and pay no attention to the log in your own eye?" ◀ Matthew 7:3 ▶ [GNT]

"Take also seven pairs of each kind of bird. Do this so that every kind of animal and bird will be kept alive to reproduce again on the earth." ◀ Genesis 7:3 ▶ [GNT]

"Do whatever You have in mind, because the LORD is with You." ◀ 2 Samuel 7:3 ▶ [GNT]

Powerful Manifestation Prayer:

I BLESS myself, my family and everyone born on this date with GOD's MOST POWERFUL PURE LOVING LIGHT, HIS MOST POWERFUL PURE SOURCE HEALING ENERGY, and an ABUNDANCE OF HIS AMAZING GREATER GRACE in the POWER, the ANOINTING, the AUTHORITY and the WISDOM of the HOLY SPIRIT, in JESUS' MOST HOLY NAME. AMEN INDEED!

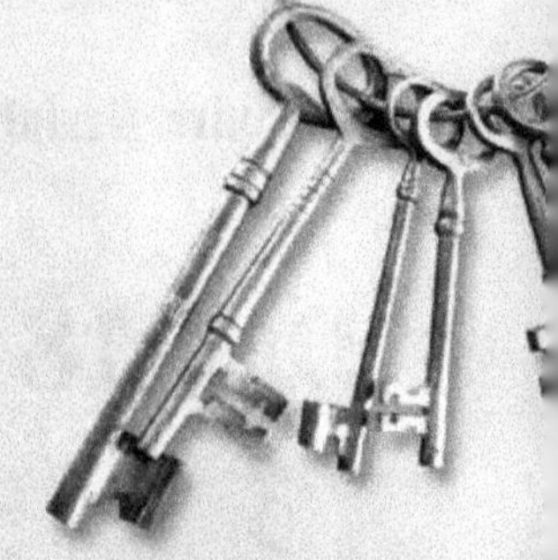

Day 185
7:4

"Don't fool yourselves! **MY** temple is here in Jerusalem, but that doesn't mean **I Will** protect **You**."
◄ Jeremiah 7:4 ► [CEV]

"People don't hide what they are doing if they want to be well known. Since **You** are doing these things, let the whole world know about **You**!"
◄ John 7:4 ► [GNT]

"Notice how great **Melchizedek** was! Our famous ancestor Abraham gave him a tenth of what he had taken from his enemies."
◄ Hebrews 7:4 ► [CEV]

"How can **You** say, "My friend, let me take the speck out of your eye," when **You** don't see the log in your own eye?"
◄ Matthew 7:4 ► [CEV]

"Say to **Wisdom**, '**You** are my sister,' and call understanding your intimate friend."
◄ Proverbs 7:4 ► [NASB]

"The mind of the wise is in the house of mourning, while the mind of fools is in the house of pleasure."
◄ Ecclesiastes 7:4 ► [NASB]

Powerful Manifestation Prayer:

I BLESS myself, my family and everyone born on this date with GOD's MOST POWERFUL PURE LOVING LIGHT, HIS MOST POWERFUL PURE SOURCE HEALING ENERGY, and an ABUNDANCE OF HIS AMAZING GREATER GRACE in the POWER, the ANOINTING, the AUTHORITY and the WISDOM of the HOLY SPIRIT, in JESUS' MOST HOLY NAME. AMEN INDEED!

Day 186
7:5

"When I raise **MY Powerful Hand** and bring out the Israelites, the Egyptians will know that **I AM** the **LORD**."
◄ Exodus 7:5 ► [NLT]

"Even **JESUS' OWN Brothers** had not yet become **HIS** followers." ◄ John 7:5 ► [CEV]

"The **Law** teaches that even Abraham's descendants must give a tenth of what they possess. And they are to give this to their own relatives, who are the descendants of Levi and are **Priests**."
◄ Hebrews 7:5 ► [CEV]

"**You** hypocrite first take the log out of your own eye, and then **You** will see clearly to take the speck out of your brother's eye."
◄ Matthew 7:5 ► [NASB]

"Correction from someone wise is better by far than praise from fools."
◄ Ecclesiastes 7:5 ► [CEV]

"Change the way **You** are living and stop doing the things **You** are doing. Be fair in your treatment of one another."
◄ Jeremiah 7:5 ► [GNT]

Powerful Manifestation Prayer:

I BLESS myself, my family and everyone born on this date with GOD's MOST POWERFUL PURE LOVING LIGHT, HIS MOST POWERFUL PURE SOURCE HEALING ENERGY, and an ABUNDANCE OF HIS AMAZING GREATER GRACE in the POWER, the ANOINTING, the AUTHORITY and the WISDOM of the HOLY SPIRIT, in JESUS' MOST HOLY NAME. AMEN INDEED!

Day 187
7:6

"Don't give to dogs what belongs to **GOD**. They will only turn and attack **You**. Don't throw pearls down in front of pigs. They will trample all over them." ◀ Matthew 7:6 ▶ [CEV]

"Although **Melchizedek** wasn't a descendant of Levi, Abraham gave him a tenth of what he had. Then **Melchizedek Blessed** Abraham, who had been given **GOD's Promise**." ◀ Hebrews 7:6 ▶ [CEV]

"In these times sons treat their fathers like fools, daughters oppose their mothers, and young women quarrel with their mothers-in-law; your enemies are the members of your own family." ◀ Micah 7:6 ▶ [GNT]

"**JESUS** replied: **You** are nothing but show-offs! The **Prophet** Isaiah was right when he wrote that **GOD** had said, "All of **You** praise **ME** with your words, but **You** never really think about **ME**." ◀ Mark 7:6 ▶ [CEV]

"Do this because **You** belong to the **LORD** your **GOD**. From all the peoples on earth **HE Chose You** to be **HIS OWN** special people." ◀ Deuteronomy 7:6 ▶ [GNT]

"Rise in **YOUR** anger, **O LORD**! Stand up against the fury of my enemies; rouse **YOURSELF** and help me! Justice is what **YOU** demand." ◀ Psalm 7:6 ▶ [GNT]

Powerful Manifestation Prayer:

I BLESS myself, my family and everyone born on this date with GOD's MOST POWERFUL PURE LOVING LIGHT, HIS MOST POWERFUL PURE SOURCE HEALING ENERGY, and an ABUNDANCE OF HIS AMAZING GREATER GRACE in the POWER, the ANOINTING, the AUTHORITY and the WISDOM of the HOLY SPIRIT, in JESUS' MOST HOLY NAME. AMEN INDEED!

Day 188
7:7

"It is no use for them to worship ME, because they teach human rules as though they were MY Laws."
◀ Mark 7:7 ▶ [GNT]

"Make the nations come to YOU, as YOU sit on YOUR throne above them all."
◀ Psalm 7:7 ▶ [CEV]

"The LORD did not set HIS Love on You nor choose You because You were more in number than any of the peoples, for You were the fewest of all peoples." ◀ Deuteronomy 7:7 ▶ [NASB]

"Then I Will let You dwell in this place, in the land that I gave to your fathers forever and ever."
◀ Jeremiah 7:7 ▶ [NASB]

"But as for me, I will watch expectantly for the LORD; I will wait for the GOD of my Salvation. My GOD Will hear me."
◀ Micah 7:7 ▶ [NASB]

"There is no doubt that the one who Blesses is greater than the one who is Blessed."
◀ Hebrews 7:7 ▶ [GNT]

Powerful Manifestation Prayer:

I BLESS myself, my family and everyone born on this date with GOD's MOST POWERFUL PURE LOVING LIGHT, HIS MOST POWERFUL PURE SOURCE HEALING ENERGY, and an ABUNDANCE OF HIS AMAZING GREATER GRACE in the POWER, the ANOINTING, the AUTHORITY and the WISDOM of the HOLY SPIRIT, in JESUS' MOST HOLY NAME. AMEN INDEED!

Day 189
7:8

"For everyone who **ASKs** receives, and he who seeks finds, and to him who knocks it will be opened."
◄ Matthew 7:8 ► [NASB]

"David, this is what **I**, the **LORD All-Powerful**, say to **You**. I brought **You** in from the fields where **You** took care of sheep, and **I** made **You** the leader of **MY** people." ◄ 2 Samuel 7:8 ► [CEV]

"In the case of the priests the tenth is collected by men who die; but as for **Melchizedek** the tenth was collected by **One Who** lives, as the **Scripture** says." ◄ Hebrews 7:8 ► [GNT]

"Do not rejoice over me, O my enemy. Though I fall I will rise; Though I dwell in darkness, the **LORD** is a **LIGHT** for me." ◄ Micah 7:8 ► [NASB]

"**You** disobey **GOD's Commands** in order to obey what humans have taught."
◄ Mark 7:8 ► [CEV]

"The end of something is better than its beginning. Patience is better than pride."
◄ Ecclesiastes 7:8 ► [GNT]

Powerful Manifestation Prayer:

I BLESS myself, my family and everyone born on this date with GOD's MOST POWERFUL PURE LOVING LIGHT, HIS MOST POWERFUL PURE SOURCE HEALING ENERGY, and an ABUNDANCE OF HIS AMAZING GREATER GRACE in the POWER, the ANOINTING, the AUTHORITY and the WISDOM of the HOLY SPIRIT, in JESUS' MOST HOLY NAME. AMEN INDEED!

Day 190
7:9

"YOU are a Righteous GOD and judge our thoughts and desires. Stop the wickedness of evildoers and reward those who are GOoD."
◀ Psalm 7:9 ▶ [GNT]

"If You will not believe, You surely shall not last."
◀ Isaiah 7:9 ▶ [NASB]

"You steal and murder; You lie in court and are unfaithful in marriage. You worship idols and offer incense to Baal, when these gods have never done anything for You."
◀ Jeremiah 7:9 ▶ [CEV]

"And JESUS continued, "You have a clever way of rejecting GOD's Law in order to uphold your own teaching."
◀ Mark 7:9 ▶ [GNT]

"Be not quick in your Spirit to become angry, for anger lodges in the hearts of fools."
◀ Ecclesiastes 7:9 ▶ [ESV]

"We have sinned against the LORD, so now we must endure HIS anger for a while. But in the end HE Will defend us and right the wrongs that have been done to us. HE Will bring us out to the Light; we will live to see HIM save us."
◀ Micah 7:9 ▶ [GNT]

Powerful Manifestation Prayer:

I BLESS myself, my family and everyone born on this date with GOD's MOST POWERFUL PURE LOVING LIGHT, HIS MOST POWERFUL PURE SOURCE HEALING ENERGY, and an ABUNDANCE OF HIS AMAZING GREATER GRACE in the POWER, the ANOINTING, the AUTHORITY and the WISDOM of the HOLY SPIRIT, in JESUS' MOST HOLY NAME. AMEN INDEED!

Day 191
7:10

"Honor your father and your mother'; and, 'Whoever reviles father or mother must surely die'."
◀ Mark 7:10 ▶ [ESV]

"But to the married I give instructions, not I, but the **LORD**, that the wife should not leave her husband."
◀ 1 Corinthians 7:10 ▶ [NASB]

"Do not say, "Why is it that the former days were better than these?" For it is not from **Wisdom** that **You** ask about this."
◀ Ecclesiastes 7:10 ▶ [NASB]

"Moreover, **I Will** appoint a place for **MY** people Israel, and **Will** plant them, that they may dwell in a place of their own and move no more; nor shall the sons of wickedness oppress them anymore, as previously."
◀ 2 Samuel 7:10 ▶ [NKJV]

"Then our enemies will see this and be disgraced--the same enemies who taunted us by asking, "Where is the **LORD** your **GOD**?" We will see them defeated, trampled down like mud in the streets."
◀ Micah 7:10 ▶ [GNT]

"And they cry out with a loud voice, saying, "**Salvation** to our **GOD WHO** sits on the throne, and to the **LAMB**!"
◀ Revelation 7:10 ▶ [NASB]

Powerful Manifestation Prayer:

I BLESS myself, my family and everyone born on this date with GOD's MOST POWERFUL PURE LOVING LIGHT, HIS MOST POWERFUL PURE SOURCE HEALING ENERGY, and an ABUNDANCE OF HIS AMAZING GREATER GRACE in the POWER, the ANOINTING, the AUTHORITY and the WISDOM of the HOLY SPIRIT, in JESUS' MOST HOLY NAME. AMEN INDEED!

Day 192
7:11

"Do You think that MY Temple is a hiding place for robbers? I have seen what You are doing."
◀ Jeremiah 7:11 ▶ [GNT]

"And all the Angels were standing around the throne and around the elders and the four living creatures; and they fell on their faces before the throne and worshiped GOD."
◀ Revelation 7:11 ▶ [NASB]

"GOD is a Righteous Judge and always condemns the wicked." ◀ Psalm 7:11 ▶ [GNT]

"If You then, being evil, know how to give GOoD gifts to your children, how much more will your FATHER WHO is in Heaven give what is GOoD to those who ASK HIM!"
◀ Matthew 7:11 ▶ [NASB]

"Everyone who lives ought to be wise; it is as GOoD as receiving an inheritance."
◀ Ecclesiastes 7:11 ▶ [GNT]

"Even from the day that I Commanded judges to be over MY people Israel; and I Will give You rest from all your enemies. The LORD also declares to You that the LORD Will make a house for You."
◀ 2 Samuel 7:11 ▶ [NASB]

Powerful Manifestation Prayer:

I BLESS myself, my family and everyone born on this date with GOD's MOST POWERFUL PURE LOVING LIGHT, HIS MOST POWERFUL PURE SOURCE HEALING ENERGY, and an ABUNDANCE OF HIS AMAZING GREATER GRACE in the POWER, the ANOINTING, the AUTHORITY and the WISDOM of the HOLY SPIRIT, in JESUS' MOST HOLY NAME. AMEN INDEED!

Day 193
7:12

"So, in everything, do to others what **You** would have them do to **You**, for this sums up the **Law** and the **Prophets**." ◄ Matthew 7:12 ► [NIV]

"For when **You** die and are buried with your ancestors, **I Will** raise up one of your descendants, your own offspring, and **I Will** make his kingdom strong." ◄ 2 Samuel 7:12 ► [NLT]

"For when the priesthood is changed, the **Law** must be changed also." ◄ Hebrews 7:12 ► [NIV]

"They sang, "**Amen**! **Blessing** and **Glory** and **Wisdom** and **Thanksgiving** and **Honor** and **Power** and **Strength** belong to our **GOD** forever and ever! Amen." ◄ Revelation 7:12 ► [NLT]

"If a person does not repent, **GOD Will** sharpen **HIS** sword; **HE Will** bend and string **HIS** bow." ◄ Psalm 7:12 ► [NLT]

"**Wisdom** and money can get **You** almost anything, but only **Wisdom** can save your life." ◄ Ecclesiastes 7:12 ► [NLT]

Powerful Manifestation Prayer:

I BLESS myself, my family and everyone born on this date with GOD's MOST POWERFUL PURE LOVING LIGHT, HIS MOST POWERFUL PURE SOURCE HEALING ENERGY, and an ABUNDANCE OF HIS AMAZING GREATER GRACE in the POWER, the ANOINTING, the AUTHORITY and the WISDOM of the HOLY SPIRIT, in JESUS' MOST HOLY NAME. AMEN INDEED!

Day 194
7:13

"Go in through the narrow gate, because the gate to hell is wide and the road that leads to it is easy, and there are many who travel it." ◀ Matthew 7:13 ▶ [GNT]

"But the earth will become a desert because of the wickedness of those who live on it."
◀ Micah 7:13 ▶ [GNT]

"HE has prepared HIS deadly weapons; HE tips HIS arrows with fire."
◀ Psalm 7:13 ▶ [CSB]

"But the people were afraid of their leaders, and none of them talked in public about HIM."
◀ John 7:13 ▶ [CEV]

"Woe to them, for they have strayed from ME! Destruction is theirs, for they have rebelled against ME! I would redeem them, but they speak lies against ME." ◀ Hosea 7:13 ▶ [NASB]

"When the LORD saw her, HE felt compassion for her, and said to her, 'Do not weep'."
◀ Luke 7:13 ▶ [NASB]

Powerful Manifestation Prayer:

I BLESS myself, my family and everyone born on this date with GOD's MOST POWERFUL PURE LOVING LIGHT, HIS MOST POWERFUL PURE SOURCE HEALING ENERGY, and an ABUNDANCE OF HIS AMAZING GREATER GRACE in the POWER, the ANOINTING, the AUTHORITY and the WISDOM of the HOLY SPIRIT, in JESUS' MOST HOLY NAME. AMEN INDEED!

Day 195
7:14

“But the gate to life is very narrow. The road that leads there is so hard to follow that only a few people find it.”
◀ Matthew 7:14 ▶ [CEV]

“If **MY OWN** people will humbly **Pray** and turn back to **ME** and stop sinning, then **I Will** answer them from **Heaven**. **I Will** forgive them and make their land fertile once again.”
◀ 2 Chronicles 7:14 ▶ [CEV]

“**JESUS** went over and touched the stretcher on which the people were carrying the dead boy. They stopped, and **JESUS** said, "Young man, get up."”
◀ Luke 7:14 ▶ [CEV]

“**I Will** be his **FATHER**, and he will be **MY** son. When he does wrong, **I Will** punish him as a father punishes his son.”
◀ 2 Samuel 7:14 ▶ [GNT]

“For it is evident that our **LORD** was descended from Judah, a tribe with reference to which Moses spoke nothing concerning priests.”
◀ Hebrews 7:14 ▶ [NASB]

“Be a **Shepherd** to **YOUR** people, **LORD**, the people **YOU** have **Chosen**. Although they live apart in the wilderness, there is fertile land around them. Let them go and feed in the rich pastures of Bashan and Gilead, as they did long ago.”
◀ Micah 7:14 ▶ [GNT]

Powerful Manifestation Prayer:

I BLESS myself, my family and everyone born on this date with GOD’s MOST POWERFUL PURE LOVING LIGHT, HIS MOST POWERFUL PURE SOURCE HEALING ENERGY, and an ABUNDANCE OF HIS AMAZING GREATER GRACE in the POWER, the ANOINTING, the AUTHORITY and the WISDOM of the HOLY SPIRIT, in JESUS’ MOST HOLY NAME. AMEN INDEED!

Day 196
7:15

"There is nothing that goes into You from the outside which can make You ritually unclean. Rather, it is what comes out of You that makes You unclean." ◄ Mark 7:15 ► [GNT]

"Watch out for false prophets! They dress up like sheep, but inside they are wolves who have come to attack You." ◄ Matthew 7:15 ► [CEV]

"But I Will not withdraw MY support from him as I did from Saul, whom I removed so that You could be king." ◄ 2 Samuel 7:15 ► [GNT]

"The matter becomes even plainer; a different PRIEST has appeared, WHO is like Melchizedek." ◄ Hebrews 7:15 ► [GNT]

"That is why they stand before GOD's Throne and serve HIM day and night in HIS Temple. HE WHO sits on the throne will protect them with HIS presence." ◄ Revelation 7:15 ► [GNT]

"As in the days when You came out from the land of Egypt, I Will show You miracles." ◄ Micah 7:15 ► [NASB]

Powerful Manifestation Prayer:

I BLESS myself, my family and everyone born on this date with GOD's MOST POWERFUL PURE LOVING LIGHT, HIS MOST POWERFUL PURE SOURCE HEALING ENERGY, and an ABUNDANCE OF HIS AMAZING GREATER GRACE in the POWER, the ANOINTING, the AUTHORITY and the WISDOM of the HOLY SPIRIT, in JESUS' MOST HOLY NAME. AMEN INDEED!

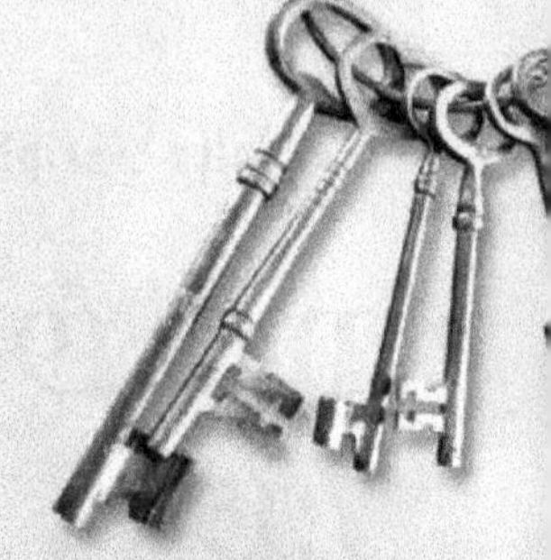

Day 197
7:16

"JESUS became a PRIEST, not by meeting the physical requirement of belonging to the tribe of Levi, but by the Power of a Life that cannot be destroyed." ◀ Hebrews 7:16 ▶ [NLT]

"So JESUS answered them and said, "MY teaching is not MINE, but HIS WHO sent ME." ◀ John 7:16 ▶ [NASB]

"Your house and your kingdom shall endure before ME forever; your throne shall be established forever." ◀ 2 Samuel 7:16 ▶ [NASB]

"They will never hunger or thirst again, and they won't be troubled by the sun or any scorching heat." ◀ Revelation 7:16 ▶ [CEV]

"The nations will see this and be frustrated in spite of all their strength. In dismay they will close their mouths and cover their ears." ◀ Micah 7:16 ▶ [GNT]

"I rejoice that in everything I have confidence in You." ◀ 2 Corinthians 7:16 ▶ [NASB]

Powerful Manifestation Prayer:

I BLESS myself, my family and everyone born on this date with GOD's MOST POWERFUL PURE LOVING LIGHT, HIS MOST POWERFUL PURE SOURCE HEALING ENERGY, and an ABUNDANCE OF HIS AMAZING GREATER GRACE in the POWER, the ANOINTING, the AUTHORITY and the WISDOM of the HOLY SPIRIT, in JESUS' MOST HOLY NAME. AMEN INDEED!

Day 198
7:17

"For the Scripture says, "YOU Will be a PRIEST forever, in the priestly order of Melchizedek."
◄ Hebrews 7:17 ► [GNT]

"Whoever is willing to do what GOD wants will know whether what I teach comes from GOD or whether I speak on MY OWN authority." ◄ John 7:17 ► [GNT]

"For the LAMB in the center of the throne will be their Shepherd, and will guide them to springs of the water of life; and GOD Will wipe every tear from their eyes." ◄ Revelation 7:17 ► [NASB]

"They will crawl in the dust like snakes; they will come from their fortresses, trembling and afraid. They will turn in fear to the LORD our GOD." ◄ Micah 7:17 ► [GNT]

"What is man that YOU magnify him, and that YOU are concerned about him?"
◄ Job 7:17 ► [NASB]

"I thank the LORD for HIS justice; I sing praises to the LORD, the Most High."
◄ Psalm 7:17 ► [GNT]

Powerful Manifestation Prayer:

I BLESS myself, my family and everyone born on this date with GOD's MOST POWERFUL PURE LOVING LIGHT, HIS MOST POWERFUL PURE SOURCE HEALING ENERGY, and an ABUNDANCE OF HIS AMAZING GREATER GRACE in the POWER, the ANOINTING, the AUTHORITY and the WISDOM of the HOLY SPIRIT, in JESUS' MOST HOLY NAME. AMEN INDEED!

Day 199
7:18

"Yes, the old requirement about the priesthood was set aside because it was weak and useless."
◄ Hebrews 7:18 ► [NLT]

"Those who speak on their own authority are trying to gain **Glory** for themselves. But **HE WHO** wants **Glory** for **The ONE WHO** sent **HIM** is honest, and there is nothing false in **HIM**."
◄ John 7:18 ► [GNT]

"Then David the king went in and sat before the **LORD**, and he said, 'Who **AM I**, **O Sovereign LORD**, and what is my house, that **YOU** have brought me this far?" ◄ 2 Samuel 7:18 ► [NASB]

"For **YOU** examine us every morning and test us every moment." ◄ Job 7:18 ► [NLT]

"I know that **GOoD** does not live in me--that is, in my human nature. For even though the desire to do **GOoD** is in me, I am not able to do it." ◄ Romans 7:18 ► [GNT]

"There is no other god like **YOU**, **O LORD; YOU** forgive the sins of **YOUR** people who have survived. **YOU** do not stay angry forever, but **YOU** take pleasure in showing us **YOUR** constant **Love**."
◄ Micah 7:18 ► [GNT]

Powerful Manifestation Prayer:

I BLESS myself, my family and everyone born on this date with GOD's MOST POWERFUL PURE LOVING LIGHT, HIS MOST POWERFUL PURE SOURCE HEALING ENERGY, and an ABUNDANCE OF HIS AMAZING GREATER GRACE in the POWER, the ANOINTING, the AUTHORITY and the WISDOM of the HOLY SPIRIT, in JESUS' MOST HOLY NAME. AMEN INDEED!

Day 200
7:19

"Every tree that does not bear **GOoD** fruit is cut down and thrown into the fire."
◀ Matthew 7:19 ▶ [NASB]

"Instead of doing what I know is right, I do wrong." ◀ Romans 7:19 ▶ [CEV]

"For the **Law** of Moses could not make anything perfect. And now a better **HOPE** has been provided through which we come near to **GOD**." ◀ Hebrews 7:19 ▶ [GNT]

"Joshua said to him, 'My son, tell the **Truth** here before the **LORD**, the **GOD** of Israel, and confess. Tell me now what **You** have done. Don't try to hide it from me'." ◀ Joshua 7:19 ▶ [GNT]

"**HE Will** again have compassion on us; **HE Will** tread our iniquities under foot. Yes, **YOU Will** cast all their sins into the depths of the sea!" ◀ Micah 7:19 ▶ [NASB]

"Yet now **YOU** are doing even more, **Sovereign LORD**; **YOU** have made **Promises** about my descendants in the years to come. And **YOU** let a man see this, **Sovereign LORD**!"
◀ 2 Samuel 7:19 ▶ [GNT]

Powerful Manifestation Prayer:

I BLESS myself, my family and everyone born on this date with GOD's MOST POWERFUL PURE LOVING LIGHT, HIS MOST POWERFUL PURE SOURCE HEALING ENERGY, and an ABUNDANCE OF HIS AMAZING GREATER GRACE in the POWER, the ANOINTING, the AUTHORITY and the WISDOM of the HOLY SPIRIT, in JESUS' MOST HOLY NAME. AMEN INDEED!

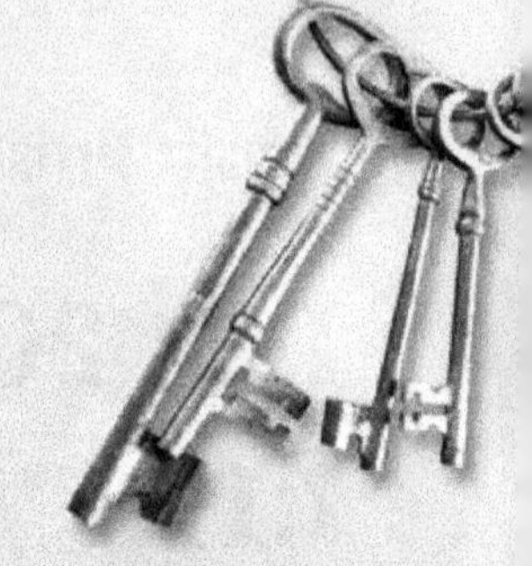

Day 201
7:20

"**You** can tell who the false prophets are by their deeds." ◀ Matthew 7:20 ▶ [CEV]

"Some of them may try to survive by hiding from **You**, but the **LORD Will** make them panic, and **SOON** they will be dead!" ◀ Deuteronomy 7:20 ▶ [CEV]

"If I have sinned, what have I done to **YOU**, **YOU WHO** see everything we do? Why have **YOU** made me **YOUR** target? Have I become a burden to **YOU**?" ◀ Job 7:20 ▶ [NIV]

"There is no one on earth who does what is right all the time and never makes a mistake." ◀ Ecclesiastes 7:20 ▶ [GNT]

"What more can I say to **YOU**? **YOU** know what **YOUR** servant is really like, **Sovereign LORD**." ◀ 2 Samuel 7:20 ▶ [NLT]

"**YOU Will** show us **YOUR Faithfulness** and constant **Love** to **YOUR** people, the descendants of Abraham and of Jacob, as **YOU Promised** our ancestors long ago." ◀ Micah 7:20 ▶ [GNT]

Powerful Manifestation Prayer:

I BLESS myself, my family and everyone born on this date with GOD's MOST POWERFUL PURE LOVING LIGHT, HIS MOST POWERFUL PURE SOURCE HEALING ENERGY, and an ABUNDANCE OF HIS AMAZING GREATER GRACE in the POWER, the ANOINTING, the AUTHORITY and the WISDOM of the HOLY SPIRIT, in JESUS' MOST HOLY NAME. AMEN INDEED!

Day 202
7:21

"Can't YOU ever forgive my sin? Can't YOU pardon the wrong I do? **SOON** I will be in my grave, and I'll be gone when YOU look for me." ◀ Job 7:21 ▶ [GNT]

"So don't be frightened when You meet them in battle. The **LORD** your **GOD** is great and fearsome, and **HE Will** fight at your side." ◀ Deuteronomy 7:21 ▶ [CEV]

"So, I find it to be a law that when I want to do right, evil lies close at hand." ◀ Romans 7:21 ▶ [ESV]

"Not everyone who says to **ME**, "**LORD, LORD**" will enter the **Kingdom** of **Heaven**, but he who does the **Will** of **MY FATHER WHO** is in **Heaven Will** enter." ◀ Matthew 7:21 ▶ [NASB]

"But **JESUS** became a **PRIEST** by means of a vow when **GOD** said to **HIM**, 'The **LORD** has made a **Solemn Promise** and will not take it back: **YOU Will** be a **PRIEST** forever.'" ◀ Hebrews 7:21 ▶ [GNT]

"At that very time **HE** cured many people of diseases and afflictions and evil spirits; and **HE** gave sight to many who were blind." ◀ Luke 7:21 ▶ [NASB]

"**YOU** have done this wonderful thing, and **YOU** have let me know about it, because **YOU** wanted to keep **YOUR Promise**." ◀ 2 Samuel 7:21 ▶ [CEV]

Powerful Manifestation Prayer:

I BLESS myself, my family and everyone born on this date with GOD's MOST POWERFUL PURE LOVING LIGHT, HIS MOST POWERFUL PURE SOURCE HEALING ENERGY, and an ABUNDANCE OF HIS AMAZING GREATER GRACE in the POWER, the ANOINTING, the AUTHORITY and the WISDOM of the HOLY SPIRIT, in JESUS' MOST HOLY NAME. AMEN INDEED!

Day 203
7:22

"I gave your ancestors no commands about burnt offerings or any other kinds of sacrifices when I brought them out of Egypt." ◀ Jeremiah 7:22 ▶ [GNT]

"The LORD your GOD Will clear away these nations before You little by little; You will not be able to put an end to them quickly, for the wild beasts would grow too numerous for You." ◀ Deuteronomy 7:22 ▶ [NASB]

"For this reason, YOU are great, O LORD GOD; for there is none like YOU, and there is no GOD besides YOU, according to all that we have heard with our ears." ◀ 2 Samuel 7:22 ▶ [NASB]

"Many will say to ME on that day, 'LORD! LORD! did we not prophesy in YOUR Name and in YOUR Name cast out demons, and in YOUR Name perform many miracles'?" ◀ Matthew 7:22 ▶ [NASB]

"This means that JESUS guarantees us a better agreement with GOD." ◀ Hebrews 7:22 ▶ [CEV]

"With my whole heart I agree with the Law of GOD." ◀ Romans 7:22 ▶ [CEV]

Powerful Manifestation Prayer:

I BLESS myself, my family and everyone born on this date with GOD's MOST POWERFUL PURE LOVING LIGHT, HIS MOST POWERFUL PURE SOURCE HEALING ENERGY, and an ABUNDANCE OF HIS AMAZING GREATER GRACE in the POWER, the ANOINTING, the AUTHORITY and the WISDOM of the HOLY SPIRIT, in JESUS' MOST HOLY NAME. AMEN INDEED!

Day 204
7:23

"I tested all this with **Wisdom**, and I said, "I will be wise," but it was far from me."
◀ Ecclesiastes 7:23 ▶ [NASB]

"But in every part of me I discover something fighting against my mind, and it makes me a prisoner of sin that controls everything I do."
◀ Romans 7:23 ▶ [CEV]

"But **I Will** tell them, "**I Will** have nothing to do with **You**! Get out of my sight, **You** evil people!"
◀ Matthew 7:23 ▶ [CEV]

"**You** must be careful to provide everything which the **GOD** of **Heaven** requires for **HIS Temple**, and so make sure that **HE** is never angry with me or with those who reign after me."
◀ Ezra 7:23 ▶ [GNT]

"But the **LORD** your **GOD Will** deliver them before **You** and will throw them into great confusion until they are destroyed."
◀ Deuteronomy 7:23 ▶ [NASB]

"Instead, **I** told them, 'If **You** listen to **ME** and do what **I** tell **You**, **I Will** be your **GOD**, **You** will be **MY** people, and all will go well for **You**.'"
◀ Jeremiah 7:23 ▶ [CEV]

Powerful Manifestation Prayer:

I BLESS myself, my family and everyone born on this date with GOD's MOST POWERFUL PURE LOVING LIGHT, HIS MOST POWERFUL PURE SOURCE HEALING ENERGY, and an ABUNDANCE OF HIS AMAZING GREATER GRACE in the POWER, the ANOINTING, the AUTHORITY and the WISDOM of the HOLY SPIRIT, in JESUS' MOST HOLY NAME. AMEN INDEED!

Day 205
7:24

"Don't judge by appearances. Judge by what is right." ◀ John 7:24 ▶ [CEV]

"How can anyone discover what life means? It is too deep for us, too hard to understand." ◀ Ecclesiastes 7:24 ▶ [GNT]

"But **JESUS**, on the other hand, because **HE** continues forever, holds **HIS PRIESTHOOD** permanently." ◀ Hebrews 7:24 ▶ [NASB]

"Therefore, everyone who hears these **WORDS** of **MINE** and acts on them, may be compared to a wise man who built his house on the rock." ◀ Matthew 7:24 ▶ [NASB]

"**YOU** have **Chosen** Israel to be **YOUR** people forever, and **YOU** have become their **GOD**." ◀ 2 Samuel 7:24 ▶ [CEV]

"**HE Will** put their kings in your power. **You** will kill them, and they will be forgotten. No one will be able to stop **You**; **You** will destroy everyone." ◀ Deuteronomy 7:24 ▶ [GNT]

Powerful Manifestation Prayer:

I BLESS myself, my family and everyone born on this date with GOD's MOST POWERFUL PURE LOVING LIGHT, HIS MOST POWERFUL PURE SOURCE HEALING ENERGY, and an ABUNDANCE OF HIS AMAZING GREATER GRACE in the POWER, the ANOINTING, the AUTHORITY and the WISDOM of the HOLY SPIRIT, in JESUS' MOST HOLY NAME. AMEN INDEED!

Day 206
7:25

“So I decided to learn everything I could and become wise enough to discover what life is all about. At the same time, I wanted to understand why it's stupid and senseless to be an evil fool.”
◄ Ecclesiastes 7:25 ► [CEV]

“And the rain fell, and the floods came, and the winds blew and slammed against that house; and yet it did not fall, for it had been founded on the rock.” ◄ Matthew 7:25 ► [NASB]

“Thank **GOD**! **JESUS CHRIST Will** rescue me. So with my mind I serve the **Law** of **GOD**, although my selfish desires make me serve the law of sin.” ◄ Romans 7:25 ► [CEV]

“Now therefore, O **LORD GOD**, the **WORD** that **YOU** have spoken concerning **YOUR** servant and his house, confirm it forever, and do as **YOU** have spoken.” ◄ 2 Samuel 7:25 ► [NASB]

“And so **HE** is able, now and always, to save those who come to **GOD** through **HIM**, because **HE** lives forever to plead with **GOD** for them.” ◄ Hebrews 7:25 ► [GNT]

“Use the **Wisdom GOD** has given **You** and choose officials and leaders to govern the people... These leaders should know **GOD's Laws** and have them taught to anyone who doesn't know them.”
◄ Ezra 7:25 ► [CEV]

Powerful Manifestation Prayer:

I BLESS myself, my family and everyone born on this date with GOD's MOST POWERFUL PURE LOVING LIGHT, HIS MOST POWERFUL PURE SOURCE HEALING ENERGY, and an ABUNDANCE OF HIS AMAZING GREATER GRACE in the POWER, the ANOINTING, the AUTHORITY and the WISDOM of the HOLY SPIRIT, in JESUS' MOST HOLY NAME. AMEN INDEED!

Day 207
7:26

“That YOUR Name may be magnified forever, by saying, ‘The LORD of Hosts is GOD over Israel’; and may the house of YOUR servant David be established before YOU.’”

◀ 2 Samuel 7:26 ▶ [NASB]

“Look! HE is talking in public, and they say nothing against HIM! Can it be that they really know that HE is The MESSIAH?” ◀ John 7:26 ▶ [GNT]

“JESUS, then, is the HIGH PRIEST that meets our needs. HE is Holy; HE has no fault or sin in HIM; HE has been set apart from sinners and raised above the Heavens.” ◀ Hebrews 7:26 ▶ [GNT]

“I found something more bitter than death--the woman who is like a trap. The love she offers You will catch You like a net, and her arms around You will hold You like a chain. A man who pleases GOD can get away, but she will catch the sinner.” ◀ Ecclesiastes 7:26 ▶ [GNT]

“Everyone who fails to obey GOD’s Law or the king's law will be punished without pity. They will either be executed or put in prison or forced to leave their country or have all they own taken away.”

◀ Ezra 7:26 ▶ [CEV]

“Everyone who hears these WORDS of MINE and does not act on them, will be like a foolish man who built his house on the sand.” ◀Matthew 7:26 ▶ [NASB]

“The LORD turned from the fierceness of HIS anger.” ◀ Joshua 7:26 ▶ [NASB]

Powerful Manifestation Prayer:

I BLESS myself, my family and everyone born on this date with GOD’s MOST POWERFUL PURE LOVING LIGHT, HIS MOST POWERFUL PURE SOURCE HEALING ENERGY, and an ABUNDANCE OF HIS AMAZING GREATER GRACE in the POWER, the ANOINTING, the AUTHORITY and the WISDOM of the HOLY SPIRIT, in JESUS’ MOST HOLY NAME. AMEN INDEED!

Day 208
7:27

“Blessed be the LORD, the GOD of our fathers, who has put such a thing as this in the king's heart, to adorn the House of the LORD, which is in Jerusalem.” ◀ Ezra 7:27 ▶ [NASB]

“For YOU, O LORD of Hosts, the GOD of Israel, have made a revelation to YOUR servant, saying, ‘I Will build YOU a house’; therefore, YOUR servant has found courage to Pray this Prayer to YOU.” ◀ 2 Samuel 7:27 ▶ [NASB]

“In the Scriptures, GOD calls John HIS Messenger and says, ‘I AM sending MY Messenger ahead of YOU to get things ready for YOU.” ◀ Luke 7:27 ▶ [CEV]

“HE is not like other high priests; HE does not need to offer sacrifices every day for HIS OWN sins first and then for the sins of the people. HE offered One Sacrifice, once and for all, when HE offered HIMSELF.” ◀ Hebrews 7:27 ▶ [GNT]

“Even your king and his officials will lose hope and cry in despair. Your hands will tremble with fear. I Will punish You for your sins and treat You the same way You have treated others. Then You will know that I AM The LORD.” ◀ Ezekiel 7:27 ▶ [CEV]

“Then the Greatest Kingdom of all will be given to the Chosen ones of GOD MOST HIGH. HIS Kingdom Will be eternal, and all others will serve and obey HIM.” ◀ Daniel 7:27 ▶ [CEV]

Powerful Manifestation Prayer:

I BLESS myself, my family and everyone born on this date with GOD’s MOST POWERFUL PURE LOVING LIGHT, HIS MOST POWERFUL PURE SOURCE HEALING ENERGY, and an ABUNDANCE OF HIS AMAZING GREATER GRACE in the POWER, the ANOINTING, the AUTHORITY and the WISDOM of the HOLY SPIRIT, in JESUS’ MOST HOLY NAME. AMEN INDEED!

Day 209
7:28

"Now, O LORD GOD, YOU are GOD, and YOUR WORDS are Truth, and YOU have Promised this GOoD thing to YOUR servant." ◄ 2 Samuel 7:28 ► [NASB]

"The Law appoints priests who have weaknesses. But GOD's Promise, which came later than the Law, appoints HIS SON. And HE is the perfect High Priest forever." ◄ Hebrews 7:28 ► [CEV]

"As JESUS taught in the Temple, HE said in a loud voice, "Do You really know ME and know where I AM from? I have not come on MY OWN Authority. HE WHO sent ME, however, is Truthful. You do not know HIM." ◄ John 7:28 ► [GNT]

"When JESUS had finished these WORDS, the crowds were amazed at HIS teaching." ◄ Matthew 7:28 ► [NASB]

"I say to You, among those born of women there is no one greater than John; yet he who is least in the Kingdom of GOD is greater than he." ◄ Luke 7:28 ► [NASB]

"And praise HIM for demonstrating such unfailing Love to me by honoring me before the king, his council, and all his mighty nobles! I felt encouraged because the Gracious Hand of the LORD my GOD was on me." ◄ Ezra 7:28 ► [NLT]

Powerful Manifestation Prayer:

I BLESS myself, my family and everyone born on this date with GOD's MOST POWERFUL PURE LOVING LIGHT, HIS MOST POWERFUL PURE SOURCE HEALING ENERGY, and an ABUNDANCE OF HIS AMAZING GREATER GRACE in the POWER, the ANOINTING, the AUTHORITY and the WISDOM of the HOLY SPIRIT, in JESUS' MOST HOLY NAME. AMEN INDEED!

Day 210
7:29

"I know **HIM** because **I AM** from **HIM**, and **HE** sent **ME**." ◀ John 7:29 ▶ [NASB]

"**HE** taught them like someone with **Authority**, and not like their teachers of the **Law** of Moses."
◀ Matthew 7:29 ▶ [CEV]

"When all the people and the tax collectors heard this, they acknowledged **GOD's** justice, having been baptized with the baptism of John." ◀ Luke 7:29 ▶ [NASB]

"I did learn one thing: We were completely honest when **GOD Created** us, but now we have twisted minds." ◀ Ecclesiastes 7:29 ▶ [CEV]

"**GOoD** answer!" **HE** said. "Now go home, for the demon has left your daughter."
◀ Mark 7:29 ▶ [NLT]

"Now therefore, may it please **YOU** to **Bless** the house of **YOUR** servant, that it may continue forever before **YOU**. For **YOU**, O **LORD GOD**, have spoken; and with **YOUR Blessing** may the house of **YOUR** servant be **Blessed** forever." ◀ 2 Samuel 7:29 ▶ [NASB]

Powerful Manifestation Prayer:

I BLESS myself, my family and everyone born on this date with GOD's MOST POWERFUL PURE LOVING LIGHT, HIS MOST POWERFUL PURE SOURCE HEALING ENERGY, and an ABUNDANCE OF HIS AMAZING GREATER GRACE in the POWER, the ANOINTING, the AUTHORITY and the WISDOM of the HOLY SPIRIT, in JESUS' MOST HOLY NAME. AMEN INDEED!

Day 211
7:30

"You have disobeyed ME by putting your disgusting idols in MY Temple, and now the Temple itself is disgusting to ME."
◀ Jeremiah 7:30 ▶ [CEV]

"So they were seeking to seize HIM; and no man laid his hand on HIM, because HIS hour had not yet come."
◀ John 7:30 ▶ [NASB]

"And she went home and found the child lying in bed and the demon gone." ◀ Mark 7:30 ▶ [ESV]

"But the Pharisees and the lawyers rejected GOD's Purpose for themselves, not having been baptized by John."
◀ Luke 7:30 ▶ [NASB]

"Present it to the LORD with your own hands as a special gift to the LORD. Bring…and lift up…as a special offering to the LORD."
◀ Leviticus 7:30 ▶ [NLT]

"Those who weep or who rejoice or who buy things should not be absorbed by their weeping or their joy or their possessions."
◀ 1 Corinthians 7:30 ▶ [NLT]

"Forty years later, an Angel appeared to Moses from a burning bush in the desert near Mount Sinai."
◀ Acts 7:30 ▶ [CEV]

Powerful Manifestation Prayer:

I BLESS myself, my family and everyone born on this date with GOD's MOST POWERFUL PURE LOVING LIGHT, HIS MOST POWERFUL PURE SOURCE HEALING ENERGY, and an ABUNDANCE OF HIS AMAZING GREATER GRACE in the POWER, the ANOINTING, the AUTHORITY and the WISDOM of the HOLY SPIRIT, in JESUS' MOST HOLY NAME. AMEN INDEED!

Day 212
7:31

"I have never commanded such a horrible deed; it never even crossed MY mind to command such a thing!"
◀ Jeremiah 7:31 ▶ [NLT]

"But many in the crowd believed in HIM and said, "When the MESSIAH comes, Will HE perform more miracles than THIS MAN has?"
◀ John 7:31 ▶ [GNT]

"His offering was one silver dish … one silver bowl … both of them full of fine flour mixed with oil for a grain offering."
◀ Numbers 7:31 ▶ [NASB]

"When Moses saw it, he marveled at the sight; and as he approached to look more closely, there came the Voice of the LORD."
◀ Acts 7:31 ▶ [NASB]

"JESUS continued, 'Now to what can I compare the people of this day? What are they like?'"
◀ Luke 7:31 ▶ [GNT]

"It won't make any difference how much GOoD You are getting from this world or how much You like it. This world as we know it is now passing away."
◀ 1 Corinthians 7:31 ▶ [CEV]

Powerful Manifestation Prayer:

I BLESS myself, my family and everyone born on this date with GOD's MOST POWERFUL PURE LOVING LIGHT, HIS MOST POWERFUL PURE SOURCE HEALING ENERGY, and an ABUNDANCE OF HIS AMAZING GREATER GRACE in the POWER, the ANOINTING, the AUTHORITY and the WISDOM of the HOLY SPIRIT, in JESUS' MOST HOLY NAME. AMEN INDEED!

August
8

~ I **Pray** for **You** and **You Pray** for Me!

"After Job had prayed for his friends, the **LORD** restored his fortunes and gave him twice as much as he had before." ◀ Job 42:10 ▶ [NIV]

"**You** haven't done this before. **A.S.K.** using **MY NAME**, and **You** will receive, and **You** will have abundant joy." ◀ John 16:24 ▶ [NLT]

Powerful Manifestation Prayer:

I BLESS myself, my family and everyone born in this month with GOD's MOST POWERFUL PURE LOVING LIGHT, HIS MOST POWERFUL PURE SOURCE HEALING ENERGY, and an ABUNDANCE OF HIS AMAZING GREATER GRACE in the POWER, the ANOINTING, the AUTHORITY and the WISDOM of the HOLY SPIRIT, in JESUS' MOST HOLY NAME.
AMEN INDEED!

A.S.K.- Additional Scripture Knowledge

Write Additional Scriptures here.

Day 213
8:1

"Then the **LORD** said to Moses, "Go to Pharaoh and say to him, 'Thus says the **LORD**, "Let **MY** people go, that they may serve **ME**."
◄ Exodus 8:1 ► [NASB]

"O **LORD**, our **LORD**, how **Majestic** is **YOUR Name** in all the earth, **WHO** have displayed **YOUR** splendor above the **Heavens**!"
◄ Psalm 8:1 ► [NASB]

"All the **Commandments** that **I AM Commanding You** today **You** shall be careful to do, that **You** may live and multiply, and go in and possess the land which the **LORD** swore to give to your forefathers."
◄ Deuteronomy 8:1 ► [NASB]

"Who is smart enough to explain everything? **Wisdom** makes **You** cheerful and gives **You** a smile."
◄ Ecclesiastes 8:1► [CEV]

"Therefore, there is now no condemnation for those who are in **CHRIST JESUS**."
◄ Romans 8:1 ► [NASB]

"Here is the main point: We have a **HIGH PRIEST WHO** sat down in the **Place of Honor** beside the throne of the **Majestic GOD** in **Heaven**."
◄ Hebrews 8:1 ► [NLT]

Powerful Manifestation Prayer:

I BLESS myself, my family and everyone born on this date with GOD's MOST POWERFUL PURE LOVING LIGHT, HIS MOST POWERFUL PURE SOURCE HEALING ENERGY, and an ABUNDANCE OF HIS AMAZING GREATER GRACE in the POWER, the ANOINTING, the AUTHORITY and the WISDOM of the HOLY SPIRIT, in JESUS' MOST HOLY NAME. AMEN INDEED!

Day 214
8:2

"On top of the heights beside the way, where the paths meet, she takes her stand."
◄ Proverbs 8:2 ► [NASB]

"I have longed to help Jerusalem because of MY deep Love for her people, a Love which has made ME angry with her enemies."
◄ Zechariah 8:2 ► [GNT]

"I looked up and saw a vision of a fiery human form. From the waist down HIS Body looked like fire, and from the waist up HE was shining like polished bronze."
◄ Ezekiel 8:2 ► [GNT]

"And I saw the seven Angels who stand before GOD, and seven trumpets were given to them."
◄ Revelations 8:2 ► [NASB]

"HE serves as HIGH PRIEST in the Most Holy Place, that is, in the real tent, which was put up by the LORD, not by human hands."
◄ Hebrews 8:2 ► [GNT]

"YOU have taught children and infants to tell of YOUR strength, silencing YOUR enemies and all who oppose YOU."
◄ Psalm 8:2 ► [NLT]

Powerful Manifestation Prayer:

I BLESS myself, my family and everyone born on this date with GOD's MOST POWERFUL PURE LOVING LIGHT, HIS MOST POWERFUL PURE SOURCE HEALING ENERGY, and an ABUNDANCE OF HIS AMAZING GREATER GRACE in the POWER, the ANOINTING, the AUTHORITY and the WISDOM of the HOLY SPIRIT, in JESUS' MOST HOLY NAME. AMEN INDEED!

Day 215
8:3

"If I send them away hungry to their homes, they will faint on the way; and some of them have come from a great distance." ◀ Mark 8:3 ▶ [NASB]

"And HE humbled You and let You hunger and fed You with manna, which You did not know, nor did your fathers know, that HE might make You know that man does not live by bread alone, but man lives by every WORD that comes from the Mouth of the LORD." ◀ Deuteronomy 8:3 ▶ [ESV]

"But the person who Loves GOD is known by HIM." ◀ 1 Corinthians 8:3 ▶ [GNT]

"JESUS stretched out HIS Hand and touched him, saying, 'I AM Willing; be cleansed.' And immediately his leprosy was cleansed." ◀ Matthew 8:3 ▶ [NASB]

"For every High Priest is appointed to offer both gifts and sacrifices; so, it is necessary that this HIGH PRIEST also have something to offer." ◀ Hebrews 8:3 ▶ [NASB]

"For I testify that according to their ability, and beyond their ability, they gave of their own accord." ◀ 2 Corinthians 8:3 ▶ [NLT]

Powerful Manifestation Prayer:

I BLESS myself, my family and everyone born on this date with GOD's MOST POWERFUL PURE LOVING LIGHT, HIS MOST POWERFUL PURE SOURCE HEALING ENERGY, and an ABUNDANCE OF HIS AMAZING GREATER GRACE in the POWER, the ANOINTING, the AUTHORITY and the WISDOM of the HOLY SPIRIT, in JESUS' MOST HOLY NAME. AMEN INDEED!

Day 216
8:4

"And **HIS Disciples** answered **HIM**, "Where will anyone be able to find enough bread here in this desolate place to satisfy these people?"
◀ Mark 8:4 ▶ [NASB]

"They even asked and begged us to let them have the joy of giving their money for **GOD's** people."
◀ 2 Corinthians 8:4 ▶ [CEV]

"And behold, the **Glory** of the **GOD** of Israel was there, like the vision that I saw in the valley."
◀ Ezekiel 8:4 ▶ [NASB]

"Even though food is offered to idols, we know that none of the idols in this world are alive. After all, there is only **ONE GOD**."
◀ 1 Corinthians 8:4 ▶ [CEV]

"What is man that **YOU** take thought of him, And the son of man that **YOU** care for him?"
◀ Psalm 8:4 ▶ [NASB]

"**JESUS** told him, "Don't tell anyone about this, but go and show the priest that **You** are well. Then take a gift to the temple just as Moses commanded, and everyone will know that **You** have been healed."
◀ Matthew 8:4 ▶ [CEV]

"**You** shall say to them, "Thus says the **LORD**, 'Do men fall and not get up again? Does one turn away and not repent?'"
◀ Jeremiah 8:4 ▶ [NASB]

Powerful Manifestation Prayer:

I BLESS myself, my family and everyone born on this date with GOD's MOST POWERFUL PURE LOVING LIGHT, HIS MOST POWERFUL PURE SOURCE HEALING ENERGY, and an ABUNDANCE OF HIS AMAZING GREATER GRACE in the POWER, the ANOINTING, the AUTHORITY and the WISDOM of the HOLY SPIRIT, in JESUS' MOST HOLY NAME. AMEN INDEED!

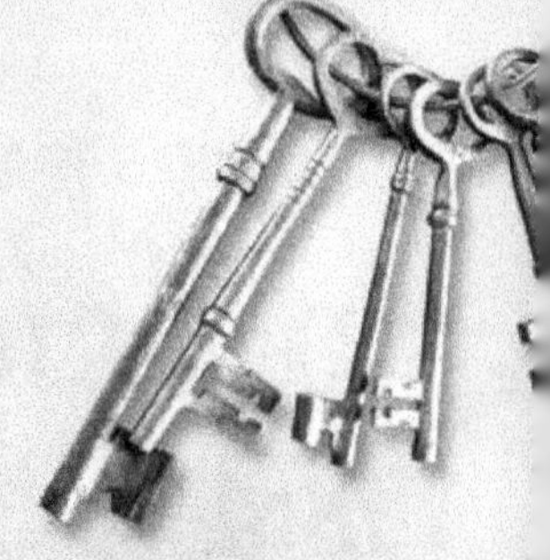

Day 217
8:5

"YOU made us a little lower than YOU YOURSELF, and YOU have crowned us with Glory and Honor." ◄ Psalm 8:5 ► [CEV]

"The LORD spoke to me again." ◄ Isaiah 8:5 ► [ESV]

"If You will seek GOD and plead with the Almighty for mercy." ◄ Job 8:5 ► [ESV]

"As long as You obey HIS commands, You are safe, and a wise person knows how and when to do it." ◄ Ecclesiastes 8:5 ► [GNT]

"There may be so-called gods both in Heaven and on earth, and some people actually worship many gods and many lords." ◄ 1 Corinthians 8:5 ► [NLT]

"For those who live according to the flesh set their minds on the things of the flesh, but those who live according to the SPIRIT set their minds on the things of the SPIRIT." ◄ Romans 8:5 ► [ESV]

Powerful Manifestation Prayer:

I BLESS myself, my family and everyone born on this date with GOD's MOST POWERFUL PURE LOVING LIGHT, HIS MOST POWERFUL PURE SOURCE HEALING ENERGY, and an ABUNDANCE OF HIS AMAZING GREATER GRACE in the POWER, the ANOINTING, the AUTHORITY and the WISDOM of the HOLY SPIRIT, in JESUS' MOST HOLY NAME. AMEN INDEED!

Day 218
8:6

"Listen, because what I say is worthwhile and right." ◄ Proverbs 8:6 ► [CEV]

"If You are so honest and pure, then GOD Will come and help You and RESTORE your household as your reward." ◄ Job 8:6 ► [GNT]

"Then Ezra Blessed The LORD, The Great GOD. And all the people answered, 'Amen, Amen!' while lifting up their hands; then they bowed low and worshiped the LORD with their faces to the ground." ◄ Nehemiah 8:6 ► [NASB]

"Yet there is for us only ONE GOD, The FATHER, WHO is the Creator of all things and for WHOM we live; and there is only ONE LORD, JESUS CHRIST, through WHOM all things were created and through WHOM we live." ◄ 1 Corinthians 8:6 ► [GNT]

"But now, JESUS, has been given priestly work, which is superior to theirs, just as the covenant which HE arranged between GOD and HIS people is a better one, because it is based on Promises of better things." ◄ Hebrews 8:6 ► [GNT]

"YOU make HIM to rule over the works of YOUR Hands; YOU have put all things under HIS feet." ◄ Psalm 8:6 ► [NASB]

Powerful Manifestation Prayer:

I BLESS myself, my family and everyone born on this date with GOD's MOST POWERFUL PURE LOVING LIGHT, HIS MOST POWERFUL PURE SOURCE HEALING ENERGY, and an ABUNDANCE OF HIS AMAZING GREATER GRACE in the POWER, the ANOINTING, the AUTHORITY and the WISDOM of the HOLY SPIRIT, in JESUS' MOST HOLY NAME. AMEN INDEED!

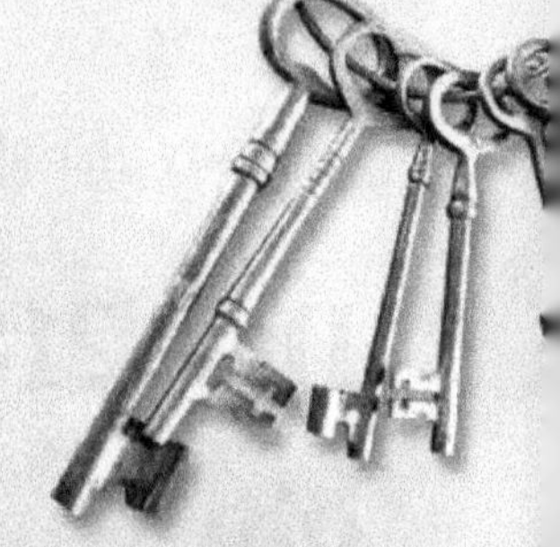

Day 219
8:7

"They also had a few small fish; and after HE had Blessed them, HE ordered these to be served as well." ◄ Mark 8:7 ► [NASB]

"For my mouth will utter Truth; and wickedness is an abomination to my lips." ◄ Proverbs 8:7 ► [NASB]

"For the LORD your GOD is bringing You into a GOoD land, a land of brooks of water, of fountains and springs, flowing out in the valleys and hills." ◄ Deuteronomy 8:7 ► [ESV]

"If there had been nothing wrong with the first covenant, there would have been no need for a second one." ◄ Hebrews 8:7 ► [GNT]

"But as You excel in everything—in Faith, in speech, in Knowledge, in all earnestness, and in our Love for You—see that You excel in this act of Grace also." ◄ 2 Corinthians 8:7 ► [ESV]

"And though your beginning was small, your latter days will be very great." ◄ Job 8:7 ► [ESV]

Powerful Manifestation Prayer:

I BLESS myself, my family and everyone born on this date with GOD's MOST POWERFUL PURE LOVING LIGHT, HIS MOST POWERFUL PURE SOURCE HEALING ENERGY, and an ABUNDANCE OF HIS AMAZING GREATER GRACE in the POWER, the ANOINTING, the AUTHORITY and the WISDOM of the HOLY SPIRIT, in JESUS' MOST HOLY NAME. AMEN INDEED!

Day 220
8:8

"For HE finds fault with them when HE says: "Behold, the days are coming, declares the LORD, when I Will establish a new covenant with the house of Israel and with the house of Judah."

◀ Hebrews 8:8 ▶ [ESV]

"All the words of my mouth are righteous; there is nothing twisted or crooked in them."

◀ Proverbs 8:8 ▶ [ESV]

"I am not ordering You to do this. I am simply testing how real your Love is by comparing it with the concern that others have shown."

◀ 2 Corinthians 8:8 ▶ [CEV]

"A land of wheat and barley, of vines and fig trees and pomegranates, a land of olive oil and honey."

◀ Deuteronomy 8:8 ▶ [NASB]

"And they ate and were satisfied; and they picked up seven large baskets full of what was left over of the broken pieces."

◀ Mark 8:8 ▶ [NASB]

"Our ancestors were wise, so learn from them."

◀ Job 8:8 ▶ [CEV]

Powerful Manifestation Prayer:

I BLESS myself, my family and everyone born on this date with GOD's MOST POWERFUL PURE LOVING LIGHT, HIS MOST POWERFUL PURE SOURCE HEALING ENERGY, and an ABUNDANCE OF HIS AMAZING GREATER GRACE in the POWER, the ANOINTING, the AUTHORITY and the WISDOM of the HOLY SPIRIT, in JESUS' MOST HOLY NAME. AMEN INDEED!

Day 221
8:9

"O LORD, our LORD, how majestic is YOUR Name in all the earth!" ◀ Psalm 8:9 ▶ [NASB]

"This day is Holy to the LORD your GOD; do not mourn or weep. "For all the people were weeping when they heard the words of the Law."" ◀ Nehemiah 8:9 ▶ [NASB]

"For I, too, am a man under authority, with soldiers under me. And I say to one, 'Go,' and he goes, and to another, 'Come,' and he comes, and to my servant, 'Do this,' and he does it."
◀ Matthew 8:9 ▶ [ESV]

"If You have understanding, You will see that MY WORDS are just what You need."
◀ Proverbs 8:9 ▶ [CEV]

"There You will never go hungry or ever be in need. Its rocks have iron in them, and from its hills You can mine copper." ◀ Deuteronomy 8:9 ▶ [GNT]

"For You know the Grace of our LORD JESUS CHRIST, that though HE was rich, yet for your sake HE became poor, so that You through HIS poverty might become rich."
◀ 2 Corinthians 8:9 ▶ [NASB]

Powerful Manifestation Prayer:

I BLESS myself, my family and everyone born on this date with GOD's MOST POWERFUL PURE LOVING LIGHT, HIS MOST POWERFUL PURE SOURCE HEALING ENERGY, and an ABUNDANCE OF HIS AMAZING GREATER GRACE in the POWER, the ANOINTING, the AUTHORITY and the WISDOM of the HOLY SPIRIT, in JESUS' MOST HOLY NAME. AMEN INDEED!

Day 222
8:10

"Let instruction and Knowledge mean more to You than silver or the finest gold."
◀ Proverbs 8:10 ▶ [CEV]

"Go, eat of the fat, drink of the sweet, and send portions to him who has nothing prepared; for this day is Holy to our LORD. Do not be grieved, for the joy of the LORD is your strength."
◀ Nehemiah 8:10 ▶ [NASB]

"For this is the covenant that I Will make with the house of Israel after those days, declares the LORD: I Will put MY Laws into their minds, and write them on their hearts, and I Will be their GOD, and they shall be MY people."
◀ Hebrews 8:10 ▶ [ESV]

"But let the ancient wise people teach You; listen to what they had to say."
◀ Job 8:10 ▶ [GNT]

"My opinion is that it is better for You to finish now what You began last year. You were the first, not only to act, but also to be willing to act."
◀ 2 Corinthians 8:10 ▶ [GNT]

"When You have eaten and are satisfied, You shall Bless the LORD your GOD for the GOoD land which HE has given You."
◀ Deuteronomy 8:10 ▶ [NASB]

Powerful Manifestation Prayer:

I BLESS myself, my family and everyone born on this date with GOD's MOST POWERFUL PURE LOVING LIGHT, HIS MOST POWERFUL PURE SOURCE HEALING ENERGY, and an ABUNDANCE OF HIS AMAZING GREATER GRACE in the POWER, the ANOINTING, the AUTHORITY and the WISDOM of the HOLY SPIRIT, in JESUS' MOST HOLY NAME. AMEN INDEED!

Day 223
8:11

"The Pharisees came out and started an argument with **JESUS**. They wanted to test **HIM** by asking for a sign from **Heaven**."
◄ Mark 8:11 ► [CEV]

"This is a sacred day, so don't worry or mourn!" ◄ Nehemiah 8:11 ► [CEV]

"None of them will have to teach their friends or tell their neighbors, 'Know the **LORD**.' For they will all know **ME**, from the least to the greatest." ◄ Hebrews 8:11 ► [GNT]

"**I AM Wisdom**, **I AM** better than jewels; nothing **You** want can compare with **ME**."
◄ Proverbs 8:11 ► [NASB]

"I think **You** should finish what **You** started. If **You** give according to what **You** have, **You** will prove **You** are as eager to give as **You** were to think about giving." ◄ 2 Corinthians 8:11 ► [CEV]

"Beware that **You** do not forget the **LORD** your **GOD** by not keeping **HIS Commandments** and **HIS Ordinances** and **HIS Statutes** which **I AM Commanding You** today."
◄ Deuteronomy 8:11 ► [NASB]

Powerful Manifestation Prayer:

I BLESS myself, my family and everyone born on this date with GOD's MOST POWERFUL PURE LOVING LIGHT, HIS MOST POWERFUL PURE SOURCE HEALING ENERGY, and an ABUNDANCE OF HIS AMAZING GREATER GRACE in the POWER, the ANOINTING, the AUTHORITY and the WISDOM of the HOLY SPIRIT, in JESUS' MOST HOLY NAME. AMEN INDEED!

Day 224
8:12

"It doesn't matter how much You have. What matters is how much You are willing to give from what You have." ◄ 2 Corinthians 8:12 ► [CEV]

"They will plant their crops in peace. Their vines will bear grapes, the earth will produce crops, and there will be plenty of rain. I Will give all these Blessings to the people of MY nation who survive." ◄ Zechariah 8:12 ► [GNT]

"Although a sinner does evil a hundred times and may lengthen his life, still I know that it will be well for those who fear GOD, who fear HIM openly." ◄ Ecclesiastes 8:12 ► [NASB]

"All the people went away to eat, to drink, to send portions and to celebrate a great festival, because they understood the Words which had been made known to them." ◄ Nehemiah 8:12 ► [NASB]

"For I Will be merciful toward their iniquities, and I Will remember their sins no more." ◄ Hebrews 8:12 ► [ESV]

"I AM Wisdom--Common Sense is my closest friend; I possess Knowledge and sound judgment." ◄ Proverbs 8:12 ► [CEV]

Powerful Manifestation Prayer:

I BLESS myself, my family and everyone born on this date with GOD's MOST POWERFUL PURE LOVING LIGHT, HIS MOST POWERFUL PURE SOURCE HEALING ENERGY, and an ABUNDANCE OF HIS AMAZING GREATER GRACE in the POWER, the ANOINTING, the AUTHORITY and the WISDOM of the HOLY SPIRIT, in JESUS' MOST HOLY NAME. AMEN INDEED!

Day 225
8:13

"I am not trying to make life easier for others by making life harder for **You**. But it is only fair."
◄ 2 Corinthians 8:13 ► [CEV]

"By speaking of a **New Covenant**, **GOD** has made the first one old; and anything that becomes old and worn out will **SOON** disappear."
◄ Hebrews 8:13 ► [GNT]

"Such are the paths of all who forget **GOD**; the **HOPE** of the godless shall perish."
◄ Job 8:13 ► [ESV]

"But it will not be well for the evil man and he will not lengthen his days like a shadow, because he does not fear **GOD**."
◄ Ecclesiastes 8:13 ► [NASB]

"**I AM** the **ONE You** should fear and respect. **I AM** the **Holy GOD**, the **LORD All-Powerful**!"
◄ Isaiah 8:13 ► [CEV]

"The fear of the **LORD** is hatred of evil. Pride and arrogance and the way of evil and perverted speech **I** hate."
◄ Proverbs 8:13 ► [ESV]

Powerful Manifestation Prayer:

I BLESS myself, my family and everyone born on this date with GOD's MOST POWERFUL PURE LOVING LIGHT, HIS MOST POWERFUL PURE SOURCE HEALING ENERGY, and an ABUNDANCE OF HIS AMAZING GREATER GRACE in the POWER, the ANOINTING, the AUTHORITY and the WISDOM of the HOLY SPIRIT, in JESUS' MOST HOLY NAME. AMEN INDEED!

Day 226
8:14

"And trust in something as frail as a spider's web--." ◄ Job 8:14 ► [CEV]

"Counsel is **MINE** and sound **Wisdom**; **I AM Understanding**, **Power** is **MINE**."
◄ Proverbs 8:14 ► [NASB]

"The **Disciples** had forgotten to bring any bread, and they had only one loaf with them in the **BOAT**."
◄ Mark 8:14 ► [CEV]

"For **You** to share with them when **You** have so much, and they have so little. Later, when they have more than enough, and **You** are in need, they can share with **You**. Then everyone will have a fair share." ◄ 2 Corinthians 8:14 ► [CEV]

"**HE Will** keep **You** safe. But to Israel and Judah **HE Will** be a stone that makes people stumble, a rock that makes them fall. And for the people of Jerusalem **HE Will** be a trap and a snare."
◄ Isaiah 8:14 ► [NLT]

"Then your heart will become proud and **You** will forget the **LORD** your **GOD WHO** brought **You** out from the land of Egypt, out of the house of slavery." ◄ Deuteronomy 8:14 ► [NLT]

Powerful Manifestation Prayer:

I BLESS myself, my family and everyone born on this date with GOD's MOST POWERFUL PURE LOVING LIGHT, HIS MOST POWERFUL PURE SOURCE HEALING ENERGY, and an ABUNDANCE OF HIS AMAZING GREATER GRACE in the POWER, the ANOINTING, the AUTHORITY and the WISDOM of the HOLY SPIRIT, in JESUS' MOST HOLY NAME. AMEN INDEED!

Day 227
8:15

"As it is written, "Whoever gathered much had nothing left over, and whoever gathered little had no lack." ◀ 2 Corinthians 8:15 ▶ [ESV]

"He trusts in his house, but it does not stand; He holds fast to it, but it does not endure." ◀ Job 8:15 ▶ [NASB]

"So, I am convinced that we should enjoy ourselves, because the only pleasure we have in this life is eating and drinking and enjoying ourselves. We can at least do this as we labor during the life that **GOD** has given us in this world." ◀ Ecclesiastes 8:15 ▶ [GNT]

"For the **SPIRIT** that **GOD** has given **You** does not make **You** slaves and cause **You** to be afraid; instead, the **SPIRIT** makes **You GOD's** children, and by the **SPIRIT's Power** we cry out to **GOD**, "**FATHER**! my **FATHER**!"" ◀ Romans 8:15 ▶ [GNT]

"He said, "**Blessed** be the **LORD**, the **GOD** of Israel, **WHO** spoke with **HIS** mouth to my father David and has fulfilled it with **HIS Hand**." ◀ 1 Kings 8:15 ▶ [NASB]

"Do not forget that **HE** led **You** through the great and terrifying wilderness with its poisonous snakes and scorpions, where it was so hot and dry. **HE** gave **You** water from the rock!" ◀ Deuteronomy 8:15 ▶ [NLT]

Powerful Manifestation Prayer:

I BLESS myself, my family and everyone born on this date with GOD's MOST POWERFUL PURE LOVING LIGHT, HIS MOST POWERFUL PURE SOURCE HEALING ENERGY, and an ABUNDANCE OF HIS AMAZING GREATER GRACE in the POWER, the ANOINTING, the AUTHORITY and the WISDOM of the HOLY SPIRIT, in JESUS' MOST HOLY NAME. AMEN INDEED!

Day 228
8:16

"Evil people sprout like **WEEDS** in the sun, like **WEEDS** that spread all through the garden."
◄ Job 8:16 ► [GNT]

"These are the things which You should do: speak the Truth to one another; judge with Truth and judgment for Peace in your gates."
◄ Zechariah 8:16 ► [NASB]

"The SPIRIT HIMSELF testifies with our Spirit that we are children of GOD."
◄ Romans 8:16 ► [NASB]

"You, MY Disciples, are to guard and preserve the messages that GOD has given ME."
◄ Isaiah 8:16 ► [GNT]

"But thanks be to GOD WHO puts the same earnestness on your behalf in the heart of Titus."
◄ 2 Corinthians 8:16 ► [NASB]

"In the wilderness HE fed You manna which your fathers did not know, that HE might humble You and that HE might test You, to do GOoD for You in the end."
◄ Deuteronomy 8:16 ► [NASB]

Powerful Manifestation Prayer:

I BLESS myself, my family and everyone born on this date with GOD's MOST POWERFUL PURE LOVING LIGHT, HIS MOST POWERFUL PURE SOURCE HEALING ENERGY, and an ABUNDANCE OF HIS AMAZING GREATER GRACE in the POWER, the ANOINTING, the AUTHORITY and the WISDOM of the HOLY SPIRIT, in JESUS' MOST HOLY NAME. AMEN INDEED!

Day 229
8:17

"Do not devise evil in your hearts against one another, and love no false oath, for all these things **I** hate, declares the **LORD**."
◄ Zechariah 8:17 ► [ESV]

"This was to fulfill what was spoken by the prophet Isaiah: "**HE** took our illnesses and bore our diseases."
◄ Matthew 8:17 ► [ESV]

"**I LOVE** those who **Love ME**; and those who diligently seek **ME Will** find **ME**."
◄ Proverbs 8:17 ► [NASB]

"I will wait for the **LORD**, **WHO** is hiding **HIS Face** from the house of Jacob, and I will **HOPE** in **HIM**."
◄ Isaiah 8:17 ► [ESV]

"I saw everything **GOD** does, and I realized no one can really understand what happens. We may be very wise, but no matter how much we try or how much we claim to know, we cannot understand it all."
◄ Ecclesiastes 8:17 ► [CEV]

"So then, **You** must never think that **You** have made yourselves wealthy by your own power and strength."
◄ Deuteronomy 8:17 ► [GNT]

Powerful Manifestation Prayer:

I BLESS myself, my family and everyone born on this date with GOD's MOST POWERFUL PURE LOVING LIGHT, HIS MOST POWERFUL PURE SOURCE HEALING ENERGY, and an ABUNDANCE OF HIS AMAZING GREATER GRACE in the POWER, the ANOINTING, the AUTHORITY and the WISDOM of the HOLY SPIRIT, in JESUS' MOST HOLY NAME. AMEN INDEED!

Day 230
8:18

"Because the gracious **Hand** of our **GOD** was on us." ◄ Ezra 8:18 ► [NIV]

"Riches and honor are with me, enduring wealth and **Righteousness**." ◄ Proverbs 8:18 ► [NASB]

"**YOU WHO** are my **Comforter** in sorrow, my heart is faint within me." ◄ Jeremiah 8:18 ► [NIV]

"But **You** shall remember the **LORD** your **GOD**, for it is **HE WHO** is giving **You** power to make wealth, that **HE** may confirm **HIS Covenant** which **HE** swore to your fathers, as it is this day."
◄ Deuteronomy 8:18 ► [NASB]

"For I consider that the sufferings of this present time are not worthy to be compared with the **Glory** that is to be revealed to us." ◄ Romans 8:18 ► [NASB]

"Behold, I and the children whom the **LORD** has given me are for signs and wonders in Israel from the **LORD** of **Hosts**, **WHO** dwells on Mount Zion." ◄ Isaiah 8:18 ► [NASB]

Powerful Manifestation Prayer:

I BLESS myself, my family and everyone born on this date with GOD's MOST POWERFUL PURE LOVING LIGHT, HIS MOST POWERFUL PURE SOURCE HEALING ENERGY, and an ABUNDANCE OF HIS AMAZING GREATER GRACE in the POWER, the ANOINTING, the AUTHORITY and the WISDOM of the HOLY SPIRIT, in JESUS' MOST HOLY NAME. AMEN INDEED!

Day 231
8:19

"When I broke the five loaves for the five thousand, how many baskets full of broken pieces did You take up?" They said to HIM, "Twelve." ◀ Mark 8:19 ▶ [ESV]

"MY fruit is better than gold, even pure gold, and MY yield better than choicest silver."
◀ Proverbs 8:19 ▶ [NASB]

"And besides that, he has been Chosen and appointed by the churches to travel with us as we carry out this service of Love for the sake of the LORD's Glory and in order to show that we want to help."
◀ 2 Corinthians 8:19 ▶ [GNT]

"And if You forget the LORD your GOD and go after other gods and serve them and worship them, I solemnly warn You today that You shall surely perish." ◀ Deuteronomy 8:19 ▶ [ESV]

"So, they were saying to HIM, 'Where is YOUR FATHER?' JESUS answered, 'You know neither ME nor MY FATHER; if You knew ME, You would know MY FATHER also.'"
◀ John 8:19 ▶ [NASB]

"A teacher of the Law came to HIM. 'TEACHER,' he said, "I am ready to go with YOU wherever YOU go." ◀ Matthew 8:19 ▶ [GNT]

Powerful Manifestation Prayer:

I BLESS myself, my family and everyone born on this date with GOD's MOST POWERFUL PURE LOVING LIGHT, HIS MOST POWERFUL PURE SOURCE HEALING ENERGY, and an ABUNDANCE OF HIS AMAZING GREATER GRACE in the POWER, the ANOINTING, the AUTHORITY and the WISDOM of the HOLY SPIRIT, in JESUS' MOST HOLY NAME. AMEN INDEED!

Day 232
8:20

"I walk in the way of **Righteousness**, along the paths of justice." ◀ Proverbs 8:20 ▶ [NIV]

"Surely **GOD** does not reject one who is blameless or strengthen the hands of evildoers." ◀ Job 8:20 ▶ [NIV]

"And when **I** broke the seven loaves for the four thousand, how many basketfuls of pieces did **You** pick up?" They answered, "Seven." ◀ Mark 8:20 ▶ [NIV]

"Look to **GOD's** instructions and teachings! People who contradict **HIS WORD** are completely in the dark." ◀ Isaiah 8:20 ▶ [NLT]

"Just as the **LORD** has destroyed other nations in your path, **You** also will be destroyed if **You** refuse to obey the **LORD** your **GOD**." ◀ Deuteronomy 8:20 ▶ [NLT]

"**JESUS** made these statements while **HE** was teaching in the section of the Temple known as the Treasury. But **HE** was not arrested, because **HIS** time had not yet come." ◀ John 8:20 ▶ [NLT]

Powerful Manifestation Prayer:

I BLESS myself, my family and everyone born on this date with GOD's MOST POWERFUL PURE LOVING LIGHT, HIS MOST POWERFUL PURE SOURCE HEALING ENERGY, and an ABUNDANCE OF HIS AMAZING GREATER GRACE in the POWER, the ANOINTING, the AUTHORITY and the WISDOM of the HOLY SPIRIT, in JESUS' MOST HOLY NAME. AMEN INDEED!

Day 233
8:21

"And **HE** was saying to them, "Do **You** not yet understand?" ◄ Mark 8:21 ► [NASB]

"I proclaimed a **Fast**, so that we might humble ourselves before our **GOD** and ask **HIM** for a safe journey for us and our children, with all our possessions." ◄ Ezra 8:21 ► [NIV]

"**HE Will** once again fill your mouth with laughter and your lips with shouts of joy." ◄ Job 8:21 ► [NLT]

"And **I** give great riches to everyone who **Loves ME.**" ◄ Proverbs 8:21 ► [CEV]

"For we aim at what is honorable not only in the **LORD's** sight but also in the sight of man." ◄ 2 Corinthians 8:21 ► [ESV]

"The **LORD** smelled the soothing aroma; and the **LORD** said to **HIMSELF**, "**I Will** never again curse the ground on account of man, for the intent of man's heart is evil from his youth; and **I Will** never again destroy every living thing, as **I** have done." ◄ Genesis 8:21 ► [NASB]

Powerful Manifestation Prayer:

I BLESS myself, my family and everyone born on this date with GOD's MOST POWERFUL PURE LOVING LIGHT, HIS MOST POWERFUL PURE SOURCE HEALING ENERGY, and an ABUNDANCE OF HIS AMAZING GREATER GRACE in the POWER, the ANOINTING, the AUTHORITY and the WISDOM of the HOLY SPIRIT, in JESUS' MOST HOLY NAME. AMEN INDEED!

Day 234
8:22

"The **LORD** created **ME** first of all, the first of **HIS** works, long ago." ◀ Proverbs 8:22 ▶ [GNT]

"Those who hate **You** will be clothed with shame, and the tent of the wicked will be no more."
◀ Job 8:22 ▶ [ESV]

"When they arrived…some people brought a blind man to **JESUS**, and they begged **HIM** to touch the man and heal him."
◀ Mark 8:22 ▶ [NLT]

"The **Gracious Hand** of our **GOD** is on everyone who looks to **HIM**, but **HIS** great anger is against all who forsake **HIM**."
◀ Ezra 8:22 ▶ [NIV]

"But **JESUS** said to him, "Follow **ME**, and allow the dead to bury their own dead."
◀ Matthew 8:22 ▶ [NASB]

"While the earth remains, seedtime and harvest, cold and heat, summer and winter, day and night, shall not cease."
◀ Genesis 8:22 ▶ [ESV]

Powerful Manifestation Prayer:

I BLESS myself, my family and everyone born on this date with GOD's MOST POWERFUL PURE LOVING LIGHT, HIS MOST POWERFUL PURE SOURCE HEALING ENERGY, and an ABUNDANCE OF HIS AMAZING GREATER GRACE in the POWER, the ANOINTING, the AUTHORITY and the WISDOM of the HOLY SPIRIT, in JESUS' MOST HOLY NAME. AMEN INDEED!

Day 235
8:23

"So, we **Fasted** and **Prayed** for **GOD** to protect us, and **HE** answered our **Prayers**."
◄ Ezra 8:23 ► [GNT]

"Taking the blind man by the hand, **HE** brought him out of the village; and after spitting on his eyes and laying **HIS Hands** on him, **HE** asked him, "Do **You** see anything?" ◄ Mark 8:23 ► [NASB]

"He said, "O **LORD**, the **GOD** of Israel, there is no **GOD** like **YOU** in **Heaven** above or on earth beneath, keeping covenant and showing lovingkindness to **YOUR** servants who walk before **YOU** with all their heart." ◄ 1 Kings 8:23 ► [NASB]

"**I** was made in the very beginning, at the first, before the world began." ◄ Proverbs 8:23 ► [GNT]

"Thus, says the **LORD** of **Hosts**, 'In those days ten men from all the nations will grasp the garment of a Jew, saying, "Let us go with **YOU**, for we have heard that **GOD** is with **YOU**."
◄ Zechariah 8:23 ► [NASB]

"And when **HE** got into the **BOAT HIS Disciples** followed **HIM**." ◄ Matthew 8:23 ► [ESV]

Powerful Manifestation Prayer:

I BLESS myself, my family and everyone born on this date with GOD's MOST POWERFUL PURE LOVING LIGHT, HIS MOST POWERFUL PURE SOURCE HEALING ENERGY, and an ABUNDANCE OF HIS AMAZING GREATER GRACE in the POWER, the ANOINTING, the AUTHORITY and the WISDOM of the HOLY SPIRIT, in JESUS' MOST HOLY NAME. AMEN INDEED!

Day 236
8:24

"YOU have kept the Promise YOU made to my father David; today every WORD has been fulfilled."
◄ 1 Kings 8:24 ► [GNT]

"A terrible storm suddenly struck the lake, and waves started splashing into their BOAT. JESUS was sound asleep."
◄ Matthew 8:24 ► [CEV]

"They came to JESUS and woke HIM up, saying, "MASTER, MASTER, we are perishing!" And HE got up and rebuked the wind and the surging waves, and they stopped, and it became calm."
◄ Luke 8:24 ► [NASB]

"I was born before the oceans, when there were no springs of water." ◄ Proverbs 8:24 ► [GNT]

"That is why I told You that You will die in your sins. And You will die in your sins if You do not believe that I AM WHO I AM."
◄ John 8:24 ► [GNT]

"Treat them in such a way that the churches will see your Love and will know why we bragged about You."
◄ 2 Corinthians 8:24 ► [CEV]

Powerful Manifestation Prayer:

I BLESS myself, my family and everyone born on this date with GOD's MOST POWERFUL PURE LOVING LIGHT, HIS MOST POWERFUL PURE SOURCE HEALING ENERGY, and an ABUNDANCE OF HIS AMAZING GREATER GRACE in the POWER, the ANOINTING, the AUTHORITY and the WISDOM of the HOLY SPIRIT, in JESUS' MOST HOLY NAME. AMEN INDEED!

Day 237
8:25

"I was born before the mountains, before the hills were set in place." ◀ Proverbs 8:25 ▶ [GNT]

"'WHO are YOU?' they asked JESUS. JESUS answered, "I AM exactly WHO I told You at the beginning.'" ◀ John 8:25 ▶ [CEV]

"LORD GOD of Israel, YOU Promised my father that someone from his family would always be king of Israel if they do their best to obey YOU, just as he did." ◀ 1 Kings 8:25 ▶ [CEV]

"So, the Disciples went over to HIM and woke HIM up. They said, 'LORD, wake up! Save us before we drown!" ◀ Matthew 8:25 ▶ [CEV]

"HE said to them, "Where is your Faith?" And they were afraid, and they marveled, saying to one another, 'WHO then is this, that HE Commands even winds and water, and they obey HIM'?" ◀ Luke 8:25 ▶ [ESV]

"Then JESUS laid HIS Hands on his eyes again; and he opened his eyes, his sight was restored, and he saw everything clearly." ◀ Mark 8:25 ▶ [ESV]

Powerful Manifestation Prayer:

I BLESS myself, my family and everyone born on this date with GOD's MOST POWERFUL PURE LOVING LIGHT, HIS MOST POWERFUL PURE SOURCE HEALING ENERGY, and an ABUNDANCE OF HIS AMAZING GREATER GRACE in the POWER, the ANOINTING, the AUTHORITY and the WISDOM of the HOLY SPIRIT, in JESUS' MOST HOLY NAME. AMEN INDEED!

Day 238
8:26

"It happened long before GOD had made the earth or any of its fields or even the dust."
◀ Proverbs 8:26 ▶ [CEV]

"Now therefore, O GOD of Israel, let YOUR WORD, I Pray, be confirmed which YOU have spoken to YOUR servant, my father David."
◀ 1 Kings 8:26 ▶ [NASB]

"And HE said to them, "Why are You afraid, O You of little Faith?" Then HE rose and rebuked the winds and the sea, and there was a great calm."
◀ Matthew 8:26 ▶ [ESV]

"There is a lot more I could say to condemn You. But the ONE WHO sent ME is Truthful, and I tell the people of this world only what I have heard from HIM."
◀ John 8:26 ▶ [CEV]

"In the same way the SPIRIT also helps our weakness; for we do not know how to Pray as we should, but the SPIRIT HIMSELF intercedes for us with groanings too deep for words."
◀ Romans 8:26 ▶ [NASB]

"The vision of the evenings and mornings which has been told is True; but keep the vision secret for it pertains to many days in the future."
◀ Daniel 8:26 ▶ [NASB]

Powerful Manifestation Prayer:

I BLESS myself, my family and everyone born on this date with GOD's MOST POWERFUL PURE LOVING LIGHT, HIS MOST POWERFUL PURE SOURCE HEALING ENERGY, and an ABUNDANCE OF HIS AMAZING GREATER GRACE in the POWER, the ANOINTING, the AUTHORITY and the WISDOM of the HOLY SPIRIT, in JESUS' MOST HOLY NAME. AMEN INDEED!

Day 239
8:27

"I was there when the LORD put the Heavens in place and stretched the sky over the surface of the sea."
◀ Proverbs 8:27 ▶ [CEV]

"But will GOD indeed dwell on the earth? Behold, Heaven and the highest Heaven cannot contain YOU, how much less this house which I have built!"
◀ 1 Kings 8:27 ▶ [NASB]

"JESUS went out along with HIS Disciples to the villages of Caesarea Philippi; and on the way HE questioned HIS Disciples, saying to them, 'WHO do people say that I AM'?"
◀ Mark 8:27 ▶ [NASB]

"The men were amazed, and said, 'What kind of a MAN is this, that even the winds and the sea obey HIM'?"
◀ Matthew 8:27 ▶ [NASB]

"They did not understand that HE was telling them about HIS FATHER."
◀ John 8:27 ▶ [NIV]

"And GOD, WHO sees into our hearts, knows what the thought of the SPIRIT is; because the SPIRIT pleads with GOD on behalf of HIS people and in accordance with HIS Will."
◀ Romans 8:27 ▶ [GNT]

Powerful Manifestation Prayer:

I BLESS myself, my family and everyone born on this date with GOD's MOST POWERFUL PURE LOVING LIGHT, HIS MOST POWERFUL PURE SOURCE HEALING ENERGY, and an ABUNDANCE OF HIS AMAZING GREATER GRACE in the POWER, the ANOINTING, the AUTHORITY and the WISDOM of the HOLY SPIRIT, in JESUS' MOST HOLY NAME. AMEN INDEED!

Day 240
8:28

"Pharaoh said, "I will let You go to offer sacrifices to the LORD your GOD in the wilderness, but You must not go very far. Now Pray for me." ◄ Exodus 8:28 ► [NIV]

"LORD my GOD, I am YOUR servant. Listen to my Prayer and grant the requests I make to YOU today." ◄ 1 Kings 8:28 ► [GNT]

"I was with HIM when HE placed the clouds in the sky and created the springs that fill the ocean." ◄ Proverbs 8:28 ► [CEV]

"So, JESUS said, "When You lift up the SON of Man, then You will know that I AM HE, and I do nothing on MY OWN initiative, but I speak these things as the FATHER taught ME." ◄ John 8:28 ► [NASB]

"This was the ordination offering. It was a pleasing aroma, a special gift presented to the LORD." ◄ Leviticus 8:28 ► [NLT]

"And we know that GOD causes all things to work together for GOoD to those who Love GOD, to those who are called according to HIS Purpose." ◄ Romans 8:28 ► [NASB]

Powerful Manifestation Prayer:

I BLESS myself, my family and everyone born on this date with GOD's MOST POWERFUL PURE LOVING LIGHT, HIS MOST POWERFUL PURE SOURCE HEALING ENERGY, and an ABUNDANCE OF HIS AMAZING GREATER GRACE in the POWER, the ANOINTING, the AUTHORITY and the WISDOM of the HOLY SPIRIT, in JESUS' MOST HOLY NAME. AMEN INDEED!

Day 241
8:29

"For those GOD foreknew HE also predestined to be conformed to the image of HIS SON, that he might be the firstborn among many brothers and sisters." ◀ Romans 8:29 ▶ [NIV]

"I was there when HE set boundaries for the sea to make it obey HIM, and when HE laid foundations to support the earth." ◀ Proverbs 8:29 ▶ [CEV]

"For JESUS had commanded the impure spirit to come out of the man." ◀ Luke 8:29 ▶ [NIV]

"The ONE WHO sent ME is with ME; HE has not left ME alone, for I always do what pleases HIM." ◀ John 8:29 ▶ [NIV]

"But what about You?" HE asked. "WHO do You say I AM?" Peter answered, 'YOU are the MESSIAH'." ◀ Mark 8:29 ▶ [NIV]

"Moses answered, "As **SOON** as I leave, I will Pray to the LORD that tomorrow the flies will leave You, your officials, and your people. But You must not deceive us again and prevent the people from going to sacrifice to the LORD." ◀ Exodus 8:29 ▶ [GNT]

"May YOUR eyes be open toward this temple night and day, this place of which YOU said, "MY Name shall be there," so that YOU Will hear the Prayer YOUR servant Prays toward this place." ◀ 1 Kings 8:29 ▶ [NIV]

Powerful Manifestation Prayer:

I BLESS myself, my family and everyone born on this date with GOD's MOST POWERFUL PURE LOVING LIGHT, HIS MOST POWERFUL PURE SOURCE HEALING ENERGY, and an ABUNDANCE OF HIS AMAZING GREATER GRACE in the POWER, the ANOINTING, the AUTHORITY and the WISDOM of the HOLY SPIRIT, in JESUS' MOST HOLY NAME. AMEN INDEED!

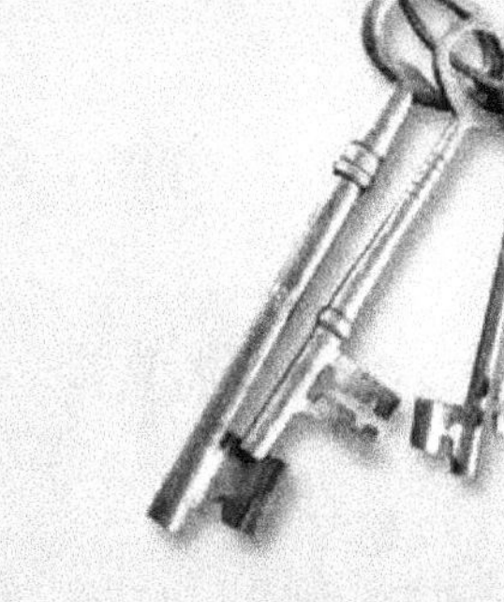

Day 242
8:30

"So Moses went out from Pharaoh and Prayed to the LORD." ◀ Exodus 8:30 ▶ [ESV]

"Hear my Prayers and the Prayers of YOUR people when they face this place and Pray. In YOUR home in Heaven hear us and forgive us." ◀ 1Kings 8:30 ▶ [GNT]

"I was right beside the LORD, helping HIM plan and build. I made HIM happy each day, and I was happy at HIS side." ◀ Proverbs 8:30 ▶ [CEV]

"As HE spoke these things, many came to believe in HIM." ◀ John 8:30 ▶ [NASB]

"And those whom HE predestined HE also called, and those whom HE called HE also justified, and those whom HE justified HE also Glorified." ◀ Romans 8:30 ▶ [ESV]

"JESUS warned the Disciples not to tell anyone about HIM." ◀ Mark 8:30 ▶ [CEV]

Powerful Manifestation Prayer:

I BLESS myself, my family and everyone born on this date with GOD's MOST POWERFUL PURE LOVING LIGHT, HIS MOST POWERFUL PURE SOURCE HEALING ENERGY, and an ABUNDANCE OF HIS AMAZING GREATER GRACE in the POWER, the ANOINTING, the AUTHORITY and the WISDOM of the HOLY SPIRIT, in JESUS' MOST HOLY NAME. AMEN INDEED!

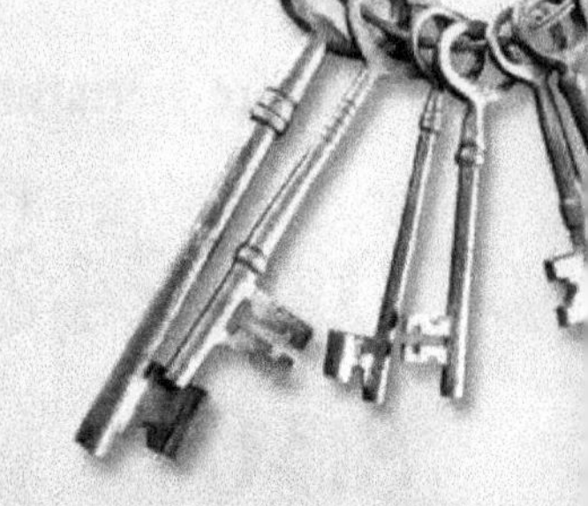

Day 243
8:31

He **[Joshua]** followed the commands that Moses, the **LORD's** servant, had written in the Book of Instruction: 'Make **ME** an altar from stones that are uncut and have not been shaped with iron tools.' Then on the altar they presented burnt offerings and peace offerings to the **LORD**."

◀ Joshua 8:31 ▶ [NLT]

"The demons kept begging **JESUS** not to send them into the bottomless pit."

◀ Luke 8:31 ▶ [NLT]

"What then shall we say to these things? If **GOD** is for us, who can be against us?"

◀ Romans 8:31 ▶ [ESV]

"And how happy **I** was with the world **HE** created; how **I** rejoiced with the human family!"

◀ Proverbs 8:31 ▶ [NLT]

"Then **JESUS** began to tell them that the **SON** of **Man** must suffer many terrible things and be rejected by the elders, the leading priests, and the teachers of religious law. **HE** would be killed, but three days later **HE** would rise from the dead."

◀ Mark 8:31 ▶ [NLT]

"So, **JESUS** said to the Jews who had believed **HIM**, "If **You** abide in **MY WORD**, **You** are truly **MY Disciples**."

◀ John 8:31 ▶ [ESV]

Powerful Manifestation Prayer:

I BLESS myself, my family and everyone born on this date with GOD's MOST POWERFUL PURE LOVING LIGHT, HIS MOST POWERFUL PURE SOURCE HEALING ENERGY, and an ABUNDANCE OF HIS AMAZING GREATER GRACE in the POWER, the ANOINTING, the AUTHORITY and the WISDOM of the HOLY SPIRIT, in JESUS' MOST HOLY NAME. AMEN INDEED!

September
9

~ I Pray for You and You Pray for Me!

"After Job had prayed for his friends, the LORD restored his fortunes and gave him twice as much as he had before." ◄ Job 42:10 ► [NIV]

"You haven't done this before. A.S.K. using MY NAME, and You will receive, and You will have abundant joy." ◄ John 16:24 ► [NLT]

Powerful Manifestation Prayer:

I BLESS myself, my family and everyone born in this month with GOD's MOST POWERFUL PURE LOVING LIGHT, HIS MOST POWERFUL PURE SOURCE HEALING ENERGY, and an ABUNDANCE OF HIS AMAZING GREATER GRACE in the POWER, the ANOINTING, the AUTHORITY and the WISDOM of the HOLY SPIRIT, in JESUS' MOST HOLY NAME.
AMEN INDEED!

A.S.K.- Additional Scripture Knowledge

Write Additional Scriptures here.

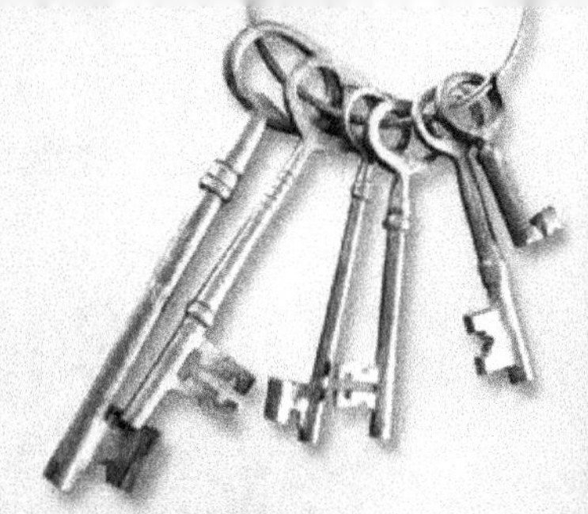

Day 244
9:1

"On this day their enemies had hoped to overpower them, but now the tables were turned, and they got the upper hand over those who hated them." ◀ Esther 9:1 ▶ [NIV]

"**JESUS** called together **HIS** twelve **Apostles** and gave them complete **Power** over all demons and diseases." ◀ Luke 9:1 ▶ [CEV]

"I will praise **YOU, LORD**, with all my heart; I will tell of all the wonderful things **YOU** have done." ◀ Psalm 9:1 ▶ [GNT]

"This, too, I carefully explored: Even though the actions of **GODly** and wise people are in **GOD's Hands**, no one knows whether **GOD Will** show them **Favor**." ◀ Ecclesiastes 9:1 ▶ [NLT]

"But there will be no more gloom for her who was in anguish." ◀ Isaiah 9:1 ▶ [NASB]

"I am telling the **Truth** in **CHRIST**, I am not lying, my conscience testifies with me in the **HOLY SPIRIT**." ◀ Romans 9:1 ▶ [NASB]

Powerful Manifestation Prayer:

I BLESS myself, my family and everyone born on this date with GOD's MOST POWERFUL PURE LOVING LIGHT, HIS MOST POWERFUL PURE SOURCE HEALING ENERGY, and an ABUNDANCE OF HIS AMAZING GREATER GRACE in the POWER, the ANOINTING, the AUTHORITY and the WISDOM of the HOLY SPIRIT, in JESUS' MOST HOLY NAME. AMEN INDEED!

Day 245
9:2

"The people who walk in darkness will see a great **Light**; Those who live in a dark land, the **Light** will shine on them." ◀ Isaiah 9:2 ▶ [NASB]

"I will be glad and exult in **YOU**; I will sing praise to **YOUR Name, O Most High**." ◀ Psalm 9:2 ▶ [NASB]

"Yes, I know all this is true in principle. But how can a person be declared innocent in **GOD's** sight?" ◀ Job 9:2 ▶ [NLT]

"And in the cities of every province they came together to attack their enemies. Everyone was afraid of the Jews, and no one could do anything to oppose them." ◀ Esther 9:2 ▶ [CEV]

"And they brought to **HIM** a paralytic lying on a bed. Seeing their **Faith**, **JESUS** said to the paralytic, 'Take courage, son; your sins are forgiven'." ◀ Matthew 9:2 ▶ [NASB]

"Then **HE** sent them to tell about **GOD's Kingdom** and to heal the sick." ◀ Luke 9:2 ▶ [CEV]

Powerful Manifestation Prayer:

I BLESS myself, my family and everyone born on this date with GOD's MOST POWERFUL PURE LOVING LIGHT, HIS MOST POWERFUL PURE SOURCE HEALING ENERGY, and an ABUNDANCE OF HIS AMAZING GREATER GRACE in the POWER, the ANOINTING, the AUTHORITY and the WISDOM of the HOLY SPIRIT, in JESUS' MOST HOLY NAME. AMEN INDEED!

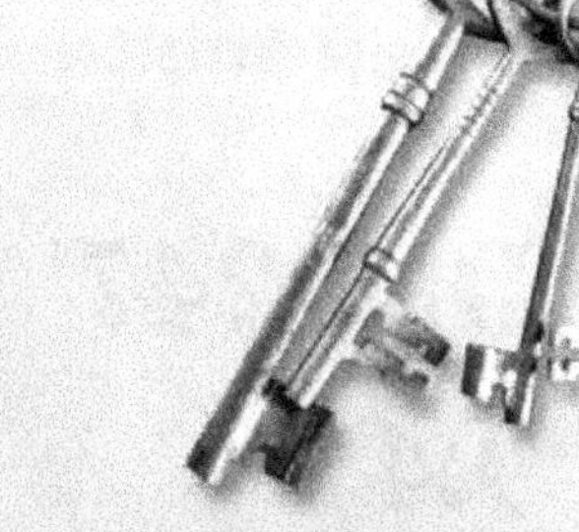

Day 246
9:3

"The LORD replied: Lies come from the mouths of MY people, like arrows from a bow. With each dishonest deed their power increases, and not one of them will admit that I AM GOD."
◄ Jeremiah 9:3 ► [CEV]

"When my enemies turn back, they stumble and perish before YOU." ◄ Psalm 9:3 ► [NASB]

"And the LORD said to him, "I have heard your Prayer and your plea, which You have made before ME. I have consecrated this house that You have built, by putting MY Name there forever. MY Eyes and MY Heart Will be there for all time." ◄ 1 Kings 9:3 ► [ESV]

"For three hours they stood and listened to the Law of the LORD their GOD, and then for the next three hours they confessed their sins and worshiped the LORD." ◄ Nehemiah 9:3 ► [CEV]

"JESUS answered, 'It was neither that this man sinned, nor his parents; but it was so that the works of GOD might be displayed in him." ◄ John 9:3 ► [NASB]

"Now as HE went on HIS way…suddenly a Light from Heaven shone around HIM."
◄ Acts 9:3 ► [ESV]

Powerful Manifestation Prayer:

I BLESS myself, my family and everyone born on this date with GOD's MOST POWERFUL PURE LOVING LIGHT, HIS MOST POWERFUL PURE SOURCE HEALING ENERGY, and an ABUNDANCE OF HIS AMAZING GREATER GRACE in the POWER, the ANOINTING, the AUTHORITY and the WISDOM of the HOLY SPIRIT, in JESUS' MOST HOLY NAME. AMEN INDEED!

Day 247
9:4

"YOU have broken the power of those who abused and enslaved your people. YOU have rescued them just as YOU saved your people from Midian." ◀ Isaiah 9:4 ▶ [CEV]

"And they cried with a loud voice to the LORD their GOD." ◀ Nehemiah 9:4 ▶ [ESV]

"YOU are fair and honest in your judgments, and YOU have judged in my Favor." ◀ Psalm 9:4 ▶ [GNT]

"For Mordecai was great in the king's house, and his fame spread throughout all the provinces, for the man Mordecai grew more and more powerful." ◀ Esther 9:4 ▶ [ESV]

"We must work the works of HIM WHO sent ME as long as it is day; night is coming when no one can work." ◀ John 9:4 ▶ [NASB]

"Whatever house You enter, stay there until You leave that city." ◀ Luke 9:4 ▶ [NASB]

Powerful Manifestation Prayer:

I BLESS myself, my family and everyone born on this date with GOD's MOST POWERFUL PURE LOVING LIGHT, HIS MOST POWERFUL PURE SOURCE HEALING ENERGY, and an ABUNDANCE OF HIS AMAZING GREATER GRACE in the POWER, the ANOINTING, the AUTHORITY and the WISDOM of the HOLY SPIRIT, in JESUS' MOST HOLY NAME. AMEN INDEED!

Day 248
9:5

"If anyone takes human life, he will be punished. **I Will** punish with death any animal that takes a human life."
◀ Genesis 9:5 ▶ [GNT]

"**YOU** have rebuked the nations, **YOU** have destroyed the wicked; **YOU** have blotted out their name forever and ever."
◀ Psalm 9:5 ▶ [NASB]

"Yes, the living know they are going to die, but the dead know nothing. They have no further reward; they are completely forgotten."
◀ Ecclesiastes 9:5 ▶ [GNT]

"Arise, **Bless** the **LORD** your **GOD** forever and ever! O may **YOUR Glorious Name** be **Blessed** and exalted above all **Blessing** and **Praise**."
◀ Nehemiah 9:5 ▶ [NASB]

"And as for those who do not receive **You**, as **You** go out from that city, shake the dust off your feet as a testimony against them."
◀ Luke 9:5 ▶ [NASB]

"While **I AM** in the world, **I AM** the **Light** of the world."
◀ John 9:5 ▶ [NASB]

Powerful Manifestation Prayer:

I BLESS myself, my family and everyone born on this date with GOD's MOST POWERFUL PURE LOVING LIGHT, HIS MOST POWERFUL PURE SOURCE HEALING ENERGY, and an ABUNDANCE OF HIS AMAZING GREATER GRACE in the POWER, the ANOINTING, the AUTHORITY and the WISDOM of the HOLY SPIRIT, in JESUS' MOST HOLY NAME. AMEN INDEED!

Day 249
9:6

"And then the people of Israel **Prayed** this **Prayer**: '**YOU**, **LORD**, **YOU Alone** are **LORD**; **YOU** made the **Heavens** and the stars of the sky. **YOU** made land and sea and everything in them; **YOU** gave life to all. The **Heavenly Powers** bow down and worship **YOU**." ◀ Nehemiah 9:6 ▶ [GNT]

"For to us a **CHILD** is born, to us a **SON** is given; and the government shall be upon **HIS Shoulder**, and **HIS Name** shall be called **Wonderful Counselor, Mighty GOD, Everlasting FATHER, Prince of Peace**." ◀ Isaiah 9:6 ▶ [ESV]

"Departing, they began going throughout the villages, preaching the **Gospel** and healing everywhere." ◀ Luke 9:6 ▶ [NASB]

"Indeed, their **Love**, their hate and their zeal have already perished, and they will no longer have a share in all that is done under the sun." ◀ Ecclesiastes 9:6 ▶ [NASB]

"Our enemies are destroyed completely for all time. Their cities are torn down, and they will never be remembered again." ◀ Psalm 9:6 ▶ [CEV]

"The point is this: whoever sows sparingly will also reap sparingly, and whoever sows bountifully will also reap bountifully." ◀ 2 Corinthians 9:6 ▶ [ESV]

Powerful Manifestation Prayer:

I BLESS myself, my family and everyone born on this date with GOD's MOST POWERFUL PURE LOVING LIGHT, HIS MOST POWERFUL PURE SOURCE HEALING ENERGY, and an ABUNDANCE OF HIS AMAZING GREATER GRACE in the POWER, the ANOINTING, the AUTHORITY and the WISDOM of the HOLY SPIRIT, in JESUS' MOST HOLY NAME. AMEN INDEED!

Day 250
9:7

"**HE** told him, "Go wash yourself in the pool of Siloam" (Siloam means "sent"). So the man went and washed and came back seeing!" ◀ John 9:7 ▶ [NLT]

"**YOU** rule forever, **LORD**, and **YOU** are on **YOUR** throne, ready for judgment." ◀ Psalm 9:7 ▶ [CEV]

"Each person should do as he has decided in his heart--not reluctantly or out of compulsion, since **GOD Loves** a cheerful giver." ◀ 2 Corinthians 9:7 ▶ [CSB]

"There will be no end to the increase of **HIS** government or of peace, On the throne of **David** and over his kingdom, To establish it and to uphold it with justice and **Righteousness** from then on and forevermore. The zeal of the **LORD** of **Hosts Will** accomplish this." ◀ Isaiah 9:7 ▶ [NASB]

"Nor are all of Abraham's descendants the **Children** of **GOD**. **GOD** said to Abraham, "It is through Isaac that **You** will have the descendants **I Promised You**."" ◀ Romans 9:7 ▶ [GNT]

"As for **You**, be fruitful and multiply; populate the earth abundantly and multiply in it." ◀ Genesis 9:7 ▶ [NASB]

"Go then, eat your bread in happiness and drink your wine with a cheerful heart; for **GOD** has already approved your works." ◀ Ecclesiastes 9:7 ▶ [NASB]

Powerful Manifestation Prayer:

I BLESS myself, my family and everyone born on this date with GOD's MOST POWERFUL PURE LOVING LIGHT, HIS MOST POWERFUL PURE SOURCE HEALING ENERGY, and an ABUNDANCE OF HIS AMAZING GREATER GRACE in the POWER, the ANOINTING, the AUTHORITY and the WISDOM of the HOLY SPIRIT, in JESUS' MOST HOLY NAME. AMEN INDEED!

Day 251
9:8

"And Moses said to them, "Wait, that I may hear what the **LORD Will** command concerning **You**."
◄ Numbers 9:8 ► [ESV]

"Because he was **Faithful**, **YOU** made an agreement to give his descendants the land .... Now **YOU** have kept **YOUR Promise**, just as **YOU** always do."
◄ Nehemiah 9:8 ► [CEV]

"And **GOD** is able to make all **Grace** abound to **You**, so that always having all sufficiency in everything, **You** may have an abundance for every **GOoD** deed."
◄ 2 Corinthians 9:8 ► [NASB]

"And **HE Will** judge the world in **Righteousness**; **HE Will** execute judgment for the peoples with equity."
◄ Psalm 9:8 ► [NASB]

"**GOD** says, '**I Will** stand guard to protect **MY Temple** from those who come to attack. **I** know what's happening, and no one will mistreat **MY** people ever again."
◄ Zechariah 9:8 ► [CEV]

"Let your garments be always white. Let not oil be lacking on your head."
◄ Ecclesiastes 9:8 ► [ESV]

Powerful Manifestation Prayer:

I BLESS myself, my family and everyone born on this date with GOD's MOST POWERFUL PURE LOVING LIGHT, HIS MOST POWERFUL PURE SOURCE HEALING ENERGY, and an ABUNDANCE OF HIS AMAZING GREATER GRACE in the POWER, the ANOINTING, the AUTHORITY and the WISDOM of the HOLY SPIRIT, in JESUS' MOST HOLY NAME. AMEN INDEED!

Day 252
9:9

"Everyone in Jerusalem, celebrate and shout! Your **KING** has won a victory, and **HE** is coming to **You**. **HE** is humble and rides on a donkey; **HE** comes on the colt of a donkey."
◀ Zechariah 9:9 ▶ [CEV]

"As it is written, "**HE** has distributed **Freely**, **HE** has given to the poor; **HIS Righteousness** endures forever."
◀ 2 Corinthians 9:9 ▶ [ESV]

"The **LORD** is a stronghold for the oppressed, a stronghold in times of trouble."
◀ Psalm 9:9 ▶ [ESV]

"**YOU** saw the affliction of our fathers in Egypt and heard their cry by the Red Sea."
◀ Nehemiah 9:9 ▶ [NASB]

"Enjoy life with your wife, whom **You Love**, all the days of your vain life that **HE** has given **You** under the sun, because that is your portion in life and in your toil at which **You** toil under the sun."
◀ Ecclesiastes 9:9 ▶ [ESV]

"And as they were coming down the mountain, **HE** charged them to tell no one what they had seen, until the **SON** of **Man** had risen from the dead."
◀ Mark 9:9 ▶ [ESV]

Powerful Manifestation Prayer:

I BLESS myself, my family and everyone born on this date with GOD's MOST POWERFUL PURE LOVING LIGHT, HIS MOST POWERFUL PURE SOURCE HEALING ENERGY, and an ABUNDANCE OF HIS AMAZING GREATER GRACE in the POWER, the ANOINTING, the AUTHORITY and the WISDOM of the HOLY SPIRIT, in JESUS' MOST HOLY NAME. AMEN INDEED!

Day 253
9:10

"The fear of the **LORD** is the beginning of **Wisdom**, and the **Knowledge** of the **Holy ONE** is **Understanding**." ◄ Proverbs 9:10 ► [NASB]

"And **GOD**, **WHO** supplies seed for the sower and bread to eat, will also supply **You** with all the seed **You** need and will make it grow and produce a rich harvest from your generosity."
◄ 2 Corinthians 9:10 ► [GNT]

"And those who know **YOUR Name Will** put their trust in **YOU**, for **YOU, O LORD**, have not forsaken those who seek **YOU**." ◄ Psalm 9:10 ► [NASB]

"**YOU** worked amazing miracles against the king, against his officials and the people of his land, because **YOU** knew how they oppressed **YOUR** people. **YOU** won then the fame **YOU** still have today." ◄ Nehemiah 9:10 ► [GNT]

"Work hard at whatever **You** do, because there will be no action, no thought, no **Knowledge**, no **Wisdom** in the world of the dead--and that is where **You** are going." ◄ Ecclesiastes 9:10 ► [GNT]

"If any of **You** or your descendants touch a dead body and become unfit to worship **ME**, or if **You** are away on a long journey, **You** may still celebrate **Passover**." ◄ Numbers 9:10 ► [CEV]

Powerful Manifestation Prayer:

I BLESS myself, my family and everyone born on this date with GOD's MOST POWERFUL PURE LOVING LIGHT, HIS MOST POWERFUL PURE SOURCE HEALING ENERGY, and an ABUNDANCE OF HIS AMAZING GREATER GRACE in the POWER, the ANOINTING, the AUTHORITY and the WISDOM of the HOLY SPIRIT, in JESUS' MOST HOLY NAME. AMEN INDEED!

Day 254
9:11

"Again, I saw that under the sun the race is not to the swift, nor the battle to the strong, nor bread to the wise, nor riches to the intelligent, nor **Favor** to those with **Knowledge**, but time and chance happen to them all."
◄ Ecclesiastes 9:11 ► [ESV]

"**You** will be enriched in every way to be generous in every way, which through us will produce thanksgiving to **GOD**."
◄ 2 Corinthians 9:11 ► [ESV]

"But when **CHRIST** appeared as a **High Priest** of the **GOoD** things to come, **HE** entered through the greater and more perfect **Tabernacle**, not made with hands, that is to say, not of this creation."
◄ Hebrews 9:11 ► [NASB]

"**YOU** divided the deep sea, and **YOUR** people walked through on dry land. But **YOU** tossed their enemies in, and they sank down like a heavy stone."
◄ Nehemiah 9:11 ► [CEV]

"When the crowds heard about it, they followed **HIM**. **HE** welcomed them, spoke to them about the **Kingdom** of **GOD**, and healed those who needed it."
◄ Luke 9:11 ► [GNT]

"Sing praise to the **LORD**, **WHO** rules in Zion! Tell every nation what **HE** has done!"
◄ Psalm 9:11 ► [GNT]

Powerful Manifestation Prayer:

I BLESS myself, my family and everyone born on this date with GOD's MOST POWERFUL PURE LOVING LIGHT, HIS MOST POWERFUL PURE SOURCE HEALING ENERGY, and an ABUNDANCE OF HIS AMAZING GREATER GRACE in the POWER, the ANOINTING, the AUTHORITY and the WISDOM of the HOLY SPIRIT, in JESUS' MOST HOLY NAME. AMEN INDEED!

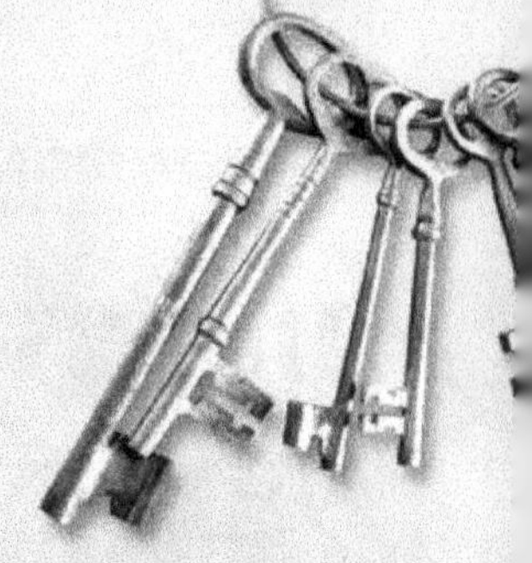

Day 255
9:12

"Each day **YOU** led **YOUR** people with a thick cloud, and at night **YOU** showed the way with a flaming fire." ◄ Nehemiah 9:12 ► [CEV]

"If others have the right to do this, we have an even greater right. But we haven't used this right of ours. We are willing to put up with anything to keep from causing trouble for the message about **CHRIST**." ◄ 2 Corinthians 9:12 ► [CEV]

"**HE** entered once for all into the **Holy Places**, not by means of the blood of goats and calves but by means of **HIS OWN Blood**, thus securing an **Eternal Redemption**." ◄ Hebrews 9:12 ► [ESV]

"For **HE WHO** avenges blood is mindful of them; **HE** does not forget the cry of the afflicted." ◄ Psalm 9:12 ► [ESV]

"What then have they done in the rest of the king's provinces! Now what is your petition? It shall even be granted **You**. And what is your further request? It shall also be done." ◄ Esther 9:12 ► [NASB]

"Come back to the place of safety, all **You** prisoners who still have **HOPE**! **I Promise** this very day that **I Will** repay two **Blessings** for each of your troubles." ◄ Zechariah 9:12 ► [NLT]

Powerful Manifestation Prayer:

I BLESS myself, my family and everyone born on this date with GOD's MOST POWERFUL PURE LOVING LIGHT, HIS MOST POWERFUL PURE SOURCE HEALING ENERGY, and an ABUNDANCE OF HIS AMAZING GREATER GRACE in the POWER, the ANOINTING, the AUTHORITY and the WISDOM of the HOLY SPIRIT, in JESUS' MOST HOLY NAME. AMEN INDEED!

Day 256
9:13

“Don't You know that people who work in the temple make their living from what is brought to the temple? Don't You know that a person who serves at the altar is given part of what is offered?”
◀ 1 Corinthians 9:13 ▶ [CEV]

“The way in which You have proved yourselves by this service will bring honor and Praise to GOD. You believed the message about CHRIST, and You obeyed it by sharing generously with GOD's people and with everyone else.” ◀ 2 Corinthians 9:13 ▶ [CEV]

“Be merciful to me, O LORD! See the sufferings my enemies cause me! Rescue me from death, O LORD.” ◀ Psalm 9:13 ▶ [GNT]

“Then YOU came down on Mount Sinai and spoke with them from Heaven; YOU gave them just ordinances and True Laws, GOoD statutes and commandments.” ◀ Nehemiah 9:13 ▶ [NASB]

“But the man who is clean and is not on a journey, and yet neglects to observe the Passover, that person shall then be cut off from his people, for he did not present the offering of the LORD at its appointed time. That man will bear his sin.” ◀ Numbers 9:13 ▶ [NASB]

“I have placed MY Rainbow in the clouds. It is the sign of MY Covenant with You and with all the earth.” ◀ Genesis 9:13 ▶ [NLT]

Powerful Manifestation Prayer:

I BLESS myself, my family and everyone born on this date with GOD's MOST POWERFUL PURE LOVING LIGHT, HIS MOST POWERFUL PURE SOURCE HEALING ENERGY, and an ABUNDANCE OF HIS AMAZING GREATER GRACE in the POWER, the ANOINTING, the AUTHORITY and the WISDOM of the HOLY

SPIRIT, in JESUS' MOST HOLY NAME. AMEN INDEED!

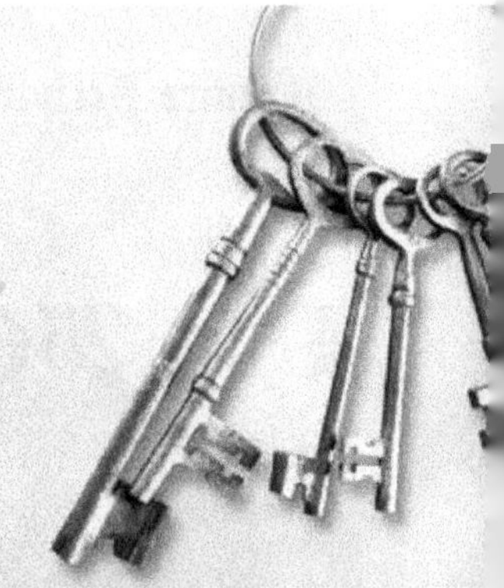

Day 257
9:14

"And so, with deep affection they will **Pray** for **You** because of the extraordinary **Grace GOD** has shown **You**." ◄ 2 Corinthians 9:14 ► [GNT]

"Just think how much more the **Blood** of **CHRIST Will** purify our consciences from sinful deeds so that we can worship the **Living GOD**. For by the **Power** of the **Eternal SPIRIT**, **CHRIST** offered **HIMSELF** to **GOD** as a perfect sacrifice for our sins." ◄ Hebrews 9:14 ► [NLT]

"That I may stand before the people of Jerusalem and tell them all the things for which I **Praise YOU**. I will rejoice because **YOU** saved me." ◄ Psalm 9:14 ► [GNT]

"**YOU** commanded them to respect **YOUR Holy Sabbath**, and **YOU** instructed **YOUR** servant Moses to teach them **YOUR Laws**." ◄ Nehemiah 9:14 ► [CEV]

"In the same way, **The LORD** wants everyone who preaches the **GOoD News** to make a living from preaching this message." ◄ 1 Corinthians 9:14 ► [CEV]

"Then **The LORD Will** appear over them, and **HIS** arrow will go forth like lightning; **The LORD GOD Will** sound the trumpet and will march forth in the whirlwinds of the south." ◄ Zechariah 9:14 ► [ESV]

Powerful Manifestation Prayer:

I BLESS myself, my family and everyone born on this date with GOD's MOST POWERFUL PURE LOVING LIGHT, HIS MOST POWERFUL PURE SOURCE HEALING ENERGY, and an ABUNDANCE OF HIS AMAZING GREATER GRACE in the POWER, the ANOINTING, the AUTHORITY and the WISDOM of the HOLY SPIRIT, in JESUS' MOST HOLY NAME. AMEN INDEED!

Day 258
9:15

"JESUS answered, "Do You expect the guests at a wedding party to be sad as long as the bridegroom is with them? Of course not! But the day will come when the Bridegroom will be taken away from them, and then they will fast." ◀ Matthew 9:15 ▶ [GNT]

"YOU gave them bread from Heaven for their hunger and brought water for them out of the rock for their thirst, and YOU told them to go in to possess the land that YOU had sworn to give them." ◀ Nehemiah 9:15 ▶ [ESV]

"I will remember MY Promise to You and to all other living creatures. Never again will I let floodwaters destroy all life." ◀ Genesis 9:15 ▶ [CEV]

"But the LORD said to him, 'Go, for he is a Chosen instrument of MINE, to bear MY Name before the Gentiles and kings and the sons of Israel.'" ◀ Acts 9:15 ▶ [NASB]

"CHRIST died to rescue those who had sinned and broken the old agreement. Now HE brings HIS Chosen ones a new agreement with its guarantee of GOD's Eternal Blessings!" ◀ Hebrews 9:15 ▶ [CEV]

"Thank GOD for HIS Gift that is too wonderful for words!" ◀ 2 Corinthians 9:15 ▶ [CEV]

Powerful Manifestation Prayer:

I BLESS myself, my family and everyone born on this date with GOD's MOST POWERFUL PURE LOVING LIGHT, HIS MOST POWERFUL PURE SOURCE HEALING ENERGY, and an ABUNDANCE OF HIS AMAZING GREATER GRACE in the POWER, the ANOINTING, the AUTHORITY and the WISDOM of the HOLY SPIRIT, in JESUS' MOST HOLY NAME. AMEN INDEED!

Day 259
9:16

"I don't have any reason to brag about preaching the **GOoD News**. Preaching is something **GOD** told me to do, and if I don't do it, I am doomed." ◀ 1 Corinthians 9:16 ▶ [CEV]

"When the rainbow appears in the clouds, **I Will** see it and remember the everlasting covenant between **ME** and all living beings on earth." ◀ Genesis 9:16 ▶ [GNT]

"**The LORD** has made **HIMSELF** known; **HE** has executed judgment. In the work of **HIS OWN Hands** the wicked is snared." ◀ Psalm 9:16 ▶ [NASB]

"No one patches up an old coat with a piece of new cloth, for the new patch will shrink and make an even bigger hole in the coat." ◀ Matthew 9:16 ▶ [GNT]

"On that day the **LORD** their **GOD Will** save them, as the flock of **HIS** people; for like the jewels of a crown they shall shine on **HIS** land." ◀ Zechariah 9:16 ▶ [ESV]

"**JESUS** took the five loaves and the two fish. **HE** looked up toward **Heaven** and **Blessed** the food. Then **HE** broke the bread and fish and handed them to **HIS Disciples** to give to the people." ◀ Luke 9:16 ▶ [CEV]

Powerful Manifestation Prayer:

I BLESS myself, my family and everyone born on this date with GOD's MOST POWERFUL PURE LOVING LIGHT, HIS MOST POWERFUL PURE SOURCE HEALING ENERGY, and an ABUNDANCE OF HIS AMAZING GREATER GRACE in the POWER, the ANOINTING, the AUTHORITY and the WISDOM of the HOLY SPIRIT, in JESUS' MOST HOLY NAME. AMEN INDEED!

Day 260
9:17

"For a Will takes effect only at death, since it is not in force as long as the one who made it is alive."
◀ Hebrews 9:17 ▶ [ESV]

"Death is the destiny of all the wicked, of all those who reject GOD." ◀ Psalm 9:17 ▶ [GNT]

"My GOD Will reject them because they have not listened to HIM; they shall be wanderers among the nations."
◀ Hosea 9:17 ▶ [ESV]

"They refused to obey and were not mindful of the wonders that YOU performed among them, but they stiffened their neck and appointed a leader to return to their slavery in Egypt. But YOU are a GOD ready to forgive, gracious and merciful, slow to anger and abounding in steadfast Love, and did not forsake them."
◀ Nehemiah 9:17 ▶ [ESV]

"If I did my work as a matter of Free choice, then I could expect to be paid; but I do it as a matter of duty, because GOD has entrusted me with this task." ◀ 1 Corinthians 9:17 ▶ [GNT]

"Words of Wisdom spoken softly make much more sense than the shouts of a ruler to a crowd of fools."
◀ Ecclesiastes 9:17 ▶ [CEV]

Powerful Manifestation Prayer:

I BLESS myself, my family and everyone born on this date with GOD's MOST POWERFUL PURE LOVING LIGHT, HIS MOST POWERFUL PURE SOURCE HEALING ENERGY, and an ABUNDANCE OF HIS AMAZING GREATER GRACE in the POWER, the ANOINTING, the AUTHORITY and the WISDOM of the HOLY SPIRIT, in JESUS' MOST HOLY NAME. AMEN INDEED!

Day 261
9:18

"The people answered, "Let them come quickly and cry for us, until our own eyes are flooded with tears."
◀ Jeremiah 9:18 ▶ [CEV]

"Wisdom does more GOoD than weapons, but one sinner can undo a lot of GOoD."
◀ Ecclesiastes 9:18 ▶ [GNT]

"And it happened that while HE was Praying alone, the Disciples were with HIM, and HE questioned them, saying, "WHO do people say that I AM?"
◀ Luke 9:18 ▶ [NASB]

"For the needy shall not always be forgotten, and the HOPE of the poor shall not perish forever."
◀ Psalm 9:18 ▶ [ESV]

"What pay AM I given? It is the chance to preach the GOoD News Free of charge and not to use the privileges that are mine because I am a preacher."
◀ 1 Corinthians 9:18 ▶ [CEV]

"So, then HE has mercy on whomever HE Wills, and HE hardens whomever HE Wills."
◀ Romans 9:18 ▶ [ESV]

Powerful Manifestation Prayer:

I BLESS myself, my family and everyone born on this date with GOD's MOST POWERFUL PURE LOVING LIGHT, HIS MOST POWERFUL PURE SOURCE HEALING ENERGY, and an ABUNDANCE OF HIS AMAZING GREATER GRACE in the POWER, the ANOINTING, the AUTHORITY and the WISDOM of the HOLY SPIRIT, in JESUS' MOST HOLY NAME. AMEN INDEED!

Day 262
9:19

"Someone may ask, "How can **GOD** blame us, if **HE** makes us behave in the way **HE** wants us to?"
◄ Romans 9:19 ► [CEV]

"For though **I AM Free** from all, I have made myself a servant to all, that I might win more of them."
◄ 1 Corinthians 9:19 ► [ESV]

"O **LORD**, hear! O **LORD**, forgive! O **LORD**, listen and take action! For **YOUR OWN** sake, O my **GOD**, do not delay, because **YOUR** city and **YOUR** people are called by **YOUR Name**."
◄ Daniel 9:19 ► [NASB]

"**YOU**, in **YOUR** great compassion, did not forsake them in the wilderness; the pillar of cloud did not leave them by day to guide them on their way, nor the pillar of fire by night to **Light** for them the way in which they were to go."
◄ Nehemiah 9:19 ► [NASB]

"When the cloud stayed over the tent for a long time, they obeyed the **LORD** and did not move on."
◄ Numbers 9:19 ► [GNT]

"Arise, O **LORD**! Let not man prevail; let the nations be judged before **YOU**!"
◄ Psalm 9:19 ► [ESV]

"**JESUS** got up and went with him, and so did **HIS Disciples**."
◄ Matthew 9:19 ► [NIV]

Powerful Manifestation Prayer:

I BLESS myself, my family and everyone born on this date with GOD's MOST POWERFUL PURE LOVING LIGHT, HIS MOST POWERFUL PURE SOURCE HEALING ENERGY, and an ABUNDANCE OF HIS AMAZING GREATER GRACE in the POWER, the ANOINTING, the AUTHORITY and the WISDOM of the HOLY SPIRIT, in JESUS' MOST HOLY NAME. AMEN INDEED!

Day 263
9:20

"YOU sent YOUR GOoD SPIRIT to instruct them, and YOU did not stop giving them manna from Heaven or water for their thirst." ◀ Nehemiah 9:20 ▶ [NLT]

"JESUS then asked, "WHO do You say I AM?" Peter answered, "YOU are the MESSIAH sent from GOD."" ◀ Luke 9:20 ▶ [CEV]

"But, my friend, I ask, "Who do You think You are to question GOD? Does the clay have the right to ask the potter why he shaped it the way he did?" ◀ Romans 9:20 ▶ [CEV]

"HE told the people, 'With this Blood GOD makes HIS Agreement with You'." ◀ Hebrews 9:20 ▶ [CEV]

"And behold, a woman who had suffered from a discharge of blood for twelve years came up behind HIM and touched the fringe of HIS garment." ◀ Matthew 9:20 ▶ [ESV]

"I went on Praying, confessing my sins and the sins of my people Israel and pleading with the LORD my GOD to restore HIS Holy Temple." ◀ Daniel 9:20 ▶ [GNT]

Powerful Manifestation Prayer:

I BLESS myself, my family and everyone born on this date with GOD's MOST POWERFUL PURE LOVING LIGHT, HIS MOST POWERFUL PURE SOURCE HEALING ENERGY, and an ABUNDANCE OF HIS AMAZING GREATER GRACE in the POWER, the ANOINTING, the AUTHORITY and the WISDOM of the HOLY SPIRIT, in JESUS' MOST HOLY NAME. AMEN INDEED!

Day 264
9:21

"Forty years **YOU** sustained them in the wilderness, and they lacked nothing. Their clothes did not wear out and their feet did not swell." ◀ Nehemiah 9:21 ▶ [ESV]

"I took your sinful thing, the calf which **You** had made, and burned it with fire and crushed it, grinding it very small until it was as fine as dust; and I threw its dust into the brook that came down from the mountain." ◀ Deuteronomy 9:21 ▶ [NASB]

"Or does not the **Potter** have a right over the clay, to make from the same lump one vessel for honorable use and another for common use?" ◀ Romans 9:21 ▶ [NASB]

"But we do not know how it is that he is now able to see, nor do we know who cured him of his blindness. **ASK** him; he is old enough, and he can answer for himself!" ◀ John 9:21 ▶ [GNT]

"She said to herself, "If I only touch **HIS** cloak, I will be healed." ◀ Matthew 9:21 ▶ [NIV]

"**JESUS** warned **HIS Disciples** not to tell anyone **WHO HE** was." ◀ Luke 9:21 ▶ [NLT]

Powerful Manifestation Prayer:

I BLESS myself, my family and everyone born on this date with GOD's MOST POWERFUL PURE LOVING LIGHT, HIS MOST POWERFUL PURE SOURCE HEALING ENERGY, and an ABUNDANCE OF HIS AMAZING GREATER GRACE in the POWER, the ANOINTING, the AUTHORITY and the WISDOM of the HOLY SPIRIT, in JESUS' MOST HOLY NAME. AMEN INDEED!

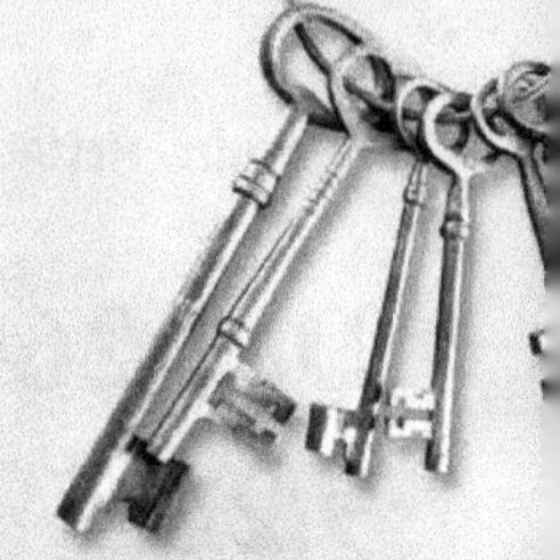

Day 265
9:22

"Indeed, under the **Law** almost everything is purified with blood, and without the shedding of **Blood** there is no forgiveness of sins." ◀ Hebrews 9:22 ▶ [ESV]

"Then **YOU** helped our ancestors conquer kingdoms and nations, and **YOU** placed **YOUR** people in every corner of the land." ◀ Nehemiah 9:22 ▶ [NLT]

"Celebrate these days with feasting and gladness and by giving gifts of food to each other and presents to the poor… commemorate a time when they gained relief from their enemies, when their sorrow was turned into gladness and their mourning into joy." ◀ Esther 9:22 ▶ [NLT]

"The **SON** of **Man** must suffer many terrible things," **HE** said. "**HE Will** be rejected by the elders, the leading priests, and the teachers of religious law. **HE Will** be killed, but on the third day **HE Will** be raised from the dead." ◀ Luke 9:22 ▶ [NLT]

"To the weak **I** became weak, to win the weak. **I** have become **ALL THINGS** to all people so that by all possible means **I** might save some." ◀ 1 Corinthians 9:22 ▶ [ESV]

"Saul preached with such power that he completely confused the Jewish people in Damascus, as he tried to show them that **JESUS** is the **MESSIAH**." ◀ Acts 9:22 ▶ [CEV]

Powerful Manifestation Prayer:

I BLESS myself, my family and everyone born on this date with GOD's MOST POWERFUL PURE LOVING LIGHT, HIS MOST POWERFUL PURE SOURCE HEALING ENERGY, and an ABUNDANCE OF HIS AMAZING GREATER GRACE in the POWER, the ANOINTING, the AUTHORITY and the WISDOM of the HOLY SPIRIT, in JESUS' MOST HOLY NAME. AMEN INDEED!

Day 266
9:23

"When many days had elapsed, the Jews plotted together to do away with HIM."
◀ Acts 9:23 ▶ [NASB]

"And HE said to all, "If anyone would come after ME, let him deny himself and take up his cross daily and follow ME."
◀ Luke 9:23 ▶ [ESV]

"And JESUS said to him, 'If You can! All things are possible for one who believes.'"
◀ Mark 9:23 ▶ [ESV]

"YOU multiplied their children as the stars of Heaven, and YOU brought them into the land that YOU had told their fathers to enter and possess."
◀ Nehemiah 9:23 ▶ [ESV]

"I do it all for the sake of the Gospel, that I may share with them in its Blessings."
◀ 1 Corinthians 9:23 ▶ [ESV]

"And HE did so to make known the Riches of HIS Glory upon vessels of mercy, which HE prepared beforehand for Glory."
◀ Romans 9:23 ▶ [NASB]

Powerful Manifestation Prayer:

I BLESS myself, my family and everyone born on this date with GOD's MOST POWERFUL PURE LOVING LIGHT, HIS MOST POWERFUL PURE SOURCE HEALING ENERGY, and an ABUNDANCE OF HIS AMAZING GREATER GRACE in the POWER, the ANOINTING, the AUTHORITY and the WISDOM of the HOLY SPIRIT, in JESUS' MOST HOLY NAME. AMEN INDEED!

Day 267
9:24

"Surely You know that many runners take part in a race, but only one of them wins the prize. Run, then, in such a way as to win the prize." ◀ 1 Corinthians 9:24 ▶ [GNT]

"For whoever would save his life will lose it, but whoever loses his life for MY sake will save it." ◀ Luke 9:24 ▶ [ESV]

"Immediately the father of the child cried out and said, "I believe; help my unbelief!" ◀ Mark 9:24 ▶ [ESV]

"For CHRIST has entered, not into Holy Places made with hands, which are copies of the true things, but into Heaven itself, now to appear in the presence of GOD on our behalf." ◀ Hebrews 9:24 ▶ [ESV]

"Then their descendants conquered the land. YOU helped them defeat the kings and nations and treat their enemies however they wished." ◀ Nehemiah 9:24 ▶ [NLT]

"Give Glory to GOD by telling the Truth." ◀ John 9:24 ▶ [NIV]

Powerful Manifestation Prayer:

I BLESS myself, my family and everyone born on this date with GOD's MOST POWERFUL PURE LOVING LIGHT, HIS MOST POWERFUL PURE SOURCE HEALING ENERGY, and an ABUNDANCE OF HIS AMAZING GREATER GRACE in the POWER, the ANOINTING, the AUTHORITY and the WISDOM of the HOLY SPIRIT, in JESUS' MOST HOLY NAME. AMEN INDEED!

Day 268
9:25

"And now, behold, we are in your hand. Whatever seems GOoD and right in your sight to do to us, do it."
◀ Joshua 9:25 ▶ [ESV]

"He gave orders in writing that his evil plan that he had devised against them should return on his own head."
◀ Esther 9:25 ▶ [ESV]

"CHRIST did not have to offer HIMSELF many times. HE wasn't like a high priest who goes into the Most Holy Place each year to offer the blood of an animal."
◀ Hebrews 9:25 ▶ [CEV]

"Athletes work hard to win a crown that cannot last, but we do it for a crown that will last forever."
◀ 1 Corinthians 9:25 ▶ [CEV]

"For what does it profit a man if he gains the whole world and loses or forfeits himself?"
◀ Luke 9:25 ▶ [ESV]

"He answered, "Whether HE is a sinner I do not know. One thing I do know, that though I was blind, now I see."
◀ John 9:25 ▶ [ESV]

Powerful Manifestation Prayer:

I BLESS myself, my family and everyone born on this date with GOD's MOST POWERFUL PURE LOVING LIGHT, HIS MOST POWERFUL PURE SOURCE HEALING ENERGY, and an ABUNDANCE OF HIS AMAZING GREATER GRACE in the POWER, the ANOINTING, the AUTHORITY and the WISDOM of the HOLY SPIRIT, in JESUS' MOST HOLY NAME. AMEN INDEED!

Day 269
9:26

"If HE had offered HIMSELF every year, HE would have suffered many times since the creation of the world. But instead, near the end of time HE offered HIMSELF once and for all, so HE could be a sacrifice that does away with sin." ◀ Hebrews 9:26 ▶ [CEV]

"For whoever is ashamed of ME and MY WORDS, the SON of Man Will be ashamed of him when HE comes in HIS Glory, and the Glory of the FATHER and of the Holy Angels." ◀ Luke 9:26 ▶ [NASB]

"When Saul arrived in Jerusalem, he tried to join the followers. But they were all afraid of him, because they did not believe he was a true follower." ◀ Acts 9:26 ▶ [CEV]

"Therefore, I run in such a way, as not without aim; I box in such a way, as not beating the air." ◀ 1 Corinthians 9:26 ▶ [NASB]

"And in the very place where they were told, 'You are not MY people,' there they will be called the children of the Living GOD." ◀ Romans 9:26 ▶ [GNT]

"The report of this miracle swept through the entire countryside." ◀ Matthew 9:26 ▶ [NLT]

Powerful Manifestation Prayer:

I BLESS myself, my family and everyone born on this date with GOD's MOST POWERFUL PURE LOVING LIGHT, HIS MOST POWERFUL PURE SOURCE HEALING ENERGY, and an ABUNDANCE OF HIS AMAZING GREATER GRACE in the POWER, the ANOINTING, the AUTHORITY and the WISDOM of the HOLY SPIRIT, in JESUS' MOST HOLY NAME. AMEN INDEED!

Day 270
9:27

"And Isaiah exclaims about Israel: "Even if the people of Israel are as many as the grains of sand by the sea, yet only a few of them will be saved." ◀ Romans 9:27 ▶ [GNT]

"Everyone must die once, and after that be judged by **GOD**." ◀ Hebrews 9:27 ▶ [GNT]

"But **I** say to **You Truthfully**, there are some of those standing here who will not taste death until they see the **Kingdom** of **GOD**." ◀ Luke 9:27 ▶ [NASB]

"Therefore, **YOU** gave them into the hand of their enemies, who made them suffer. And in the time of their suffering they cried out to **YOU** and **YOU** heard them from **Heaven**, and according to **YOUR Great Mercies YOU** gave them saviors who saved them from the hand of their enemies."
◀ Nehemiah 9:27 ▶ [ESV]

"I discipline my body like an athlete, training it to do what it should. Otherwise, I fear that after preaching to others I myself might be disqualified." ◀ 1 Corinthians 9:27 ▶ [NLT]

"But **JESUS** took the boy by the hand and helped him rise, and he **STOOD** up."
◀ Mark 9:27 ▶ [GNT]

Powerful Manifestation Prayer:

I BLESS myself, my family and everyone born on this date with GOD's MOST POWERFUL PURE LOVING LIGHT, HIS MOST POWERFUL PURE SOURCE HEALING ENERGY, and an ABUNDANCE OF HIS AMAZING GREATER GRACE in the POWER, the ANOINTING, the AUTHORITY and the WISDOM of the HOLY SPIRIT, in JESUS' MOST HOLY NAME. AMEN INDEED!

Day 271
9:28

"So, he went in and out among them at Jerusalem, preaching boldly in the Name of the LORD."
◄ Acts 9:28 ► [ESV]

"So, CHRIST, having been offered once to bear the sins of many, will appear a second time, not to deal with sin but to save those who are eagerly waiting for HIM." ◄ Hebrews 9:28 ► [ESV]

"When HE entered the house, the blind men came up to HIM, and JESUS said to them, "Do You believe that I AM able to do this?" They said to HIM, 'Yes, LORD'." ◄ Matthew 9:28 ► [NASB]

"But when they were at peace, they would turn against YOU, and YOU would hand them over to their enemies. Then they would beg for help, and because YOU are merciful, YOU rescued them over and over again."
◄ Nehemiah 9:28 ► [CEV]

"The LORD Will be quick and sure to do on earth what HE has warned HE Will do."
◄ Romans 9:28 ► [CEV]

"Pray to the LORD! We have had enough of this thunder and hail! I Promise to let You go; You don't have to stay here any longer." ◄ Exodus 9:28 ► [GNT]

Powerful Manifestation Prayer:

I BLESS myself, my family and everyone born on this date with GOD's MOST POWERFUL PURE LOVING LIGHT, HIS MOST POWERFUL PURE SOURCE HEALING ENERGY, and an ABUNDANCE OF HIS AMAZING GREATER GRACE in the POWER, the ANOINTING, the AUTHORITY and the WISDOM of the HOLY SPIRIT, in JESUS' MOST HOLY NAME. AMEN INDEED!

Day 272
9:29

"**YOU** warned them to obey **YOUR** teachings, but in pride they rejected **YOUR Laws**, although keeping your **Law** is the way to life. Hard-headed and stubborn, they refused to obey."
◀ Nehemiah 9:29 ▶ [GNT]

"As **HE** was **Praying**, the appearance of **HIS Face** changed, and **HIS** clothes became as bright as a flash of lightning."
◀ Luke 9:29 ▶ [NIV]

"But they are **YOUR** people and **YOUR** special possession, whom **YOU** brought out of Egypt by **YOUR Great Strength** and **Powerful Arm**."
◀ Deuteronomy 9:29 ▶ [NLT]

"If the **LORD All-Powerful** had not spared some of our descendants, we would have been destroyed like the cities of Sodom and Gomorrah."
◀ Romans 9:29 ▶ [CEV]

"**JESUS** answered, "Only **Prayer** can force out this kind of demon."
◀ Mark 9:29 ▶ [CEV]

"**JESUS** touched their eyes and said, "Because of your **Faith**, **You** will be healed."
◀ Matthew 9:29 ▶ [CEV]

Powerful Manifestation Prayer:

I BLESS myself, my family and everyone born on this date with GOD's MOST POWERFUL PURE LOVING LIGHT, HIS MOST POWERFUL PURE SOURCE HEALING ENERGY, and an ABUNDANCE OF HIS AMAZING GREATER GRACE in the POWER, the ANOINTING, the AUTHORITY and the WISDOM of the HOLY SPIRIT, in JESUS' MOST HOLY NAME. AMEN INDEED!

Day 273
9:30

"**JESUS** and **HIS Disciples** left that place and went on through Galilee. **JESUS** did not want anyone to know where **HE** was." ◄ Mark 9:30 ► [GNT]

"The man answered and said to them, 'Well, here is an amazing thing, that **You** do not know where **HE** is from, and yet **HE** opened my eyes'." ◄ John 9:30 ► [NASB]

"They were able to see, and **JESUS** strictly warned them not to tell anyone about **HIM**." ◄ Matthew 9:30 ► [CEV]

"For years, **YOU** were patient, and **YOUR SPIRIT** warned them with messages spoken by **YOUR Prophets**. Still they refused to listen, and **YOU** handed them over to their enemies." ◄ Nehemiah 9:30 ► [CEV]

"But I know that **You** and your officials do not yet fear the **LORD GOD**." ◄ Exodus 9:30 ► [GNT]

"So, we say that the Gentiles, who were not trying to put themselves right with **GOD**, were put right with **HIM** through **Faith**." ◄ Romans 9:30 ► [GNT]

Powerful Manifestation Prayer:

I BLESS myself, my family and everyone born on this date with GOD's MOST POWERFUL PURE LOVING LIGHT, HIS MOST POWERFUL PURE SOURCE HEALING ENERGY, and an ABUNDANCE OF HIS AMAZING GREATER GRACE in the POWER, the ANOINTING, the AUTHORITY and the WISDOM of the HOLY SPIRIT, in JESUS' MOST HOLY NAME. AMEN INDEED!

October 10

~ I Pray for You and You Pray for Me!

"After Job had prayed for his friends, the LORD restored his fortunes and gave him twice as much as he had before." ◀ Job 42:10 ▶ [NIV]

"You haven't done this before. A.S.K. using MY NAME, and You will receive, and You will have abundant joy." ◀ John 16:24 ▶ [NLT]

Powerful Manifestation Prayer:

I BLESS myself, my family and everyone born in this month with GOD's MOST POWERFUL PURE LOVING LIGHT, HIS MOST POWERFUL PURE SOURCE HEALING ENERGY, and an ABUNDANCE OF HIS AMAZING GREATER GRACE in the POWER, the ANOINTING, the AUTHORITY and the WISDOM of the HOLY SPIRIT, in JESUS' MOST HOLY NAME.
AMEN INDEED!

A.S.K.- Additional Scripture Knowledge

Write Additional **Scriptures** here.

Day 274
10:1

"I am disgusted with my life. Let me complain Freely. My bitter Soul must complain."
◄ Job 10:1 ► [NLT]

"Oh LORD, why do YOU stand so far away? Why do YOU hide when I am in trouble?"
◄ Psalm 10:1 ► [NLT]

"Then the LORD said to Moses, 'Return to Pharaoh and make your demands again. I have made him and his officials stubborn so I can display MY miraculous signs among them." ◄ Exodus 10:1 ► [NIV]

"ASK the LORD for rain in the spring, for HE makes the storm clouds. And HE Will send showers of rain so every field becomes a lush pasture." ◄ Zechariah 10:1 ► [NLT]

"The old system under the Law of Moses was only a shadow, a dim preview of the GOoD things to come, not the GOoD things themselves. The sacrifices under that system were repeated again and again, year after year, but they were never able to provide perfect cleansing for those who came to worship."
◄ Hebrews 10:1 ► [NLT]

"A wise child brings joy to a father, but a foolish child brings grief to a mother." ◄ Proverbs 10:1 ► [NIV]

Powerful Manifestation Prayer:

I BLESS myself, my family and everyone born on this date with GOD's MOST POWERFUL PURE LOVING LIGHT, HIS MOST POWERFUL PURE SOURCE HEALING ENERGY, and an ABUNDANCE OF HIS AMAZING GREATER GRACE in the POWER, the ANOINTING, the AUTHORITY and the WISDOM of the HOLY SPIRIT, in JESUS' MOST HOLY NAME. AMEN INDEED!

Day 275
10:2

"Household gods give worthless advice, fortune-tellers predict only lies, and interpreters of dreams pronounce falsehoods that give no comfort. So **MY** people are wandering like lost sheep; they are attacked because they have no shepherd." ◄ Zechariah 10:2 ► [NLT]

"If they could have provided perfect cleansing, the sacrifices would have stopped, for the worshipers would have been purified once for all time, and their feelings of guilt would have disappeared." ◄ Hebrews 10:2 ► [NLT]

"Tainted wealth has no lasting value, but right living can save your life." ◄ Proverbs 10:2 ► [NLT]

"I say to **GOD**: Do not declare me guilty, but tell me what charges **YOU** have against me." ◄ Job 10:2 ► [NIV]

"The wicked arrogantly hunt down the poor. Let them be caught in the evil they plan for others." ◄ Psalm 10:2 ► [NLT]

"We have been unfaithful to our **GOD**…But in spite of this, there is still **HOPE** for Israel." ◄ Ezra 10:2 ► [NLT]

Powerful Manifestation Prayer:

I BLESS myself, my family and everyone born on this date with GOD's MOST POWERFUL PURE LOVING LIGHT, HIS MOST POWERFUL PURE SOURCE HEALING ENERGY, and an ABUNDANCE OF HIS AMAZING GREATER GRACE in the POWER, the ANOINTING, the AUTHORITY and the WISDOM of the HOLY SPIRIT, in JESUS' MOST HOLY NAME. AMEN INDEED!

Day 276
10:3

"Let us now make a covenant with our GOD…We will follow the advice given…by the others who respect the commands of our GOD. Let it be done according to the Law of GOD."
◀ Ezra 10:3 ▶ [NLT]

"MY anger burns against the shepherds, and I Will punish the leaders; for the LORD Almighty Will care for HIS flock, the people of Judah, and make them like a proud horse in battle."
◀Zechariah 10:3 ▶ [NIV]

"What do YOU gain by oppressing me? Why do YOU reject me, the work of YOUR OWN HANDS, while smiling on the schemes of the wicked?" ◀ Job 10:3 ▶ [NLT]

"Among those who approach ME, I Will be proved Holy; in the sight of all the people I Will be honored." ◀ Leviticus 10:3 ▶ [NIV]

"For the wicked boasts of the desires of his Soul, and the one greedy for gain curses and renounces the LORD." ◀ Psalm 10:3 ▶ [ESV]

"The LORD Will not let the GODly go hungry, but HE refuses to satisfy the craving of the wicked."
◀ Proverbs 10:3 ▶ [NLT]

"I ate no choice food; no meat or wine touched my lips; and I used no lotions at all until the three weeks were over." ◀ Daniel 10:3 ▶ [NIV]

Powerful Manifestation Prayer:

I BLESS myself, my family and everyone born on this date with GOD's MOST POWERFUL PURE LOVING LIGHT, HIS MOST POWERFUL PURE SOURCE HEALING ENERGY, and an ABUNDANCE OF HIS AMAZING GREATER GRACE in the POWER, the ANOINTING, the AUTHORITY and the WISDOM of the HOLY SPIRIT, in JESUS' MOST HOLY NAME. AMEN INDEED!

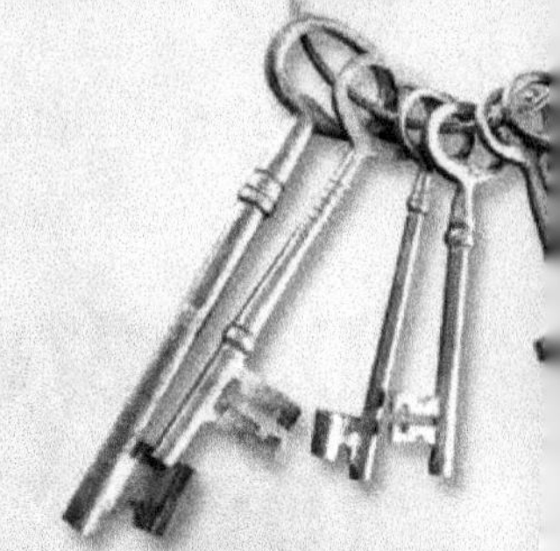

Day 277
10:4

"Lazy hands make for poverty, but diligent hands bring wealth." ◀ Proverbs 10:4 ▶ [NIV]

"Rise up; this matter is in your hands. We will support **You**, so take courage and do it."
◀ Ezra 10:4 ▶ [NIV]

"It is impossible for the blood of bulls and goats to take away sins." ◀ Hebrews 10:4 ▶ [NIV]

"The weapons we fight with are not the weapons of the world. On the contrary, they have **Divine Power** to demolish strongholds."
◀ 2 Corinthians 10:4 ▶ [NIV]

"**CHRIST** is the culmination of the **Law** so that there may be **Righteousness** for everyone who believes."
◀ Romans 10:4 ▶ [NIV]

"After **HE** has gathered **HIS OWN Flock**, **HE** walks ahead of them, and they follow **HIM** because they know **HIS Voice**."
◀ John 10:4 ▶ [NLT]

Powerful Manifestation Prayer:

I BLESS myself, my family and everyone born on this date with GOD's MOST POWERFUL PURE LOVING LIGHT, HIS MOST POWERFUL PURE SOURCE HEALING ENERGY, and an ABUNDANCE OF HIS AMAZING GREATER GRACE in the POWER, the ANOINTING, the AUTHORITY and the WISDOM of the HOLY SPIRIT, in JESUS' MOST HOLY NAME. AMEN INDEED!

Day 278
10:5

“We demolish arguments and every pretension that sets itself up against the **Knowledge** of **GOD**, and we take captive every thought to make it obedient to **CHRIST**.” ◀ 2 Corinthians 10:5 ▶ [NIV]

“Yet they succeed in everything they do. They do not see **YOUR** punishment awaiting them. They sneer at all their enemies.” ◀ Psalm 10:5 ▶ [NLT]

“What sorrow awaits … the rod of **MY** anger. **I** use it as a club to express **MY** anger.” ◀ Isaiah 10:5 ▶ [NLT]

“A wise youth harvests in the summer, but one who sleeps during harvest is a disgrace.” ◀ Proverbs 10:5 ▶ [NLT]

“Then the **Angel** I saw standing on the sea and on the land raised **His Right Hand** toward **Heaven**.” ◀ Revelation 10:5 ▶ [NLT]

“They will be like mighty warriors in battle, trampling their enemies in the mud under their feet. Since the **LORD** is with them as they fight, they will overthrow even the enemy’s horsemen.” ◀ Zechariah 10:5 ▶ [NLT]

Powerful Manifestation Prayer:

I BLESS myself, my family and everyone born on this date with GOD’s MOST POWERFUL PURE LOVING LIGHT, HIS MOST POWERFUL PURE SOURCE HEALING ENERGY, and an ABUNDANCE OF HIS AMAZING GREATER GRACE in the POWER, the ANOINTING, the AUTHORITY and the WISDOM of the HOLY SPIRIT, in JESUS’ MOST HOLY NAME. AMEN INDEED!

Day 279
10:6

"No one is like **YOU**, **LORD; YOU** are **Great,** and **YOUR Name** is **Mighty** in **Power**."
◄ Jeremiah 10:6 ► [NIV]

"But '**GOD** made them male and female' from the beginning of creation." ◄ Mark 10:6 ► [NLT]

"**Blessings** crown the head of the **Righteous**, but violence overwhelms the mouth of the wicked."
◄ Proverbs 10:6 ► [NIV]

"And he swore by **HIM WHO** lives for ever and ever, **WHO** created the **Heavens** and all that is in them, the earth and all that is in it, and the sea and all that is in it, and said, "There will be no more delay!"
◄ Revelation 10:6 ► [NIV]

"**I Will** strengthen Judah and save the tribes of Joseph. **I Will RESTORE** them because **I** have compassion on them. They will be as though **I** had not rejected them, for **I AM The LORD** their **GOD** and **I Will** answer them."
◄ Zechariah 10:6 ► [NIV]

"Now these things occurred as examples to keep us from setting our hearts on evil things as they did."
◄ 1 Corinthians 10:6 ► [NIV]

Powerful Manifestation Prayer:

I BLESS myself, my family and everyone born on this date with GOD's MOST POWERFUL PURE LOVING LIGHT, HIS MOST POWERFUL PURE SOURCE HEALING ENERGY, and an ABUNDANCE OF HIS AMAZING GREATER GRACE in the POWER, the ANOINTING, the AUTHORITY and the WISDOM of the HOLY SPIRIT, in JESUS' MOST HOLY NAME. AMEN INDEED!

Day 280
10:7

"Do not leave the entrance to the tent of meeting or **You** will die, because the **LORD's Anointing Oil** is on **You**."
◀ Leviticus 10:7 ▶ [NIV]

"Then **I** said, 'Here **I AM**—it is written about **ME** in the scroll—**I** have come to do **YOUR Will, MY GOD**."
◀ Hebrews 10:7 ▶ [NIV]

"If **You** are **GOoD** to these people and do your best to please them and give them a favorable answer, they will always be your loyal subjects."
◀ 2 Chronicles 10:7 ▶ [NLT]

"The **Name** of the **Righteous** is used in **Blessings**, but the name of the wicked will rot."
◀ Proverbs 10:7 ▶ [NIV]

"Their mouths are full of cursing, lies, and threats. Trouble and evil are on the tips of their tongues."
◀ Psalm 10:7 ▶ [NLT]

"Go and announce to them that the **Kingdom** of **Heaven** is near."
◀ Matthew 10:7 ▶ [NLT]

Powerful Manifestation Prayer:

I BLESS myself, my family and everyone born on this date with GOD's MOST POWERFUL PURE LOVING LIGHT, HIS MOST POWERFUL PURE SOURCE HEALING ENERGY, and an ABUNDANCE OF HIS AMAZING GREATER GRACE in the POWER, the ANOINTING, the AUTHORITY and the WISDOM of the HOLY SPIRIT, in JESUS' MOST HOLY NAME. AMEN INDEED!

Day 281
10:8

"They lurk in ambush in the villages, waiting to murder innocent people. They are always searching for helpless victims." ◀ Psalm 10:8 ▶ [NLT]

"Then the **Voice** from **Heaven** spoke to me again: "Go and take the open scroll from the hand of the **Angel** who is standing on the sea and on the land." ◀ Revelation 10:8 ▶ [NLT]

"The **LORD** said…,"Do not be afraid of them; **I** have given them into your hand. Not one of them will be able to withstand **You**."" ◀ Joshua 10:8 ▶ [NIV]

"First **HE** said, "Sacrifices and offerings, burnt offerings and sin offerings **YOU** did not desire, nor were **YOU** pleased with them"—though they were offered in accordance with the **Law**." ◀ Hebrews 10:8 ▶ [NIV]

"The wise are glad to be instructed, but babbling fools fall flat on their faces." ◀ Proverbs 10:8 ▶ [NLT]

"Heal the sick, raise the dead, cure those with leprosy, and cast out demons. Give as **Freely** as **You** have received!" ◀ Matthew 10:8 ▶ [NLT]

Powerful Manifestation Prayer:

I BLESS myself, my family and everyone born on this date with GOD's MOST POWERFUL PURE LOVING LIGHT, HIS MOST POWERFUL PURE SOURCE HEALING ENERGY, and an ABUNDANCE OF HIS AMAZING GREATER GRACE in the POWER, the ANOINTING, the AUTHORITY and the WISDOM of the HOLY SPIRIT, in JESUS' MOST HOLY NAME. AMEN INDEED!

Day 282
10:9

"If You declare with your mouth, "JESUS is LORD," and believe in your heart that GOD raised HIM from the dead, You will be saved." ◄ Romans 10:9 ► [NIV]

"Then HE said, "Here I AM, I have come to do YOUR Will." HE sets aside the first to establish the second." ◄ Hebrews 10:9 ► [NIV]

"People with integrity walk safely, but those who follow crooked paths will be exposed." ◄ Proverbs 10:9 ► [NLT]

"Like lions crouched in hiding, they wait to pounce on the helpless. Like hunters they capture the helpless and drag them away in nets." ◄ Psalm 10:9 ► [NLT]

"So I went to the Angel and asked Him to give me the little scroll. He said to me, 'Take it and eat it. It will turn your stomach sour, but in your mouth it will be as sweet as honey'." ◄ Revelation 10:9 ► [NIV]

"Though I scatter them among the peoples, yet in distant lands they will remember ME. They and their children will survive, and they will return." ◄ Zechariah 10:9 ► [NIV]

Powerful Manifestation Prayer:

I BLESS myself, my family and everyone born on this date with GOD's MOST POWERFUL PURE LOVING LIGHT, HIS MOST POWERFUL PURE SOURCE HEALING ENERGY, and an ABUNDANCE OF HIS AMAZING GREATER GRACE in the POWER, the ANOINTING, the AUTHORITY and the WISDOM of the HOLY SPIRIT, in JESUS' MOST HOLY NAME. AMEN INDEED!

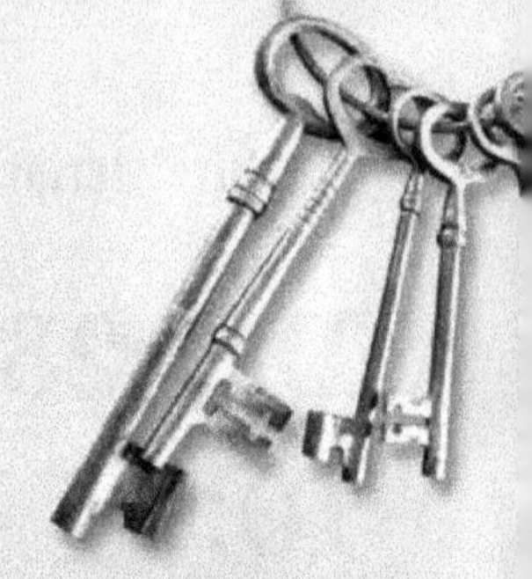

Day 283
10:10

"But the **LORD** is the **True GOD**; **HE** is the **Living GOD**, the **Eternal King**. When **HE** is angry, the earth trembles; the nations cannot endure **HIS** wrath." ◄ Jeremiah 10:10 ► [NIV]

"For it is with your heart that **You** believe and are justified, and it is with your mouth that **You** profess your **Faith** and are saved." ◄ Romans 10:10 ► [NIV]

"Now I had stayed on the mountain forty days and forty nights, as I did the first time, and the **LORD** listened to me at this time also. It [is] not **HIS Will** to destroy **You**." ◄ Deuteronomy 10:10 ► [NIV]

"And by that **WILL**, we have been made **Holy** through the sacrifice of the **Body** of **JESUS CHRIST** once for all." ◄ Hebrews 10:10 ► [NIV]

"His victims are crushed, they collapse; they fall under his strength." ◄ Psalm 10:10 ► [NIV]

"People who wink at wrong cause trouble, but a bold reproof promotes **Peace**." ◄ Proverbs 10:10 ► [NLT]

Powerful Manifestation Prayer:

I BLESS myself, my family and everyone born on this date with GOD's MOST POWERFUL PURE LOVING LIGHT, HIS MOST POWERFUL PURE SOURCE HEALING ENERGY, and an ABUNDANCE OF HIS AMAZING GREATER GRACE in the POWER, the ANOINTING, the AUTHORITY and the WISDOM of the HOLY SPIRIT, in JESUS' MOST HOLY NAME. AMEN INDEED!

Day 284
10:11

"I AM the GOoD Shepherd. The GOoD Shepherd lays down HIS Life for the sheep."
◀ John 10:11 ▶ [NIV]

"Day after day every priest stands and performs his religious duties; again and again he offers the same sacrifices, which can never take away sins."
◀ Hebrews 10:11 ▶ [NIV]

"So now confess your sin to the LORD, the GOD of your ancestors, and do what HE demands. Separate yourselves from the people of the land and from these pagan women."
◀ Ezra 10:11 ▶ [NLT]

"The wicked think, "GOD isn't watching us! HE has closed HIS eyes and won't even see what we do!"
◀ Psalm 10:11 ▶ [NLT]

"The Words of the GODly are a life-giving fountain; the words of the wicked conceal violent intentions."
◀ Proverbs 10:11 ▶ [NLT]

"Whenever You enter a city or village, search for a worthy person and stay in his home until You leave town."
◀ Matthew 10:11 ▶ [NLT]

"Then the LORD said to me, 'Get up and resume the journey, and lead the people to the land I swore to give to their ancestors, so they may take possession of it."
◀ Deuteronomy 10:11 ▶ [NLT]

Powerful Manifestation Prayer:

I BLESS myself, my family and everyone born on this date with GOD's MOST POWERFUL PURE LOVING LIGHT, HIS MOST POWERFUL PURE SOURCE HEALING ENERGY, and an ABUNDANCE OF HIS AMAZING GREATER GRACE in the POWER, the ANOINTING, the AUTHORITY and the WISDOM of the HOLY SPIRIT, in JESUS' MOST HOLY NAME. AMEN INDEED!

Day 285
10:12

"But **GOD** made the earth by **HIS Power**; **HE** founded the world by **HIS Wisdom** and stretched out the **Heavens** by **HIS Understanding**." ◄ Jeremiah 10:12 ► [NIV]

"Arise, O **LORD**! Punish the wicked, O **GOD**! Do not ignore the helpless." ◄ Psalm 10:12 ► [NLT]

"For there is no difference between Jew and Gentile--the same **LORD** is **LORD** of all and richly **Blesses** all who call on **HIM**." ◄ Romans 10:12 ► [NIV]

"Hatred stirs up conflict, but **Love** covers over all wrongs." ◄ Proverbs 10:12 ► [NIV]

"**YOU** gave me life and showed me kindness, and in **YOUR** providence watched over my **Spirit**." ◄ Job 10:12 ► [NIV]

"By **MY Power I Will** make **MY People** strong, and by **MY Authority** they will go wherever they wish. **I, The LORD**, have spoken!" ◄ Zechariah 10:12 ► [NLT]

Powerful Manifestation Prayer:

I BLESS myself, my family and everyone born on this date with GOD's MOST POWERFUL PURE LOVING LIGHT, HIS MOST POWERFUL PURE SOURCE HEALING ENERGY, and an ABUNDANCE OF HIS AMAZING GREATER GRACE in the POWER, the ANOINTING, the AUTHORITY and the WISDOM of the HOLY SPIRIT, in JESUS' MOST HOLY NAME. AMEN INDEED!

Day 286
10:13

"Everyone who calls on the **Name** of the **LORD Will** be saved." ◄ Romans 10:13 ► [NLT]

"No temptation has overtaken **You** except what is common to mankind. And **GOD** is **Faithful**; **HE Will** not let **You** be tempted beyond what **You** can bear. But when **You** are tempted, **HE Will** also provide a way out so that **You** can endure it." ◄ 1 Corinthians 10:13 ► [NIV]

"Why do the wicked get away with despising **GOD**? They think, "**GOD Will** never call us to account." ◄ Psalm 10:13 ► [NLT]

"There **HE** waits until **HIS** enemies are humbled and made a footstool under **HIS Feet**." ◄ Hebrews 10:13 ► [NLT]

"**Wisdom** is found on the lips of the discerning, but a rod is for the back of one who has no sense." ◄ Proverbs 10:13 ► [NIV]

"If the home is deserving, let your **Peace** rest on it; if it is not, let your **Peace** return to **You**." ◄ Matthew 10:13 ► [NIV]

Powerful Manifestation Prayer:

I BLESS myself, my family and everyone born on this date with GOD's MOST POWERFUL PURE LOVING LIGHT, HIS MOST POWERFUL PURE SOURCE HEALING ENERGY, and an ABUNDANCE OF HIS AMAZING GREATER GRACE in the POWER, the ANOINTING, the AUTHORITY and the WISDOM of the HOLY SPIRIT, in JESUS' MOST HOLY NAME. AMEN INDEED!

Day 287
10:14

"But **YOU**, **GOD**, see the trouble of the afflicted, **YOU** consider their grief and take it in **Hand**. The victims commit themselves to **YOU**; **YOU** are the **Helper** of the fatherless." ◄ Psalm 10:14 ► [NIV]

"There has never been a day like it before or since, a day when the **LORD** listened to a human being. Surely the **LORD** was fighting for Israel." ◄ Joshua 10:14 ► [NIV]

"To the **LORD** your **GOD** belong the **Heavens**, even the highest **Heavens**, the earth and everything in it." ◄ Deuteronomy 10:14 ► [NIV]

"When **JESUS** saw what was happening, **HE** was angry with **HIS Disciples**. **HE** said to them, "Let the children come to **ME**. Don't stop them! For the **Kingdom** of **GOD** belongs to those who are like these children." ◄ Mark 10:14 ► [NIV]

"If anyone will not welcome **You** or listen to your **Words**, leave that home or town and shake the dust off your feet." ◄ Matthew 10:14 ► [NIV]

"For by **ONE Sacrifice HE** has made perfect forever those who are being made **Holy**." ◄ Hebrews 10:14 ► [NIV]

"Wise people treasure **Knowledge**, but the babbling of a fool invites disaster." ◄ Proverbs 10:14 ► [NLT]

Powerful Manifestation Prayer:

I BLESS myself, my family and everyone born on this date with GOD's MOST POWERFUL PURE LOVING LIGHT, HIS MOST POWERFUL PURE SOURCE HEALING ENERGY, and an ABUNDANCE OF HIS AMAZING GREATER GRACE in the POWER, the ANOINTING, the AUTHORITY and the WISDOM of the HOLY SPIRIT, in JESUS' MOST HOLY NAME. AMEN INDEED!

Day 288
10:15

"Yet the **LORD** set **HIS** affection on your ancestors and **Loved** them, and **HE Chose You**, their descendants, above all the nations—as it is today." ◄ Deuteronomy 10:15 ► [NIV]

"The **HOLY SPIRIT** also testifies to us about this." ◄ Hebrews 10:15 ► [NIV]

"Break the arms of these wicked, evil people! Go after them until the last one is destroyed." ◄ Psalm 10:15 ► [NIV]

"The wealth of the rich is their fortress; the poverty of the poor is their destruction." ◄ Proverbs 10:15 ► [NLT]

"**I** tell **You** the **Truth**, anyone who doesn't receive the **Kingdom** of **GOD** like a child will never enter it." ◄ Mark 10:15 ► [NLT]

"Just as **MY FATHER** knows **ME** and **I** know **The FATHER**. So, **I Sacrifice MY Life** for the sheep." ◄ John 10:15 ► [NLT]

Powerful Manifestation Prayer:

I BLESS myself, my family and everyone born on this date with GOD's MOST POWERFUL PURE LOVING LIGHT, HIS MOST POWERFUL PURE SOURCE HEALING ENERGY, and an ABUNDANCE OF HIS AMAZING GREATER GRACE in the POWER, the ANOINTING, the AUTHORITY and the WISDOM of the HOLY SPIRIT, in JESUS' MOST HOLY NAME. AMEN INDEED!

Day 289
10:16

"The LORD is KING forever and ever! The GODless nations will vanish from the land."
◀ Psalm 10:16 ▶ [NLT]

"This is the New Covenant I Will make with MY people on that day, says the LORD: I Will put MY Laws in their hearts, and I Will write them on their minds." ◀ Hebrews 10:16 ▶ [NLT]

"The wages of the Righteous is life, but the earnings of the wicked are sin and death."
◀ Proverbs 10:16 ▶ [NIV]

"Then HE took the children in HIS Arms and placed HIS Hands on their heads and Blessed them."
◀ Mark 10:16 ▶ [NLT]

"Whoever listens to You listens to ME; whoever rejects You rejects ME; but whoever rejects ME rejects HIM WHO sent ME." ◀ Luke 10:16 ▶ [NIV]

"I have other sheep, too, that are not in this sheepfold. I must bring them also. They will listen to MY Voice, and there will be one flock with ONE SHEPHERD." ◀ John 10:16 ▶ [NLT]

Powerful Manifestation Prayer:

I BLESS myself, my family and everyone born on this date with GOD's MOST POWERFUL PURE LOVING LIGHT, HIS MOST POWERFUL PURE SOURCE HEALING ENERGY, and an ABUNDANCE OF HIS AMAZING GREATER GRACE in the POWER, the ANOINTING, the AUTHORITY and the WISDOM of the HOLY SPIRIT, in JESUS' MOST HOLY NAME. AMEN INDEED!

Day 290
10:17

"For the **LORD** your **GOD** is **GOD** of gods and **LORD** of lords, the **Great GOD**, **Mighty** and **Awesome**, **WHO** shows no partiality and accepts no bribes." ◀ Deuteronomy 10:17 ▶ [NIV]

"Now, forgive my sin once more and **Pray** to the **LORD** your **GOD** to take this deadly plague away from me." ◀ Exodus 10:17 ▶ [NIV]

"**YOU**, **LORD**, hear the desire of the afflicted; **YOU** encourage them, and **YOU** listen to their cry." ◀ Psalm 10:17 ▶ [NIV]

"Then **HE** says, "**I Will** never again remember their sins and lawless deeds." ◀ Hebrews 10:17 ▶ [NLT]

"But, 'Let the one who boasts, boast in the **LORD**.'" ◀ 2 Corinthians 10:17 ▶ [NIV]

"People who accept discipline are on the pathway to life, but those who ignore correction will go astray." ◀ Proverbs 10:17 ▶ [NLT]

"When the seventy-two disciples returned, they joyfully reported to **HIM**, "**LORD**, even the demons obey us when we use **YOUR Name**!" ◀ Luke 10:17 ▶ [NLT]

Powerful Manifestation Prayer:

I BLESS myself, my family and everyone born on this date with GOD's MOST POWERFUL PURE LOVING LIGHT, HIS MOST POWERFUL PURE SOURCE HEALING ENERGY, and an ABUNDANCE OF HIS AMAZING GREATER GRACE in the POWER, the ANOINTING, the AUTHORITY and the WISDOM of the HOLY SPIRIT, in JESUS' MOST HOLY NAME. AMEN INDEED!

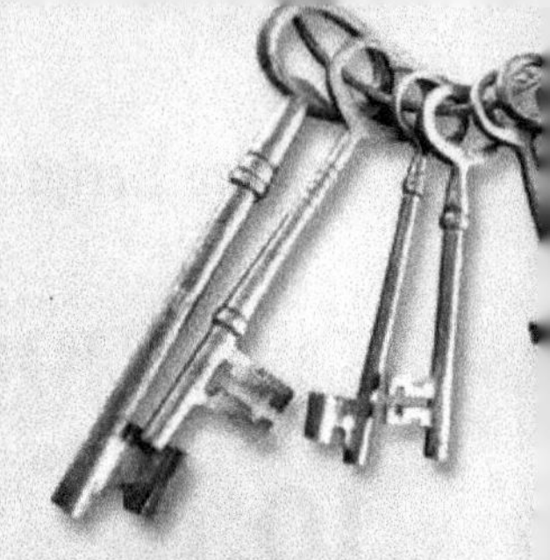

Day 291
10:18

"Yes," **HE** told them, "I saw Satan fall from **Heaven** like lightning"!" ◀ Luke 10:18 ▶ [NLT]

"**HE** defends the cause of the fatherless and the widow, and **Loves** the foreigner residing among **You**, giving them food and clothing." ◀ Deuteronomy 10:18 ▶ [NIV]

"**YOU Will** bring justice to the orphans and the oppressed, so mere people can no longer terrify them." ◀ Psalm 10:18 ▶ [NLT]

"And when sins have been forgiven, there is no need to offer any more sacrifices." ◀ Hebrews 10:18 ▶ [NLT]

"Hiding hatred makes **You** a liar; slandering others makes **You** a fool." ◀ Proverbs 10:18 ▶ [NLT]

"Why do **YOU** call **ME GOoD?**" **JESUS** asked. "**Only GOD** is **Truly GOoD**." ◀ Mark 10:18 ▶ [NLT]

Powerful Manifestation Prayer:

I BLESS myself, my family and everyone born on this date with GOD's MOST POWERFUL PURE LOVING LIGHT, HIS MOST POWERFUL PURE SOURCE HEALING ENERGY, and an ABUNDANCE OF HIS AMAZING GREATER GRACE in the POWER, the ANOINTING, the AUTHORITY and the WISDOM of the HOLY SPIRIT, in JESUS' MOST HOLY NAME. AMEN INDEED!

Day 292
10:19

"And You are to Love those who are foreigners, for You yourself were foreigners in Egypt."
◄ Deuteronomy 10:19 ► [NIV]

"But when they arrest You, do not worry about what to say or how to say it. At that time, You will be given what to say."
◄ Matthew 10:19 ► [NIV]

"A party gives laughter, wine gives happiness, and money gives everything!"
◄ Ecclesiastes 10:19 ► [NLT]

"Too much talk leads to sin. Be sensible and keep your mouth shut." ◄ Proverbs 10:19 ► [NLT]

"And so, dear brothers and sisters, we can boldly enter **Heaven's Most Holy Place** because of the **BLOOD OF JESUS**."
◄ Hebrews 10:19 ► [NLT]

"I have given You authority to trample on snakes and scorpions and to overcome all the power of the enemy; nothing will harm You."
◄ Luke10:19 ► [NIV]

Powerful Manifestation Prayer:

I BLESS myself, my family and everyone born on this date with GOD's MOST POWERFUL PURE LOVING LIGHT, HIS MOST POWERFUL PURE SOURCE HEALING ENERGY, and an ABUNDANCE OF HIS AMAZING GREATER GRACE in the POWER, the ANOINTING, the AUTHORITY and the WISDOM of the HOLY SPIRIT, in JESUS' MOST HOLY NAME. AMEN INDEED!

Day 293
10:20

"For it will not be You speaking, but the SPIRIT of your FATHER speaking through You."
◄ Matthew 10:20 ► [NIV]

"However, do not rejoice that the spirits submit to You, but rejoice that your names are written in Heaven."
◄ Luke 10:20 ► [NIV]

"Fear the LORD your GOD and serve HIM. Hold fast to HIM and take your oaths in HIS Name."
◄ Deuteronomy 10:20 ► [NIV]

"By HIS death, JESUS opened a new and life-giving way through the curtain into the Most Holy Place."
◄ Hebrews 10:20 ► [NLT]

"TEACHER," the man replied, "I've obeyed all these commandments since I was young."
◄ Mark 10:20 ► [NLT]

"The Words of the GODly are like sterling silver; the heart of a fool is worthless."
◄ Proverbs 10:20 ► [NLT]

Powerful Manifestation Prayer:

I BLESS myself, my family and everyone born on this date with GOD's MOST POWERFUL PURE LOVING LIGHT, HIS MOST POWERFUL PURE SOURCE HEALING ENERGY, and an ABUNDANCE OF HIS AMAZING GREATER GRACE in the POWER, the ANOINTING, the AUTHORITY and the WISDOM of the HOLY SPIRIT, in JESUS' MOST HOLY NAME. AMEN INDEED!

Day 294
10:21

"But others said, "These are not the sayings of a man possessed by a demon. Can a demon open the eyes of the blind?"
◀ John 10:21 ▶ [NIV]

"You cannot drink the cup of the LORD and the cup of demons too; You cannot have a part in both the LORD's table and the table of demons."
◀ 1 Corinthians 10:21 ▶ [NIV]

"HE is the ONE You Praise; HE is your GOD, WHO performed for You those great and awesome wonders You saw with your own eyes."
◀ Deuteronomy 10:21 ▶ [NIV]

"The Words of the GODly encourage many, but fools are destroyed by their lack of common sense."
◀ Proverbs 10:21 ▶ [NLT]

"JESUS looked at him and Loved him. "One thing You lack," HE said. "Go, sell everything You have and give to the poor, and You will have treasure in Heaven. Then come follow ME."
◀ Mark 10:21 ▶ [NIV]

"At that time JESUS, full of joy through the HOLY SPIRIT said, "I Praise YOU, FATHER, LORD of Heaven and earth, because YOU have hidden these things from the wise and learned, and revealed them to little children. Yes, FATHER, for this is what YOU were pleased to do."
◀ Luke 10:21 ▶ [NIV]

Powerful Manifestation Prayer:

I BLESS myself, my family and everyone born on this date with GOD's MOST POWERFUL PURE LOVING LIGHT, HIS MOST POWERFUL PURE SOURCE HEALING ENERGY, and an ABUNDANCE OF HIS AMAZING GREATER GRACE in the POWER, the ANOINTING, the AUTHORITY and the WISDOM of the HOLY SPIRIT, in JESUS' MOST HOLY NAME. AMEN INDEED!

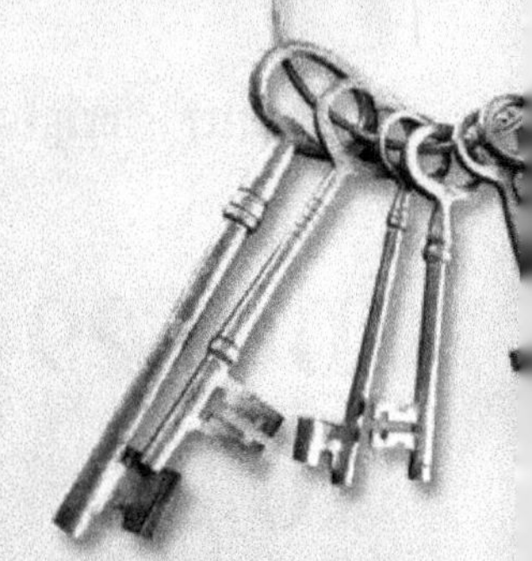

Day 295
10:22

"Are we trying to arouse the **LORD's** jealousy? Are we stronger than **HE**?"
◄ 1 Corinthians 10:22 ► [NIV]

"**You** will be hated by everyone because of **ME**, but the one who stands firm to the end will be saved."
◄ Matthew 10:22 ► [NIV]

"When your ancestors went down into Egypt, there were only seventy of them. But now the **LORD** your **GOD** has made **You** as numerous as the stars in the sky!" ◄ Deuteronomy 10:22 ► [NLT]

"Let us go right into the presence of **GOD** with sincere hearts fully trusting **HIM**. For our guilty consciences have been sprinkled with **CHRIST's Blood** to make us clean, and our bodies have been washed with pure water."
◄ Hebrews 10:22 ► [NLT]

"The **Blessing** of the **LORD** makes a person rich, and **HE** adds no sorrow with it."
◄ Proverbs 10:22 ► [NLT]

"**MY FATHER** has entrusted everything to **ME**. No one **Truly** knows the **SON** except the **FATHER**, and no one truly knows the **FATHER** except the **SON** and those to whom the **SON Chooses** to reveal **HIM**."
◄ Luke 10:22 ► [NLT]

Powerful Manifestation Prayer:

I BLESS myself, my family and everyone born on this date with GOD's MOST POWERFUL PURE LOVING LIGHT, HIS MOST POWERFUL PURE SOURCE HEALING ENERGY, and an ABUNDANCE OF HIS AMAZING GREATER GRACE in the POWER, the ANOINTING, the AUTHORITY and the WISDOM of the HOLY SPIRIT, in JESUS' MOST HOLY NAME. AMEN INDEED!

Day 296
10:23

"**You** say, "I am allowed to do anything"—but not everything is **GOoD** for **You**. **You** say, "I am allowed to do anything"—but not everything is beneficial." ◀ 1 Corinthians 10:23 ▶ [NLT]

"Let us hold tightly without wavering to the **HOPE** we affirm, for **GOD** can be trusted to keep **HIS Promise**." ◀ Hebrews 10:23 ▶ [NLT]

"A fool finds pleasure in wicked schemes, but a person of **Understanding** delights in **Wisdom**." ◀ Proverbs 10:23 ▶ [NIV]

"I know, **LORD**, that our lives are not our own. We are not able to plan our own course." ◀ Jeremiah 10:23 ▶ [NLT]

"**JESUS** looked around and said to **HIS Disciples**, "How hard it is for the rich to enter the **Kingdom** of **GOD**!" ◀ Mark 10:23 ▶ [NLT]

"Then **HE** turned to **HIS Disciples** and said privately, "**Blessed** are the eyes that see what **You** see." ◀ Luke 10:23 ▶ [NIV]

Powerful Manifestation Prayer:

I BLESS myself, my family and everyone born on this date with GOD's MOST POWERFUL PURE LOVING LIGHT, HIS MOST POWERFUL PURE SOURCE HEALING ENERGY, and an ABUNDANCE OF HIS AMAZING GREATER GRACE in the POWER, the ANOINTING, the AUTHORITY and the WISDOM of the HOLY SPIRIT, in JESUS' MOST HOLY NAME. AMEN INDEED!

Day 297
10:24

"What the wicked dread will overtake them; what the **Righteous** desire will be granted."
◄ Proverbs 10:24 ► [NIV]

"Discipline me, **LORD**, but only in due measure—not in **YOUR** anger, or **YOU Will** reduce me to nothing."
◄ Jeremiah 10:24 ► [NIV]

"Let us think of ways to motivate one another to acts of **Love** and **GOoD** works."
◄ Hebrews 10:24 ► [NLT]

"The **Disciples** were amazed at **HIS WORDS**, but **JESUS** said again, "Children, how hard it is to enter the **Kingdom** of **GOD**!"
◄ Mark 10:24 ► [NIV]

"The people surrounded **HIM** and asked, "How long are **YOU** going to keep us in suspense? If **YOU** are the **MESSIAH**, tell us plainly."
◄ John 10:24 ► [NLT]

"**I** tell **You**, many prophets and kings longed to see what **You** see, but they didn't see it. And they longed to hear what **You** hear, but they didn't hear it."
◄ Luke 10:24 ► [NLT]

Powerful Manifestation Prayer:

I BLESS myself, my family and everyone born on this date with GOD's MOST POWERFUL PURE LOVING LIGHT, HIS MOST POWERFUL PURE SOURCE HEALING ENERGY, and an ABUNDANCE OF HIS AMAZING GREATER GRACE in the POWER, the ANOINTING, the AUTHORITY and the WISDOM of the HOLY SPIRIT, in JESUS' MOST HOLY NAME. AMEN INDEED!

Day 298
10:25

"Do not be afraid; do not be discouraged. Be strong and courageous. This is what the **LORD Will** do to all the enemies **You** are going to fight." ◀ Joshua 10:25 ▶ [NIV]

"And let us not neglect our meeting together, as some people do, but encourage one another, especially now that the day of **HIS** return is drawing near." ◀ Hebrews 10:25 ▶ [NLT]

"When the storms of life come, the wicked are whirled away, but the **GODly** have a lasting foundation." ◀ Proverbs 10:25 ▶ [NLT]

"One day an expert in religious law stood up to test **JESUS** by asking **HIM** this question: "**TEACHER**, what should I do to inherit **Eternal Life**?" ◀ Luke 10:25 ▶ [NLT]

"In fact, it is easier for a camel to go through the eye of a needle than for a rich person to enter the **Kingdom** of **GOD**!" ◀ Mark 10:25 ▶ [NLT]

"**JESUS** replied, '**I** have already told **You**, and **You** don't believe **ME**. The proof is the work **I** do in **MY FATHER's Name**." ◀ John 10:25 ▶ [NLT]

Powerful Manifestation Prayer:

I BLESS myself, my family and everyone born on this date with GOD's MOST POWERFUL PURE LOVING LIGHT, HIS MOST POWERFUL PURE SOURCE HEALING ENERGY, and an ABUNDANCE OF HIS AMAZING GREATER GRACE in the POWER, the ANOINTING, the AUTHORITY and the WISDOM of the HOLY SPIRIT, in JESUS' MOST HOLY NAME. AMEN INDEED!

Day 299
10:26

"So, do not be afraid of them, for there is nothing concealed that will not be disclosed, or hidden that will not be made known."
◀ Matthew 10:26 ▶ [NIV]

"Lazy people irritate their employers, like vinegar to the teeth or smoke in the eyes."
◀ Proverbs 10:26 ▶ [NLT]

"And we won't know how we are to worship the **LORD** until we get there."
◀ Exodus 10:26 ▶ [NLT]

"If we deliberately keep on sinning after we have received the **Knowledge** of the **Truth**, no sacrifice for sins is left."
◀ Hebrews 10:26 ▶ [NIV]

"The **LORD** of **Heaven's Armies** will lash them with **HIS** whip, as **HE** did when Gideon triumphed over the Midianites at the rock of Oreb, or when the **LORD's Staff** was raised to drown the Egyptian army in the sea."
◀ Isaiah 10:26 ▶ [NLT]

"For, 'The earth is the **LORD's**, and everything in it'."
◀ 1 Corinthians 10:26 ▶ [NLT]

"The **Disciples** were even more amazed, and said to each other, "Who then can be saved?"
◀ Mark 10:26 ▶ [NIV]

Powerful Manifestation Prayer:

I BLESS myself, my family and everyone born on this date with GOD's MOST POWERFUL PURE LOVING LIGHT, HIS MOST POWERFUL PURE SOURCE HEALING ENERGY, and an ABUNDANCE OF HIS AMAZING GREATER GRACE in the POWER, the ANOINTING, the AUTHORITY and the WISDOM of the HOLY SPIRIT, in JESUS' MOST HOLY NAME. AMEN INDEED!

Day 300
10:27

"The fear of the LORD adds length to life, but the years of the wicked are cut short."
◄ Proverbs 10:27 ► [NIV]

"There is only the terrible expectation of GOD's judgment and the raging fire that will consume HIS enemies."
◄ Hebrews 10:27 ► [NLT]

"JESUS looked at them intently and said, "Humanly speaking, it is impossible. But not with GOD. Everything is possible with GOD."
◄ Mark 10:27 ► [NLT]

"HE answered, 'Love the LORD your GOD with all your heart and with all your Soul and with all your strength and with all your mind'; and, 'Love your neighbor as yourself.'"
◄ Luke 10:27 ► [NIV]

"MY Sheep listen to MY Voice; I know them, and they follow ME."
◄ John 10:27 ► [NIV]

"If an unbeliever invites You to a meal and You want to go, eat whatever is put before You without raising questions of conscience."
◄ 1 Corinthians 10:27 ► [NIV]

Powerful Manifestation Prayer:

I BLESS myself, my family and everyone born on this date with GOD's MOST POWERFUL PURE LOVING LIGHT, HIS MOST POWERFUL PURE SOURCE HEALING ENERGY, and an ABUNDANCE OF HIS AMAZING GREATER GRACE in the POWER, the ANOINTING, the AUTHORITY and the WISDOM of the HOLY SPIRIT, in JESUS' MOST HOLY NAME. AMEN INDEED!

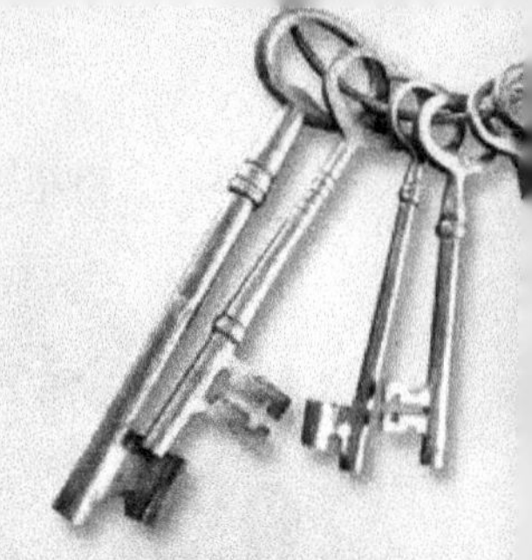

Day 301
10:28

"But **GOD** has shown me that I should not call anyone impure or unclean." ◄ Acts 10:28 ► [NIV]

"The **HOPES** of the **GODly** result in happiness, but the expectations of the wicked come to nothing." ◄ Proverbs 10:28 ► [NLT]

"And do not fear those who kill the body but cannot kill the **Soul**. Rather fear him who can destroy both **Soul** and body in hell." ◄ Matthew 10:28 ► [NIV]

"Then Peter spoke up, "We have left everything to follow **YOU**!" ◄ Mark 10:28 ► [NIV]

"'Right'! **JESUS** told him. "Do this and **You** will live!" ◄ Luke 10:28 ► [NLT]

"**I** give them **Eternal Life**, and they will never perish. No one can snatch them away from **ME**." ◄ John 10:28 ► [NLT]

Powerful Manifestation Prayer:

I BLESS myself, my family and everyone born on this date with GOD's MOST POWERFUL PURE LOVING LIGHT, HIS MOST POWERFUL PURE SOURCE HEALING ENERGY, and an ABUNDANCE OF HIS AMAZING GREATER GRACE in the POWER, the ANOINTING, the AUTHORITY and the WISDOM of the HOLY SPIRIT, in JESUS' MOST HOLY NAME. AMEN INDEED!

Day 302
10:29

"The man wanted to justify his actions, so he asked **JESUS**, "And who is my neighbor?"
◀ Luke 10:29 ▶ [NLT]

"It might not be a matter of conscience for **You**, but it is for the other person. For why should my **Freedom** be limited by what someone else thinks?" ◀ 1 Corinthians 10:29 ▶ [NLT]

"Just think how much worse the punishment will be for those who have trampled on the **SON** of **GOD**, and have treated the **Blood** of the **Covenant**, which made us **Holy**, as if it were common and unholy, and have insulted and disdained the **HOLY SPIRIT** who brings **GOD's** mercy to us."
◀ Hebrews 10:29 ▶ [NLT]

"What is the price of two sparrows—one copper coin? But not a single sparrow can fall to the ground without your **FATHER** knowing it." ◀ Matthew 10:29 ▶ [NLT]

"So, I came without objection as soon as I was sent for. Now tell me why **You** sent for me."
◀ Acts 10:29 ▶ [NLT]

"**MY FATHER**, **WHO** has given them to **ME**, is **Greater** than all; no one can snatch them out of **MY FATHER's Hand**." ◀ John 10:29 ▶ [NIV]

Powerful Manifestation Prayer:

I BLESS myself, my family and everyone born on this date with GOD's MOST POWERFUL PURE LOVING LIGHT, HIS MOST POWERFUL PURE SOURCE HEALING ENERGY, and an ABUNDANCE OF HIS AMAZING GREATER GRACE in the POWER, the ANOINTING, the AUTHORITY and the WISDOM of the HOLY SPIRIT, in JESUS' MOST HOLY NAME. AMEN INDEED!

Day 303
10:30

"Four days ago, I was Praying in my house about this same time, three o'clock in the afternoon. Suddenly, a MAN in dazzling clothes was standing in front of me." ◀ Acts 10:30 ▶ [NLT]

"I and MY FATHER are ONE." ◀ John 10:30 ▶ [NLT]

"For we know HIM WHO said, "It is MINE to avenge; I Will repay," and again, "The LORD Will judge HIS people." ◀ Hebrews 10:30 ▶ [NIV]

"If I can thank GOD for the food and enjoy it, why should I be condemned for eating it?" ◀ 1 Corinthians 10:30 ▶ [NLT]

"And even the very hairs of your head are all numbered." ◀ Matthew 10:30 ▶ [NIV]

"But he shall receive a hundredfold now in this time, houses, and brethren, and sisters, and mothers, and children, and lands, with persecutions; and in the world to come Eternal Life." ◀ Mark 10:30 ▶ [KJV]

Powerful Manifestation Prayer:

I BLESS myself, my family and everyone born on this date with GOD's MOST POWERFUL PURE LOVING LIGHT, HIS MOST POWERFUL PURE SOURCE HEALING ENERGY, and an ABUNDANCE OF HIS AMAZING GREATER GRACE in the POWER, the ANOINTING, the AUTHORITY and the WISDOM of the HOLY SPIRIT, in JESUS' MOST HOLY NAME. AMEN INDEED!

Day 304
10:31

"It is a terrible thing to fall into the Hands of the Living GOD." ◀ Hebrews 10:31 ▶ [NLT]

"By chance a priest came along. But when he saw the man lying there, he crossed to the other side of the road and passed him by." ◀ Luke 10:31 ▶ [NLT]

"But many who are first will be last, and the last, first." ◀ Mark 10:31 ▶ [NIV]

"So, don't be afraid; You are worth more than many sparrows." ◀ Matthew 10:31 ▶ [NIV]

"HE told me… your Prayer has been heard, and your gifts to the poor have been noticed by GOD!" ◀ Acts 10:31 ▶ [NLT]

"So, whether You eat or drink or whatever You do, do it all for the Glory of GOD." ◀ 1 Corinthians 10:31 ▶ [NIV]

Powerful Manifestation Prayer:

I BLESS myself, my family and everyone born on this date with GOD's MOST POWERFUL PURE LOVING LIGHT, HIS MOST POWERFUL PURE SOURCE HEALING ENERGY, and an ABUNDANCE OF HIS AMAZING GREATER GRACE in the POWER, the ANOINTING, the AUTHORITY and the WISDOM of the HOLY SPIRIT, in JESUS' MOST HOLY NAME. AMEN INDEED!

November
11

~ I Pray for You and You Pray for Me!

"After Job had prayed for his friends, the LORD restored his fortunes and gave him twice as much as he had before." ◀ Job 42:10 ▶ [NIV]

"You haven't done this before. A.S.K. using MY NAME, and You will receive, and You will have abundant joy." ◀ John 16:24 ▶ [NLT]

Powerful Manifestation Prayer:

I BLESS myself, my family and everyone born in this month with GOD's MOST POWERFUL PURE LOVING LIGHT, HIS MOST POWERFUL PURE SOURCE HEALING ENERGY, and an ABUNDANCE OF HIS AMAZING GREATER GRACE in the POWER, the ANOINTING, the AUTHORITY and the WISDOM of the HOLY SPIRIT, in JESUS' MOST HOLY NAME.
AMEN INDEED!

A.S.K.- Additional Scripture Knowledge

Write Additional Scriptures here.

Day 305
11:1

"One day **JESUS** was **Praying** in a certain place. When **HE** finished, one of **HIS Disciples** said to **HIM**, "**LORD**, teach us to **Pray**, just as John taught his disciples." ◀ Luke 11:1 ▶ [NIV]

"And **You** should imitate me, just as I imitate **CHRIST**." ◀ 1 Corinthians 11:1 ▶ [NLT]

"**Love** the **LORD** your **GOD** and keep **HIS Requirements**, **HIS Decrees**, **HIS Laws** and **HIS Commands** always." ◀ Deuteronomy 11:1 ▶ [NIV]

"Now **Faith** is confidence in what we **HOPE** for and assurance about what we do not see." ◀ Hebrews 11:1 ▶ [NIV]

"I trust in the **LORD** for protection. So why do **You** say to me, "Fly like a bird to the mountains for safety!" ◀ Psalm 11:1 ▶ [NLT]

"Then the **SPIRIT** lifted me up and brought me to the gate of the house of the **LORD** that faces east." ◀ Ezekiel 11:1 ▶ [NIV]

Powerful Manifestation Prayer:

I BLESS myself, my family and everyone born on this date with GOD's MOST POWERFUL PURE LOVING LIGHT, HIS MOST POWERFUL PURE SOURCE HEALING ENERGY, and an ABUNDANCE OF HIS AMAZING GREATER GRACE in the POWER, the ANOINTING, the AUTHORITY and the WISDOM of the HOLY SPIRIT, in JESUS' MOST HOLY NAME. AMEN INDEED!

Day 306
11:2

"Remember today that your children were not the ones who saw and experienced the discipline of the LORD your GOD: HIS majesty, HIS Mighty Hand, HIS outstretched Arm."

◀ Deuteronomy 11:2 ▶ [NIV]

"I am so glad that You always keep me in your thoughts, and that You are following the teachings I passed on to You."

◀ 1 Corinthians 11:2 ▶ [NLT]

"Pride leads to disgrace, but with humility comes Wisdom."

◀ Proverbs 11:2 ▶ [NLT]

"But divide your investments among many places, for You do not know what risks might lie ahead."

◀ Ecclesiastes 11:2 ▶ [NLT]

"The LORD said to me, 'Son of man, these are the men who are plotting evil and giving wicked advice in this city.'"

◀ Ezekiel 11:2 ▶ [NIV]

"The SPIRIT of the LORD Will rest on HIM-- the SPIRIT of Wisdom and of Understanding, the SPIRIT of Counsel and of Might, the SPIRIT of the Knowledge and fear of the LORD."

◀ Isaiah 11:2 ▶ [NIV]

Powerful Manifestation Prayer:

I BLESS myself, my family and everyone born on this date with GOD's MOST POWERFUL PURE LOVING LIGHT, HIS MOST POWERFUL PURE SOURCE HEALING ENERGY, and an ABUNDANCE OF HIS AMAZING GREATER GRACE in the POWER, the ANOINTING, the AUTHORITY and the WISDOM of the HOLY SPIRIT, in JESUS' MOST HOLY NAME. AMEN INDEED!

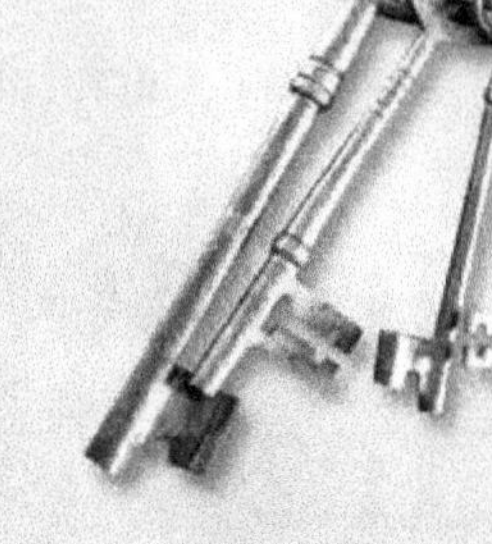

Day 307
11:3

"By **Faith** we understand that the universe was formed at **GOD's Command**, so that what is seen was not made out of what was visible." ◀ Hebrews 11:3 ▶ [NIV]

"They didn't see the miraculous signs and wonders **HE** performed in Egypt against Pharaoh and all his land." ◀ Deuteronomy 11:3 ▶ [NLT]

"Honesty guides **GOoD** people; dishonesty destroys treacherous people." ◀ Proverbs 11:3 ▶ [NLT]

"**HE Will** delight in obeying **The LORD**. **HE Will** not judge by appearance nor make a decision based on hearsay." ◀ Isaiah 11:3 ▶ [NLT]

"Tell them that this is what **The LORD**, **The GOD** of Israel, says: 'Cursed is the one who does not obey the terms of this **Covenant**.'" ◀ Jeremiah 11:3 ▶ [NIV]

"But I want **You** to realize that the head of every man is **CHRIST**, the head of woman is man, and the head of **CHRIST** is **GOD**." ◀ 1 Corinthians 11:3 ▶ [NIV]

Powerful Manifestation Prayer:

I BLESS myself, my family and everyone born on this date with GOD's MOST POWERFUL PURE LOVING LIGHT, HIS MOST POWERFUL PURE SOURCE HEALING ENERGY, and an ABUNDANCE OF HIS AMAZING GREATER GRACE in the POWER, the ANOINTING, the AUTHORITY and the WISDOM of the HOLY SPIRIT, in JESUS' MOST HOLY NAME. AMEN INDEED!

Day 308
11:4

"The **LORD** is in **HIS Holy Temple**; the **LORD** is on **HIS Heavenly Throne**. **HE** observes everyone on earth; **HIS** eyes examine them." ◀ Psalm 11:4 ▶ [NIV]

"They didn't see what the **LORD** did to the armies of Egypt and to their horses and chariots—how **HE** drowned them in the Red Sea as they were chasing **You**. **HE** destroyed them, and they have not recovered to this very day!" ◀ Deuteronomy 11:4 ▶ [NLT]

"Riches won't help on the day of judgment, but right living can save **You** from death." ◀ Proverbs 11:4 ▶ [NLT]

"Farmers who wait for perfect weather never plant. If they watch every cloud, they never harvest." ◀ Ecclesiastes 11:4 ▶ [NLT]

"**HE Will** give justice to the poor and make fair decisions for the exploited. The earth will shake at the force of **HIS WORD**, and one breath from **HIS** mouth will destroy the wicked." ◀ Isaiah 11:4 ▶ [NLT]

"Obey **ME** and do everything **I** command **You**, and **You** will be **MY** people, and **I Will** be your **GOD**." ◀ Jeremiah 11:4 ▶ [NIV]

Powerful Manifestation Prayer:

I BLESS myself, my family and everyone born on this date with GOD's MOST POWERFUL PURE LOVING LIGHT, HIS MOST POWERFUL PURE SOURCE HEALING ENERGY, and an ABUNDANCE OF HIS AMAZING GREATER GRACE in the POWER, the ANOINTING, the AUTHORITY and the WISDOM of the HOLY SPIRIT, in JESUS' MOST HOLY NAME. AMEN INDEED!

Day 309
11:5

"It was by **Faith** that Enoch was taken up to **Heaven** without dying—'he disappeared, because **GOD** took him.' For before he was taken up, he was known as a person who pleased **GOD**."

◀ Hebrews 11:5 ▶ [NLT]

"Now **JESUS Loved** Martha and her sister [Mary] and Lazarus." ◀ John 11:5 ▶ [NIV]

"Your children didn't see how the **LORD** cared for **You** in the wilderness until **You** arrived here."

◀ Deuteronomy 11:5 ▶ [NLT]

"The **LORD** examines both the **Righteous** and the wicked. **HE** hates those who love violence."

◀ Psalm 11:5 ▶ [NLT]

"As **You** do not know the path of the wind, or how the body is formed in a mother's womb, so **You** cannot understand the work of **GOD**, the **Maker** of all things." ◀ Ecclesiastes 11:5 ▶ [NIV]

"**HE Will** wear **Righteousness** like a belt and **Truth** like an undergarment." ◀ Isaiah 11:5 ▶ [NLT]

"**I** said this so **I** could keep **MY Promise** to your ancestors to give **You** a land flowing with milk and honey—the land **You** live in today. Then I replied, "Amen, **LORD**! May it be so."

◀ Jeremiah 11:5 ▶ [NLT]

Powerful Manifestation Prayer:

I BLESS myself, my family and everyone born on this date with GOD's MOST POWERFUL PURE LOVING LIGHT, HIS MOST POWERFUL PURE SOURCE HEALING ENERGY, and an ABUNDANCE OF HIS AMAZING GREATER GRACE in the POWER, the ANOINTING, the AUTHORITY and the WISDOM of the HOLY SPIRIT, in JESUS' MOST HOLY NAME. AMEN INDEED!

Day 310
11:6

"And without **Faith** it is impossible to please **GOD**, because anyone who comes to **HIM** must believe that **HE** exists and that **HE** rewards those who earnestly seek **HIM**." ◀ Hebrews 11:6 ▶ [NIV]

"**HE Will** rain down blazing coals and burning sulfur on the wicked, punishing them with scorching winds." ◀ Psalm 11:6 ▶ [NLT]

"Plant your seed in the morning and keep busy all afternoon, for **You** don't know if profit will come from one activity or another—or maybe both." ◀ Ecclesiastes 11:6 ▶ [NLT]

"The **LORD** said to me, "Proclaim all these **Words** in the towns of Judah and in the streets of Jerusalem: "Listen to the terms of this **Covenant** and follow them." ◀ Jeremiah 11:6 ▶ [NIV]

"They answered as **JESUS** had told them to, and the people let them go." ◀ Mark 11:6 ▶ [NIV]

"I may indeed be untrained as a speaker, but I do have **Knowledge**. We have made this perfectly clear to **You** in every way." ◀ 2 Corinthians 11:6 ▶ [NIV]

Powerful Manifestation Prayer:

I BLESS myself, my family and everyone born on this date with GOD's MOST POWERFUL PURE LOVING LIGHT, HIS MOST POWERFUL PURE SOURCE HEALING ENERGY, and an ABUNDANCE OF HIS AMAZING GREATER GRACE in the POWER, the ANOINTING, the AUTHORITY and the WISDOM of the HOLY SPIRIT, in JESUS' MOST HOLY NAME. AMEN INDEED!

Day 311
11:7

"It was by **Faith** that Noah built a large **BOAT** to save his family from the flood. He obeyed **GOD, WHO** warned him about things that had never happened before. By his **Faith** Noah condemned the rest of the world, and he received the **Righteousness** that comes by **Faith**." ◀ Hebrews 11:7 ▶ [NLT]

"Can **You** solve the mysteries of **GOD**? Can **You** discover everything about the **ALMIGHTY**?"
◀ Job 11:7 ▶ [NLT]

"For the **LORD** is **Righteous**, **HE Loves** justice; the upright will see **HIS Face**."
◀ Psalm 11:7 ▶ [NIV]

"From the time **I** brought your ancestors up from Egypt until today, **I** warned them again and again, saying, "Obey **ME**." ◀ Jeremiah 11:7 ▶ [NIV]

"Was I wrong when I humbled myself and honored **You** by preaching **GOD's GOoD News** to **You** without expecting anything in return?" ◀ 2 Corinthians 11:7 ▶ [NLT]

"**Light** is sweet; how pleasant to see a new day dawning." ◀ Ecclesiastes 11:7 ▶ [NLT]

Powerful Manifestation Prayer:

I BLESS myself, my family and everyone born on this date with GOD's MOST POWERFUL PURE LOVING LIGHT, HIS MOST POWERFUL PURE SOURCE HEALING ENERGY, and an ABUNDANCE OF HIS AMAZING GREATER GRACE in the POWER, the ANOINTING, the AUTHORITY and the WISDOM of the HOLY SPIRIT, in JESUS' MOST HOLY NAME. AMEN INDEED!

Day 312
11:8

"The **Righteous** person is rescued from trouble, and it falls on the wicked instead."
◀ Proverbs 11:8 ▶ [NIV]

"When people live to be very old, let them rejoice in every day of life. But let them also remember there will be many dark days."
◀ Ecclesiastes 11:8 ▶ [NLT]

"I replied, 'Surely not, **LORD**! Nothing impure or unclean has ever entered my mouth.'"
◀ Acts 11:8 ▶ [NIV]

"It was by **Faith** that Abraham obeyed when **GOD** called him to leave home and go to another land that **GOD** would give him as his inheritance. He went without knowing where he was going."
◀ Hebrews 11:8 ▶ [NLT]

"The sky is no limit for **GOD**, but it lies beyond your reach. **GOD** knows the world of the dead, but **You** do not know it."
◀ Job 11:8 ▶ [GNT]

"But I tell **You** this—though he won't do it for friendship's sake, if **You** keep knocking long enough, he will get up and give **You** whatever **You** need because of your shameless persistence."
◀ Luke 11:8 ▶ [NLT]

Powerful Manifestation Prayer:

I BLESS myself, my family and everyone born on this date with GOD's MOST POWERFUL PURE LOVING LIGHT, HIS MOST POWERFUL PURE SOURCE HEALING ENERGY, and an ABUNDANCE OF HIS AMAZING GREATER GRACE in the POWER, the ANOINTING, the AUTHORITY and the WISDOM of the HOLY SPIRIT, in JESUS' MOST HOLY NAME. AMEN INDEED!

Day 313
11:9

"So, I say to You: ASK and it will be given to You; seek and You will find; knock and the door will be opened to You." ◄ Luke 11:9 ► [NIV]

"Young people, it's wonderful to be young! Enjoy every minute of it. Do everything You want to do; take it all in. But remember that You must give an account to GOD for everything You do." ◄ Ecclesiastes 11:9 ► [NLT]

"Likewise, David said, 'Let their bountiful table become a snare, a trap that makes them think all is well. Let their Blessings cause them to stumble and let them get what they deserve.'" ◄ Romans 11:9 ► [NLT]

"Nothing will hurt or destroy in all MY Holy mountain, for as the waters fill the sea, so the earth will be filled with people who know the LORD." ◄ Isaiah 11:9 ► [NLT]

"But the Voice from Heaven spoke again: 'Do not call something unclean if GOD has made it clean." ◄ Acts 11:9 ► [NLT]

"JESUS replied, "There are twelve hours of daylight every day. During the day people can walk safely. They can see because they have the Light of this world." ◄ John 11:9 ► [NLT]

Powerful Manifestation Prayer:

I BLESS myself, my family and everyone born on this date with GOD's MOST POWERFUL PURE LOVING LIGHT, HIS MOST POWERFUL PURE SOURCE HEALING ENERGY, and an ABUNDANCE OF HIS AMAZING GREATER GRACE in the POWER, the ANOINTING, the AUTHORITY and the WISDOM of the HOLY SPIRIT, in JESUS' MOST HOLY NAME. AMEN INDEED!

Day 314
11:10

"So, refuse to worry, and keep your body healthy. But remember that youth, with a whole life before You, is meaningless."
◀ Ecclesiastes 11:10 ▶ [NLT]

"They have returned to the sins of their ancestors, who refused to listen to **MY WORDS**. They have followed other gods to serve them. Both Israel and Judah have broken the **Covenant I** made with their ancestors."
◀ Jeremiah 11:10 ▶ [NIV]

"May their eyes be darkened so they cannot see, and their backs be bent forever."
◀ Romans 11:10 ▶ [NIV]

"As surely as the **Truth** of **CHRIST** is in me, no one in all of Greece will ever stop me from boasting about this."
◀ 2 Corinthians 11:10 ▶ [NLT]

"For everyone who **ASKs** receives; the one who seeks finds; and to the one who knocks, the door will be opened."
◀ Luke 11:10 ▶ [NIV]

"This happened three times, and then it was all pulled up to **Heaven** again."
◀ Acts 11:10 ▶ [NLT]

Powerful Manifestation Prayer:

I BLESS myself, my family and everyone born on this date with GOD's MOST POWERFUL PURE LOVING LIGHT, HIS MOST POWERFUL PURE SOURCE HEALING ENERGY, and an ABUNDANCE OF HIS AMAZING GREATER GRACE in the POWER, the ANOINTING, the AUTHORITY and the WISDOM of the HOLY SPIRIT, in JESUS' MOST HOLY NAME. AMEN INDEED!

Day 315
11:11

"Upright citizens are **GOoD** for a city and make it prosper, but the talk of the wicked tears it apart."
◀ Proverbs 11:11 ▶ [NLT]

"He asked the **LORD**, "Why have **YOU** brought this trouble on your servant? What have I done to displease **YOU** that **YOU** put the burden of all these people on me?"
◀ Numbers 11:11 ▶ [NIV]

"Why? Because I do not **Love You**? **GOD** knows I do!" ◀ 2 Corinthians 11:11 ▶ [NIV]

"For **HE** knows those who are false, and **HE** takes note of all their sins."
◀ Job 11:11 ▶ [NLT]

"Therefore, this is what the **LORD** says: '**I Will** bring on them a disaster they cannot escape. Although they cry out to **ME**, **I Will** not listen to them." ◀ Jeremiah 11:11 ▶ [NIV]

"It was by **Faith** that even Sarah was able to have a child, though she was barren and was too old. She believed that **GOD** would keep **HIS Promise**." ◀ Hebrews 11:11 ▶ [NLT]

"**I** tell **You** the **Truth**, of all who have ever lived, none is greater than John the Baptist. Yet even the least person in the **Kingdom** of **Heaven** is greater than he is!" ◀ Matthew 11:11 ▶ [NLT]

Powerful Manifestation Prayer:

I BLESS myself, my family and everyone born on this date with GOD's MOST POWERFUL PURE LOVING LIGHT, HIS MOST POWERFUL PURE SOURCE HEALING ENERGY, and an ABUNDANCE OF HIS AMAZING GREATER GRACE in the POWER, the ANOINTING, the AUTHORITY and the WISDOM of the HOLY SPIRIT, in JESUS' MOST HOLY NAME. AMEN INDEED!

Day 316
11:12

"Then the people of Judah and Jerusalem will pray to their idols and burn incense before them. But the idols will not save them when disaster strikes!" ◀ Jeremiah 11:12 ▶ [NLT]

"An empty-headed person won't become wise any more than a wild donkey can bear a human child." ◀ Job 11:12 ▶ [NLT]

"The **Disciples** said, "**LORD**, if he is sleeping, he will **SOON** get better!" ◀ John 11:12 ▶ [NLT]

"And so, a whole nation came from this one man [Abraham] who was as **GOoD** as dead—a nation with so many people that, like the stars in the sky and the sand on the seashore, there is no way to count them." ◀ Hebrews 11:12 ▶ [NLT]

"And from the time John the Baptist began preaching until now, the **Kingdom** of **Heaven** has been forcefully advancing, and violent people are attacking it." ◀ Matthew 11:12 ▶ [NLT]

"The **SPIRIT** told me to have no hesitation about going with them." ◀ Acts 11:12 ▶ [NIV]

Powerful Manifestation Prayer:

I BLESS myself, my family and everyone born on this date with GOD's MOST POWERFUL PURE LOVING LIGHT, HIS MOST POWERFUL PURE SOURCE HEALING ENERGY, and an ABUNDANCE OF HIS AMAZING GREATER GRACE in the POWER, the ANOINTING, the AUTHORITY and the WISDOM of the HOLY SPIRIT, in JESUS' MOST HOLY NAME. AMEN INDEED!

Day 317
11:13

"A gossip betrays a confidence, but a trustworthy person keeps a secret."

◀ Proverbs 11:13 ▶ [NIV]

"Look now, people of Judah; **You** have as many gods as **You** have towns. **You** have as many altars of shame—altars for burning incense to your god Baal—as there are streets in Jerusalem."

◀ Jeremiah 11:13 ▶ [NLT]

"Then at last the jealousy …will end. They will not be rivals anymore." ◀ Isaiah 11:13 ▶ [NLT]

"All these people died still believing what **GOD** had **Promised** them. They did not receive what was **Promised**, but they saw it all from a distance and welcomed it. They agreed that they were foreigners and nomads here on earth."

◀ Hebrews 11:13 ▶ [NLT]

"If **You** then, though **You** are evil, know how to give **GOoD** gifts to your children, how much more will your **FATHER** in **Heaven** give the **HOLY SPIRIT** to those who **ASK HIM**!"

◀ Luke 11:13 ▶ [NIV]

"If only **You** would prepare your heart and lift up your hands to **HIM** in **Prayer**!"

◀ Job 11:13 ▶ [NLT]

Powerful Manifestation Prayer:

I BLESS myself, my family and everyone born on this date with GOD's MOST POWERFUL PURE LOVING LIGHT, HIS MOST POWERFUL PURE SOURCE HEALING ENERGY, and an ABUNDANCE OF HIS AMAZING GREATER GRACE in the POWER, the ANOINTING, the AUTHORITY and the WISDOM of the HOLY SPIRIT, in JESUS' MOST HOLY NAME. AMEN INDEED!

Day 318
11:14

"The WORD of the LORD came to me." ◀ Ezekiel 11:14 ▶ [NIV]

"Without wise leadership, a nation falls; there is safety in having many advisers."
◀ Proverbs 11:14 ▶ [NLT]

"In those times many shall rise against the king of the south, and the violent among your own people shall lift themselves up in order to fulfill the vision, but they shall fail."
◀ Daniel 11:14 ▶ [ESV]

"JESUS was driving out a demon that was mute. When the demon left, the man who had been mute spoke, and the crowd was amazed." ◀ Luke 11:14 ▶ [NIV]

"Get rid of your sins and leave all iniquity behind You." ◀ Job 11:14 ▶ [NLT]

"HE Will bring You a message through which You and all your household will be saved."
◀ Acts 11:14 ▶ [NIV]

Powerful Manifestation Prayer:

I BLESS myself, my family and everyone born on this date with GOD's MOST POWERFUL PURE LOVING LIGHT, HIS MOST POWERFUL PURE SOURCE HEALING ENERGY, and an ABUNDANCE OF HIS AMAZING GREATER GRACE in the POWER, the ANOINTING, the AUTHORITY and the WISDOM of the HOLY SPIRIT, in JESUS' MOST HOLY NAME. AMEN INDEED!

Day 319
11:15

"There's danger in putting up security for a stranger's debt; it's safer not to guarantee another person's debt."
◀ Proverbs 11:15 ▶ [NLT]

"For since their rejection meant that **GOD** offered **Salvation** to the rest of the world, their acceptance will be even more wonderful. It will be life for those who were dead!"
◀ Romans 11:15 ▶ [NLT]

"And isn't long hair a woman's pride and joy? For it has been given to her as a covering."
◀ 1 Corinthians 11:15 ▶ [NLT]

"**HE Will** give **You** lush pastureland for your livestock, and **You** yourselves will have all **You** want to eat."
◀ Deuteronomy 11:15 ▶ [NLT]

"The **LORD** examines both the righteous and the wicked. He hates those who love violence."
◀ Psalm 11:15 ▶ [NLT]

"Then your face will brighten with innocence. **You** will be strong and **Free** of fear."
◀ Job 11:15 ▶ [NLT]

Powerful Manifestation Prayer:

I BLESS myself, my family and everyone born on this date with GOD's MOST POWERFUL PURE LOVING LIGHT, HIS MOST POWERFUL PURE SOURCE HEALING ENERGY, and an ABUNDANCE OF HIS AMAZING GREATER GRACE in the POWER, the ANOINTING, the AUTHORITY and the WISDOM of the HOLY SPIRIT, in JESUS' MOST HOLY NAME. AMEN INDEED!

Day 320
11:16

"You will forget your misery; it will be like water flowing away." ◀ Job 11:16 ▶ [NLT]

"Others, trying to test JESUS, demanded that HE show them a miraculous sign from Heaven to prove HIS Authority." ◀ Luke 11:16 ▶ [NLT]

"Instead, they were longing for a better country--a Heavenly one. Therefore, GOD is not ashamed to be called their GOD, for HE has prepared a city for them." ◀ Hebrews 11:16 ▶ [NIV]

"But if anyone wants to argue about this, I simply say that we have no other custom than this, and neither do GOD's other churches." ◀ 1 Corinthians 11:16 ▶ [NLT]

"But be careful. Don't let your heart be deceived so that You turn away from the LORD and serve and worship other gods." ◀ Deuteronomy 11:16 ▶ [NLT]

"A kindhearted woman gains honor, but ruthless men gain only wealth." ◀ Proverbs 11:16 ▶ [NIV]

Powerful Manifestation Prayer:

I BLESS myself, my family and everyone born on this date with GOD's MOST POWERFUL PURE LOVING LIGHT, HIS MOST POWERFUL PURE SOURCE HEALING ENERGY, and an ABUNDANCE OF HIS AMAZING GREATER GRACE in the POWER, the ANOINTING, the AUTHORITY and the WISDOM of the HOLY SPIRIT, in JESUS' MOST HOLY NAME. AMEN INDEED!

Day 321
11:17

"Your life will be brighter than the noonday. Even darkness will be as bright as morning."
◀ Job 11:17 ▶ [NLT]

"**JESUS** knew their thoughts and said to them: 'Any kingdom divided against itself will be ruined, and a house divided against itself will fall.'"
◀ Luke 11:17 ▶ [NIV]

"By **Faith** Abraham, when **GOD** tested him, offered Isaac as a sacrifice. He who had embraced the **Promises** was about to sacrifice his one and only son."
◀ Hebrews 11:17 ▶ [NIV]

"But in the following instructions, I cannot praise **You.** For it sounds as if more harm than **GOoD** is done when **You** meet together."
◀ 1 Corinthians 11:17 ▶ [NLT]

"**I Will** come down and talk to **You** there. **I Will** take some of the **SPIRIT** that is upon **You**, and **I Will** put the **SPIRIT** upon them also. They will bear the burden of the people along with **You**, so **You** will not have to carry it alone."
◀ Numbers 11:17 ▶ [NLT]

"Your kindness will reward **You**, but your cruelty will destroy **You**."
◀ Proverbs 11:17 ▶ [NLT]

Powerful Manifestation Prayer:

I BLESS myself, my family and everyone born on this date with GOD's MOST POWERFUL PURE LOVING LIGHT, HIS MOST POWERFUL PURE SOURCE HEALING ENERGY, and an ABUNDANCE OF HIS AMAZING GREATER GRACE in the POWER, the ANOINTING, the AUTHORITY and the WISDOM of the HOLY SPIRIT, in JESUS' MOST HOLY NAME. AMEN INDEED!

Day 322
11:18

"Having **HOPE** will give **You** courage. **You** will be protected and will rest in safety."
◀ Job 11:18 ▶ [NLT]

"**You** say **I AM** empowered by Satan. But if Satan is divided and fighting against himself, how can his kingdom survive?
◀ Luke 11:18 ▶ [NLT]

"First, I hear that there are divisions among **You** when **You** meet as a church, and to some extent I believe it."
◀ 1 Corinthians 11:18 ▶ [NLT]

"So commit yourselves wholeheartedly to these **WORDS** of **MINE**. Tie them to your hands and wear them on your forehead as reminders."
◀ Deuteronomy 11:18 ▶ [NLT]

"And say to the people, 'Purify yourselves, for tomorrow **You** will have meat to eat. **You** were whining, and the **LORD** heard **You** when **You** cried…. Now the **LORD Will** give **You** meat, and **You** will have to eat it."
◀ Numbers 11:18 ▶ [NLT]

"Evil people get rich for the moment, but the reward of the **GODly Will** last." ◀ Proverbs 11:18 ▶ [NLT]

Powerful Manifestation Prayer:

I BLESS myself, my family and everyone born on this date with GOD's MOST POWERFUL PURE LOVING LIGHT, HIS MOST POWERFUL PURE SOURCE HEALING ENERGY, and an ABUNDANCE OF HIS AMAZING GREATER GRACE in the POWER, the ANOINTING, the AUTHORITY and the WISDOM of the HOLY SPIRIT, in JESUS' MOST HOLY NAME. AMEN INDEED!

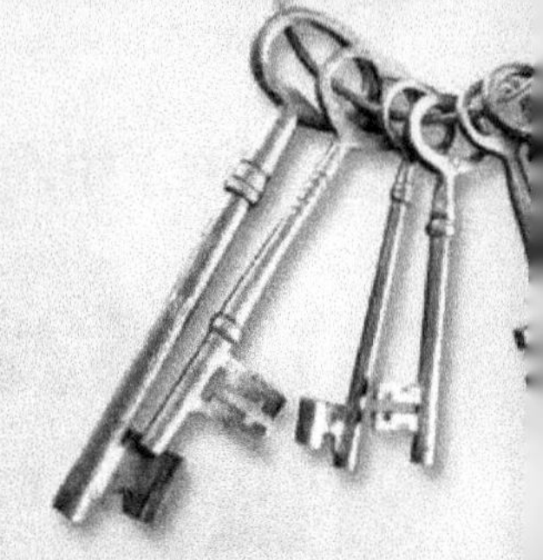

Day 323
11:19

"You will lie down unafraid, and many will look to You for help." ◀ Job 11:19 ▶ [NLT]

"Truly the Righteous attain life, but whoever pursues evil finds death." ◀ Proverbs 11:19 ▶ [NIV]

"Abraham reasoned that GOD could even raise the dead, and so in a manner of speaking he did receive Isaac back from death." ◀ Hebrews 11:19 ▶ [NIV]

"But, of course, there must be divisions among You so that You who have GOD's approval will be recognized!" ◀ 1 Corinthians 11:19 ▶ [NLT]

"Teach Them to your children. Talk about Them when You are at home and when You are on the road, when You are going to bed and when You are getting up." [Them = **The WORD of GOD**] ◀ Deuteronomy 11:19 ▶ [NLT]

"I Will give them an undivided heart and put a new SPIRIT in them; I Will remove from them their heart of stone and give them a heart of flesh." ◀ Ezekiel 11:19 ▶ [NIV]

Powerful Manifestation Prayer:

I BLESS myself, my family and everyone born on this date with GOD's MOST POWERFUL PURE LOVING LIGHT, HIS MOST POWERFUL PURE SOURCE HEALING ENERGY, and an ABUNDANCE OF HIS AMAZING GREATER GRACE in the POWER, the ANOINTING, the AUTHORITY and the WISDOM of the HOLY SPIRIT, in JESUS' MOST HOLY NAME. AMEN INDEED!

Day 324
11:20

"Then **JESUS** began to denounce the towns where **HE** had done so many of **HIS** miracles, because they hadn't repented of their sins and turned to **GOD**." ◀ Matthew 11:20 ▶ [NLT]

"The **LORD** detests those whose hearts are perverse, but **HE** delights in those whose ways are blameless." ◀ Proverbs 11:20 ▶ [NIV]

"But the wicked will be blinded. They will have no escape. Their only hope is death." ◀ Job 11:20 ▶ [NLT]

"But if **I AM** casting out demons by the **Power** of **GOD**, then the **Kingdom** of **GOD** has arrived among **You**." ◀ Luke 11:20 ▶ [NLT]

"By **Faith** Isaac **Blessed** Jacob and Esau in regard to their future." ◀ Hebrews 11:20 ▶ [NIV]

"Then they will follow **MY Decrees** and be careful to keep **MY Laws**. They will be **MY People**, and **I Will** be their **GOD**." ◀ Ezekiel 11:20 ▶ [NIV]

Powerful Manifestation Prayer:

I BLESS myself, my family and everyone born on this date with GOD's MOST POWERFUL PURE LOVING LIGHT, HIS MOST POWERFUL PURE SOURCE HEALING ENERGY, and an ABUNDANCE OF HIS AMAZING GREATER GRACE in the POWER, the ANOINTING, the AUTHORITY and the WISDOM of the HOLY SPIRIT, in JESUS' MOST HOLY NAME. AMEN INDEED!

Day 325
11:21

"For some of **You** hurry to eat your own meal without sharing with others. As a result, some go hungry while others get drunk."
◄ 1 Corinthians 11:21 ► [NLT]

"Be sure of this: The wicked will not go unpunished, but those who are **Righteous** will go **Free**."
◄ Proverbs 11:21 ► [NIV]

"But as for those who long for vile images and detestable idols, **I Will** repay them fully for their sins. **I, The Sovereign LORD**, have spoken!"
◄ Ezekiel 11:21 ► [NLT]

"When a strong man, fully armed, guards his own house, his possessions are safe."
◄ Luke 11:21 ► [NIV]

"Martha said to **JESUS**, '**LORD**, if only **YOU** had been here, my brother would not have died.'"
◄ John 11:21 ► [NLT]

"So that your days and the days of your children may be many in the land the **LORD** swore to give your ancestors, as many as the days that the **Heavens** are above the earth."
◄ Deuteronomy 11:21 ► [NIV]

Powerful Manifestation Prayer:

I BLESS myself, my family and everyone born on this date with GOD's MOST POWERFUL PURE LOVING LIGHT, HIS MOST POWERFUL PURE SOURCE HEALING ENERGY, and an ABUNDANCE OF HIS AMAZING GREATER GRACE in the POWER, the ANOINTING, the AUTHORITY and the WISDOM of the HOLY SPIRIT, in JESUS' MOST HOLY NAME. AMEN INDEED!

Day 326
11:22

"It was by **Faith** that Joseph, when he was about to die, said confidently that the people of Israel would leave Egypt." ◄ Hebrews 11:22 ► [NLT]

"Then the cherubim, with the wheels beside them, spread their wings, and the **Glory** of **The GOD** of Israel was above them." ◄ Ezekiel 11:22 ► [NIV]

"A beautiful woman who lacks discretion is like a gold ring in a pig's snout." ◄ Proverbs 11:22 ► [NLT]

"But when someone stronger attacks and overpowers him, he takes away the armor in which the man trusted and divides up his plunder." ◄ Luke 11:22 ► [NIV]

"Be careful to obey all these **Commands I AM** giving **You**. Show **Love** to the **LORD** your **GOD** by walking in **HIS** ways and holding tightly to **HIM**." ◄ Deuteronomy 11:22 ► [NLT]

"But I know that even now **GOD Will** give **You** whatever **You ASK**." ◄ John 11:22 ► [NIV]

Powerful Manifestation Prayer:

I BLESS myself, my family and everyone born on this date with GOD's MOST POWERFUL PURE LOVING LIGHT, HIS MOST POWERFUL PURE SOURCE HEALING ENERGY, and an ABUNDANCE OF HIS AMAZING GREATER GRACE in the POWER, the ANOINTING, the AUTHORITY and the WISDOM of the HOLY SPIRIT, in JESUS' MOST HOLY NAME. AMEN INDEED!

Day 327
11:23

"Anyone who isn't with **ME** opposes **ME**, and anyone who isn't working with **ME** is actually working against **ME**." ◄ Luke 11:23 ► [NLT]

"**JESUS** said to her, "Your brother will rise again." ◄ John 11:23 ► [NIV]

"It was by **Faith** that Moses' parents hid him for three months when he was born. They saw that **GOD** had given them an unusual child, and they were not afraid to disobey the king's command." ◄ Hebrews 11:23 ► [NLT]

"For I pass on to **You** what I received from the **LORD HIMSELF**. On the night when **HE** was betrayed, the **LORD JESUS** took some bread." ◄ 1 Corinthians 11:23 ► [NLT]

"Then the **LORD** said to Moses, 'Has **MY Arm** lost its **Power**? Now **You** will see whether or not **MY WORD** comes **True**!'" ◄ Numbers 11:23 ► [NLT]

"Then the **LORD Will** drive out all the nations ahead of **You**, though they are much greater and stronger than **You**, and **You** will take over their land." ◄ Deuteronomy 11:23 ► [NLT]

Powerful Manifestation Prayer:

I BLESS myself, my family and everyone born on this date with GOD's MOST POWERFUL PURE LOVING LIGHT, HIS MOST POWERFUL PURE SOURCE HEALING ENERGY, and an ABUNDANCE OF HIS AMAZING GREATER GRACE in the POWER, the ANOINTING, the AUTHORITY and the WISDOM of the HOLY SPIRIT, in JESUS' MOST HOLY NAME. AMEN INDEED!

Day 328
11:24

"Give **Freely** and become more wealthy; be stingy and lose everything." ◀ Proverbs 11:24 ▶ [NLT]

"When an evil spirit leaves a person, it goes into the desert, searching for rest. But when it finds none, it says, 'I will return to the person I came from." ◀ Luke 11:24 ▶ [NLT]

"Martha answered, I know he [Lazarus] will rise again in the **Resurrection** at the last day." ◀ John 11:24 ▶ [NIV]

"By **Faith** Moses, when he had grown up, refused to be known as the son of Pharaoh's daughter." ◀ Hebrews 11:24 ▶ [NIV]

"And when **HE** had given thanks, **HE** broke it and said, "This is **MY BODY**, which is given for **You**; do this in remembrance of **ME**." ◀ 1 Corinthians 11:24 ▶ [NIV]

"Every place where **You** set your foot will be yours: Your territory will extend from the desert…and from the...River to the... Sea." ◀ Deuteronomy 11:24 ▶ [NIV]

Powerful Manifestation Prayer:

I BLESS myself, my family and everyone born on this date with GOD's MOST POWERFUL PURE LOVING LIGHT, HIS MOST POWERFUL PURE SOURCE HEALING ENERGY, and an ABUNDANCE OF HIS AMAZING GREATER GRACE in the POWER, the ANOINTING, the AUTHORITY and the WISDOM of the HOLY SPIRIT, in JESUS' MOST HOLY NAME. AMEN INDEED!

Day 329
11:25

"**JESUS** said to her, "**I AM** the **Resurrection** and the **Life**. The one who believes in **ME Will** live, even though they die." ◀ John 11:25 ▶ [NIV]

"And when **You** stand **Praying**, if **You** hold anything against anyone, forgive them, so that your **FATHER** in **Heaven** may forgive **You** your sins." ◀ Mark 11:25 ▶ [NIV]

"So, it **[unclean spirit]** returns and finds that its former home is all swept and in order." ◀ Luke 11:25 ▶ [NLT]

"He [Moses] chose to be mistreated along with the people of **GOD** rather than to enjoy the fleeting pleasures of sin." ◀ Hebrews 11:25 ▶ [NIV]

"In the same way, **HE** took the cup of wine after supper, saying, "This cup is the **New Covenant** between **GOD** and **HIS** people—an **Agreement** confirmed with **MY BLOOD**. Do this in remembrance of **ME** as often as **You** drink it." ◀ 1 Corinthians 11:25 ▶ [NLT]

"No one will be able to stand against **You**. The **LORD** your **GOD**, as **HE Promised You**, will put the terror and fear of **You** on the whole land, wherever **You** go." ◀ Deuteronomy 11:25 ▶ [NIV]

Powerful Manifestation Prayer:

I BLESS myself, my family and everyone born on this date with GOD's MOST POWERFUL PURE LOVING LIGHT, HIS MOST POWERFUL PURE SOURCE HEALING ENERGY, and an ABUNDANCE OF HIS AMAZING GREATER GRACE in the POWER, the ANOINTING, the AUTHORITY and the WISDOM of the HOLY SPIRIT, in JESUS' MOST HOLY NAME. AMEN INDEED!

Day 330
11:26

"People curse the one who hoards grain, but they **Pray GOD's Blessing** on the one who is willing to sell."
◀ Proverbs 11:26 ▶ [NIV]

"Then the spirit finds seven other spirits more evil than itself, and they all enter the person and live there. And so that person is worse off than before."
◀ Luke 11:26 ▶ [NLT]

"He thought it was better to suffer for the sake of **CHRIST** than to own the treasures of Egypt, for he was looking ahead to his great reward."
◀ Hebrews 11:26 ▶ [NLT]

"And whoever lives by believing in **ME Will** never die. Do **You** believe this?"
◀ John 11:26 ▶ [NIV]

"For every time **You** eat this **Bread** and drink this **Cup**, **You** are announcing the **LORD's** death until **HE** comes again."
◀ 1 Corinthians 11:26 ▶ [NLT]

"Look, today **I AM** giving **You** the choice between a **Blessing** and a curse!"
◀ Deuteronomy 11:26 ▶ [NLT]

Powerful Manifestation Prayer:

I BLESS myself, my family and everyone born on this date with GOD's MOST POWERFUL PURE LOVING LIGHT, HIS MOST POWERFUL PURE SOURCE HEALING ENERGY, and an ABUNDANCE OF HIS AMAZING GREATER GRACE in the POWER, the ANOINTING, the AUTHORITY and the WISDOM of the HOLY SPIRIT, in JESUS' MOST HOLY NAME. AMEN INDEED!

Day 331
11:27

"If You search for GOoD, You will find Favor; but if You search for evil, it will find You!"
◄ Proverbs 11:27 ► [NLT]

"As HE was speaking, a woman in the crowd called out, 'GOD Bless YOUR MOTHER—the Womb from which YOU came, and the breasts that nursed YOU!'"
◄ Luke 11:27 ► [NLT]

"Yes, LORD," she replied, 'I believe that YOU are the MESSIAH, the SON of GOD, WHO is to come into the world.'"
◄ John 11:27 ► [NLT]

"It was by Faith that Moses left the land of Egypt, not fearing the king's anger. He kept right on going because he kept his eyes on the ONE WHO is Invisible."
◄ Hebrews 11:27 ► [NLT]

"Whoever, therefore, eats the Bread or drinks the Cup of the LORD in an unworthy manner will be guilty concerning the Body and Blood of the LORD."
◄ 1 Corinthians 11:27 ► [ESV]

"You will be Blessed if You obey the Commands of the LORD your GOD that I AM giving You today."
◄ Deuteronomy 11:27 ► [NLT]

Powerful Manifestation Prayer:

I BLESS myself, my family and everyone born on this date with GOD's MOST POWERFUL PURE LOVING LIGHT, HIS MOST POWERFUL PURE SOURCE HEALING ENERGY, and an ABUNDANCE OF HIS AMAZING GREATER GRACE in the POWER, the ANOINTING, the AUTHORITY and the WISDOM of the HOLY SPIRIT, in JESUS' MOST HOLY NAME. AMEN INDEED!

Day 332
11:28

"Now the man Jeroboam was capable, and Solomon noticed the young man because he was getting things done. So he appointed him over the entire labor force of the house of Joseph." ◀ 1 Kings 11:28 ▶ [CSB]

"Then **JESUS** said, 'Come to **ME**, all of **You** who are weary and carry heavy burdens, and **I Will** give **You** rest'." ◀ Matthew 11:28 ▶ [NLT]

"Trust in your money and down **You** go! But the **GODly** flourish like leaves in spring." ◀ Proverbs 11:28 ▶ [NLT]

"It was by **Faith** that Moses commanded the people of Israel to keep the **Passover** and to sprinkle blood on the doorposts so that the angel of death would not kill their firstborn sons." ◀ Hebrews 11:28 ▶ [NLT]

"That is why **You** should examine yourself before eating the **Bread** and drinking the **Cup**." ◀ 1 Corinthians 11:28 ▶ [NLT]

"But **You** will be cursed if **You** reject the **Commands** of the **LORD** your **GOD** and turn away from **HIM** and worship gods **You** have not known before." ◀ Deuteronomy 11:28 ▶ [NLT]

"**HE** replied, '**Blessed** rather are those who hear the **WORD** of **GOD** and obey it.'" ◀ Luke 11:28 ▶ [NIV]

Powerful Manifestation Prayer:

I BLESS myself, my family and everyone born on this date with GOD's MOST POWERFUL PURE LOVING LIGHT, HIS MOST POWERFUL PURE SOURCE HEALING ENERGY, and an ABUNDANCE OF HIS AMAZING GREATER GRACE in the POWER, the ANOINTING, the AUTHORITY and the WISDOM of the HOLY SPIRIT, in JESUS' MOST HOLY NAME. AMEN INDEED!

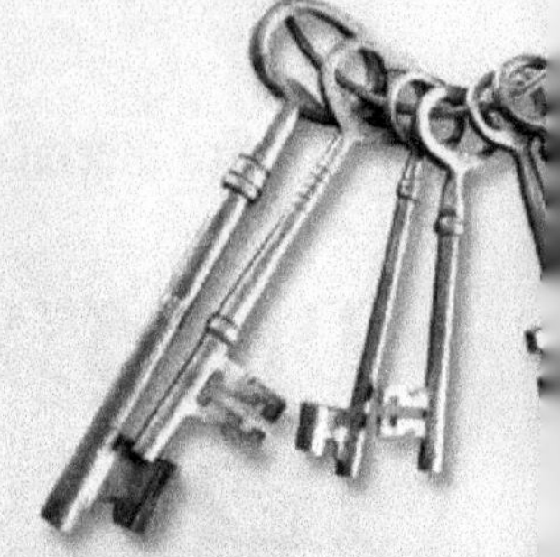

Day 333
11:29

"Take MY Yoke upon You and learn from ME, for I AM gentle and humble in heart, and You will find rest for your Souls." ◀ Matthew 11:29 ▶ [NIV]

"As the crowds increased, JESUS said, 'This is a wicked generation. It asks for a sign, but none will be given it except the sign of Jonah.'" ◀ Luke 11:29 ▶ [NIV]

"Whoever brings ruin on their family will inherit only wind, and the fool will be servant to the wise." ◀ Proverbs 11:29 ▶ [NIV]

"For GOD's gifts and HIS call can never be withdrawn." ◀ Romans 11:29 ▶ [NLT]

"And when she heard it, she rose quickly and went to HIM." ◀ John 11:29 ▶ [ESV]

"It was by Faith that the people of Israel went right through the Red Sea as though they were on dry ground. But when the Egyptians tried to follow, they were all drowned." ◀ Hebrews 11:29 ▶ [NLT]

"For if You eat the Bread or drink the Cup without honoring the Body of CHRIST, You are eating and drinking GOD's judgment upon yourself." ◀1 Corinthians 11:29 ▶ [NLT]

Powerful Manifestation Prayer:

I BLESS myself, my family and everyone born on this date with GOD's MOST POWERFUL PURE LOVING LIGHT, HIS MOST POWERFUL PURE SOURCE HEALING ENERGY, and an ABUNDANCE OF HIS AMAZING GREATER GRACE in the POWER, the ANOINTING, the AUTHORITY and the WISDOM of the HOLY SPIRIT, in JESUS' MOST HOLY NAME. AMEN INDEED!

Day 334
11:30

"That is why many among You are weak and sick, and a number of You have fallen asleep."
◀ 1 Corinthians 11:30 ▶ [NIV]

"Did John's authority to baptize come from Heaven, or was it merely human? Answer me!"
◀ Mark 11:30 ▶ [NLT]

"What happened to him [Jonah] was a sign to the people of Nineveh that GOD had sent him. What happens to the SON of Man will be a sign to these people that HE was sent by GOD."
◀ Luke 11:30 ▶ [NLT]

"The seeds of GOoD deeds become a tree of life; a wise person wins friends."
◀ Proverbs 11:30 ▶ [NLT]

"By Faith the walls of Jericho fell, after the army had marched around them for seven days."
◀ Hebrews 11:30 ▶ [NIV]

"For MY Yoke is easy to bear, and the burden I give You is light." ◀ Matthew 11:30 ▶ [NLT]

Powerful Manifestation Prayer:

I BLESS myself, my family and everyone born on this date with GOD's MOST POWERFUL PURE LOVING LIGHT, HIS MOST POWERFUL PURE SOURCE HEALING ENERGY, and an ABUNDANCE OF HIS AMAZING GREATER GRACE in the POWER, the ANOINTING, the AUTHORITY and the WISDOM of the HOLY SPIRIT, in JESUS' MOST HOLY NAME. AMEN INDEED!

December 12

~ I **Pray** for **You** and **You Pray** for Me!

"After Job had prayed for his friends, the **LORD** restored his fortunes and gave him twice as much as he had before." ◄ Job 42:10 ► [NIV]

"**You** haven't done this before. **A.S.K.** using **MY NAME**, and **You** will receive, and **You** will have abundant joy." ◄ John 16:24 ► [NLT]

Powerful Manifestation Prayer:

I BLESS myself, my family and everyone born in this month with GOD's MOST POWERFUL PURE LOVING LIGHT, HIS MOST POWERFUL PURE SOURCE HEALING ENERGY, and an ABUNDANCE OF HIS AMAZING GREATER GRACE in the POWER, the ANOINTING, the AUTHORITY and the WISDOM of the HOLY SPIRIT, in JESUS' MOST HOLY NAME.
AMEN INDEED!

A.S.K.- Additional Scripture Knowledge

Write Additional Scriptures here.

Day 335
12:1

"Don't let the excitement of youth cause You to forget your CREATOR. Honor HIM in your youth before You grow old and say, 'Life is not pleasant anymore.'" ◀ Ecclesiastes 12:1 ▶ [NLT]

"These are the decrees and regulations You must be careful to obey when You live in the land that the LORD, the GOD of your ancestors, is giving You. You must obey them as long as You live." ◀ Deuteronomy 12:1 ▶ [NLT]

"Whoever Loves discipline Loves Knowledge, but whoever hates correction is stupid." ◀ Proverbs 12:1 ▶ [NIV]

"Therefore, I urge You, brothers and sisters, in view of GOD's mercy, to offer your bodies as a living sacrifice, holy and pleasing to GOD--this is your true and proper worship." ◀ Romans 12:1 ▶ [NIV]

"In that day You will sing: "I will Praise YOU, O LORD! YOU were angry with me, but not anymore. Now YOU comfort me." ◀ Isaiah 12:1 ▶ [NLT]

"Therefore, since we are surrounded by such a great cloud of witnesses, let us throw off everything that hinders and the sin that so easily entangles. And let us run with perseverance the race marked out for us." ◀ Hebrews 12:1 ▶ [NIV]

Powerful Manifestation Prayer:

I BLESS myself, my family and everyone born on this date with GOD's MOST POWERFUL PURE LOVING LIGHT, HIS MOST POWERFUL PURE SOURCE HEALING ENERGY, and an ABUNDANCE OF HIS AMAZING GREATER GRACE in the POWER, the ANOINTING, the AUTHORITY and the WISDOM of the HOLY SPIRIT, in JESUS' MOST HOLY NAME. AMEN INDEED!

Day 336
12:2

"Everyone lies to their neighbor; they flatter with their lips but harbor deception in their hearts."
◀ Psalm 12:2 ▶ [NIV]

"**GOoD** people obtain **Favor** from the **LORD**, but **HE** condemns those who devise wicked schemes."
◀ Proverbs 12:2 ▶ [NIV]

"Fixing our eyes on **JESUS** the pioneer and perfecter of **Faith**. For the joy set before **HIM, HE** endured the **Cross**, scorning its shame, and sat down at the **Right Hand** of the throne of **GOD**."
◀ Hebrews 12:2 ▶ [NIV]

"Do not conform to the pattern of this world, but be transformed by the renewing of your mind. Then **You** will be able to test and approve what **GOD's Will** is—**HIS GOoD**, pleasing and perfect **Will**."
◀ Romans 12:2 ▶ [NIV]

"Surely **GOD** is my **Salvation**; I will trust and not be afraid. **The LORD**, **The LORD HIMSELF**, is my strength and my defense; **HE** has become my **Salvation**."
◀ Isaiah 12:2 ▶ [NIV]

"**I Will** make **You** into a great nation. **I Will Bless You** and make **You** famous, and **You** will be a **Blessing** to others."
◀ Genesis 12:2 ▶ [NLT]

Powerful Manifestation Prayer:

I BLESS myself, my family and everyone born on this date with GOD's MOST POWERFUL PURE LOVING LIGHT, HIS MOST POWERFUL PURE SOURCE HEALING ENERGY, and an ABUNDANCE OF HIS AMAZING GREATER GRACE in the POWER, the ANOINTING, the AUTHORITY and the WISDOM of the HOLY SPIRIT, in JESUS' MOST HOLY NAME. AMEN INDEED!

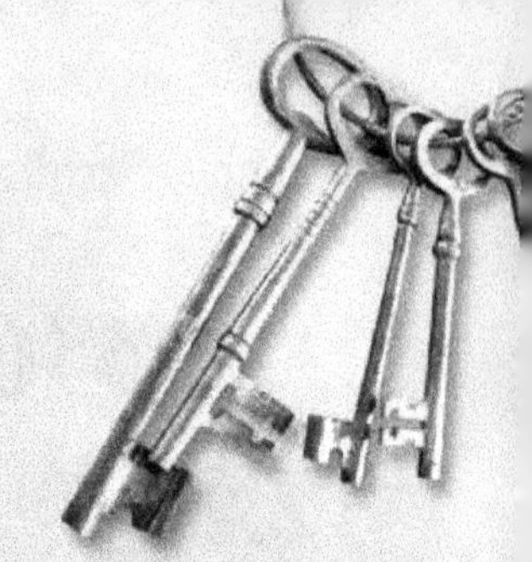

Day 337
12:3

"May the **LORD** cut off their flattering lips and silence their boastful tongues."
◄ Psalm 12:3 ► [NLT]

"No one can be established through wickedness, but the **Righteous** cannot be uprooted."
◄ Proverbs 12:3 ► [NIV]

"But as for me, **LORD**, **YOU** know my heart. **YOU** see me and test my thoughts. Drag these people away like sheep to be butchered! Set them aside to be slaughtered!" ◄ Jeremiah 12:3 ► [NLT]

"With joy **You** will drink deeply from the fountain of **Salvation**!" ◄ Isaiah12:3 ► [NLT]

"Think of all the hostility **HE** endured from sinful people; then **You** won't become weary and give up."
◄ Hebrews 12:3 ► [NLT]

"**I Will Bless** those who **Bless You**, and whoever curses **You I Will** curse; and all peoples on earth will be **Blessed** through **You**." ◄ Genesis 12:3 ► [NIV]

Powerful Manifestation Prayer:

I BLESS myself, my family and everyone born on this date with GOD's MOST POWERFUL PURE LOVING LIGHT, HIS MOST POWERFUL PURE SOURCE HEALING ENERGY, and an ABUNDANCE OF HIS AMAZING GREATER GRACE in the POWER, the ANOINTING, the AUTHORITY and the WISDOM of the HOLY SPIRIT, in JESUS' MOST HOLY NAME. AMEN INDEED!

Day 338
12:4

"But You, Daniel, keep this prophecy a secret; seal up the book until the time of the end, when many will rush here and there, and Knowledge will increase." ◄ Daniel 12:4 ► [NLT]

"There are different kinds of Spiritual gifts, but the same SPIRIT is the SOURCE of them all." ◄ 1 Corinthians 12:4 ► [NLT]

"We have many parts in the one body, and all these parts have different functions." ◄ Romans 12:4 ► [GNT]

"I have become a laughingstock to my friends, though I called on GOD and HE answered— a mere laughingstock, though Righteous and blameless." ◄ Job 12:4 ► [NIV]

"Do not worship the LORD your GOD in the way these pagan peoples worship their gods." ◄ Deuteronomy 12:4 ► [NLT]

"They say, "We will lie to our hearts' content. Our lips are our own—who can stop us?" ◄ Psalm 12:4 ► [NLT]

"In that day You will say: "Give Praise to the LORD, proclaim HIS Name; make known among the nations what HE has done, and proclaim that HIS Name is exalted." ◄ Isaiah 12:4 ► [NIV]

Powerful Manifestation Prayer:

I BLESS myself, my family and everyone born on this date with GOD's MOST POWERFUL PURE LOVING LIGHT, HIS MOST POWERFUL PURE SOURCE HEALING ENERGY, and an ABUNDANCE OF HIS AMAZING GREATER GRACE in the POWER, the ANOINTING, the AUTHORITY and the WISDOM of the HOLY SPIRIT, in JESUS' MOST HOLY NAME. AMEN INDEED!

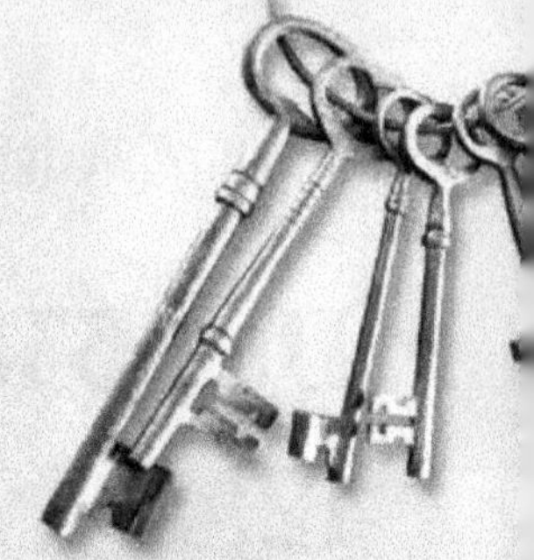

Day 339
12:5

"There are different kinds of service, but we serve the same **LORD**." ◀ 1 Corinthians 12:5 ▶ [NLT]

"Sing to the **LORD**, for **HE** has done wonderful things. Make known **HIS Praise** around the world." ◀ Isaiah 12:5 ▶ [NLT]

"Rather, **You** must seek the **LORD** your **GOD** at the place of worship **HE HIMSELF Will Choose** from among all the tribes—the place where **HIS Name Will** be honored." ◀ Deuteronomy 12:5 ▶ [NLT]

"The plans of the **Righteous** are just, but the advice of the wicked is deceitful." ◀ Proverbs 12:5 ▶ [NIV]

"The **LORD** replies, "**I** have seen violence done to the helpless, and **I** have heard the groans of the poor. Now **I Will** rise up to rescue them, as they have longed for **ME** to do." ◀ Psalm 12:5 ▶ [NLT]

"So, in **CHRIST** we, though many, form one body, and each member belongs to all the others." ◀ Romans 12:5 ▶ [NIV]

Powerful Manifestation Prayer:

I BLESS myself, my family and everyone born on this date with GOD's MOST POWERFUL PURE LOVING LIGHT, HIS MOST POWERFUL PURE SOURCE HEALING ENERGY, and an ABUNDANCE OF HIS AMAZING GREATER GRACE in the POWER, the ANOINTING, the AUTHORITY and the WISDOM of the HOLY SPIRIT, in JESUS' MOST HOLY NAME. AMEN INDEED!

Day 340
12:6

"We have different gifts, according to the **Grace** given to each of us. If your gift is prophesying, then prophesy in accordance with your **Faith**." ◄ Romans 12:6 ► [NIV]

"Let all the people of Jerusalem shout **HIS Praise** with joy! For great is the **HOLY ONE** of Israel **WHO Lives** among **You**." ◄ Isaiah 12:6 ► [NLT]

"There **You** will bring your burnt offerings, your sacrifices, your tithes, your sacred offerings, your offerings to fulfill a vow, your voluntary offerings." ◄ Deuteronomy 12:6 ► [NLT]

"The **LORD's Promises** are pure, like silver refined in a furnace, purified seven times over."
◄ Psalm 12:6 ► [NLT]

"The words of the wicked are like a murderous ambush, but the **WORDS** of the **GODly** save lives."
◄ Proverbs 12:6 ► [NLT]

"**I** tell **You**, there is **ONE** here **WHO** is even **Greater** than the **Temple**!"
◄ Matthew 12:6 ► [NLT]

Powerful Manifestation Prayer:

I BLESS myself, my family and everyone born on this date with GOD's MOST POWERFUL PURE LOVING LIGHT, HIS MOST POWERFUL PURE SOURCE HEALING ENERGY, and an ABUNDANCE OF HIS AMAZING GREATER GRACE in the POWER, the ANOINTING, the AUTHORITY and the WISDOM of the HOLY SPIRIT, in JESUS' MOST HOLY NAME. AMEN INDEED!

Day 341
12:7

"There, in the presence of the **LORD** your **GOD**, **You** and your families shall eat and shall rejoice in everything **You** have put your hand to, because the **LORD** your **GOD** has **Blessed You**."
◀ Deuteronomy 12:7 ▶ [NIV]

"If your gift is serving others, serve them well. If **You** are a teacher, teach well."
◀ Romans 12:7 ▶ [NLT]

"The wicked are overthrown and are no more, but the house of the **Righteous** stands firm."
◀ Proverbs 12:7 ▶ [NIV]

"If **You** had known what these **WORDS** mean, '**I** desire mercy, not sacrifice,' **You** would not have condemned the innocent."
◀ Matthew 12:7 ▶ [NIV]

"**YOU**, **LORD**, **Will** keep the needy safe and **Will** protect us forever from the wicked."
◀ Psalm 12:7 ▶ [NIV]

"For then the dust will return to the earth, and the **Spirit** will return to **GOD WHO** gave it."
◀ Ecclesiastes 12:7 ▶ [NLT]

Powerful Manifestation Prayer:

I BLESS myself, my family and everyone born on this date with GOD's MOST POWERFUL PURE LOVING LIGHT, HIS MOST POWERFUL PURE SOURCE HEALING ENERGY, and an ABUNDANCE OF HIS AMAZING GREATER GRACE in the POWER, the ANOINTING, the AUTHORITY and the WISDOM of the HOLY SPIRIT, in JESUS' MOST HOLY NAME. AMEN INDEED!

Day 342
12:8

"A sensible person wins admiration, but a warped mind is despised." ◄ Proverbs 12:8 ► [NLT]

"If your gift is to encourage, then give encouragement; if it is giving, then give generously; if it is to lead, do it diligently; if it is to show mercy, do it cheerfully." ◄ Romans 12:8 ► [NLT]

"The wicked prowl on every side, when vileness is exalted among the sons of men." ◄ Psalm 12:8 ► [NKJV]

"Three different times I begged the LORD to take it away." ◄ 2 Corinthians 12:8 ► [NLT]

"There he **[Abram]** built an altar to the LORD and called on the Name of the LORD." ◄ Genesis 12:8 ► [NIV]

"For the SON of Man is LORD, even over the Sabbath!" ◄ Matthew 12:8 ► [NLT]

Powerful Manifestation Prayer:

I BLESS myself, my family and everyone born on this date with GOD's MOST POWERFUL PURE LOVING LIGHT, HIS MOST POWERFUL PURE SOURCE HEALING ENERGY, and an ABUNDANCE OF HIS AMAZING GREATER GRACE in the POWER, the ANOINTING, the AUTHORITY and the WISDOM of the HOLY SPIRIT, in JESUS' MOST HOLY NAME. AMEN INDEED!

Day 343
12:9

"Not only was the Teacher wise, but he also imparted **Knowledge** to the people. He pondered and searched out and set in order many proverbs." ◀ Ecclesiastes 12:9 ▶ [NIV]

"**Love** must be sincere. Hate what is evil; cling to what is **GOoD**." ◀ Romans 12:9 ▶ [NIV]

"**You** have not yet arrived at the place of rest, the land the **LORD** your **GOD** is giving **You** as your special possession." ◀ Deuteronomy 12:9 ▶ [NLT]

"Better to be an ordinary person with a servant than to be self-important but have no food." ◀ Proverbs 12:9 ▶ [NLT]

"The same **SPIRIT** gives great **Faith** to another, and to someone else the **ONE SPIRIT** gives the gift of healing." ◀ 1 Corinthians 12:9 ▶ [NLT]

"But **HE** said to me, "**MY Grace** is sufficient for **You**, for **MY Power** is made perfect in weakness." Therefore I will boast all the more gladly about my weaknesses, so that **CHRIST's Power** may rest on me." ◀ 2 Corinthians 12:9 ▶ [NIV]

Powerful Manifestation Prayer:

I BLESS myself, my family and everyone born on this date with GOD's MOST POWERFUL PURE LOVING LIGHT, HIS MOST POWERFUL PURE SOURCE HEALING ENERGY, and an ABUNDANCE OF HIS AMAZING GREATER GRACE in the POWER, the ANOINTING, the AUTHORITY and the WISDOM of the HOLY SPIRIT, in JESUS' MOST HOLY NAME. AMEN INDEED!

Day 344
12:10

"The Teacher searched to find just the right **Words**, and what he wrote was upright and **True**."
◄ Ecclesiastes 12:10 ► [NIV]

"Be devoted to one another in **Love**. Honor one another above yourselves."
◄ Romans 12:10 ► [NIV]

"But **You** will cross the Jordan and settle in the land the **LORD** your **GOD** is giving **You** as an inheritance, and **HE Will** give **You** rest from all your enemies around **You** so that **You** will live in safety."
◄ Deuteronomy 12:10 ► [NIV]

"The **GODly** care for their animals, but the wicked are always cruel." ◄ Proverbs 12:10 ► [NLT]

"**HE** gives one person the **Power** to perform miracles, and another the ability to prophesy. **HE** gives someone else the ability to discern whether a message is from the **SPIRIT** of **GOD** or from another spirit. Still another person is given the ability to speak in unknown languages, while another is given the ability to interpret what is being said."
◄ 1 Corinthians 12:10 ► [NLT]

"That is why, for **CHRIST's** sake, I delight in weaknesses, in insults, in hardships, in persecutions, in difficulties. For when I am weak, then **I AM** strong."
◄ 2 Corinthians 12:10 ► [NIV]

Powerful Manifestation Prayer:

I BLESS myself, my family and everyone born on this date with GOD's MOST POWERFUL PURE LOVING LIGHT, HIS MOST POWERFUL PURE SOURCE HEALING ENERGY, and an ABUNDANCE OF HIS AMAZING GREATER GRACE in the POWER, the ANOINTING, the AUTHORITY and the WISDOM of the HOLY SPIRIT, in JESUS' MOST HOLY NAME. AMEN INDEED!

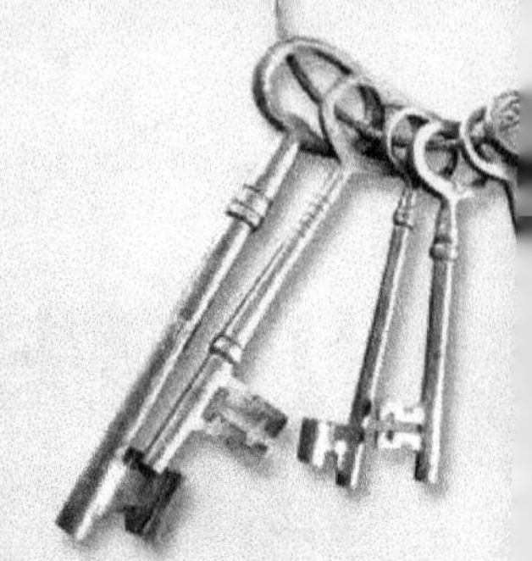

Day 345
12:11

"Never be lazy, but work hard and serve the LORD enthusiastically." ◀ Romans 12:11 ▶ [NLT]

"Then to the place the LORD your GOD Will choose as a dwelling for HIS Name--there You are to bring everything I Command You: your burnt offerings and sacrifices, your tithes and special gifts, and all the choice possessions You have vowed to the LORD." ◀ Deuteronomy 12:11 ▶ [NIV]

"The Words of the wise are like cattle prods—painful but helpful. Their collected sayings are like a nail-studded stick with which a shepherd drives the sheep." ◀ Ecclesiastes 12:11 ▶ [NLT]

"A hard worker has plenty of food, but a person who chases fantasies has no sense."
◀ Proverbs 12:11 ▶ [NLT]

"You have made me act like a fool. You ought to be writing commendations for me, for I am not at all inferior to these 'super apostles', even though **I am Nothing** at all."
◀ 2 Corinthians 12:11 ▶ [NLT]

"It is the ONE and ONLY SPIRIT WHO distributes all these gifts. HE alone decides which gift each person should have." ◀ 1 Corinthians 12:11 ▶ [NLT]

Powerful Manifestation Prayer:

I BLESS myself, my family and everyone born on this date with GOD's MOST POWERFUL PURE LOVING LIGHT, HIS MOST POWERFUL PURE SOURCE HEALING ENERGY, and an ABUNDANCE OF HIS AMAZING GREATER GRACE in the POWER, the ANOINTING, the AUTHORITY and the WISDOM of the HOLY SPIRIT, in JESUS' MOST HOLY NAME. AMEN INDEED!

Day 346
12:12

"Be **Joyful** in **HOPE**, **Patient** in affliction, **Faithful** in **Prayer**." ◀ Romans 12:12 ▶ [NIV]

"**You** must celebrate there in the presence of the **LORD** your **GOD** with your sons and daughters and all your servants." ◀ Deuteronomy 12:12 ▶ [NLT]

"The human body has many parts, but the many parts make up one whole body. So it is with the **BODY** of **CHRIST**." ◀ 1 Corinthians 12:12 ▶ [NLT]

"I persevered in demonstrating among **You** the marks of a **True Apostle**, including **Signs**, **Wonders** and **Miracles**." ◀ 2 Corinthians 12:12 ▶ [NIV]

"But, my child, let me give **You** some further advice: Be careful, for writing books is endless, and much study wears **You** out." ◀ Ecclesiastes 12:12 ▶ [NLT]

"For the **HOLY SPIRIT** will teach **You** at that time what needs to be said." ◀ Luke 12:12 ▶ [NLT]

Powerful Manifestation Prayer:

I BLESS myself, my family and everyone born on this date with GOD's MOST POWERFUL PURE LOVING LIGHT, HIS MOST POWERFUL PURE SOURCE HEALING ENERGY, and an ABUNDANCE OF HIS AMAZING GREATER GRACE in the POWER, the ANOINTING, the AUTHORITY and the WISDOM of the HOLY SPIRIT, in JESUS' MOST HOLY NAME. AMEN INDEED!

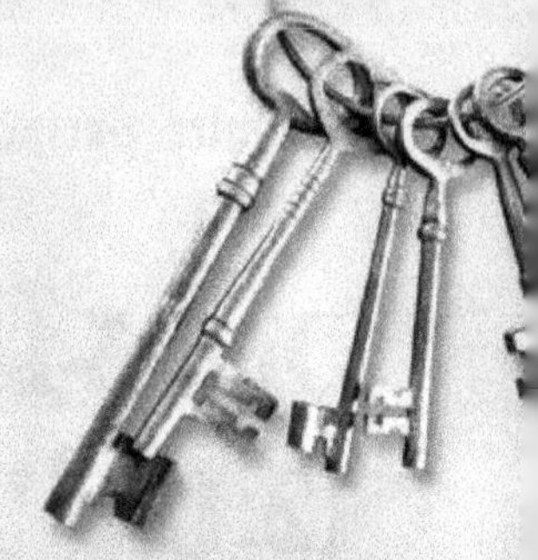

Day 347
12:13

"To **GOD** belong **Wisdom** and **Power**; **Counsel** and **Understanding** are **HIS**."
◀ Job 12:13 ▶ [NIV]

"As for **You**, go your way till the end. **You** will rest, and then at the end of the days **You** will rise to receive your allotted inheritance."
◀ Daniel 12:13 ▶ [NIV]

"Share with the **LORD's** people who are in need. Practice hospitality." ◀ Romans 12:13 ▶ [NIV]

"The wicked are trapped by their own words, but the **GODly** escape such trouble."
◀ Proverbs 12:13 ▶ [NLT]

"Some of us are Jews, some are Gentiles, some are slaves, and some are **Free**. But we have all been baptized into **One Body** by **One Spirit**, and we all share the same **SPIRIT**."
◀ 1 Corinthians 12:13 ▶ [NLT]

"That's the whole story. Here now is my final conclusion: Fear **GOD** and obey **HIS Commands**, for this is everyone's duty."
◀ Ecclesiastes 12:13 ▶ [NLT]

Powerful Manifestation Prayer:

I BLESS myself, my family and everyone born on this date with GOD's MOST POWERFUL PURE LOVING LIGHT, HIS MOST POWERFUL PURE SOURCE HEALING ENERGY, and an ABUNDANCE OF HIS AMAZING GREATER GRACE in the POWER, the ANOINTING, the AUTHORITY and the WISDOM of the HOLY SPIRIT, in JESUS' MOST HOLY NAME. AMEN INDEED!

Day 348
12:14

"Bless those who persecute You; Bless and do not curse." ◄ Romans 12:14 ► [NIV]

"Now I am coming to You for the third time, and I will not be a burden to You. I don't want what You have—I want You. After all, children don't provide for their parents. Rather, parents provide for their children." ◄ 2 Corinthians 12:14 ► [NLT]

"For GOD Will bring every deed into judgment, including every hidden thing, whether it is GOoD or evil." ◄ Ecclesiastes 12:14 ► [NIV]

"This is a day to remember. Each year, from generation to generation, You must celebrate it as a special festival to the LORD. This is a Law for all time." ◄ Exodus 12:14 ► [NLT]

"Yes, the body has many different parts, not just one part." ◄ 1 Corinthians 12:14 ► [NLT]

"Wise Words bring many benefits, and hard work brings rewards." ◄ Proverbs 12:14 ► [NLT]

Powerful Manifestation Prayer:

I BLESS myself, my family and everyone born on this date with GOD's MOST POWERFUL PURE LOVING LIGHT, HIS MOST POWERFUL PURE SOURCE HEALING ENERGY, and an ABUNDANCE OF HIS AMAZING GREATER GRACE in the POWER, the ANOINTING, the AUTHORITY and the WISDOM of the HOLY SPIRIT, in JESUS' MOST HOLY NAME. AMEN INDEED!

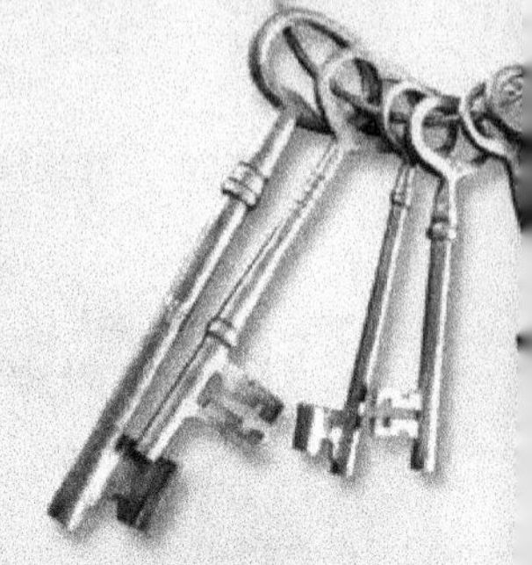

Day 349
12:15

"Rejoice with those who rejoice; mourn with those who mourn." ◄ Romans 12:15 ► [NIV]

"I will gladly spend myself and all I have for You, even though it seems that the more I Love You, the less You Love me." ◄ 2 Corinthians 12:15 ► [NLT]

"Then HE said, "Beware! Guard against every kind of greed. Life is not measured by how much You own." ◄ Luke 12:15 ► [NLT]

"The way of fools seems right to them, but the wise listen to advice." ◄ Proverbs 12:15 ► [NIV]

"If the foot says, "I am not a part of the body because I am not a hand," that does not make it any less a part of the body." ◄ 1 Corinthians 12:15 ► [NLT]

"But afterward I Will return and have compassion on all of them. I Will bring them home to their own lands again, each nation to its own possession." ◄ Jeremiah 12:15 ► [NLT]

Powerful Manifestation Prayer:

I BLESS myself, my family and everyone born on this date with GOD's MOST POWERFUL PURE LOVING LIGHT, HIS MOST POWERFUL PURE SOURCE HEALING ENERGY, and an ABUNDANCE OF HIS AMAZING GREATER GRACE in the POWER, the ANOINTING, the AUTHORITY and the WISDOM of the HOLY SPIRIT, in JESUS' MOST HOLY NAME. AMEN INDEED!

Day 350
12:16

"But granting that I myself did not burden You, I was crafty, You say, and got the better of You by deceit." ◀ 2 Corinthians 12:16 ▶ [NLT]

"To HIM belong strength and insight; both deceived and deceiver are HIS." ◀ Job 12:16 ▶ [NIV]

"And if the ear should say, 'Because I am not an eye, I do not belong to the body', it would not for that reason stop being part of the body." ◀ 1 Corinthians 12:16 ▶ [NIV]

"Live in harmony with one another. Do not be proud, but be willing to associate with people of low position. Do not be conceited." ◀ Romans 12:16 ▶ [NIV]

"A fool is quick-tempered, but a wise person stays calm when insulted." ◀ Proverbs 12:16 ▶ [NLT]

"And if these nations Truly learn the ways of MY people, and if they learn to swear by MY Name, saying, 'As surely as the LORD Lives' (just as they taught MY people to swear by the name of Baal), then they will be given a place among MY people." ◀ Jeremiah 12:16 ▶ [NLT]

"See that no one is sexually immoral, or is godless like Esau, who for a single meal sold his inheritance rights as the oldest son." ◀ Hebrews 12:16 ▶ [NIV]

Powerful Manifestation Prayer:

I BLESS myself, my family and everyone born on this date with GOD's MOST POWERFUL PURE LOVING LIGHT, HIS MOST POWERFUL PURE SOURCE HEALING ENERGY, and an ABUNDANCE OF HIS AMAZING GREATER GRACE in the POWER, the ANOINTING, the AUTHORITY and the WISDOM of the HOLY SPIRIT, in JESUS' MOST HOLY NAME. AMEN INDEED!

Day 351
12:17

"Celebrate this Festival of Unleavened Bread, for it will remind You that I brought your forces out of the land of Egypt on this very day. This festival will be a permanent Law for You; celebrate this day from generation to generation." ◀ Exodus 12:17 ▶ [NIV]

"An honest witness tells the Truth, but a false witness tells lies." ◀ Proverbs 12:17 ▶ [NIV]

"He leads counselors away, stripped of GOoD judgment; wise judges become fools." ◀ Job 12:17 ▶ [NLT]

"Never pay back evil with more evil. Do things in such a way that everyone can see You are honorable." ◀ Romans 12:17 ▶ [NLT]

"If the whole body were an eye, how would You hear? Or if your whole body were an ear, how would You smell anything?" ◀ 1 Corinthians 12:17 ▶ [NLT]

"Then JESUS said to them, 'Give back to Caesar what is Caesar's and to GOD what is GOD's.' And they were amazed at HIM." ◀ Mark 12:17 ▶ [NIV]

Powerful Manifestation Prayer:

I BLESS myself, my family and everyone born on this date with GOD's MOST POWERFUL PURE LOVING LIGHT, HIS MOST POWERFUL PURE SOURCE HEALING ENERGY, and an ABUNDANCE OF HIS AMAZING GREATER GRACE in the POWER, the ANOINTING, the AUTHORITY and the WISDOM of the HOLY SPIRIT, in JESUS' MOST HOLY NAME. AMEN INDEED!

Day 352
12:18

"The words of the reckless pierce like swords, but the tongue of the wise brings healing."
◀ Proverbs 12:18 ▶ [NIV]

"Then he said, 'This is what I'll do. I will tear down my barns and build bigger ones, and there I will store my surplus grain."
◀ Luke 12:18 ▶ [NIV]

"No! For we have the same SPIRIT and walk in each other's steps, doing things the same way."
◀ 2 Corinthians 12:18 ▶ [NLT]

"But in fact, GOD has placed the parts in the body, every one of them, just as HE wanted them to be."
◀ 1 Corinthians 12:18 ▶ [NIV]

"Here is MY Servant WHOM I have Chosen, the One I Love, in WHOM I delight; I Will put MY SPIRIT on HIM, and HE Will proclaim justice to the nations."
◀ Matthew 12:18 ▶ [NIV]

"Do all that You can to live in Peace with everyone."
◀ Romans 12:18 ▶ [NLT]

Powerful Manifestation Prayer:

I BLESS myself, my family and everyone born on this date with GOD's MOST POWERFUL PURE LOVING LIGHT, HIS MOST POWERFUL PURE SOURCE HEALING ENERGY, and an ABUNDANCE OF HIS AMAZING GREATER GRACE in the POWER, the ANOINTING, the AUTHORITY and the WISDOM of the HOLY SPIRIT, in JESUS' MOST HOLY NAME. AMEN INDEED!

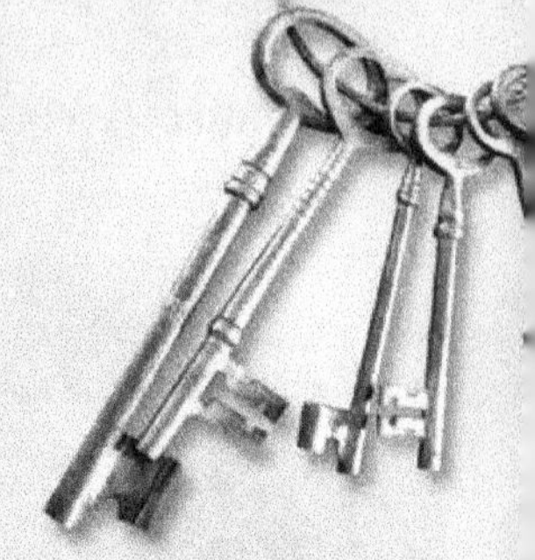

Day 353
12:19

"How strange a body would be if it had only one part!" ◄ 1 Corinthians 12:19 ► [NLT]

"**Truthful** lips endure forever, but a lying tongue lasts only a moment." ◄ Proverbs 12:19 ► [NIV]

"**Pray** to the **LORD** your **GOD**, for your servants that we will not die, for we have added to all our other sins this evil." ◄ 1 Samuel 12:19 ► [NLT]

"Beloved, never avenge yourselves, but leave it to the wrath of **GOD**, for it is written, "Vengeance is **MINE**, **I Will** repay, says the **LORD**." ◄ Romans 12:19 ► [ESV]

"**HE** leads priests away, stripped of status; he overthrows those with long years in **Power**." ◄ Job 12:19 ► [NLT]

"And I will say to my **Soul**, '**Soul**, **You** have ample **GOoDs** laid up for many years; relax, eat, drink, be merry.'" ◄ Luke 12:19 ► [ESV]

"Perhaps **You** think we're saying these things just to defend ourselves. No, we tell **You** this as **CHRIST's Servants**, and with **GOD** as our witness. Everything we do, dear friends, is to strengthen **You**." ◄ 2 Corinthians 12:19 ► [NLT]

Powerful Manifestation Prayer:

I BLESS myself, my family and everyone born on this date with GOD's MOST POWERFUL PURE LOVING LIGHT, HIS MOST POWERFUL PURE SOURCE HEALING ENERGY, and an ABUNDANCE OF HIS AMAZING GREATER GRACE in the POWER, the ANOINTING, the AUTHORITY and the WISDOM of the HOLY SPIRIT, in JESUS' MOST HOLY NAME. AMEN INDEED!

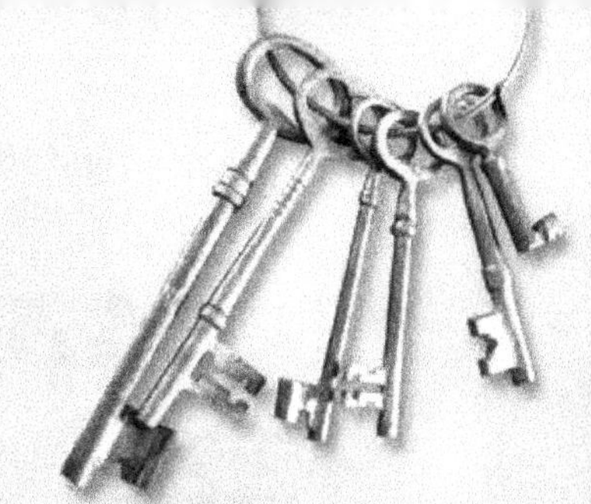

Day 354
12:20

"When the **LORD** your **GOD** expands your territory as **HE** has **Promised**, and **You** have the urge to eat meat, **You** may **Freely** eat meat whenever **You** want." ◀ Deuteronomy 12:20 ▶ [NLT]

"Deceit is in the hearts of those who plot evil, but those who promote **Peace** have joy." ◀ Proverbs 12:20 ▶ [NIV]

"Instead, "If your enemies are hungry, feed them. If they are thirsty, give them something to drink. In doing this, **You** will heap burning coals of shame on their heads." ◀ Romans 12:20 ▶ [NLT]

"Yes, there are many parts, but only **ONE BODY**." ◀ 1 Corinthians 12:20 ▶ [NLT]

"For I am afraid that when I come I won't like what I find, and **You** won't like my response. I am afraid that I will find quarreling, jealousy, anger, selfishness, slander, gossip, arrogance, and disorderly behavior." ◀ 2 Corinthians 12:20 ▶ [NLT]

"**HE Will** not crush the weakest reed or put out a flickering candle. Finally, **HE Will** cause justice to be victorious." ◀ Matthew 12:20 ▶ [NLT]

Powerful Manifestation Prayer:

I BLESS myself, my family and everyone born on this date with GOD's MOST POWERFUL PURE LOVING LIGHT, HIS MOST POWERFUL PURE SOURCE HEALING ENERGY, and an ABUNDANCE OF HIS AMAZING GREATER GRACE in the POWER, the ANOINTING, the AUTHORITY and the WISDOM of the HOLY SPIRIT, in JESUS' MOST HOLY NAME. AMEN INDEED!

Day 355
12:21

"Do not be overcome by evil but overcome evil with **GOoD**." ◄ Romans 12:21 ► [NIV]

"No harm overtakes the **Righteous**, but the wicked have their fill of trouble."
◄ Proverbs 12:21 ► [NIV]

"The eye can never say to the hand, 'I don't need **You**.' The head can't say to the feet, 'I don't need **You**.'" ◄ 1 Corinthians 12:21 ► [NLT]

"Yes, I am afraid that when I come again, **GOD Will** humble me in your presence. And I will be grieved because many of **You** have not given up your old sins. **You** have not repented of your impurity, sexual immorality, and eagerness for lustful pleasure." ◄ 2 Corinthians 12:21 ► [NLT]

"In **HIS Name** the nations will put their **HOPE**." ◄ Matthew 12:21 ► [NIV]

"Yes, a person is a fool to store up earthly wealth but not have a rich relationship with **GOD**."
◄ Luke 12:21 ► [NLT]

Powerful Manifestation Prayer:

I BLESS myself, my family and everyone born on this date with GOD's MOST POWERFUL PURE LOVING LIGHT, HIS MOST POWERFUL PURE SOURCE HEALING ENERGY, and an ABUNDANCE OF HIS AMAZING GREATER GRACE in the POWER, the ANOINTING, the AUTHORITY and the WISDOM of the HOLY SPIRIT, in JESUS' MOST HOLY NAME. AMEN INDEED!

Day 356
12:22

"The LORD detests lying lips, but HE delights in those who tell the Truth."
◄ Proverbs 12:22 ► [NLT]

"In fact, some parts of the body that seem weakest and least important are actually the most necessary."
◄ 1 Corinthians 12:22 ► [NLT]

"Then a demon-possessed man, who was blind and couldn't speak, was brought to JESUS. HE healed the man so that he could both speak and see."
◄ Matthew 12:22 ► [NLT]

"Then JESUS said to HIS Disciples: 'Therefore I tell You, do not worry about your life, what You will eat; or about your body, what You will wear.'"
◄ Luke 12:22 ► [NIV]

"Son of man, You have heard that proverb they quote in Israel: 'Time passes, and prophecies come to nothing."
◄ Ezekiel 12:22 ► [NLT]

"HE reveals the deep things of darkness and brings utter darkness into the Light."
◄ Job 12:22 ► [NIV]

Powerful Manifestation Prayer:

I BLESS myself, my family and everyone born on this date with GOD's MOST POWERFUL PURE LOVING LIGHT, HIS MOST POWERFUL PURE SOURCE HEALING ENERGY, and an ABUNDANCE OF HIS AMAZING GREATER GRACE in the POWER, the ANOINTING, the AUTHORITY and the WISDOM of the HOLY SPIRIT, in JESUS' MOST HOLY NAME. AMEN INDEED!

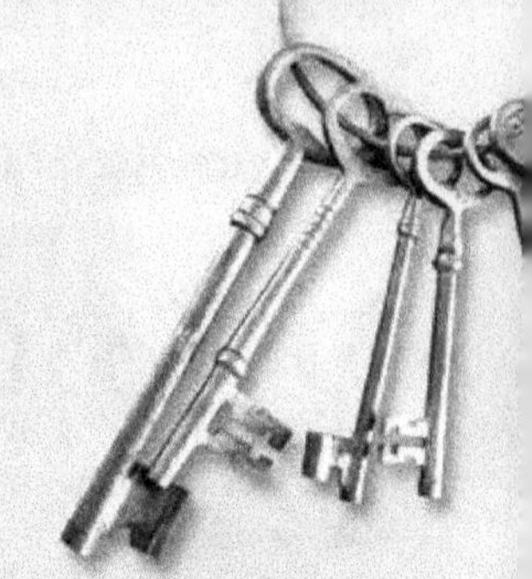

Day 357
12:23

"For life is more than food, and your body more than clothing." ◄ Luke 12:23 ► [NLT]

"And the parts we regard as less honorable are those we clothe with the greatest care. So we carefully protect those parts that should not be seen." ◄ 1 Corinthians 12:23 ► [NLT]

"The wise don't make a show of their **Knowledge**, but fools broadcast their foolishness."
◄ Proverbs 12:23 ► [NLT]

"The crowd was amazed and asked, "Could it be that **JESUS** is the **SON** of **David**, **The MESSIAH**?"
◄ Matthew 12:23 ► [NLT]

"**HE** builds up nations, and **HE** destroys them. **HE** expands nations, and **HE** abandons them."
◄ Job 12:23 ► [NLT]

"**JESUS** replied, "Now the time has come for the **SON** of **Man** to enter into **HIS Glory**."
◄ John 12:23 ► [NLT]

Powerful Manifestation Prayer:

I BLESS myself, my family and everyone born on this date with GOD's MOST POWERFUL PURE LOVING LIGHT, HIS MOST POWERFUL PURE SOURCE HEALING ENERGY, and an ABUNDANCE OF HIS AMAZING GREATER GRACE in the POWER, the ANOINTING, the AUTHORITY and the WISDOM of the HOLY SPIRIT, in JESUS' MOST HOLY NAME. AMEN INDEED!

Day 358
12:24

"While our presentable parts need no special treatment. But GOD has put the body together, giving greater honor to the parts that lacked it." ◀ 1 Corinthians 12:24 ▶ [NIV]

"Look at the ravens. They don't plant or harvest or store food in barns, for GOD feeds them. And You are far more valuable to HIM than any birds!" ◀ Luke 12:24 ▶ [NLT]

"HE strips kings of understanding and leaves them wandering in a pathless wasteland." ◀ Job 12:24 ▶ [NLT]

"I tell You the Truth, unless a kernel of wheat is planted in the soil and dies, it remains alone. But its death will produce many new kernels—a plentiful harvest of new lives." ◀ John 12:24 ▶ [NLT]

"For there will be no more false visions or flattering divinations among the people of Israel." ◀ Ezekiel 12:24 ▶ [NLT]

"Work hard and become a leader; be lazy and become a slave." ◀ Proverbs 12:24 ▶ [NLT]

Powerful Manifestation Prayer:

I BLESS myself, my family and everyone born on this date with GOD's MOST POWERFUL PURE LOVING LIGHT, HIS MOST POWERFUL PURE SOURCE HEALING ENERGY, and an ABUNDANCE OF HIS AMAZING GREATER GRACE in the POWER, the ANOINTING, the AUTHORITY and the WISDOM of the HOLY SPIRIT, in JESUS' MOST HOLY NAME. AMEN INDEED!

Day 359
12:25

"But I the LORD Will speak what I Will, and it shall be fulfilled without delay. For in your days, You rebellious people, I Will fulfill whatever I say, declares the Sovereign LORD."
◀ Ezekiel 12:25 ▶ [NIV]

"Worry weighs a person down; an encouraging Word cheers a person up."
◀ Proverbs 12:25 ▶ [NLT]

"This makes for harmony among the members, so that all the members care for each other."
◀ 1 Corinthians 12:25 ▶ [NLT]

" knew their thoughts and said to them, "Every Kingdom divided against itself will be ruined, and every city or household divided against itself will not stand."
◀ Matthew 12:25 [NIV]

"Can all your worries add a single moment to your life?"
◀ Luke 12:25 [NLT]

"Those who ove their life in this world will lose it. Those who care nothing for their life in this world will keep it for Eternity."
◀ John 12:25 [NLT]

"When the dead rise, they will neither marry nor be given in marriage; they will be like the in ."
◀ Mark 12:25 [NIV]

Day 360
12:26

"Whoever serves ME must follow ME; and where I AM, MY servant also will be. MY FATHER Will honor the one who serves ME."
◀ John 12:26 ▶ [NIV]

"Take your sacred gifts and your offerings given to fulfill a vow to the place the LORD Chooses."
◀ Deuteronomy 12:26 ▶ [NLT]

"The Righteous choose their friends carefully, but the way of the wicked leads them astray."
◀ Proverbs 12:26 ▶ [NIV]

"And if Satan is casting out Satan, he is divided and fighting against himself. His own kingdom will not survive."
◀ Matthew 12:26 [NLT]

"If one part suffers, every part suffers with it; if one part is honored, every part rejoices with it."
◀ 1 Corinthians 12:26 [NIV]

"And if worry can't accomplish a little thing like that, what's the use of worrying over bigger things?"
◀ Luke 12:26 [NLT]

Manifestation Prayer:

Day 361
12:27

"Lazy people don't even cook the game they catch, but the diligent make use of everything they find."
◀ Proverbs 12:27 ▶ [NLT]

"And if **I AM** empowered by Satan, what about your own exorcists? They cast out demons, too, so they will condemn **You** for what **You** have said." ◀ Matthew 12:27 ▶ [NLT]

"All of **You** together are **CHRIST's BODY**, and each of **You** is a part of **IT**."
◀ 1 Corinthians 12:27 ▶ [NLT]

"Look at the lilies and how they grow. They don't work or make their clothing, yet Solomon in all his **Glory** was not dressed as beautifully as they are." ◀ Luke 12:27 ▶ [NLT]

"Son of man, the Israelites are saying, 'The vision he sees is for many years from now, and he prophesies about the distant future.'" ◀ Ezekiel 12:27 ▶ [NIV]

"Now **MY Soul** is troubled, and what shall **I** say? '**FATHER**, save **ME** from this hour?' No, it was for this very reason **I** came to this hour." ◀ John 12:27 ▶ [NIV]

Powerful Manifestation Prayer:

I BLESS myself, my family and everyone born on this date with GOD's MOST POWERFUL PURE LOVING LIGHT, HIS MOST POWERFUL PURE SOURCE HEALING ENERGY, and an ABUNDANCE OF HIS AMAZING GREATER GRACE in the POWER, the ANOINTING, the AUTHORITY and the WISDOM of the HOLY SPIRIT, in JESUS' MOST HOLY NAME. AMEN INDEED!

Day 362
12:28

"Be careful to obey all MY Commands, so that all will go well with You and your children after You, because You will be doing what is GOoD and pleasing to the LORD your GOD."
◀ Deuteronomy 12:28 ▶ [NLT]

"The way of the GODly leads to life; that path does not lead to death." ◀ Proverbs 12:28 ▶ [NLT]

"But if I AM casting out demons by the SPIRIT of GOD, then the Kingdom of GOD has arrived among You."
◀ Matthew 12:28 ▶ [NLT]

"FATHER, Glorify YOUR Name. Then a Voice came from Heaven: 'I have Glorified IT, and I Will Glorify IT again.'"
◀ John 12:28 ▶ [ESV]

"But if GOD so clothes the grass, which is alive in the field today, and tomorrow is thrown into the oven, how much more will HE clothe You, O You of little Faith!" ◀ Luke 12:28 ▶ [ESV]

"Therefore, say to them, 'This is what the Sovereign LORD says: None of MY WORDS Will be delayed any longer; whatever I say Will be fulfilled, declares the Sovereign LORD."
◀ Ezekiel 12:28 ▶ [NIV]

Powerful Manifestation Prayer:

I BLESS myself, my family and everyone born on this date with GOD's MOST POWERFUL PURE LOVING LIGHT, HIS MOST POWERFUL PURE SOURCE HEALING ENERGY, and an ABUNDANCE OF HIS AMAZING GREATER GRACE in the POWER, the ANOINTING, the AUTHORITY and the WISDOM of the HOLY SPIRIT, in JESUS' MOST HOLY NAME. AMEN INDEED!

Day 363
12:29

" replied, "The most important is this: 'Listen, O Israel! The our is the and ." Mark 12:29 [NLT]

"Are we all ? Are we all ? Are we all ? Do we all have the to do miracles?" 1 Corinthians 12:29 [NLT]

"For who is powerful enough to enter the house of a strong man and plunder his ? Only someone even stronger—someone who could tie him up and then plunder his house." Matthew 12:29 [NLT]

"The your cut off before You the nations You are about to invade and dispossess." Deuteronomy 12:29 [NIV]

"At midnight the struck down all the firstborn in Egypt, from the firstborn of Pharaoh, who sat on the throne, to the firstborn of the prisoner, who was in the dungeon, and the firstborn of all the livestock as well." Exodus 12:29 [NIV]

"And don't be concerned about what to eat and what to drink. Don't worry about such things." Luke 12:29 [NLT]

"When the crowd heard the , some thought it was thunder, while others declared an had spoken to ." John 12:29 [NLT]

Day 364
12:30

" the your with all your heart and with all your and with all your mind and with all your strength." Mark 12:30 [NIV]

"Whoever is not with is against , and whoever does not gather with scatters." Matthew 12:30 [NIV]

"Do not fall into the trap of following their customs and worshiping their gods. Do not inquire about their gods, saying, 'How do these nations worship their gods?'" Deuteronomy 12:30 [NLT]

"Do we all have the gift of healing? Do we all have the ability to speak in unknown languages? Do we all have the ability to interpret unknown languages? Of course not!" 1 Corinthians 12:30 [NLT]

"These things dominate the thoughts of unbelievers all over the world, but your already knows your needs." Luke 12:30 [NLT]

"Then told them, "The was for your benefit, not ." John 12:30 [NLT]

Day 365
12:31

"Love your neighbor as yourself. There is no Commandment greater than these."
◀ Mark 12:31 ▶ [NIV]

"And so, I tell You, every kind of sin and slander can be forgiven, but blasphemy against the SPIRIT Will not be forgiven."
◀ Matthew 12:31 ▶ [NIV]

"You must not worship the LORD your GOD the way the other nations worship their gods, for they perform for their gods every detestable act that the LORD hates." ◀ Deuteronomy 12:31 ▶ [NLT]

"Seek the Kingdom of GOD above all else, and HE Will give You everything You need."
◀ Luke 12:31 ▶ [NLT]

"The time for judging this world has come, when Satan, the ruler of this world, will be cast out."
◀ John 12:31 ▶ [NLT]

"So, You should earnestly desire the most helpful gifts. But now let ME show You A WAY OF LIFE THAT IS BEST OF ALL."
◀ 1 Corinthians 12:31 ▶ [NLT]

Powerful Manifestation Prayer:

I BLESS myself, my family and everyone born on this date with GOD's MOST POWERFUL PURE LOVING LIGHT, HIS MOST POWERFUL PURE SOURCE HEALING ENERGY, and an ABUNDANCE OF HIS AMAZING GREATER GRACE in the POWER, the ANOINTING, the AUTHORITY and the WISDOM of the HOLY SPIRIT, in JESUS' MOST HOLY NAME. AMEN INDEED!

CPSIA information can be obtained
at www.ICGtesting.com
Printed in the USA
LVHW061058270421
685413LV00002B/3